Portrait of Sir Sydney Nicholson in Doctoral robes by J. G. L. Northmore

Sydney Nicholson and his

Musings of a Musician

by

John Henderson and Trevor Jarvis

RSCM

The Royal School of Church Music
19 The Close, Salisbury, Wilts, SP1 2EB. England
E-mail: press@rscm.com Website: www.rscm.com
Registered charity 312828

Copyright © 2013 John Henderson & Trevor Jarvis

John Henderson and Trevor Jarvis have asserted their moral rights to be identified as the authors of this work under the Copyright, Designs and Patents Act, 1988

First published 2013

All rights reserved. No part of this work may be reproduced or transmitted in any form or by any means, electronic or mechanical, including photocopy, recording or any information storage or retrieval system, without the authors' written permission.

ISBN-13: 978-0-85402-226-7

Cover Design by Heather Bamber
Type face: Trebuchet MS
Printed in Great Britain on acid-free paper by
Charlesworth Press, Wakefield

CONTENTS

Preface	By Andrew Reid, Director of the *RSCM*	iii
Foreword	By Sir Sydney Nicholson	v
Introduction	By the Editors	vi
Abbreviations and acknowledgments		vii
Chapter I	My Home	1
Chapter II	School and College life	13
Chapter III	Eton, Westgate, Carlisle	51
Chapter IV	Manchester	81
Chapter V	Westminster	105
Chapter VI	The School of English Church Music	153
Chapter VII	The present and future of church music	189
Chapter VIII	The Final Years	205

Appendix A	Nicholson's account of his ancestry	221
Appendix B	Recollections of Sir Charles Nicholson	235
Appendix C	Nicholson's observations on the role of choristers	239
Appendix D	Nicholson's observations on cathedral worship	241
Appendix E	The principal organs played by Sydney Nicholson	243
Appendix F	Nicholson as a composer, with a list of his compositions	269
Appendix G	The original hymn tunes of Sydney Nicholson	287
Appendix H	Leslie Heward	295
Appendix I	*My song is love unknown*: by Sydney Nicholson	

Preface by the Director of the *Royal School of Church Music*

John Henderson and Trevor Jarvis have done excellent work in reconstructing Sydney Nicholson's 'Musings of a Musician', including copious notes and plentiful background information. The book has significant value for those who are interested in the period of Nicholson's life, especially with regard to the Church and music, since he came into contact with so many influential people in both fields. Those interested in the various places Nicholson studied and worked, in particular Oxford University, the Royal Academy of Music, Carlisle and Manchester Cathedrals and Westminster Abbey, will no doubt find detail, ideas and assertions here which are not readily available in other publications.

For those involved in the *RSCM*, this book (together with its companion *Sydney Nicholson and the College of St Nicholas*) provides an insight into the reasons why Nicholson left his prestigious post at Westminster Abbey and founded the *School of English Church Music*. Its success to this day is largely dependent on the energy he put behind the project over 20 years, including, incredibly in the face of such difficulty, during the War years. His indefatigable travelling, single-minded focus, initiatives, flexibility in handling change, ability to steer a principled course, patience and yet forthright speaking his mind among his fellow church musicians and clergy, and his sheer determination are here brought to light within a narrative which shows humility, love and a belief in the potential of music in Christian worship to transform our corporate life. Would that we could all learn from these qualities in our own days!

Andrew Reid

Foreword by Sir Sydney Nicholson

It has long been in my mind to try and write my reminiscences, partly because I have generally found such books interesting reading, and partly because I have found life a very interesting adventure and enjoy telling other people my experiences.

I have collected papers and made notes for many years, though I have not managed to keep a regular diary: but I never had time to get them together until my work was interrupted by the outbreak of war and I had to exchange the busy life of a College for the quiet of a cottage in the depths of the country.

I can only hope that these reminiscences may prove anything like as interesting for others to read as they have been for me to write: that I can hardly expect, for so many of them are purely personal. Still it has been my good fortune to be associated with many well-known people and places, and this at least may save me from the charge of having nothing to write about, if not from that of being garrulous.

But I am rather horrified on reading through these pages to find how many sentences begin with the first person singular. Yet perhaps, after all, it is more natural - and it is certainly shorter - to write 'I think' than to use such a phrase as 'The author is of opinion'. Anyhow it is too late to alter now.

S.H.N.

Woodchurch, December 1939.

Introduction

In addition to his career as cathedral musician and composer, various labels such as; painter, poet, printer, photographer, publisher and pioneer could all be applied to polymath Sir Sydney Hugo Nicholson MVO, MA, D Mus, FRCO, ARAM. He was a man of immense energy. When the College of St Nicolas closed on the outbreak of WWII in 1939 and the winding down of related administrative matters had been achieved, he took himself for a 'rest' at his cottage in Woodchurch, Kent. In the months leading to Christmas 1939 he worked on six chapters of an autobiography. Barely was Christmas over when he was back in harness visiting large numbers of parish church choirs and arranging choir festivals. He subsequently added a seventh non-autobiographical chapter to his book — a reflection on the future of church music.

The editors present this book as a companion volume to *Sydney Nicholson and The College of St Nicolas: The Chislehurst Years* (hereafter referred to as *SNCSN*) published in 2011. The photographs used here mostly differ from those in *SNCSN*, and, in order to avoid repetition of biographical and other information, many of the footnotes will refer the reader to *SNCSN*.

With Nicholson's reminiscences and often very perceptive observations, together with contemporary photographs, what emerges is much more than the memoir of a musician: it becomes a fascinating snapshot of the changing times through which he lived. His life spanned the latter part of Queen Victoria's reign through to that of King George VI, as well as two world wars, and embraced many changes that occurred in both cathedral and parish church worship.

Nicholson left a draft copy of his autobiography together with a bound typescript, of which the latter seems closer to his final intentions[1]. In addition to this, the editors have drawn upon a wide range of material from Sir Sydney's own archive: letters, diaries, date books, photograph albums and other family writings which he so diligently kept throughout his life. His final typescript contained no illustrations apart from one musical example, but he did suggest that seven photographs were to be included, and these we have honoured. Whilst the core of our offering is Nicholson's own writing, we have attempted to place his life in context with photographs and information about his friends, colleagues and family.

This account of Nicholson's life and work is primarily a factual one and little attempt has been made to provide a critical appraisal. In 1949 The Rev Canon W K Lowther Clarke[2] began work on a biography of Nicholson. Although this was never published, the many letters he received from Nicholson's former colleagues and choristers are very revealing. Virtually all were agreed that Nicholson was likeable, persuasive, an outstanding organiser, a choir

---

1 `In his typescript, Nicholson suggested several possible titles for his autobiography: *Musings of a Musician, Musical Memories* and *Music and other things*. On the cover of the surviving bound copy he uses *Musings of a Musician* and during the final years of his life he also referred to it in other writings using this title, these suggesting that this was his preferred option.

2 See Appendix F, Footnote 1

trainer who could motivate singers (especially boys), and that he possessed a remarkable memory for people, rarely forgetting anybody. A few letters suggested that Nicholson's musical abilities were not in the premier league, but, in the words of one cathedral musician:

> He may not have been a *Great Musician*, but he was certainly a *Great Man*.

John Henderson and Trevor Jarvis, Editors

All text within line boxes and text in [ ] square brackets is editorial, as is Chapter VIII in which the editors have taken the opportunity to complete the final chapter of this remarkable life.

Abbreviations

A&M	Hymns Ancient & Modern
ACDCM	(ADCM) The Archbishop of Canterbury's Diploma in Church Music.
CBE	Commander of the British Empire
CMS	Church Music Society
ECM	*English Church Music*
FRS	Fellow of the Royal Society
MVO	Member of the Victorian Order
PMMS	Plainsong and Mediæval Music Society
RAM	Royal Academy of Music (ARAM – Associate)
RCM	Royal College of Music (ARCM – Associate, FRCM – Fellow)
RCO	Royal College of Organists (ARCO – Associate, FRCO – Fellow)
RMCM	Royal Manchester College of Music (became RNCM — Royal Northern College of Music)
RSCM	Royal School of Church Music (ARSCM – Associate, FRSCM – Fellow)
SECM	School of English Church Music
SHN	Sydney Hugo Nicholson
SNCSN	*Sydney Nicholson and The College of St Nicolas: The Chislehurst Years*[3]
SPCK	Society for Promoting Christian Knowledge

Acknowledgments

The authors would like to thank the many people who provided information, photographs and advice or who assisted in proof-reading our efforts. These include Tim Ruffer, Julian Elloway, Andrew Reid, Nigel Groome, Colin Brownlee, Mervyn Cooper and Heather Bamber.

---

[3] Published 2011: ISBN 9780952805045, available from the *RSCM* at www.rscm.com.

The homes of Nicholson's childhood

26 Devonshire Place, London,
The birthplace of Sydney Nicholson
Photographed whilst snowing on a
winter's day in 2013

The Grange at Totteridge
before the 1899 fire

Hadleigh House, Essex, after purchase by the Salvation Army in 1899

Nicholson family photograph of the gardens at Hadleigh House in 1867

Chapter I

My Home

My recollections of childhood are entirely associated with my early home at Totteridge. Though I was born in London (at 26, Devonshire Place, in 1875[4]), my parents came to live at The Grange, Totteridge, when I was only a year old, giving up at the same time their London house and their Essex home at Hadleigh[5], near Southend.

My remembrance of my father is always as an old man, for he was 67 when I was born. My mother was 30 years younger, so almost all the 'bringing-up' of their three boys, of whom I was the youngest, naturally devolved on her.

> [At this point Nicholson embarked on an extensive account of his ancestors, which can be found in Appendix A.]

It is an undoubted disadvantage of a very late marriage that at any rate the youngest child should know little of intimate companionship with his father. I only knew him as an old man, — indeed he was older when I was born than I am now! Yet no father could have been more affectionate or more anxious to enter into his children's interests.

He spoke little of his early days, except when telling his many excellent 'stories': and, as he had kept a diary since he was 21, he would say, when we asked him for reminiscences, that we should some day find it all written down: — a prophecy, alas, never to be fulfilled, for the rows of volumes, of which none of us had ever been allowed to see more than the covers, were entirely destroyed in the disastrous fire at The Grange, of which I shall speak later.

His main interest in life was undoubtedly scholarship. Though not much of a conversational linguist he could read most languages, including Hebrew; he had a real affection for the classics and a wonderful memory, so that even in old age he would quote complete Odes of Horace or portions of Virgil, as well as his favourite poets, Shakespeare, Milton, Pope, Dryden, Tennyson and others: he was also a keen student of Dante. His chief subject was Egyptology, and his one published volume *Aegyptiaca* deals with this, mainly in relation to his collection at Sydney University[6]. He possessed a fine papyrus of The Book of the Dead and several beautiful illuminated manuscripts and early printed books. He loved to show them and explain them to his friends. He was also a student of Church history and theology, and he never ceased to marvel at the wonders of science and the newest inventions. The versatility of his tastes perhaps prevented him from becoming a very profound or critical scholar; but he was essentially a man of letters, and his scholarship was a pleasure rather than a business. He had marked artistic perception and excellent judgment, as shown by the beautiful things

---

[4] The date was 9th Feb 1875. It is now a property divided into suites, two of which are the consulting rooms of medical practitioners.

[5] Hadleigh House was sold in December 1899 to the Salvation Army and renamed Victoria House. It was licensed as a voluntary retreat and opened in 1901 with accommodation for up to 25 men who paid twenty shillings per week for treatment.

[6] The Nicholson Museum.

he collected, as for example his tapestry[7] and illuminated manuscripts.

Architecture interested him greatly, and in this his eldest son[8] was able to gratify him; and it is most curious that in early days he should have been so much interested in stained glass, little dreaming that his second son[9] would devote his gifts to that form of art.

He was not, I think, in the least musical; but he loved to be played to, especially tunes (like the well-known Scotch airs and Moore's Melodies[10]) which he could associate with poetry. Though my adoption of music as a profession was always a disappointment to him, yet he never failed to show the greatest interest in my work and even gave me an organ to help me in it.

Besides all this he must have been an excellent man of business, for he was a Director of several important Companies, including the British India Steam Navigation Company, and Chairman from 1872 to 1902 of the London Board of the Liverpool and London and Globe Insurance Company, taking on this responsible office at a time of grave crisis for the Company and steering it through to wonderful success.

William Horsley

My mother was musical to the extent that she sang (as ladies did in the evenings in those days), had a good voice and a very expressive and dramatic style: she had lessons from

---

[7] SHN here refers to a French or Flemish tapestry dating from the latter half of the 17C depicting a landscape, which had been acquired in 1856 by Nicholson's father Sir Charles Nicholson. This formerly hung in the family home in Sydney, Australia, then in the Grange at Totteridge. It was rescued from the 1899 fire and later adorned a wall in the dining room of the College of St Nicolas at Chislehurst. After the College closed it was given to the Dean and Chapter of Canterbury Cathedral but was destroyed in a wartime air-raid.

[8] Charles Archibald Nicholson FRIBA (1867-1949), SHN's eldest brother was an ecclesiastical architect and, like Sir Sydney, was educated at Rugby School. Early in his career, in 1907 whilst SHN was at Carlisle, he designed new choir stalls for the boys. In 1922 he designed the Rugby School Memorial Chapel, worked on Portsmouth Cathedral and was responsible for the west front of St Anne's Cathedral in Belfast where he served as cathedral architect from 1924 to 1948. Along with his brother Archie, he also did work at St Sepulchre in Holborn. He married Evelyn Louise Olivier (see Chapter II) on 1st Oct 1895 at Winchfield and succeeded to the Baronetcy on the death of his father in 1903.

[9] Archibald Keightley Nicholson (1871-1937) was the second son of Sir Charles Nicholson and so the middle of the three brothers. Keightley was his mother's family name. Archie was a stained glass artist, responsible for over 700 windows, including several in cathedrals, most notably the Elgar Memorial Window in Worcester Cathedral. In the church of St Sepulchre, Holborn, so closely associated with the *SECM*, there is a memorial window to him inscribed:

'To the glory of God. In memory of Archibald Keightley Nicholson, Master Glass Painter, who worshipped at this church. This window is designed and carried out by the craftsmen of his studios as a thank offering for his life and friendship. 1871 - 1937'.

The window he designed for the College of St Nicolas chapel at Chislehurst (subsequently installed at Addington Palace) is still extant, but in storage. His studio was at 105, Gower Street, London, WC1, and, from Jan 1928, he provided a room there for the use of the *SECM*. He was elected to College Council in Jan 1934 and resigned in Feb 1937, just two weeks before his death. He had been ill for seven years but, according to his obituary by H C Colles, 'He never missed any [*SECM*] function of importance in which he could play a useful part'. He also founded a Scholarship to the College and left a substantial legacy to the *SECM*.

[10] Thomas Moore (1779-1852) was an Irish poet and songwriter, sometimes regarded as Ireland's national poet. Perhaps his most enduring lyric is 'The last rose of summer'. His ballads were published initially in four volumes (1808-1811) and then again in numerous volumes

William Horsley[11], who was then organist at the Charterhouse, but she was in no sense a trained musician. She certainly had her great favourites, but naturally not much real critical sense. Her artistic impulses found their expression in painting and sketching in which she was extremely gifted.

The Dowager Lady Nicholson c 1910

Lady Sarah Elizabeth Nicholson (née Keightley) was born on 30th March 1839 at Charterhouse and died on 2nd December 1923 at 7 Airlie Gardens, London. She was a student at Leigh's Academy, just off Oxford Street, the first art academy in London to accept women on equal terms as men. Many of her paintings and sketches were destroyed when The Grange burnt down, but some were rescued. She married Sir Charles Nicholson on 8th August 1865 in Charterhouse Chapel. She had a close relationship with her son Sydney and throughout her life they exchanged weekly letters. Like her son, she was also a hoarder of family memorabilia so that many of these letters survive, together with numerous newspaper clippings about her son's career. She was buried in Totteridge.

On the following page is a portrait of Sydney Nicholson as a child painted by Lady Sarah.

---

throughout his lifetime, and posthumously in 1859 as *Moore's Irish Melodies* 'with symphonies and accompaniments'.

11 William Horsley (1774-1858) was organist of there from 1838. Composer of the hymn tune 'Horsley' now associated with the words 'There is a green hill far away', he was a friend of Felix Mendelssohn. He also composed three orchestral symphonies together with many glees and part-songs. His son John Callcott Horsley designed and sent the first ever Christmas Card in 1843 and his eldest daughter married Isambard Kingdom Brunel to whom Horsley gave at least one organ lesson. Horsley was also the composer of the Charterhouse school song *Carmen Carthusianum*, much admired by Ralph Vaughan Williams, and sung by Charterhouse boys to this day.

Sydney Nicholson (aged 6¼)
Painted by his mother whilst the family were on holiday in Hythe, Kent, in August 1881.

Her beautiful sketches, especially the landscapes, dating from the time when she was a girl to when she was over 80, are a delightful record of the many places she visited: indeed she regarded her sketches as a kind of journal; and she kept three special books, one for each of her sons, in which she made sketches of places which they had visited in her company. She also liked to draw small portraits of her friends, and many of these are excellent.

Lady Nicholson painting in The Grange at Totteridge before the 1899 fire.

After her art her main interest was in theology, of which she had a profound knowledge. She was a great reader and a most thorough one; indeed if a book interested her it was her habit to 'index' it, often making copious extracts of passages that particularly struck her. Both she and my father were also greatly interested in psychical subjects.

She had a most methodical mind. Had it not been for this I should never have been able to collect material for this book. Not only did she keep together papers of general interest, but she had a large box for each of her sons in which she kept letters, newspaper cuttings and all sorts of other records concerning them which would otherwise undoubtedly have been lost[12]. It has been to me a matter of extraordinary interest to go carefully through my 'box' and to have brought to mind many happenings in my life which I had entirely forgotten. To re-read a whole series of one's own letters, extending over some 40 years, is an extraordinary and I think rather an unusual experience. Even more interesting than the actual events referred to in the letters is to recapture one's thoughts about them at the time they happened. How deeply I regret that I did not similarly preserve my mother's letters to me!

I remember some of the distinguished visitors to The Grange in the early days, when I was only a small boy; Professor Crookes, Professor Sayce, Huxley and Max Muller among them. Then there were my mother's special friends, Hilda de Bunsen (Madame von Krause and afterwards Baroness Deichmann[13]), my Godmother: Clara Lane, with her eccentric sister Emily, daughters of the artist R J Lane[14] and great-nieces of Gainsborough: Mrs (afterwards Lady) Priestley[15], daughter of Robert Chambers of Cyclopaedia fame: and above all Sophy Horsley[16], the devoted friend of Mendelssohn, to whom the composer dedicated some of his works and who played them with that rare understanding derived from first-hand knowledge of his intentions. I can almost hear her now, playing the magnificent *Prelude and Fugue in F minor*, and telling how it was written after a serious illness, — the turbulent *Prelude* representing the feverish tossing on a bed of sickness and the Chorale at the end of the *Fugue* a thanksgiving for recovery: or how the idea of the *Spring Song* came to him when playing, surrounded by children who kept snatching his hands from the keys. She also knew Chopin, and I remember her saying that few people knew how to play his music; — he himself always played it with the utmost delicacy and never loud like modern pianists. She was a most emphatic and downright old lady, and a trifle alarming. I remember one occasion when I was taken to see her and had to play some piece I had just learnt. When I had finished, she said:

> "Do you like it, my dear?"
>
> "Not very much", was my reply;
>
> "Then, my dear, why do you play it?"

Talking of famous musicians; though I never met Madame Schumann, I am very glad to remember that I heard her play the famous Pianoforte Quintett with the Joachim Quartet and to recall the impression of the old lady sitting very upright at her piano and striking those opening chords with such a sense of mastery. She was a friend of my Aunt Julia and I have in my possession many of her letters; but all of them deal with purely social matters and are of no special musical interest except for their authorship.

---

12 Her diligence in keeping all this material has been of invaluable help to the editors.

13 Baroness Deichmann (1848-1932) was born Hilda Elisabeth von Bunsen. After her first husband Hugo Berend von Krause died in 1874, she married Adolf Wilhelm Conrad Rudolph Deichmann, 1st Baron Deichmann in 1877. This caused a question to be raised in the House of Commons in 1916 and *Hansard* reported that, although married to a German national, she would be of no danger to England in wartime. Her recollection of Sir Charles Nicholson is in Appendix B. Nicholson went to stay with her at her house in Germany during his European holiday in 1908.

14 Richard James Lane (1800-1872) was an engraver and lithographer of considerable distinction who enjoyed royal patronage, having executed pencil and chalk portraits of Queen Victoria and other members of the Royal Family at various ages. He married Sophia Hodges in 1825 and they had five children including Clara Sophie (1828-1912) and Emily.

15 Sir William Overend Priestley (1829-1900) trained in medicine at Edinburgh University becoming an obstetrician and gynaecologist and accoucheur to royalty. He was also an MP for the Edinburgh and St Andrews parliamentary constituency from 1896 to 1900. He and his wife Eliza (1829-1900) lived in London from 1856 and he was knighted in 1893 in recognition of his medical services.

16 Sophy Horsley (née Sophia Hutchins) (1819-1894), concert pianist, sister-in-law of Isambard Kingdom Brunel, was a close friend of Lady Sarah Nicholson and daughter of composer William Horsley who gave Lady Nicholson singing lessons. She often visited the house. SHN found her terrifying but loved her playing.

Another great friend who constantly came to The Grange was Louisa Starr (Madame Canziani[17]) the artist, who painted my mother's portrait. Then, of course, there were many visits from old Australian friends, — chief among them the Alan Campbells.

Totteridge was a very pleasant village in those days, consisting almost entirely of rather large places occupied by big families, and there was much pleasant society for us youngsters. My mother was very fond of riding and we boys were all taught by her, with our ponies on a leading rein while Mr Gage, the coachman, followed at a respectful distance in a top-hat and blue livery coat and top-boots, mounted on one of the carriage horses; — for in those days it would have seemed odd for a lady to go out riding without a servant in attendance. Then there was our beloved Scotch gardener, Macdonald, one of the greatest friends of my boyhood, devoted to my father, but ready to help us in every enterprise, and the most delightful of companions.

The Grange was a large, old-fashioned house, with an old-world garden of some ten acres. It contained many treasures collected by my father and a remarkable library in which he spent most of his time. But perhaps the most attractive possession, and that which I most associate with my old home, was the beautiful Flemish (or French) tapestry dating from about 1670. This he had purchased somewhere about 1856 and had taken with him to his house near Sydney. On his return to England he brought it back with him (or had it sent after) and it was housed in specially built rooms first at Hadleigh and then at Totteridge. It was saved from the fire (in 1899) and is now in my possession, having been given to me by my brother Charles to hang in the College of St Nicolas[18]. There was also a fine collection of Greek statuary presented by my father's old friend Sir George Macleay[19]: this was unfortunately entirely destroyed in the fire.

I cannot remember the time when I did not love music more than anything in the world. When a tiny child I used to beg my mother to leave the drawing-room door open if there was to be music in the evening: and my supreme joy was to be allowed to sit on the floor under the piano when Miss Horsley was playing, and to put down the pedal, "to make it sound", as I said. I suppose I always strummed and picked out tunes, but my Aunt Julia first taught me my notes. I remember the first time I was taken to Church on a Christmas Day, I suppose when I was about 5 years old; when I came back I picked out the tune of 'Hark, the herald angels' (no doubt with some 'chords') much to the amazement of my adoring parents.

---

17   Madame Starr Canziani, nee Louisa Starr (1845-1909) was the first woman artist to be awarded a Royal Academy medal. She regularly exhibited at the Royal Academy, from the 1870's to the 1890's. One of SHN's juvenile piano compositions is entitled 'Estella Canziani'.
18   See footnote 7.
19   Sir George Macleay (1809-1891), explorer and zoologist, spent 1826 to 1859 in Australia and, like Sir Charles Nicholson, returned to London though he spent most of his retirement in the South of France.

The very first letter to my father that I can find, written from Malvern when I was 7 years old, in large handwriting on carefully ruled paper, reads as follows:

> 1 Bellevue Place,
> Great Malvern.
>
> My dear Father,
>
> Thank you so much for your kind letter. I hope some day I shall be able to play the organ. Thank you so much for the fruit you sent us it was so nice. It is so wet now, from Sydney.

It soon became evident in what direction my tastes lay, and I was given a very good grounding by my governess, Miss Brander, in the old-fashioned way, — scales and five-finger exercises which I duly loathed. But, though I got on well, my mother wanted a real test; and she devised a very good one. I had never heard a concert, but when I was about 8 years old she took me to — of all things — a performance of Bach's *B minor Mass* at the Albert Hall, thinking that if I could survive that experience it would be evidence of the real thing. I came out of the test triumphantly (and wakefully), and from that moment I think my mother felt that I should probably in the end become a musician. But such an ambition was never even hinted at, for it was in those days hardly considered as a possible walk in life for a 'gentleman'. My parents had in mind for me some such career as the law or perhaps diplomacy, little knowing that the small boy for whom they were planning would be about the least suitable person in the world for such a life. I think that, had I not been allowed to go in for music, I should have chosen to be an engineer.

My first instrument of my own was a Concertina (!) which was given to me by my father on the above mentioned visit to Malvern. A portrait by my mother exists, showing me playing this instrument in a velvet suit with broad lace collar and "sausage curls"! Later, to console me for having the measles, I was given a small American organ.

My first attempts at the organ proper were made in Totteridge Church[20] under the guidance of our parson, dear old Mr Squibb. By some odd arrangement Totteridge was at that time part of the parish of Hatfield, ten miles away; the Rector of Hatfield, who paid a visit about once a year, I believe gave his Curate-in-charge the magnificent stipend of £80 a year. Mr Squibb[21] was a delightful old gentleman of the Tractarian school. He had a very difficult task to minister to the peculiar congregation at Totteridge, almost exclusively composed of well-

---

[20] St Andrew's Parish Church, Totteridge became part of the newly-formed Diocese of St Albans in 1877, but it was not until 1892 that it became a separate parish with its own vicar. This would explain why the church was looked after, albeit infrequently, by the Rector of Hatfield. The census of 1892 records Totteridge had 785 residents, which certainly puts it in the category of 'village'.

[21] The Rev George Meyler Squibb MA (d 1905) came to Totteridge in 1869. A Scholar of Brasenose College, Oxford, he had been a missionary in South Africa for many years, and had obtained the small curacy of Totteridge on a very modest salary. He was the author of *The Negro Sidesman: A Sketch from Missionary Life* 1867.

to-do and extremely critical folks. He scandalized many of his flock, including my father, by his 'silken petticoat' and his adoption of the 'Eastward position'[22]. Though he was a really musical man the choir at Totteridge was, even to my childish ears, execrable; but the organ was quite a good one, and I remember how Mr Squibb gave me my first 'lesson' and I was allowed to play on it whenever I could get a blower[23]. I played my first service in Totteridge Church on St. Mark's Day in 1883 or 1884, — anyhow before I went to school; and mighty proud was I to wear a surplice and feel like a real organist!

I soon began to try my hand at composition, the first I think being a song "Ring out wild bells": but a great event was the 'Jubilee March' written in 1887 and ending with 'God Save the Queen'. This my parents thought most wonderful and I believe a copy was actually sent to Her Gracious Majesty!

Before turning from these early days I must say something of the other members of our small family. I do not remember my grandfather who died in 1877, but think of Mrs Keightley as a dear old lady in a lace cap, rather an invalid and doing an endless amount of woolwork. I also associate her with playing the piano in a very gentle and charming manner, but I can only remember her playing one piece. It was quite short and was called "The York Bells." I have no idea of its origin and never saw a copy, but as it is probably quite unknown and is a most charming little tune I write it down, just as she used to play it:

Then there were the three Aunts. "Aunt Julia[24]", the eldest, was very musical: her great disappointment in life was that Madame Schumann, whom she adored, would not give her

---

22 The reference to 'Eastward position' which so scandalized Nicholson's father, was considered a 'high church' practice, the *Book of Common Prayer* of 1662 laying down the rubric '...and the priest standing at the north side of the table.'
23 Non organists may not realise that, before the introduction of powered blowers, it was necessary for an assistant to work the pump that provided wind to the organ in order for the instrument to be played.
24 Julia Keightley b 1843 at Charterhouse. In 1901 she was living in Whitchurch, Shropshire.

lessons, on account of her hands being too small. She was, however, much in musical circles, singing in the original Bach Choir with her sister Mary under Madame Goldschmidt (Jenny Lind), and having been one of the adventurous and rather 'risky' people who attended the first Wagner Festival at Bayreuth. "Aunt Illa[25]", my godmother, was learned and greatly given to good works, and I think she was my father's favourite. "Aunt Mary[26]", the youngest, was musical and sang very well; she often accompanied us on holidays and was a delightful companion: she is happily still alive, the last member of her generation.

Waiting for the Horses[27]

Julia and Illa Keightley painted by their sister Lady Sarah Nicholson c 1862 (slightly damaged in the 1899 fire)

My two brothers, Charles and Archibald[28], were both extremely artistic as boys and were always drawing, but they were neither of them really musical. Archie and I were much thrown together, going to a school at Elstree in our little pony-cart and returning home for week-ends: we were always excellent 'pals', though we had violent quarrels and at times I

---

25   Isabella Keightley (1845-1922)
26   Mary Keightley (1854-1946)
27   A picture dated 1886 of an 11 year old Sydney Nicholson mounted on horseback and ready for the hunt exists. It is too poor for reproduction.
28   See footnotes 8 & 9.

am sure I hated him desperately! Charlie, being older, I knew less of in those days, for he was already a schoolboy when I first remember him.

I think this picture of a very happy and fortunate family life will best be completed by quoting some 'Recollections of Sir Charles Nicholson' by our beloved Clara Lane, with others by Baroness Deichmann. Such impressions of life at The Grange as they struck devoted friends are more illuminating than anything that can be written by one of the family.

[These recollections can be found in Appendix B]

In an age of motor-cars, cinemas and the 'wireless', — not to mention such products of civilization as aeroplanes and submarines, it is refreshing to look back to those Victorian days. The world was not such an exciting place as it is today, but I question whether it was not far happier.

For one thing one got to know one's friends better: and I think people were more interested in interesting things. There was more time for conversation and reading and the pursuit of art or other hobbies: people had to learn to create their own interests at home when they were not so lavishly provided for them outside. London had not become the vast place it now is, yet distances seemed greater when the only means of communication were the horse-buses or the smoky old Underground, unless one could indulge in a hansom cab or a 'growler'. It was quite pleasant to drive up to town in a carriage and pair when there were no trams, and there was still plenty of open country between Totteridge and London. We were quite content with flaring gas-jets before we became accustomed to electric light. Railway trains were slow and uncomfortable, lighted only by oil lamps and with no heating except that supplied by occasional foot-warmers and the 'Ulsters' in which we habitually travelled: corridor carriages and dining-cars were of course unknown; yet journeys and holiday visits were far more appreciated, for they were more difficult to accomplish. Life was not disturbed by the telephone and even the arrival of a telegram was considered something of an event, generally associated with bad news.

Yet it was an extraordinarily pleasant time. The world was at peace; the country was not afflicted with grievous taxation, so that money went much further and many more people seemed to be 'comfortably off'; — anyhow there were many more substantial family houses and moderate properties. Servants were perhaps under-paid and often poorly housed, but they were happy and contented and extremely faithful and there was no 'domestic problem'. Life may have been duller, but people were not 'blasé' or bored as they are today.

The present generation no doubt think the Victorian age was somewhat 'stuffy' and restricted in its outlook. But those who were brought up in it know how false such an estimate really is. In spite of all the progress that has been made in material things, the world was a happier place in those days than it now is, and I, for one, am thankful to have seen such days and to have been associated with such people.

Chapter II
School and College life

Early School Days

I went to school at Elstree when I was nine years old, with my brother Archie. This was not the famous Elstree School kept by Sanderson[1], but a small, old-fashioned place[2], very rough and 'spartan'; I think the sole reason for our being sent there was that we were allowed to come home at each week-end, and we drove to and fro in our smart little pony cart, drawn by 'Gipsy', of which we were very proud.

We held the headmaster in terror, not because he beat us (the absence of such form of punishment was supposed to be one of the attractions of the school), but for his violent temper and the appalling impositions and fines we had to endure. I learnt practically nothing except certain Latin rhymes dealing with genders:

"Common are to either sex, Artifex and opifex," etc.

I certainly learnt these thoroughly for I can remember them to this day: — not a very valuable remnant of classical studies, I fear! But I began music seriously with Mr F G M Ogbourne[3], who attended once a week, and he gave me a very good grounding in piano and the elements of harmony. I played one of the Beethoven Sonatinas at a School concert at the end of my first term, — my first appearance on a concert platform.

It is interesting to read my first music report, with the list of pieces learnt during the term: certainly they represent a good deal of work for a small boy of 9.

F G M Ogbourne

Summer Term 1884.

Sonatina in F.	- Beethoven
Studies, Bk. 1.	- Heller
Marche des Troubadours.	- Roubier
Sonatina in G.	- Beethoven
Serenade.	- Gounod
Reverie.	- Lebeau

Progress: Very satisfactory. He has considerable musical taste and works steadily.
Frank Geo Mitford Ogbourne.

---

1 The Rev Lancelot Sanderson (1838-1904), a pioneer in the development of preparatory school educations, took over and reformed Elstree School in 1869.

2 Wikipedia: The school was founded in 1784 as Totteridge Park School in Hertfordshire. In 1865 it moved to Hendon and became Brent Bridge House School, and from 1874 to 1886, it moved to Elstree and became Hillside School. In 1886 it moved to Littlehampton and became The School House, and in 1905, it merged with and became Dorset House School. It still continues as a co-educational preparatory school near Pulborough in West Sussex.

3 Frank George Mitford Ogbourne (1851-1929) was organist of several London churches, latterly at St Andrew's in Holborn for 22 years. When he tutored Nicholson he was serving at St Peter's in Paddington and he became a professor of organ at Trinity College, London in 1885.

Dating from about this time I have come across an amusing account[4] of a visit to the Inventions Exhibition[5]. (The original spelling and punctuation are preserved).

> It is a very nice place. We saw a great many things; we had a ride on the compressed air tramway[6], which goes with a very easy motion, very different to the rattling old omnibusses [sic] in London that they have now; I believe they are going to use them in the streets. There is by the side of it an electric tram but it was not going when we were there. There is a wonderful engine which is very big. There is some new dodge about it something like this, the waist [sic] steam from one lot of wheels works another lot. We heard lot of music amongst which we heard the Albert Hall[7] organ played by Coward[8], and Bailee Hamilton's Vocalion[9]. The organ is beautiful. The Vocalion has a very nice tone I think it would do very well for a small church, and it wouldn't have too much power for a house. We saw a machine for moving soot or any thing like that and another one that can be put in to a heap of anything and it will take it somewhere else; and they are both wonderful. We came along the Subway from S. Kensington Station it is for the most part lighted by Electric light[10] and is all tiled with white tiles on the roof and sides and is paved on the floor: it leads to the S. Kensington Museum and to the Natural History, as well as to the Inventions. We saw a great many pianos and

---

4   This young Nicholson's written account is extant in the Nicholson Archive.

5   The International Inventions Exhibition, a world fair held in South Kensington, opened on 4th May 1885. It was hugely popular, attracting 94,959 visitors in the first week alone and a total of 3¾ million visitors during the six months it remained open. Countries participating included the USA, the Austria-Hungary Alliance, Italy, Japan and of course the United Kingdom. In addition to the many technical exhibits there were attractions such as pleasure gardens, food, concerts and fountains. Every hour an illuminated fountain projected 70,000 gallons of water 120 feet into the air. The competitors for the Gold, Silver and Bronze medals in the various competitive categories were warned that space would be restricted, but this did not prevent most of the British organ builders showcasing their instruments and innovations, including three and four manual instruments. These, together with pianos and harmoniums were demonstrated with daily performances. It was here that the young organ virtuoso Edwin H Lemare first came to the attention of the public.

6   Of various alternatives sought for the propulsion of public transport, the Mékarski compressed air system was thought to be a serious contender. It was given a trial in London on the Caledonian Road and, though not taken up seriously by London, it was used in France in Paris and Nantes and in England (somewhat unsuccessfully) by the Wantage Tramway.

7   The Royal Albert Hall and organ (both opened in 1871) was part of the Inventions Exhibition featuring regular concerts and recitals through the summer, including the Eduard Strauss Orchestra from Vienna, hired at a cost of £6000.

8   James Munro Coward (b 1853 or 1854), a pupil of Joseph Barnby and noted improviser and performer on the Mustel harmonium, was editor of the American Organ Journal and general manager of London music publisher Metzler & Co. Also organist of St Saviour's in Pimlico, he was uncle of Noel Coward (1899-1973), playwright, composer, actor and singer. His father, also James Coward (1824-1880) and a well-known organ recitalist, served for 23 years as the first organist appointed to the Crystal Palace.

9   John (k/a James) Buchanan Baillie Hamilton (1850-1921) devised the 'Vocalion' organ around 1875. His idea was to improve the sound of a reed organ by incorporating sympathetically vibrating strings, wires, resonator boxes and tubes. It was more akin to an American organ in that it used a blower rather than the suction method of a harmonium. Thomas Hill, son of organ builder William Hill, initially built ten instruments. In 1885 Vocalion manufacture was started in Massachusetts, USA, and, though the instrument never really became established in the UK, the US market was very successful. The company went through various changes and was eventually amalgamated into the Aeolian company, who even marketed a Vocalion gramophone record label. Chapter V includes more about Baillie Hamilton.

10 Sir Joseph Swan (1828-1914) first demonstrated the electric light bulb at a lecture in Newcastle-upon-Tyne in 1878 and patented an improved version in 1880. His house in Gateshead was the first in the world lit by electric light bulbs. In 1881 the Savoy Theatre in the City of Westminster, London was lit by Swan incandescent light bulbs, the first theatre and the first public building in the world to be lit entirely by electricity. The Subway at South Kensington referred to by Nicholson was only built by the Metropolitan District Railway in 1885 and was opened on the 4th May 1885 by the Prince and Princess of Wales, the same day that they also opened the International Inventions Exhibition. The electric lighting mentioned by Nicholson was therefore quite a novelty.

harmoniums and American organs. We saw a little wee piano that is called a concert grand, and it was about half as long as an ordinary piano and all the sharps and flats were white and all the white notes were black: it was 110 years old. We saw a beautiful little model of the Polypemus[11]. It was all very nice I enjoyed it very much. I have been told that 'Old London' is all stuck over inside with advertisements, but it is the same as it was at the 'Healtheries' except the shops are different. I had my hair cut there."

This document at any rate indicates the future tastes of the writer.

I think my first school must have been in its decline when I went there, for after a year or two it entirely collapsed and I was sent to one of the most famous of preparatory schools, Temple Grove, East Sheen, where the Rev J H Edgar had recently succeeded Waterfield. Here the teaching was splendid and on the whole I was quite happy. But the educational methods were very different from those of today: the extremely repressive measures adopted towards the boys were, I daresay, a healthy discipline, but rather tended to turn people out in a mould. There was little chance of showing individuality when the slightest deviation from rules, such as even a whisper in the dormitories, would result in punishment that would nowadays be considered excessive for quite serious crimes. Here, again, it was not the rule of the stick — that was comparatively rare: the principle adopted was that the punishment (drills, impositions and curtailment of all privileges for perhaps ten days on end) was so severe for the slightest offences, that the boys were simply cowed into submission and hardly ever adventured into the paths of even the mildest wickedness. Each dormitory was presided over by a separate Matron. My particular 'wardress' was known as "Jane", and I remember how she would appear noiselessly in her velvet slippers when lights were out and we thought we might safely dare to whisper some confidence to our neighbour in the next cubicle, and would say, in highly superior tones, "Very nice this noise! Very sweet! You will all be reported in the morning to Mist' Edgar for insubordination in the dormitory!" It was I suppose a good example of the Victorian method of education. Certainly it had its merits and we all liked Edgar, though we certainly feared him. But of real enjoyment of school life we had little, except on the glorious occasions when we were taken out for walks in Richmond park by the German master, and if the weather happened to be foggy we would escape in a body and leave our guardian stranded while we chased the deer, climbed trees, and indulged in other forbidden delights. I suppose he was too frightened of losing his post, or perhaps too kind-hearted, ever to report these misdoings to headquarters.

My music made some progress with poor old Mr H L Morley, a good teacher but very jaded, and always lamenting the inaptitude of his pupils. In later years Mrs Edgar told me how she

---

11 It is possible that this is a misspelling. Nicholson is probably referring to a model of *H.M.S. Polyphemus*, an unusual ship launched by the Royal Navy in 1881 and designed to fire the newly invented torpedo. It was also designed so that, if the vessel sank, the deck would float off as two life rafts.

brought me to him as a new boy and said, "Here at last is a boy whom you will enjoy teaching!" "They all say that!" was his reply, "only one more to bring me a step nearer to the grave!" I loved singing in the school choir, though I never had a good voice: but we had no Chapel and prayers were held in the big schoolroom, where I was sometimes allowed, as a great treat, to play the American organ for services.

Temple Grove School

Temple Grove School,
An early engraving.

The Rev Joseph Haythorne Edgar (1834-1898), educated at Wadham College, Oxford, and formerly a Lieutenant in the Royal Artillery, was ordained priest in 1860. He succeeded Ottiwell Charles Waterfield (1831-1898) at Temple Grove School in 1880. His *Notebook on Practical Solid or Descriptive Geometry* of 1880 is, surprisingly, still in print. Temple Grove School was founded in 1810 when Dr William Pearson (1767-1847) moved his 'school for young gentlemen' from Fulham to East Sheen, then a rural estate. It subsequently moved to Eastbourne and finally to Heron's Ghyll near Uckfield in Sussex.

Temple Grove School,
c 1891

Rugby School (1889-1893)

I went to Rugby in 1889[12], to the School House under the commanding reign of Dr Percival. On the whole my time at Rugby was a very happy one[13]. Unfortunately I never had the slightest aptitude for, or interest in, games of any kind, and this naturally meant a certain amount of bullying at first: but after a time I was let alone as 'simply hopeless', and when I could be free of compulsory cricket I used to scour the countryside on my bicycle, getting to know every village within a radius of 15 miles or so, exploring the country churches and when possible trying their organs, and establishing an interest in seeing places which has brought me much happiness throughout my life.

At Rugby I came for the first time under the influence of a really first-rate musician. Basil Johnson, fresh from the inspiring mastership of Walter Parratt and from Magdalen choir, seemed to me something almost miraculous. His organ playing thrilled me, and especially his recitals on Sundays after Chapel[14]. He was wise enough to include in his programmes not only pure organ music but arrangements of standard orchestral pieces: at a time when orchestral concerts were rare this was of great educational value, and it was through his playing that I first became acquainted with such works as the slow movements of the Beethoven or Haydn Symphonies and even such 'modern music' as the prelude and Good Friday music from *Parsifal*.

Basil and Bessie Johnson in Wells c 1931

(Arthur) Basil (Noel) Johnson (1861-1950), 3rd son of the Dean of Wells Cathedral, was educated at Malvern College and was organist there from 1876 to 1879. After graduating from Magdalen College, Oxford, he studied at the Royal College of Music with Sir Walter Parratt, Sir Frederick Bridge and Sir Charles Stanford. After serving briefly as organist in London at St James's, Norlands, and St Gabriel's, Pimlico, he was appointed to Rugby School in 1886 where he married the headmaster's daughter Elizabeth ("Miss Bessie") Ann Percival, a painter, in 1891. He was also conductor of the Rugby Philharmonic Society for 27 years. In 1914 he succeeded C H Lloyd (1849-1919) as Precentor (choir director) of Eton College, retiring in 1926. He received a Lambeth D Mus in 1928.

The developments of school music, in which he was a pioneer, roused my enthusiasm to the highest pitch, and I well remember the wonderful occasion when we sang the *Hallelujah*

---

12 His first day was 2nd May 1889.

13 Nicholson does not mention that during his time at Rugby he was Confirmed in Rugby School Chapel on 11th March 1891 by Bishop John Perowne (1823-1904), Bishop of Worcester.

14 The Rugby Chapel organ at this time had been installed by Bryceson of London in 1872. For that time it was a very pioneering instrument with electro-pneumatic action and a detached console.

Chorus at a School Concert, and later *The Hymn of Praise*, quite certain in our own minds that there was no such school choir as at Rugby and no such conductor as B.J.

Rehearsing for a Rugby School Concert in 1902 with Basil Johnson directing.
Nicholson (standing to BJ's left) had returned to play the organ for this concert.
A fine view of the Bryceson organ installed in 1890.

With him I seriously began the organ, after watching almost daily the rise of the new instrument in Big School[15], He has since told me that he thought I should never master it, though I had dabbled on the organ for years, and he was actually on the point of advising me to give up the attempt as hopeless.

Of the other people at Rugby I think first of the dominating figure of Percival[16] — the handsomest man I ever saw (especially in old age), with his strong north-country speech and the smile that brought terror to the heart of the delinquent. By sheer force of his presence he could cow the 500 boys into awed silence on those dread occasions when he castigated us

---

15 The instrument 'rising' here was probably the new 3-manual, 40 stop instrument by Bryceson, which was completed in the 'Speech Room' (i.e. school hall) in 1890. It is still in use having been transferred to the new 'Temple Speech Room' in 1907, but it has twice been rebuilt and is now only 31 stops. It retains a tracker action with Barker Lever.

16 The Rev John Percival (1834-1918) won a scholarship to The Queen's College in Oxford in 1854 and, after obtaining first-class degrees in classics and mathematics, he was elected to a fellowship of the college in 1858. Ordained Deacon in 1860, he took a position as a master at Rugby School under headmaster Frederick Temple until his appointment as the first Headmaster of Clifton College in Bristol in 1862. Under him the school grew from 62 to 680 pupils. He returned ('head-hunted' one suspects) to Rugby as Headmaster in 1887, where he rescued the school from a bad patch following Hayman's Headmastership (see note 19). He became Bishop of Hereford in 1895, retired to Oxford in 1917 and died the following year. He is buried in the chapel crypt of Clifton College.

with his merciless tongue in Big School, or dealt with some 'social cancer' in Chapel. Yet he seldom punished, and in his own study or family circle could be as gentle and sympathetic as anyone. A very great man, but always remote, even I think from his masters. He was feared by everyone, but honoured by every decent person. As I knew him in later years, chiefly through my intimacy with his daughter who became Mrs Basil Johnson, and think of him, mellowed by old age, as a most delightful host in his Palace at Hereford, I come to appreciate more and more the greatness of his character. He was always to some extent aloof from other people and he remained at heart the schoolmaster: but his kindness (generally done in the most secret way) was unbounded, and his sympathy, even in things that were widely separated from his own pursuits, was unfailing. Though his appointment as Bishop of Hereford [in 1895] had met with the strongest opposition, chiefly owing to his pronounced political views, he grew as time went on to win the devotion of his clergy, not on account of his intellectual ability, which was unquestioned, nor of his religious opinions, which many of them detested, but for his simple goodness and kindliness to all who served under him.

The Rev John Percival

E A Scott[17], always known as "Ginger Scott", was one of my greatest friends among the masters. Appointed by Temple[18], he was one of the revolutionaries who had brought about the downfall of Hayman[19]. He [Scott] was a most original character, starting his first lesson every day by reading a short biblical passage, generally from one of the Prophets. I can see him now, standing at his desk in his gown, with somewhat bald head and red whiskers:

> "Howl ye, howl ye!" — then looking up and glaring over his pince-nez at someone who was giving a last glance at his 'prep' - "Put that book away! — Howl ye, howl ye! Cry ye to the waste places" etc. etc.

He would sometimes tell us of his wonderful dreams or of his conversations with his gardener or other out-of-school experiences, thus greatly enlivening the tedium of form work. He had a great belief in treating his form with old-fashioned courtesy, and would address us as "Now, gentlemen." But he made the lessons most interesting and I learnt more from him than any master in the school. He was much interested in music and I suppose this made him

---

17 A Housemaster appointed in 1884.
18 The Rev Dr Frederick Temple (1821-1902) was Headmaster of Rugby from 1858 to 1869, was appointed bishop of Exeter in 1869, and became Archbishop of Canterbury in 1896.
19 The Rev Henry Hayman DD (1823-1904) was appointed Headmaster of Rugby in 1870 after the departure of Frederick Temple to the bishopric of Exeter. He seems not only to have submitted out-of-date testimonials when applying for the post, but also behaved somewhat unfairly over some staff appointments. The staff as a body rose up against him, and appealed both to the School Governors and to Temple, who fully supported the staff. Hayman was dismissed, becoming the Rector of Aldingham in Lancashire. He was subsequently an Honorary Canon of Carlisle Cathedral but had died before Nicholson arrived in Carlisle.

[e]specially kind to me, and he often took me out with him for long rides on horse-back, — a very exceptional treat in those days at Rugby.

Another great friend among the masters was the Rev W H Payne Smith, who was my tutor[20]. He was one of the first who took a real interest in boys outside their school work and regular games. He encouraged such hobbies as Natural History and Architecture, and many were the delightful excursions we made with him on our bicycles to neighbouring places of interest. He was I think the most 'human' of all the masters, at least in our eyes. Then there was dear old Mr Lindsay[21], the drawing master, with whom I became most intimate: I think he always showed me special kindness owing to his affection and admiration for my eldest brother, who had preceded me at Rugby, and must have been one of the best of his pupils.

By this time it was necessary to decide what was to be my future walk in life. Many things were suggested, but at last in a heart-to-heart talk with my mother I told her that I felt I could be nothing but a musician. She, as usual full of sympathy, broached the idea to my father. To him it was a real disappointment, for it meant that none of his sons would follow the sort of career in which he had earned such distinction. Music to him meant almost nothing beyond a polite accomplishment, and as a profession seemed quite futile; — "Just being a mere fiddler!" But he was above all things a philosopher besides being a very practical man: it was therefore ordained that before my parents' consent could be given I must be tested by some eminent musician. Accordingly I was sent to Windsor and put through my paces by Sir Walter Parratt[22]. The upshot of the test was that I was given my heart's desire, with the extremely wise advice to my parents that before concentrating on music I should go and take an ordinary Arts degree at Oxford. This advice I have never for one moment regretted, for though it has meant that I have been handicapped through life as an executant, never attaining the first rank in this respect, the gain in other directions was enormous: had I concentrated at once on music I am sure that I should never have met with the success that has fallen to my lot.

Oxford University (1893-1897)

Accordingly I went up to Oxford, entering New College[23], where my eldest brother had been before me, in October 1893. Life at Oxford suited me exactly. I fear I did not do very much work, and, though I read English Literature for my final Schools with a good deal of pleasure, I only succeeded in getting a third. But I made hosts of friends and had great musical experiences.

---

20 The Rev William Henry Payne-Smith, M.A. (b 1852), educated at Marlborough College and in Oxford at Trinity College and Christ Church, was Vice-Principal of Wycliffe Hall in Oxford from 1880 until appointed to Rugby in 1884. His father was Dean of Canterbury.

21 Thomas Mitchener Lindsay (1841-1919), born in Liverpool, studied at the Royal College of Art. He was headmaster of the Roeland Street School of Art in Cape Town, South Africa, from 1864 and headmaster of the Government School of Art in Belfast from 1870. He was appointed to Rugby as a 'teacher of drawing' in 1880.

22 Following Nicholson's 'audition' and subsequent study with Sir Walter Parratt at the Royal College of Music, the two remained in contact until Parratt's death in 1924.

23 He began his studies on 10th Oct 1893.

Through my friendship with the Rev Dr J H Mee[24] I got my first practical acquaintance with Chamber music at the Musical Union and at his own house, Kettell Hall. High-class professional Chamber concerts could be heard weekly at the Musical Club[25].

Rev J H Mee 1894

Oxford University Musical Union Committee 1894/95
(SHN back right, Johnny Mee middle centre, Theodore Walrond seated on floor, front right)

---

24 Rev John Henry Mee (1852-1918) MA DMus (1888) A Fellow of Merton College. He held many posts including that of Precentor of Chichester Cathedral. A graduate in classics and music at Oxford University, he was a Founder member of the Oxford University Musical Union and also one of the founders of the today's Musicians' Union. He composed a string quartet, anthems and songs and he was a contributor to Sir George Grove's Dictionary of Music and Musicians.

25 The Oxford University Musical Club was founded by Sir Hubert Parry and C H Lloyd in 1874. It subsequently merged with 'Union' to become 'The Oxford University Musical Club and Union'. Both had similar aims, but all performers at the 'club' were amateurs.

One of the leading lights at both institutions was Edmund H Fellowes[26] who was quite the best amateur violinist I have ever heard. He has since won a European reputation for his researches in Tudor music. Another prominent member was Duncan Wilson[27] (now Sir Duncan Wilson of the Home Office): he was a brilliant pianist and we became close friends and for a time shared 'digs'. 'Johnny Mee', as he was affectionately called, had a most remarkable influence on the life of the undergraduates. Not only was he the life and soul of the Musical Union, which he had founded, but with boundless hospitality he kept open house every Sunday evening for those who liked to come and try their hands at Chamber music. And we responded with enthusiasm. Everyone was encouraged to do his bit, however feeble it might be, and, though there were some excellent performances, at times the noises were excruciating: but never once was our beloved host seen to smile or to sanction any sort of discouragement. At about 11 o'clock the music would end and then we would gather round the fire to listen to his marvellous 'stories' and to talk about everything under the sun until the last moment when a frantic rush would allow us to get back into College by midnight. Johnny Mee was a remarkable man in many ways: — considerably deformed, owing to an accident in childhood, he yet managed to play a very good game of tennis: besides being a Doctor of Music he was a Lecturer, I think either in History or Philosophy, at Worcester College and a Fellow of Queen's: he was also Precentor of Chichester Cathedral, though he only functioned actively when he was at his country home at Westbourne, Sussex: and he was I should think unique in the fact that he and his father had married two sisters, — so that, as he used to say, he was brother-in-law to his own father as well as his nephew by marriage!

I suppose it was really my Oxford days that caused my main interest to turn to Church music. Certainly this was not so at Rugby, for I am bound to say that the Chapel services there made little impression upon me, except one of boredom. A very 'low Church' tradition had been

Edmund Fellowes aged 7

---

26 The Rev Edmund Horace Fellowes (1870-1951) was indeed a fine violinist and, at the age of eight, the virtuoso violinist Joseph Joachim offered to take him to Berlin to train as a professional violinist. Instead, he (or his family) decided that he pursue a career in the Anglican Church. He studied theology in Oxford at Oriel College, was ordained deacon in 1894, priest in 1895, took a Mus Bac degree in 1896 and became Precentor of Bristol Cathedral in 1897. He was a minor canon of St George's Chapel, Windsor from 1900 until his death (through the reigns of five monarchs) and, from 1924 to 1927, he directed the choir following the death of Sir Walter Parratt. He was on the Council of the Plainsong and Mediæval Music Society from 1931 to 1946 and he is perhaps best known as a musicologist who researched and edited a vast amount of Tudor music, both sacred and secular. Further photographs of Fellowes can be found in Chapter V.

27 Sir Duncan Randolph Wilson CVO CBE (1875-1945) studied at Eton and Magdalen College, Oxford, where he took his degree with first-class honours in natural sciences. A career civil servant as an economist he was latterly chief inspector of factories until his retirement in 1940.

inherited from the days of Arnold[28], and musically the one idea was 'hearty' singing. Anything like 'ritual' would have been [an] anathema, and there was nothing whatever to appeal to any boy with an artistic sense: indeed, except for occasional visits to Cathedrals in the holidays, I had never been present at a service that really attracted me. So if I had any ideas at all about a particular form of musical career they lay, I think, in the direction of school work. But when I came to Oxford this soon changed. There were the lovely Chapel services at New College, Magdalen and Christ Church, each of the three in those days having its own Choir school and Lay Clerks, and each of them rendering two daily choral services. I was a very frequent attendee at all three places, often accompanied by my old Rugby friend, Theodore Walrond[29] who was at Balliol.

MR. THEO. WALROND, M.A., F.R.C.O.

Of the three choirs, that of Magdalen had the highest reputation: so much so that it was necessary to get a ticket of admission even for weekday services, and the Chapel was always crowded. The organist was Dr Varley Roberts[30]. He was undoubtedly a very gifted choir-trainer and had brought the choir to a high pitch of perfection. Anyone who knew musical life at Oxford in those days is full of stories of this remarkable character. So many of them have been recorded, that I will only mention two, which are perfectly authentic. The Magdalen choir assembled for their first rehearsal under the comparatively unknown Yorkshireman who had been chosen as their Director, fully conscious of the reputation they had acquired under his distinguished

Dr J V Roberts

---

28 Dr Thomas Arnold (1795-1842), regarded by many as Rugby School's greatest Head Master (serving from 1828 until 1842) is known to many for his depiction in the novel *Tom Brown's Schooldays* by Thomas Hughes (1822-1896). He reformed many school policies and invented the 'prefect' system under his ideals of "First religious and moral principle, second gentlemanly conduct, third academic ability". Today The Arnold Singers, a chamber choir at Rugby School, is named after him and there is an Arnold Foundation to provide bursaries.

29 Born in Glasgow, Theodore Hunter Hastings Walrond (1872-1935) was briefly Nicholson's assistant at Carlisle Cathedral and then succeeded him as Acting-Organist in 1908 until the appointment of F W Wadeley in 1910. After leaving Carlisle he worked for the Board of Education and became one of H M's Inspectors of Schools. Appointed to the Council of the SECM in May 1932, he resigned in June 1933 on his retirement from the Board of Education. He moved to Winchester, where he was appointed organist of St Cross and assistant at the cathedral.

30 John Varley Roberts (1882-1918) took up his first organ post at St John's in Farsley near Leeds at the age of twelve. After serving at Halifax Parish Church he became organist of Magdalen College Oxford though, according to Watkins-Shaw in *The Succession of Organists*, Varley Roberts's playing may not have been top rate. Roberts was an examiner for Oxford University and he composed many anthems together with part-songs and cantatas. He was also organist of St Giles in Oxford from 1885 to 1893.

predecessors Sir Walter Parratt and Sir John Stainer. The practice went through without much incident, and at the end Roberts addressed them thus: "Gentlemen and boys: ye have the makin's of a choir!" On one occasion, when I had gone to consult him about the advisability of taking a post in Yorkshire, he described Yorkshire folk to me thus: — "Aye, — they may drop their aitches, but they're not 'ypocrites or 'oombugs."[31] He had a great admiration for his own compositions, and he was said to have written an Oratorio called *Jonah* which had a bass solo for the Whale!

New College choir was directed by Dr James Taylor[32], an elderly gentleman with a long white beard. He was a fine organist of the old-fashioned school and had one of the most lovely organs to play on that I ever heard, — an untouched "Father Willis": but he was better known in Oxford as a really first-rate pianist. His choir was excellent: perhaps less highly finished than Magdalen, but I think more natural and spontaneous. I remember a splendid boy soloist, Ivimey[33], — one of the best boys I ever heard: I made his acquaintance again in later years when I accepted his son as a chorister at Westminster Abbey.

At Christ Church was Basil Harwood[34], who had recently succeeded Lloyd[35], He was a splendid player and was producing his fine organ compositions, — *Dithyramb*, *Paean*, *Requiem*, &c. It was a rare treat to get him to play one of these; I was constantly in his organ loft and had several lessons from him. His choir always suffered from the poor acoustics of the Cathedral, but it was very efficient and its repertoire was probably the most interesting of the three. It [the choir] contained two very heavy basses who were known to the undergraduates as 'Thunderguts' and 'Rumblebelly'.

Dr Basil Harwood

---

31 Another Anecdote of Varley Roberts is worthy of repetition. A member of the congregation had joined in with the singing of the Psalms. When rebuked by Roberts after the service, the offender claimed he had a right to sing as this was the House of God. Roberts replied "That's just where yer make a mistake young man, this is Magdalen College Chapel!"

32 James Taylor (1833-1900) was born in Gloucester and at the age of 17 became organist of St Mary-le-Crypt there. His piano skills took him to study at the Royal Academy of Music with (Sir) William Sterndale Bennett (1816-1875). In 1865 he became organist of New College, serving until his death. After appointment to New College he took an Oxford B Mus in 1873 and he received an honorary D Mus in 1894. He was also University Organist for 28 years and conducted the Oxford Philharmonic Society for 22 years. He was the leading piano teacher in Oxford at that time and gained a reputation in chamber music performances. A shy and modest man, it is clear from contemporary writings that he was greatly liked and respected by both students and colleagues.

33 Walter Thomas Ivimey also performed solos in concerts in Oxford. He went on to be an Academical Clerk (i.e. choral scholar) singing bass/baritone at Magdalen College where he was also active in theatrical performances. In 1910 he became a National Health Insurance Commissioner.

34 Basil Harwood (1859-1949) studied with George Riseley of Bristol Cathedral, at Charterhouse, Trinity College, Oxford, and in Leipzig with C Reinecke and S Jadassohn. Harwood was organist of Trinity College, Oxford, of St Barnabas, Pimlico, London, of Ely Cathedral (1887-1892) and then of Christ Church Cathedral in Oxford (1892-1909). To his choristers at Christ Church he was affectionately known as 'Billy'. He took the Oxford D Mus in 1896, but retired from professional music early (in 1909) to administer the family estates in Gloucestershire.

35 C H Lloyd (1849-1910), see Chapter III.

Nothing shows the change that has come over Cathedral music in the last 50 years better than a recollection of the choice of anthems and services in those days. We who were keen would eagerly scan the weekly service lists in order that we might not miss our favourites. I think the most popular anthem was Mendelssohn's *Hear my prayer* (an easy first): close runners were Schubert's *Song of Miriam*, Gounod's *Gallia* and Stainer's *Lead, kindly light* (a particular favourite): it will be noted that each of these contains a treble solo, without which no anthem was considered really perfect. At Magdalen some of the 'pieces de resistance' were S Wesley's *In exitu Israel* or *Exultate Deo*, when Varley Roberts would come in at the end with the organ to show that his choir had kept the pitch! Another great favourite was – of all things – Meyerbeer's *91st Psalm*. Services like those of Barnby, Gadsby, Calkin, Stainer and Martin, with some of Stanford's, appeared on every list; but the fine old Tudor music was practically unheard, and even Purcell and Blow were rarities (which I fear we thought rather dull!).

Besides the College Chapels there were certain churches much frequented by undergraduates, for in those days church-going was quite the fashion. St Barnabas, under the remarkable Father Nowell[36], met the needs of those who were ritualistically inclined, and the recently built Cowley Fathers' church[37] gave us a fine taste of plainsong: at the University Church the vicar was a young Magdalen don, Cosmo Gordon Lang[38], who drew huge crowds of undergraduates by his remarkable preaching at the popular evening services which he instituted.

The Rev Dr Sir Frederick Arthur Gore Ouseley with the Tenbury choir c 1881

---

36 Actually this was the Rev Montague Henry Noel (1840-1929), Old Etonian and the first vicar of St Barnabas from 1869 to 1899. He was a very ritualistic follower of the "Oxford Movement", so much so that a cartoonist wrote (alluding to the church's proximity to the railway) that it was "Barn'bas Junction - change here for Rome."

37 A parallel strand to the 'Oxford Movement' was a desire to re-establish religious orders within the Anglican Church. Fr Richard Meux Benson (1824-1915), the founding parish priest of the parish of Cowley St John, was a strong supporter and in 1866 he founded The Society of St John the Evangelist (SSJE). His Mission House grew rapidly and dedicated itself to national and international mission work. Locally the fathers were known as the Cowley Fathers or, more affectionately, as the 'Cowley Dads.' Missions were established in India, Canada, South Africa, Japan and Scotland. A new church was built, the Church of St John the Evangelist, dedicated by the Bishop of Oxford on 12 May 1896 (i.e. during Nicholson's time in Oxford). Today the SSJE is based in Westminster, London.

38 For more on Archibishop Cosmo Gordon Lang (1864-1945), and his important role in the first decade of the *School of English Church Music*, see *SNCSN*.

I think it must have been Johnny Mee's talks of Tenbury and Sir Gore Ouseley[39] that first planted in my mind the germ of an idea which made me wonder whether one day I might be able to found a musical College. I think I must have had the idea at the back of my mind even so long ago as this, for I remember my mother, on more than one occasion when we were discussing the future, saying, "I rather expect that one day you will start some School like Sir Gore Ouseley's": so I must have given some indication of my thoughts. Anyhow it is certain that it was at Oxford that my mind became really set on Church music.

But there were plenty of other musical interests. At Balliol was John Farmer[40], of Harrow fame, and surely one of the quaintest of people. His idol was Bach, whom he called "Boch", and he had the greatest contempt for anything like emotionalism (in spite of his own compositions): he would speak of a visit to Magdalen Chapel as 'going to get your soul shampooed', and said it was enough 'to make an Angel moult or God Almighty turn bilious'. Nevertheless he did excellent work with the Balliol concerts on Sunday evenings, which were a great feature of the musical life, and in these he was very ably seconded by Dr Ernest Walker[41] who succeeded him as Director, and often delighted us by his beautiful playing. Old John Farmer, though a great devotee of the German classical composers, had a profound contempt for anything he considered a pose: "I can't stand those people who go Brahmsing about", was one of his happiest remarks.

A don at Worcester was W H Hadow (later Sir Henry Hadow of educational fame), who had just written his delightful *Studies in Modern Music*[42]: he was a great light at the Musical Club and a splendid lecturer. The Professor of Music was Sir John Stainer. I knew him intimately, for when he was organist of St Paul's Cathedral he had been a friend of my grandparents in

---

39 At the age of 19 the Rev Dr Sir Frederick Arthur Gore Ouseley (2nd Baronet) MA, Mus D, LLD (1825-1889) inherited the baronetcy and estate from his father who had been a founder of the Royal Academy of Music. From 1850 to 1851 he was organist of St Barnabas in Pimlico and in 1854 he founded St Michael's College, Tenbury, 'for the education of boys in music'. His College continued with daily cathedral-style choral services until closure in 1985. In 1855 he became Professor of Music at Oxford University and he was a canon of Hereford Cathedral from 1886.

40 John Farmer (1835-1901), a child prodigy, came to prominence after his piano 'demonstrations' at the London International Exhibition of 1862. After teaching abroad, he was appointed organist and Music Master at Harrow School in 1864, under Henry Montague Butler. Farmer did much to elevate the place of music in the school and also discarded many mid-Victorian chants and hymns, which he nicknamed 'sweedle-pipe tunes' which had been in use in Chapel. At Harrow he composed school songs and *Willow the King*, which became a well-known cricketing song. When Butler retired in 1885, Farmer moved to Balliol College, Oxford, as organist and he founded the 'Balliol Concerts'. In his leaving speech, Butler described Farmer as a man "who made us laugh and cry almost at will; whose wit and humour and explosions and eccentricities and invariable kindnesses have made up so large a part of the charm and romance of the last 24 years." (from *Harrow* by P H M Bryant, London, Blackie & Son, 1936)

41 Born in India, Ernest Walker (1870-1949) completed his Mus.D. at Oxford University in 1898 whilst he was assistant organist (1891-1901) to John Farmer at Balliol College. On Farmer's death, he became organist of Balliol resigning in 1913 because his own views on religion were incompatible with the religious texts sung in the chapel. He continued as director of music at the college until 1925, resigning to concentrate on composition. He was an examiner for the university, a writer contributing to the second edition of Grove's Dictionary and he published a notable *History of Music in England* 1907 which remained in print until c 1980.

42 Musicologist Sir William Henry Hadow CBE (1859-1937) studied at Malvern College and Worcester College, Oxford, where he subsequently taught, becoming Dean in 1889. In 1909, he moved to Newcastle before appointment as Warden and Vice-Chancellor of the University of Durham in 1916. In 1919, he was appointed Vice-Chancellor of Sheffield University serving until 1930. He published several reports on education, notably *The Education of the Adolescent* 1926 and was a leading influence in English education at all levels in the 1920's and 1930's. He was author of books on music and music theory, especially the *Oxford History of Music* (6 vols. 1901-1905) of which he was both editor and contributor. Knighted in 1918, Hadow's series of *Studies in Modern Music*, begun in 1893, were biographies of 19C composers.

Charterhouse days. He was much amused when my mother told him how she used to draw surreptitious portraits of him during the long sermons at St Paul's, when she was a little girl and he an extremely seraphic choirboy. I am glad to take this opportunity of speaking of Stainer as an excellent and most learned musician. He is now generally thought of as a composer of Church music of a type that is out of fashion and perhaps of little serious merit. From all accounts he must have been a wonderful organist and choir-trainer, and his influence on the music of his day was quite remarkable. He was the first to bring fresh life to the dull and inadequate performances of music that were customary in Cathedrals during the first half of the nineteenth century. He revolutionised the services and the personnel of the choir at St Paul's, and every Cathedral in the land gradually followed his example. He was indeed a pioneer, and had he been alive at the present day he would certainly have been in the forefront of the workers for reform and improvement in Church music.

Sir John Stainer (1840-1901)

John Stainer, the eighth of nine children, showed musical promise from an early age, becoming a chorister at St Paul's Cathedral at the age of nine, and rising to become one of the choir's leading soloists. Grove subsequently describes him as "already a remarkable player and an excellent sight-singer". In 1857, at the age of 17, he became organist at the newly founded St Michael's College in Tenbury where he wrote the anthem *I saw the Lord*, reckoned by many to be his masterpiece.

In 1860 Stainer became organist at Magdalen College, Oxford, and then of St Paul's Cathedral in 1872. It is easy to forget that Stainer was also an academic. Knighted by Queen Victoria in 1888 for his services to church music, he became Professor of Music at Oxford University in the following year.

Stainer never regarded himself as a great composer, more of a person unable to say 'no' when approached by a succession of clergymen with commissions. E H Fellowes (in *ECM* 1951) recalled the time, on his last visit to Stainer before the latter's death, when "he suddenly stopped me in the Magdalen walks and said … he regretted ever having published most of his compositions".

Of his compositions it may be said that they were mainly written to supply a need for easy and attractive music at a time when choirs were springing up in parish churches all over the land. He did not take them very seriously, and indeed he told me that he 'did not consider himself a composer', and thought that the best thing he had ever written was the hymn-tune "The saints of God"[43]. I am sure that, had he lived longer, he would have regretted works like *The Crucifixion*, which was written for his old friend Canon Barker[44] at Marylebone Church: but it must in fairness be remembered, however much musicians may dislike the work, that no one has succeeded in writing anything to take its place in the affections of the ordinary Church-goer; and for a man of Stainer's intense religious convictions this might have meant more than mere musical success. He had an amazing knowledge of musical history, and to spend an afternoon with him among the many treasures of his library was in itself an education. He was a pioneer in the study of plainsong in this country and it was he who first directed the attention of Dr E H Fellowes to the unknown treasures of Tudor music. He also did admirable work for the improvement of music in schools under the Board of Education, when he was its Chief Inspector of Music. I only once heard him extemporize, and that was on his large harmonium, but it was enough to show his mastery in this rare art. In concluding this short tribute to a really great man I quote a letter received from him, in reference to my B Mus Exercise and his professorship, shortly before his death in 1901 at the age of sixty:

> *Education Department* *On tramp*
> *Whitehall.* *May 17 1899*
>
> My dear Nicholson,
>
> My wife and I were at Mentone till the early part of March; what a terrible loss and annoyance to you all! I cannot imagine anything more distressing than the burning of one's home, and such a home! *
>
> I presume Exercises must be sent before 1st August as usual, but as I have resigned the professorship I shall escape the work of looking through all of them. I think Exercises must be sent to Sir Hubert Parry at the R C M, — but if you do not mind sending a stamped and addressed envelope to the Clerk of the Schools, you will receive official information.
>
> I have held the post 10 years, and I now find the preparation of the Lectures too much for my long-worked head, and the examinations and exercises too much for my one faithful eye!!!
>
> Please give my best regards to Lady Nicholson,
>
> I am yours truly, John Stainer
>
> If you are in Oxford when you are here pray look us up.

* The event referred to at the beginning of his letter is the disaster that befell my old home in February 1899 in its total destruction by fire.

---

43 The tune "Rest" 8 8 8 8 8 8 (1873)

44 The Rev Canon William Barker was Rector of St Marylebone and later Dean of Carlisle.

Besides purely musical experiences in Oxford I had one of a somewhat different kind which was not without its value later on. A friend had asked me to help in what was known in those days by the not very alluring title of a 'Ragged School'[45], in which he and other undergraduates were interested. This involved taking a class on Sunday afternoons in a somewhat dilapidated building in a pretty bad slum. The boys were plentiful, but the roughest of the rough. Why they came at all I do not know, for the Vicar, who was a 'muscular Christian' of the extreme Evangelical type, made no bones about using his muscles freely when more peaceful methods failed. When the miscellaneous crowd was quelled into something like submission it was necessary to keep them so; but taking one's class was rather like sitting on a volcano, which might erupt at any moment: in fact, as we were all in one room, there was a pretty constant series of eruptions! The only chance was to manage to interest them somehow. I don't think I managed to teach them much in the way of Sunday-School lessons, but I came to like the boys in spite of their roughness, and I suggested to the Vicar that I should be of more use in trying to form a singing class to meet on a week-night, rashly promising to run it myself. This was approved and quite a good number of the boys turned up. I knew little about training their voices, and less about keeping them in order: there were some rather lurid scenes, but gradually things began to shake down and after a while we managed to give a concert to raise funds for a piano. It happened that a kindly musical don got wind of it and came himself and nobly made up the sum needed. So we got our piano and at the same time a certain reputation: several of the boys managed to get into the choirs at the smaller Colleges and the parish churches, and when the time came to leave Oxford I was quite sorry to have to give up my class.

It was a useful experience, and I advise any young man whose job it will be to manage boys to seek for a similar chance. No one can teach you how to handle boys in the lump; — you have got to find out for yourself, and it is a good thing to buy your experience in a place where it does not much matter if you meet with a few defeats. I really learnt quite a lot in that Ragged School, — a good deal more than I taught!

It was while at Oxford and during the last part of my time at Rugby that I began to develop a taste for those many 'hobbies' that have made my life, or at any rate my holidays, so pleasant. Happy indeed is the man who has plenty of hobbies, and I confess I have hardly ever known what it is to be bored by having nothing particular to do. My main recreation in those days was cycling. I used to go for long tours, mainly by myself, during the holidays, and I think I must be almost unique in being able to say that I have visited every Cathedral in England and Wales on a 'push-bike', — and a good many of them before pneumatic tyres were invented! This of course led me to know England extremely well, long before the days of

---

[45] Although there had been early individual schools, the Ragged School Union as an organised movement began in 1844. It provided free education, food, clothing, lodging and other home missionary services in working class districts. Charles Dickens wrote his Christmas Carol after experiencing the poor conditions in one such school. With better local education legislation, these schools had all but disappeared by 1900. There is now a Ragged School Museum in London near Regent's Canal, housed in what was once London's largest Ragged School.

motors, and this knowledge has been a delightful possession.

Very often these tours included visits to and short journeys on the many small independent railways that were then in existence all over the country. I have always been extremely interested in railways ever since I was a small boy and watched the 'High Barnet Train'; in fact, like many small boys, it was my firm intention to become an engine driver when I grew up! This may seem a curious taste for a musician; but it is, for some reason, one that is shared by many organists, — Walter Alcock, who has made his own private railway, Henry Ley, the late Charles Hylton Stewart of Windsor and Charles Macpherson of St Paul's are all to be numbered amongst railway enthusiasts. Though I liked express trains on main lines, I think my special interest was in the queer little railways, of which even the names are now forgotten. There was the old "East and West," which was planned to form a trunk route right across England; and the "Manchester and Milford" in the remotest depths of Wales, which started some 30 or 40 miles from Milford and never got within a hundred of Manchester. Then there was the "Eastern and Midlands" which meandered around Norfolk and always seemed to bring one to its 'hub of the universe' at a place called Melton Constable; and the delightfully primitive "Bishop's Castle" in Herefordshire, the last railway to retain the old chain brakes. The nicest of all was perhaps the Port Carlisle Railway, worked by a "Dandy Coach" drawn by a horse. The main lines were much more interesting in old days than they are now, with modern grouping. Each had its own distinctive livery for engines and carriages, and this added greatly to the interest of travelling. The sight of the splendid-looking 8 ft singles starting from King's Cross with the 'Flying Scotsman' was indeed thrilling.

'The Dandy' Port Carlisle

The 'Flying Scotsman' passing New Barnet hauled by a Stirling 8ft Single

The broad-gauge trains on the Great Western were still running, though I did not happen to know very much of that particular line. Then there were the famous races between the East and West Coast routes to Edinburgh. It was while I was at Oxford that the extension to London of the old "Manchester, Sheffield and Lincoln-shire" was being made, and I often used to bicycle over towards Buckingham to watch the work in progress. So that when the line was finally opened as the "Great Central" I was greatly interested to travel in the very first train from Marylebone station to Rugby and back. Perhaps the greatest railway thrill in my life was when the father of one of my choristers managed to arrange for me the very rare privilege of being allowed to ride on the footplate of an express engine from Marylebone to Manchester. It was rather a hair-raising experience, and in spite of the 'sweat-rag' thoughtfully provided by the driver I descended from the cab at the end of my journey looking far more like an assistant stoker than an Abbey organist. Sketching, in a very mild way, has always been one of my hobbies, a very harmless one as it costs practically nothing and the results need never be shown. Photography, too, I began in Rugby days. Other hobbies, involving use of the hands, have been a delight at various times, — carpentry, book-binding and printing have all had their turn. In the latter perhaps the most ambitious effort was *The Jackdaw of Rheims* (1896) for which the cover was designed by my eldest brother [Charles], Archie supplying excellent line drawings to illustrate the text, while I did the printing. This hobby I still greatly enjoy.

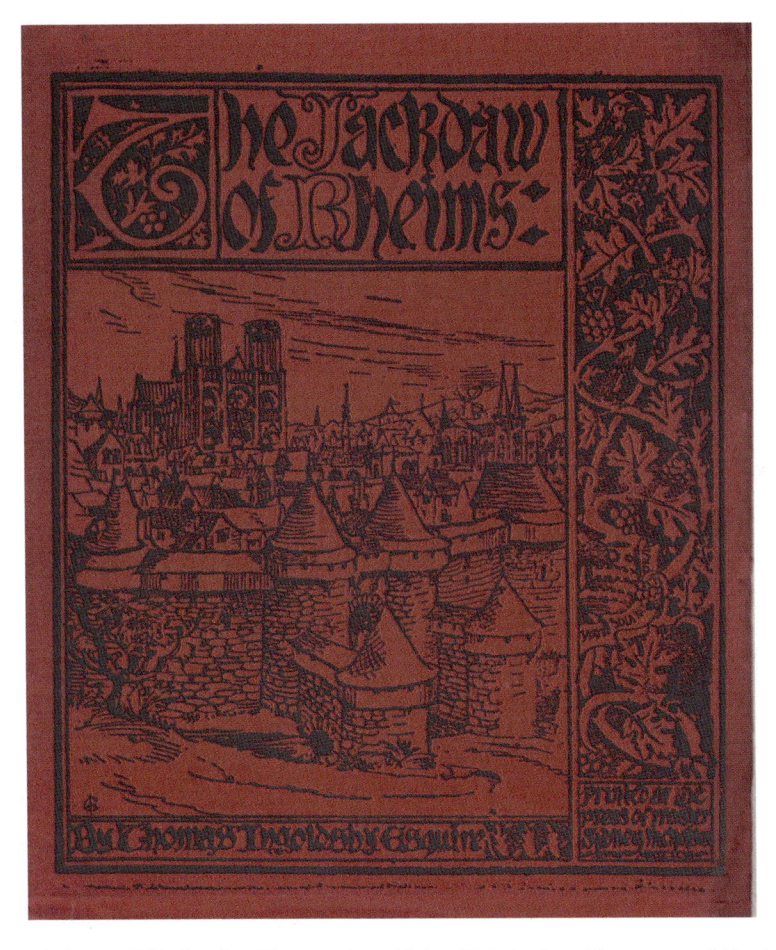

Cover of *The Jackdaw of Rheims* by Thomas Ingoldsby 'Printed on the press of Master Sydney Nicholson', with cover drawing by Sir Charles A Nicholson Bt.

The Nicholson Press

Nicholson's printing press was active from his Carlisle years right through to the time he wrote his 'Musings'. During the autumn of 1939, whilst St Nicolas College affairs were being wound up, he printed 200 copies of *A Metrical Medley* on his press at Woodchurch. The 'poems' were mostly rhymes he had previously penned to be sung in his children's operas *The Boy Bishop*, *The Children of the Chapel* and *The Guggenheimer Emerald*. The literary worth of these is somewhat mediocre. He sent copies to a number of highly placed clergymen and received very polite replies! He does offer an apologia at the end:

To THE READER:—

Reader, be 'gentle' as you scan these rhymes,
Nor think how sadly they misfit the times:
Think rather of a hobby's matchless power
To cheer the darkness of some black-out hour.
And should his hobby chance to raise a smile,
Or even lead you to forget awhile
These anxious days, how glad is he that sends
His token of goodwill, and cheers his friends.

It would appear that his intention with this publication was simply to 'cheer people up!'

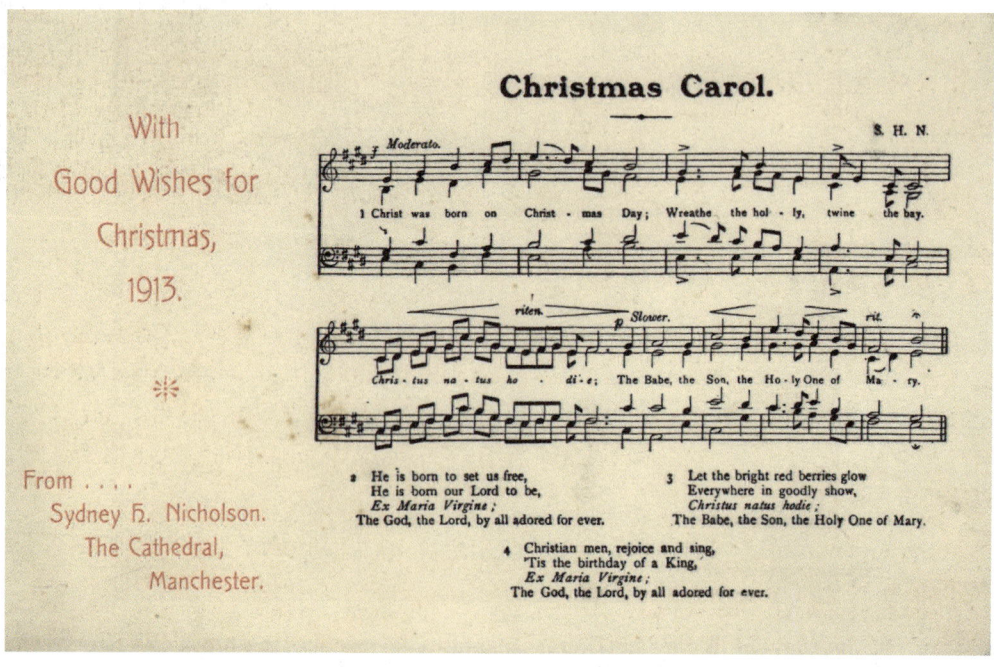

SHN sometimes printed his own Christmas cards: here is a 1913 example:

I took my degree at Oxford in 1897, after four extremely happy years, and stayed up a further term to work at music.

Royal College of Music (1898-1900)

On leaving Oxford I seriously began my musical career and entered the Royal College of Music, studying with Sir Walter Parratt (organ), Sir Charles Stanford (composition) and Walford Davies[46] (counterpoint). At the same time it happened that the organistship of the Parish Church, Chipping Barnet, two miles from my home at Totteridge, fell vacant, and I was (very trustfully) appointed to the post[47]. In this way I was able to get practical experience with a choir while pursuing my studies, and this proved a great advantage later on though at the time it rather interfered with my progress; but I think the experience gained was well worth the drawbacks, and I should recommend such a course to any young man who is intending to follow my profession. The great disadvantage of the ordinary training is that the young man emerges from his College probably as a splendid player and with a thoroughly sound theoretical knowledge of music, but when he is confronted with his first job he is completely at a loss how to handle his choir, and it takes him some years to discover how to get the best out of them. Meanwhile he may easily get discouraged, and consequently many a gifted young man will make a failure of his first post. If he has the chance to 'try his wings' while he is still a student, and has wise masters whose advice he can ask on any difficulties that may arise, it will be a great advantage to him.

Sydney Nicholson c 1898

---

[46] Sir Henry Walford Davies (1869-1941) was a chorister at St George's Chapel in Windsor. He was appointed organist of the Temple Church, London, in 1898, moving to Aberystwyth as Professor of Music at the university in 1920. Knighted in 1922, he returned to St George's, Windsor, as organist in 1927. His regular radio broadcasts to schools on music were very popular which led to his appointment as BBC Music Advisor. On the death of Sir Edward Elgar in 1934 he held the office of Master of the King's Music until his death.

[47] Nicholson took up the post from 1st Jan 1898

To be a pupil of Parratt and Stanford was a wonderful experience. Both of them were born teachers, though in very different ways.

Parratt had an almost uncanny power of detecting the slightest inaccuracy. He would walk about his room, or even outside it passing remarks perhaps to his many visitors, while his pupil went on playing: the unwary might think there was some chance of slip-shod work passing unnoticed, but the master would presently intervene with some such remark as — "I think, Mr Nicholson, if you will look carefully at the copy you will find that Bach preferred a B flat: you evidently prefer a B natural"; and he might add, in withering tones, "personally I am inclined to agree with Bach!" Another favourite *mot* was, "please observe the rests: they are so much nicer than the notes – sometimes!" He was certainly somewhat terrifying, yet he made his pupils adore him, and his high outlook on an organist's work was an inspiration to all who came into contact with him.

He was a great believer in musicians being men of all round interests (as he was himself), and he would often talk to us about literature and our own general reading and outside pursuits. One of his great recreations was chess, which he played without looking at the board, leaving his opponent to make the moves. He once told me that he learnt to do this as a method of training the memory. He apparently had a haunting dread of blindness (though I do not think that his eyesight was ever threatened), and he felt it was wise to prepare oneself so as to be able to meet such an eventuality by being as far as possible independent of one's eyes. There are amazing tales of his feats of memory. He knew the whole of the *48 Preludes and Fugues* of Bach by heart when he was a boy of 11 or 12 and played them as a 'birthday present' for his mother. It is said that on one occasion at Tenbury he directed two simultaneous games of chess while at the same time he played a Bach fugue from memory!

As a Bach player he was of course superb, and his advice on interpretation as well as his insistence on absolute accuracy was extraordinarily illuminating[48]. Though he taught us all manner of pieces, and did not even despise the lighter composers of the French school such as Guilmant or Dubois, it was of course in Bach that he was supreme.

---

48   The RSCM Colles Library contains Parratt's personal copies of Bach organ works donated by Henry G Ley. It is interesting to note that they are almost devoid of fingerings and registration markings.

Sir Walter Parratt (1841-1924)

Walter Parratt, son of the organist of Huddersfield Parish Church, was appointed organist of Armitage Bridge Church near Huddersfield at the age of 11, but was almost immediately sent off to London to the choir school of St Peter's Chapel in Palace Place, Westminster. Here he was a pupil of George Cooper Jnr (1820-1876), assistant organist of St Paul's Cathedral. He returned to Huddersfield at the age of 14 and was appointed organist of St Paul's Church there. Subsequently he served as organist to the Earl of Dudley, at Wigan Parish Church, then Magdalen College in Oxford and finally for 42 years at St George's Chapel in Windsor. The photograph (above left) is Parratt at the St George's organ c 1910. He was knighted in 1892 and the following year became Master of the Queen's Music. In 1883 he was the first professor of organ to be appointed when the Royal College of Music was founded and, from 1908 to 1918, he held the Chair of Music at Oxford University, concurrently with the post at Windsor. He was one of the foremost organ teachers of his day, with many of his students filling prestigious posts in cathedrals and public schools.

Parratt was clearly revered by his pupils and in June 1902 they arranged a dinner in his honour. In the photograph on the next page, Nicholson is second left on the second table. Note that, in this photograph, the former social convention of wearing white tie and tail coat to dinner has already started changing to that of wearing a black tie with tail-less Dinner Jacket, a semi-formal dress code which became fully established in Edwardian times.

Dinner for Sir Walter Parratt given by his pupils, 29th June 1902

One great joy was to walk with him across the Park on the way to Paddington, — striding along without overcoat and often hatless, his hair flying about in all directions, while he would talk on all manner of subjects — generally not music. And often one was invited to accompany him to Windsor for the afternoon service. The choir was most artistically trained and the accompaniment in exquisite taste: full of subtle variety but always most restrained. I remember one great occasion when the anthem was Stanford's *The Lord is my Shepherd*, exquisitely performed with Parratt playing and the composer standing by his side to listen.

He knew the power of sarcasm, and he used it to the full when roused. On one occasion he addressed one of his lay clerks, an aged alto, in his most acid tones, "Really Mr —, those sounds are scarcely human!" But with his pupils, at any rate those who really tried, he made each one feel that his progress was the one thing that mattered to him, and he spared no pains to give them of his very best: and of course in return we felt it to be almost disloyal to bring him anything that was not properly prepared. But, if we did, we heard of it; and we were not happier for the experience!

Work with Stanford was very different. Highly irascible and a man of violent moods, his lessons sometimes amounted to nothing but a series of inarticulate grumblings and abuse, emerging from behind a large cigar. But when he was in the mood there was no one like him for sheer brilliancy as a teacher. He would glance through the pages of manuscript and grasp his pupil's ideas in a few minutes: then he would set to work to pick out the weak points, suggest remedies, put in a few almost illegible scrawls, and send one away to ponder what he had said and find it invariably right.

He had the greatest dislike to slip-shod work of any kind, and this of course included illegible manuscript: "Play it slow and loud and without any pedal" was a favourite bit of advice. Anything like conceit or self-satisfaction roused his bitter anger, and he was sometimes very cruel in his treatment of those whose enthusiasm surpassed their knowledge. "Bosh! – Bosh! – Bosh!" he would say, turning over the pages of some over-facile string quartet or orchestral score, "All bosh! Take it away!" and lucky it was if he did not tear up the cherished manuscript before the composer's eyes.

But he **could** teach, and his amazing knowledge of the classics enabled him to point to the practice of the great masters and make the pupil feel that his criticisms were based not on his private opinion but upon wide experience of all that was best in his art.

At times, when in a good temper, he could be most charming and amusing, but it can seldom have happened that he was not engaged in a row with someone. Parratt, I think, never quarrelled with him and often acted as peacemaker. I, like everyone else, had an occasional 'dust-up' with him; but on the whole we were very good friends, and as a teacher I owe more to him than I can say.

Amongst others at the College I was brought into contact with Walford Davies, then a brilliant young man teaching counterpoint. I don't think we learnt much counterpoint from him, for we delighted to get him talking about the beauties of his beloved Bach and playing us preludes and fugues in his inimitable way, and with that lovely touch which still captivates his wireless listeners. Needless to say his lessons were deeply interesting, but I did not feel they led far in the direction of exams. So after enjoying a few terms of them I changed to Charles Wood[49] whom I found an excellent teacher, though very reserved and rather dry.

Charles Wood

A familiar figure at the College was Sir Frederick Bridge, whom later I was to know so well. He was always ready with some joke, and his counterpoint lessons, which I attended for a term or two, were largely taken up with performances of his latest Children's cantata or humorous part song. I do not think I ever met anyone who had such a ready wit as Bridge.

At one time his room was next to Parratt's: he was not very punctual for his classes, and his pupils were apt to congregate in Parratt's room, which was always a place of popular resort and a rather noisy one at that. One day Parratt put up a notice on his own door "WAITING

---

49 Charles Wood (1866-1926) was born in Armargh, Ireland, where he was a chorister at St Patrick's Cathedral. He studied in London at the RCM from 1883, being one of the inaugural students. He then made his home in Cambridge teaching at the university and ultimately becoming Professor of Music to the University in 1924.

ROOM FOR SIR FREDERICK BRIDGE'S PUPILS". Bridge came along and read it, tore down the notice, and substituted "THE COCKATOO HOUSE".

Once when rehearsing the Royal Choral Society a cat got into the Albert Hall and solemnly advanced up the middle aisle: the chorus began to laugh, and Bridge, turning round to see the cause, addressed the visitor, "Come along, miss, — there's your place, among the sopranos!"

On another occasion he was rehearsing the orchestra and could not get them to play as softly as he wished. "Now I was told that [at] a concert the other day you managed to get a most beautiful pianissimo: I suppose it was for one of those foreign conductors with a name as long as your arm!"
    "As a matter of fact, Sir Frederick", said the leader, "it was Mr Percy Pitt."
    "Oh", replied Bridge, "no wonder you could play soft for a fellow with those initials!"

Pervading the Royal College was the genial figure of Sir Hubert Parry. He was a most delightful person, beloved by everyone, and he drove his somewhat difficult team with wonderful success. He did little teaching himself during my time, and one only came in contact with him in occasional history lectures and at his splendid terminal addresses: but he was always accessible to those in need of advice or help. Whether he was a great administrator I do not know, but he was certainly an admirable Director.

In those days life at the College was far less of a social affair than it has since become. There was little intercourse between men and women students, who had to use separate staircases and separate waiting-rooms; and the women students were considerably in the minority. The organists were generally the most prominent among the students, though of course there were some brilliant composers who were not organists, such as Coleridge Taylor, John Ireland, T F Dunhill[50] and others. The number of students and professors was far smaller than now, and though the course of study was much less diffuse than at present I think there was more concentration on first-study work. The professors being fewer were well supplied with pupils, and consequently lessons were hardly ever missed through absence on examination tours or other outside engagements. The training was undoubtedly rather narrow: there was no attempt to teach conducting, so far as I know, and 'aural training' had not been invented: nor was it ever suggested that those who were destined to spend much of their lives in training other people's voices might with profit learn something about singing themselves. But what we set out to do we certainly did thoroughly.

---

[50] Samuel Coleridge-Taylor (1875-192) and John Ireland (1879-1962) are well known, but Thomas Dunhill (1877-1962) much less so. He was a music master at Eton (whilst Nicholson was there) before appointment as a professor at the RCM in 1905. Although Dunhill composed orchestral works and operas, he is best known now for the many easy piano pieces he composed for domestic and examination use.

Sir Charles Stanford (1852-1924)

Sir Frederick Bridge (1844-1924)
(at the Westminster Abbey organ)

Sir Hubert Parry (1848-1918)

Sir Henry Walford Davies (1869-1941)

While I was at the College I had the pleasure of seeing my first composition to appear in print and hearing it performed at St James's Hall. This was a part-song *Phyllida flouts me*[51], for which I was awarded a prize by the Magpie Madrigal Society[52]. This was followed by four [solo] songs, the only ones I have ever published. I stayed at the Royal College for three years, taking my B Mus degree in 1902.

An RCM end-of-term report signed by Parry and initialled by Parratt, Stanford and Walford Davies

---

51 Published by Laudy & Co in London in 1901, it was dedicated to Basil Johnson.
52 This was in 1900. The Magpie Madrigal Society (formerly the Magpie Minstrels), a large choir of some 200 members, flourished from 1888 to 1911 and was the idea of amateur musician and composer Sir Alfred Scott-Gatty though Lionel Benson was the conductor. The choir commissioned pieces from several famous composers including Stanford and Parry.

St John the Baptist, Chipping Barnet

Nicholson with the Barnet choristers in 1903

Meanwhile I was getting into the swing of things at Barnet. I found myself with a fine, large church, a delightful Rector, The Rev D W Barrett[53], a very well-run parish, a good though old-fashioned organ[54] and a very competent choir of some 16 boys and a good body of men, every one of whom was considerably older than myself, some of them having been in the choir long before I was born. They were a most loyal lot and put up with the inexperience of a youngster in the kindest way. This was my real introduction to what has been one of the greatest pleasures of my life, — my association with choirboys. Among the first new boys that I had to appoint were some who have remained my friends ever since: one[55] is a member of the Council of the School of English Church Music and regularly curbs me when I want to spend too much money: another is music master at one of the great public schools: others are doing useful work as organists and choirmasters in different parts of the country.

---

53 The Rev Daniel William Barrett (1848-1925) graduated at Trinity College, Dublin, in 1871. He was ordained in 1872 and served as Vicar of Nassington (near Peterborough) from 1870 to 1887 and then as Rector of Chipping Barnet.

54 By 'old-fashioned' in design Nicholson probably means 'traditional, for the organ was only 16 years old when Nicholson arrived. The specification can be found in Appendix E. For a small church it was an impressive instrument.

55 Fred Martin-Smith was elected to SECM Council 4th Dec 1930. At that time he was manager of Barclays Bank in the Brompton Road. He served as organist of the John Keble Church in Mill Hill from its opening in 1936 until his retirement to the country in 1955. He became Honorary Treasurer of the RSCM on 1st Jan 1951 retiring in 1963, whereupon he was made a Vice-President. A photograph of him as chorister is on the next page.

The Barnet boys soon became very good and the men well above the average, so that with the temerity of youthful leadership, we were able to tackle such anthems as *Hear my prayer* and Wesley's *Wilderness*, and, with the aid of an orchestral society which I conducted, performed such works as *The Hymn of Praise*; *The Creation* in which Stanley Marchant[56], (a pupil of that wonderful trainer of choirboys, James Bates[57], and afterwards organist of St Paul's Cathedral and now principal of the Royal Academy of Music), sang the solos in splendid style; and Haydn's *Seven Last Words* in which Harry Colles[58], then my fellow student at the Royal College and now Musical Critic of *The Times* played the organ. In 1899 I started the 'Barnet and District Church Choral Union', and with the neighbouring church choirs we held a series of annual Choral Festivals.

Fred Martin-Smith

It was in connection with one of these that I began my close friendship with Charles Macpherson[59], then the Sub-organist of St Paul's Cathedral, who had come to hear one of his Services which we had chosen and consented to play the organ. Here is the letter which he wrote after it:

> Your Choral Festival, at which you asked me to play, was a complete revelation to me. You seemed to obtain the best possible results with most indifferent material, and this, too, with a class of music **far** in advance of many other such festivals. If this was only your second of such services it points to a very great amount of organising power on your part, for everything was performed as though the thing were an ordinary, everyday occurrence. From a somewhat hasty and casual observation it was evident that your undoubted enthusiasm and skill had fired not only your own, but all the other choirs which took part in the service. In short you knew what was your ideal and you did your best to enforce it, and with great success.

---

56 (Sir) Stanley Marchant (1883-1949) was assistant organist at St Paul's from 1916 and full organist from 1927, retiring on his appointment as Principal of the RAM.

57 James Bates (d 1932) taught Voice Culture and Class-Singing at the Royal Academy of Music (1908-1922). He also served as choirmaster of Christ Church, Lancaster Gate (1883-1910), taught singing at many schools and was director of the London College for Choristers (1893-1919). His *Voice Culture for Children*, published in the Novello series of 'Primers', was widely admired.

58 Henry Cope (k/a 'Harry') Colles (1879-1943) studied at the RCM with Walford Davies, Hubert Parry and Walter Alcock and was then organ scholar at Worcester College in Oxford. In 1932 he received an honorary Doctorate from Oxford University. A teacher at the RCM, he was a Fellow and Governor of St Michael's College, Tenbury and Chairman of the Church Music Society. He was appointed as one of the first batch of Council Members for the School of English Church Music on 18th Sep 1930 and further appointed Deputy Chairman the following year. He remained on Council until his death. Editor of the 3rd and 4th editions of Grove's Dictionary of Music and Musicians and music critic for The Times, he published many books. He was editor of the SECM journal *English Church Music* and was responsible for the SECM *Gift Book* published in 1935. On the re-opening of St Nicolas College in Canterbury in 1946, the RSCM Library, now in Salisbury, was named after him.

59 Charles Macpherson D Mus, FRAM (1870-1927) was a chorister at St Paul's Cathedral and became organist to St Clement's, Eastcheap, at the age of 17 serving for three years. After study at the RCM, he returned to St Paul's in 1895 as sub-organist to Sir George Martin whom he succeeded in 1916, retaining the post until his death. A professor at the Royal Academy of Music, he was President of the Royal College of Organists from 1920 to 1922. Macpherson was buried in the crypt of St Paul's, next to the grave of Arthur Sullivan. His three predecessors at St Pauls Goss/Stainer/Martin and his two successors Marchant and Dykes Bower were all knighted but Macpherson was not, possibly because he died young and unexpectedly before an honour was considered.

These Choral Festivals gave me an early experience in a kind of work in which I have always interested myself throughout my life.

Charles Macpherson, after this first pleasant meeting, became a great friend of the family and a frequent visitor at The Grange, and my father was particularly fond of him.

Charles Macpherson

The 6th Barnet and District Choral Union Choir Festival 1903. SHN front centre with BA hood.

It must have been while still at Rugby that I first made the acquaintance of James Baillie Hamilton. He was a most fascinating man and we became great friends when he came to Totteridge with his wife, Lady Evelyn[60], the daughter of the Duke of Argyll. He had invented an instrument which he called the Vocalion[61]. The original idea had been a combination of a reed with a string; the vibrating reed setting the string sounding; and this idea, which I believe produced a beautiful tone, attracted a good deal of attention in scientific circles: but it was not found to be practical as applied to a keyed instrument owing to the impossibility of keeping all the strings in tune. So the original idea was abandoned, and the Vocalion had become, when I saw it, virtually a large and well-designed Harmonium, though a certain amount of variety of tone was obtained by various resonating devices. But my

---

60 Lady Evelyn Campbell (1855-1940) married Baillie Hamilton in 1886.
61 See Chapter II, Footnote 9.

purpose is not so much to describe the Vocalion as to relate a curious series of events of which it was the starting point.

Baillie Hamilton was a great friend of Dean Stanley[62] and, I suppose through this influence, a Vocalion was set up in Henry VII's Chapel. One evening, after the Abbey was closed, I was taken by my mother to see and play on the Instrument. The other members of the party, besides the Baillie Hamiltons, were Mr and Mrs Gladstone (the only time I ever saw the great man) and Lady Frances Baillie[63], who was sister of Lady Augusta Stanley[64]. My mother was introduced to Lady Frances, and conversation happened to turn on art. Lady Frances told my mother that she had made the acquaintance of a rising young artist who had painted an excellent portrait of her three sons, and suggested a visit to his studio. The invitation was accepted and my mother was much attracted by the artist, Herbert Olivier[65], and his work, and felt that he might be asked to undertake a portrait of my father. The portrait of the three sons she thought admirable: — one of the sons was the present Dean of Windsor[66] who some 40 years later became one of my intimate friends. Herbert Olivier duly came to Totteridge and made a most successful portrait of my father, besides establishing himself as a most delightful guest. My eldest brother Charles had won a travelling scholarship (for the study of architecture) and was about to start for Italy where the Olivier family were spending the winter. Naturally introductions were given, and the result was that Herbert's sister Evelyn[67] became engaged to my brother and they were married in 1895. Herbert himself met at Totteridge Margaret[68], the daughter of our neighbour Sir William Peat[69], and a few years later they too were married. Two marriages and a 40 years

Evelyn Olivier, later to become Lady C A Nicholson

---

62 The Rev Arthur Penrhyn Stanley (1815-1881) was Dean of Westminster from 1864 until his death.

63 Lady Frances Anne Bruce (1831-1894), Lady-in-Waiting to the Duchess of Edinburgh.

64 Lady Augusta Frederica Elizabeth Bruce (1822-1876), the wife of Dean Stanley (above) was the daughter of Thomas Bruce 7th Earl of Elgin (the man who removed the Elgin Marbles from the Parthenon in Athens). She was Lady-in-Waiting to HRH the Duchess of Kent and Resident Woman of the Bedchamber to Queen Victoria.

65 British artist Herbert Arnould Olivier (1861-1952) was an uncle of actor Sir Laurence Olivier. He studied at the Royal Academy Schools of Art winning the Creswick Prize in 1882. He taught at the Bombay School of Art in the 1880's and was elected to the Royal Society of British Artists in 1887. He was appointed an Official War Artist in 1917. In later life his work tended towards large ceremonial works using oils.

66 The Very Rev Albert Victor Baillie (1864-1955) was the Dean of Windsor from 1917 to 1945. He travelled with Nicholson to Canada in 1927 on the joint Westminster/Windsor choir trip, see Chapter V.

67 Evelyn Louise Olivier (1866-1927) was the aunt of actor Sir Laurence Olivier.

68 Margaret Barclay Peat married Herbert Olivier in 1903.

69 Born in Laurencekirk, Kincardineshire, Sir William Barclay Peat (1852-1936) was educated at Montrose Academy and became head of the firm of W B Peat & Co, Chartered Accountants. This very successful firm merged with others to become the giant KPMG of today. In 1927 when Nicholson launched the School of English Church Music, Sir William offered his services to Nicholson as Hon Auditor. He was good to

later friendship arising from that Vocalion! But that is not all. As we left the Abbey on that first evening we heard the sound of the big organ, and Baillie Hamilton took me up to the organ-loft. I think, but I am not sure, that it was Walter Alcock playing; anyhow, seeing that I was interested, he allowed me to put my fingers on the keys. And that was the first time I played the organ in Westminster Abbey! The old Vocalion was still in action, and occasionally used, when I became organist, but during the war it had suffered grievously through being surrounded with sand-bags, and I am afraid a good deal of the sand got into the works. Anyhow it had become practically useless; so it was given to the Rev H F Westlake[70], one of the Minor Canons, to be put in the church of the village of Warehorne[71] to which his father-in-law, Mr Raynoy, had just been appointed. And there it is still, not four miles from the village [Woodchurch] where I am writing these reminiscences!

Another Vocalion was purchased for me by my father and set up in the dining-room of the old Grange. This of course was a great pleasure to me and I found it very useful for practice. It was destroyed in the fire, and when the Grange was rebuilt, my father gave me a real organ, a most delightful little two manual instrument built by Henry Speechly[72].

This instrument accompanied me to Carlisle and later to Manchester, where it was rebuilt by Messrs Harrison. When I moved to Westminster I had to dispose of it for lack of space: it went to a preparatory school in Hertfordshire. Quite recently I discovered that this school had removed to Surrenden-Dering Park[73] in Kent, and was delighted to find that the organ from which I have had such pleasure was doing excellent duty in the School Chapel within a few miles of my country home [Woodchurch]. It is curious that two instruments which have been so closely connected with my musical life should have, almost by chance, come to anchorage in the same district as myself.

While I was living at Totteridge I became considerably interested in the "Boys Farm Home"[74] at East Barnet. This splendid institution had been founded by Col Gillum, a Crimean veteran, for whom my parents had great admiration. I was asked to look after the singing of the school and I used to visit them every week. It was interesting to try and get some musical

---

his word and although he had actually retired from accountancy in 1923, Peat, Marwick, Mitchell & Co. continued the auditing work without reward.

[70] The Rev Canon Herbert Francis Westlake, FSA (1879-1925), Custodian of Westminster Abbey. Author of books about Westminster Abbey, St Margaret's, Westminster and *The Parish Gilds of Mediæval England*.

[71] Near Ashford in Kent. The removal, by Hill Norman & Beard in 1925, cost £15.

[72] Henry Speechly (& Sons), Organbuilder active 1868-1940; a photograph of the instrument in Manchester is in Chapter IV.

[73] Founded in 1881 as Northaw School in Potters Bar, the school moved to Surrenden-Dering in Kent. In 1952 the school was destroyed by fire and moved to its present site at Norman Court where, in 1995, it was renamed Norman Court School. It closed in July 2012.

[74] In 1860 Colonel William Gillum, philanthropist and veteran of the Crimean War, purchased Church Farm for use by a school for destitute boys from London who had not been involved in crime. The Boys' Farm Home was a branch of the London Boys' Home initially founded in 1858 in Euston Road, London. Falling under the 1857 Industrial Schools Act, they were certified as industrial schools under the act and this allowed them to receive government funding. The boys were usually aged from ten to twelve on admission and were taught ordinary lessons as well as a trade so that they could become cobblers, tailors, and farm workers. At the age of fifteen they were found jobs by the school managers and for two years the school kept in contact with their former boys. There were originally only four boys when Church Farm School opened, but by the 1930s the number of boys at the school had risen to over a hundred. After East Barnet developed from a rural area into a suburb, the Church Farm School was moved to Church Hill, East Barnet, in 1937.

results out of these very rough lads, and I was not wholly unsuccessful.

But the great difficulty was to find suitable music for them to sing. Really good school song-books, such as are common to-day, were hardly to be found. So I set to work to compile a book which was published under the title *British Songs for British Boys*. The idea was to include as many as possible of the best National songs as well as the standard old ballads and a few folk-songs, always bearing in mind that they were intended for boys to sing, and should therefore express sentiments into which boys might reasonably be expected to enter. It was intended rather as a reaction against the current school songs of the day, which so often dealt with bluebells and daisies, or fairy rings, or May Queens, and other such things which Victorian children were supposed to like, but which in fact to an ordinary healthy boy seemed 'mere tripe'. The book was at once successful, getting a wide circulation among schools of all kinds[75]. The short explanatory notes accompanying each song were, I think, attractive, and also the provision made for a certain amount of part-singing if desired. Anyhow it was by far the most successful publication that I have ever embarked on, and though many much better books on similar lines have since been produced, I am glad to say it still holds its own. I think its musical success must be due to the fact that the original composition involved runs to no more than the accompaniments, and those are of the simplest kind!

The boy choristers of Church Farm School at the Barnet Choral Festival of 1902

---

[75] Originally published in 1904, it was reprinted 10 times up until 1934.

It was on 22nd February 1899 that the disastrous fire occurred at The Grange, to which I have already referred. Owing to a defective flue, fire broke out at the top of the house about 2 o'clock in the morning on a cold winter's night with a strong wind blowing. Roused by one of the servants, my brother and I went to our parents' room to wake them. When told what had happened and that it was necessary to leave at once, my father (who was then over 90) merely said "Well, I must put on my trousers first", and then came down in nightshirt, trousers and a 'tam-o-shanter cap' which he was fond of wearing. Over these garments was hurried[ly placed] a big fur coat, and the parents were placed in safety in the gardener's cottage. By the time we returned to the house it had become a roaring furnace and we were never able to get upstairs again. Of course there were no telephones in those days, so my brother Archie rode off to Barnet in his pyjamas on a bicycle to summon the local fire-brigade, while I with the willing help of neighbours tried to get as much as possible from the lower floors. We were able to get out nearly all the valuable tapestry by dragging it from the walls of the dining-room, and the bulk of the books from the Library; but many treasures were utterly destroyed, and, worst of all, the whole of my father's journal of a life-time perished. Yet his only comment when he heard of this was "perhaps it is just as well — there were a lot of things in the books which are better forgotten." Still the loss was irreparable

The Grange at Totteridge burning in the early hours of 22nd Feb 1899.
A fireman is directing his hose into the arched window.

and made it impossible to find material for writing his life, which would certainly have made a most interesting volume. Dressed as he had escaped from the fire, the wonderful old gentleman insisted on driving straight up to London, and appeared in this remarkable costume on the steps of The Athenaeum. To an old friend who greeted him with commiseration, asking whether there was anything he could do to help, his only reply was "Lend me a shirt!" We arranged to move into "Oakhurst", a new house nearly opposite The Grange, and within a week my eldest brother was making plans for a new Grange, my father taking the greatest interest in all the details, and as the work progressed making daily visits of inspection.

There cannot be many old gentlemen of 90 who are burnt out of house and home and live to superintend and thoroughly enjoy living in a new one[76]. But so it was with this grand old man, and he lived to within a few days of his 95th birthday[77], and was buried under an ancient yew tree in Totteridge Churchyard, on 12th November 1903, his friend Charles Macpherson playing the organ.

Sir Charles Nicholson laying the foundation stone of the 'new' Grange, 1900.

---

76   The family moved back into the rebuilt house on 21st June 1900.
77   Sir Charles died at 2.20pm on 8th Nov 1903 at The Grange, Totteridge.

This brought to a close what may be called the first chapter of my life, for soon after my father's death my mother decided to move her home to London, while, the ties that bound me to home being loosened, it seemed better that I should seek work farther afield.

The end of an era. In 1902, one year after Queen Victoria's death, 93 year old Sir Charles Nicholson (right) takes tea with 83 year old Sir Arthur Hodgson[78] (left).

---

[78] Australian pioneer and politician Sir Arthur Hodgson KCMG (1818-1902) went to Australia in 1839 and became general superintendent of the Australian Agricultural Company in 1856. He served in the New South Wales and Queensland Legislative Assemblies and was acting-premier during a visit by the Duke of Edinburgh. He returned to England in 1870 and lived near Stratford-upon-Avon, serving as Mayor of that town and as High Sheriff of Warwickshire. He died shortly after this photograph was taken. He was appointed KCMG in 1886 (Knight Commander of the Most Distinguished Order of Saint Michael and Saint George awarded to men and women who render extraordinary or important non-military service in a foreign country).

Chapter III
Eton, Westgate, Carlisle 1903-1907

Eton

It was obviously desirable to seek some post that was more lucrative than that of an ordinary parish church, and my thoughts again turned to school work. First I applied for the vacant music-mastership at Winchester College, but was thought too young. Then I was invited by Dr C H Lloyd[1] to join his staff at Eton as organist of the Lower Chapel. At first I went over for a few days each week from Totteridge, but I removed there permanently for the autumn term of 1903. My main duty, besides giving private lessons to the boys, was to play the organ for the services in the Lower Chapel.

I soon discovered that this was no enviable task. In the first place the organ was constructed on some special principle (fortunately I believe unique), which had the result of causing constant cyphers, so that a service seldom went through without something going wrong[2]. The service itself was not in the least attractive though the Chapel was beautiful. The boys seemed utterly bored; there was no choir and quite often I had to play through a whole hymn or psalm with 400 boys standing gaping with their hands in their pockets and not uttering a sound. In other ways, too, the conditions were tragic. Music lessons were regarded as of far less importance than, for example, watching games or even fagging. I spent most of my time waiting in a wretched old music room at the bottom of Keate's Lane for boys that did not turn up for their lessons: and there was no redress and no support from the majority of the masters. Dr Lloyd did his best and he was a most delightful person to work with, but he had inherited a bad tradition and was not strong enough to fight against it.

I soon found the position quite intolerable and told Dr Lloyd so. He, full of sympathy for my grievances, asked me to write him a letter which he could show to the Headmaster.

Dr C H Lloyd

---

1   Charles Harford Lloyd was born in 1849, educated at Rossall School and Oxford. He succeeded S S Wesley at Gloucester Cathedral in 1876, and in 1882 he moved to Christ Church Cathedral, Oxford, finally moving to Eton College in 1892 as Precentor and Musical Instructor, in succession to Joseph Barnby. He was renowned for his masterly organ improvisations. On retirement from Eton, he took the post of Organist and Composer at the Chapel Royal, remaining there until his death in 1919.

The biography *Walter Parratt: Master of the Music* by Donald Tovey and Geoffrey Parratt (OUP, 1941) quotes Sir Walter Parratt as saying "If in Eton College Chapel you heard an unknown organ voluntary manifestly above the average in rich invention and graceful form, you might be quite sure that Lloyd was extemporising".

2   The Lower Chapel organ was built by Lewis & Co. in 1891. Accoridng to *Music & Musicians of Eton College'* by Albert Mellor; London, Spottiswood, Balantyne & Co. 1929, "The mechanism was first built on the tubular-pneumatic principle, which was not a success in this particular instrument, and in consequence was altered to the old tracker action. The blowing was effected by hydraulic apparatus, and gave...trouble, owing to the water pressure being insufficient to be effective." No wonder Nicholson had problems with this instrument.

Dr Warre's reply was characteristic: "Mr Nicholson's gravamina [sic][3] can only be met by a non possumus." This being so, the obvious thing was to take my departure. I duly played my last service, when the organ (not from any revengeful tactics of mine) excelled itself by cyphering on all three manuals and the pedals; so I left my seat and told the blower to stop blowing till the cacophony ceased, and that was my grand finale at Eton![4]

In giving this rather lurid picture of Eton music at this time I must not forget to speak of the other side; of my pleasure in the College Chapel services[5] where I often played, and more often enjoyed Lloyd's beautiful playing and improvisations. Many of the boys, too, were delightful as individuals, though collectively they could be atrocious. I also had some pleasant times in taking the College Chapel choristers, and doing something to cheer their rather sad existence: and of course my intimacy with Parratt increased through many delightful visits to his house at Windsor.

I think the main cause of my unhappiness was the Lower Chapel services: they were another instance (though very much worse than Rugby) of how such bare, formal services can fail to influence or attract school-boys. A few years later when Basil Johnson had succeeded Lloyd and there had come a Lower Master (Mr A B Ramsay[6]) who was really keen to bring some life into them, the Lower Chapel services were completely revolutionized. A choir was recruited from among the Eton boys and fellows, who had been accustomed to speak of the College choristers as "Choir cads," now found themselves put into surplices and scarlet cassocks and taking part in dignified ceremonial. The result was an instantaneous and complete transformation: as the choir rapidly found its feet membership became the fashion, and the rest of the boys backed them with enthusiasm: so that the Lower Chapel service, from being a by-word became, and still remains, one of the most impressive to be heard in any public school: and solely because it was realised that boys could be interested in a service if only it was made interesting and attractive.

---

3   Gravimina = Grievances/Complaints. Non possumus = Not possible

4   Eton was the least successful period of Nicholson's career. If he and the college parted on a slightly sour note then it was not helped by events ten years later. Shortly before Lloyd's retirement on health grounds at the end of 1913, Nicholson was invited (as one of Lloyd's suggestions) by Edward Lyttleton, Headmaster of Eton, to be Lloyd's successor [letter dated 17th November]. Two days later the offer was retracted as the Provost of Eton preferred Nicholson's former mentor Basil Johnson from Rugby School, even though Johnson was now in his fifties. Follow up letters from Basil Johnson, Lloyd and Sir Walter Parratt tried to smooth the waters, but Nicholson was quite clear - he did not want to work in a school anyway and preferred the cathedral environment.

5   The College choir consisted of six lay clerks who, up until 1868, were supplied by St George's Chapel, Windsor, but since 1868 were separately supplied by the College. The Choristers were from the Eton College Choir School, set up in 1872 (until closure of the school in 1968). Both College Chapel and Lower Chapel had weekday 'morning chapel'. In addition there was Choral Evensong on Mondays, Tuesdays, Thursdays and Fridays. For Evensong on Lady Day and at the Confirmation Service both choirs combined.

6   It was A B Ramsay, appointed in 1916 as Lower Master, who ordered the Lower Chapel organ to be rebuilt (by Messrs Hunter of Clapham), and an electric blower installed. He also reconstituted the choir, and under Basil Johnson's guidance, the services improved. 'Descants are frequently used for the hymns with fine effect, and anthems for boys' voices are usually sung every Sunday' (Mellor, ibid). This highlights the lack of support that Nicholson received during his time at Eton.

Eton College Chapel steps
Painted by Nicholson 7th July 1920

Germany

Being without a job seemed to indicate a little more study. Accordingly, I went to Frankfurt-on-Main and put myself under Professor Ivan Knorr[7] for composition. Life in Germany was most pleasant in those days: opera at least two or three nights a week, at absurdly low prices: concerts available at almost any time: plenty of kind friends to whom I had introductions: and a splendid teacher. I worked mainly at orchestration, and Knorr's method of teaching was most original. He would give one a lesson on some particular instrument, explaining how it was played, what it could do and what it could not: then one had to write a little theme with variations intended to explore the possibilities of the particular instrument, and an orchestral player would be in attendance to let one hear how one's work sounded: this he was glad to do for about 3/6[8] a time! Surely there could be no better way of teaching orchestration than this very practical one, but I have never heard of it being adopted anywhere else, though I used to try and arrange something of the sort for my pupils at Manchester; I certainly found it most illuminating.

Prof Ivan Knorr

Ivan Knorr was a charming man, a Russian; he had been the intimate friend both of Brahms and Tchaikovsky. It fell to his lot to introduce the two great men to one another, and he described the scene how, each having told the other how completely he detested his music, they fraternised very happily over tankards of beer and became quite good friends. Knorr himself was a gifted, though not very prolific composer; but he was a splendid teacher and had had quite a number of English pupils, including Norman O'Neill, Percy Grainger, Cyril Scott and Balfour Gardiner.

My time in Germany was somewhat cut short by an urgent request, backed by Parratt, that I should go as music master to Wellington House Preparatory School at Westgate-on-Sea, where the Rev Herbert Bull was the highly successful headmaster; so I started work there in the Summer term of 1904.

---

7   German composer and pedagogue Ivan Knorr (1853-1916) was born in Mewe (now Gniew in Pomeranian Poland) and attended the Leipzig Conservatory where he studied with Ignaz Moscheles, Ernst Friedrich Richter and Carl Reinecke. He taught at the Imperial Conservatory in Kharkiv (Ukraine) and, in 1883, he settled he in Frankfurt on the faculty of the Hoch Conservatory. He was appointed Director here in 1908. As well as the pupils mentioned in the next paragraph he taught Ernest Bloch, Ernst Toch, Roger Quilter and Hans Pfitzner. Some unpublished ms copies of music by him (made by Nicholson) are in the RSCM Library.

8   Three shillings and sixpence (17½ pence today).

Wellington House

Wellington House was a most delightful school[9] and I would gladly have stayed on[10] but suddenly, out of the blue, came an offer (again through the good offices of Parratt) of the post of Acting Organist at Carlisle Cathedral. Happy though I was at Westgate, I knew in my own mind that school music was not my real line, and the chance of getting my foot in at a Cathedral seemed too good to be neglected[11]; so I had only one term at Wellington House.

Wellington House School Choir 1904

Sunday afternoon at Wellington House School 1904
The Headmaster reading to the boys

---

9 During the 1939-45 war the school was moved to Stringston Manor in Somerset and the school buildings were used by the Ministry of Defence. It closed in July 1970.

10 Whilst teaching there, Nicholson lived at 4 Gordon Grove, Westgate-on-Sea, Kent.

11 Letters between Nicholson and his mother suggest that he really wanted to go to Lichfield Cathedral as Assistant Organist. His mother seems to have dissuaded Nicholson, suggesting that three years as Acting Organist at Carlisle would be better for him. He deferred to her and 'telegraphed' Lichfield in July 1904 with his decision.

Rev Henry Dams, Precentor, with the choristers in the
Carlisle Cathedral Choir School c 1904.

The Carlisle Cathedral Choristers in 1905.
Head boy Arthur Reeves is seated front left, next to the Precentor, Rev Henry Dams.

Carlisle Cathedral (1904-1908)

I started at Carlisle in the autumn of 1904[12] almost at the same time[13] my mother moved to [7] Airlie Gardens, Kensington, and the old home at Totteridge was finally given up.

My predecessor at Carlisle, Dr Henry Edmund Ford, on his retirement was allowed to retain the title of Organist, to which he claimed a statutory right, till his death, so that I was only termed Acting Organist, though I had full responsibility (but not the full stipend[14]).

The choir consisted of 6 men, three of them quite good and the others rather bad, and there were about 16 boys the head of whom, Arthur Reeves[15], was an excellent singer and a tower of strength. The Precentor was the Rev Henry Dams[16], who was also Master of the Choir School, and solely responsible for the education of the boys at their varying ages, an almost hopeless task which he carried out with remarkable success. He was a most musical man and one of the best chanters I ever heard. We became extremely intimate friends and I was able to help him to carry out the many reforms that he had inaugurated before my arrival. As an assistant I had Geoffrey O'Connor Morris[17], a very gifted, very delightful and in those days a somewhat irresponsible young man.

Arthur Reeves

The Dean was Dr Henderson[18] who, when I arrived, was a confirmed invalid, and we never saw him except when he was brought into the Cathedral in a bath-chair and deposited by his

---

12 He began on 25th September 1904. In Carlisle Nicholson lived at 1 Eden Mount, Stanwix, just north of the Cathedral. He lived at 161 Warwick Road from 1906.

13 She moved in on 11th Aug 1904.

14 At this point Nicholson added "£100" in pencil, presumably the organist's stipend. He does not comment on whether this was his share or H E Ford's stipend. Judging by other stipends of the time it was the annual stipend for the full organist.

15 Arthur Reeves (photograph above and on the previous page), Head Chorister at Carlisle eventually became a lawyer and served as Town Clerk in Peterborough, retiring in 1949. In a personal letter Reeves comments that, of the 16 choristers, he and three others went on to become lawyers. Reeves' son became a chorister at the College of St Nicolas in Chislehurst in 1931.

16 The Rev Henry Dams, a graduate of Trinity College, Dublin, was appointed in 1901. From 1910 until his death in 1928 he was Vicar of Knowsley, Lancashire. His son Cyril Theodore Henry Dams, born in Carlisle in 1906, became Precentor of Westminster Abbey in 1951.

17 Born in Switzerland of Irish descent, Geoffrey O'Connor-Morris (1886-1964) studied in Dublin and became assistant organist to Carlisle Cathedral at the age of 17 out of 80 candidates. On Nicholson's departure he also became Acting Organist. He was subsequently organist in London at St Paul's, Onslow Square, then to the Seventh Church of Christ, Scientist in Kensington (for over 30 years). He was an examiner for Trinity College London and a professor at the Guildhall School of Music. His photograph is on the next page.

18 The Very Rev William George Henderson DD (1819-1905) was educated at Magdalen College in Oxford. He served as a Fellow of that College, then as a tutor at Durham University and was then Principal of Hatfield College in Durham. Ordained in 1859, he served as Headmaster of Victoria College in Jersey and of Leeds Grammar School before his appointment to Carlisle. He was Dean of Carlisle from 1884 to his death in 1905.

male nurse in an arm-chair below his stall. Though I was under him as Dean for more than two years, I never spoke to him, and I doubt whether he knew of my existence; he transacted no business whatever, and yet he drew his full salary to the day of his death. He had a large family[19] who were most kindly folks and took a good deal of interest in the choir.

My greatest friend among the Chapter was the Bishop of Barrow-in-Furness[20] (and Mrs Ware). He was one of the most saintly people I ever met, absolutely beloved by everyone, very gentle, very sympathetic and very generous. Mrs Ware, the eldest daughter of Bishop Harvey Goodwin[21], formed the greatest contrast to her husband: brim-full of energy, ready to back any good idea, she was a born leader: she was also boundlessly kind, a perfect hostess and widely beloved, even though some people were rather overwhelmed by her. The Wares backed me up in every possible way and showed me constant kindness; so it came about that any innovations had to be proposed when the Bishop was in residence, for without his help (egged on by his wife) we could get little done: great were the plottings to make the most of his three months!

Geoffrey O'Connor Morris

The Wares lived a good deal of their time at Grasmere, where I was a constant visitor at their charming house, How Foot, thus making my first proper acquaintance with the joys of the Lake District. There one met many interesting friends, especially Canon and Mrs Rawnsley of Crosthwaite, Gordon Wordsworth, the grandson of the poet, Arthur Severn, the great friend and the heir of Ruskin, and various members of the Goodwin family. Among these my greatest friend was Canon Rawnsley[22]. He was a remarkable person in many ways: a most prolific poet — it was said that he wrote a

Bishop and Mrs Ware

---

19 Dean Henderson had 14 children (in 17 years).

20 The Right Rev Henry Ware (1830-1909) studied at Trinity College in Cambridge, was ordained priest and then became a Fellow and Tutor at that college. From 1862 he was vicar of Kirby Lonsdale in Westmorland until he became the first Bishop of Barrow-in-Furness in 1888, serving until his death.

21 Bishop Harvey Goodwin (1818-1891), Bishop of Carlisle from 1869 until his death.

22 The Rev Canon Hardwicke Drummond Rawnsley (1851-1920) became Vicar of Wray near Ambleside and then, from 1883, at Crosthwaite near Keswick. He became an Honorary Canon of Carlisle Cathedral in 1891 and Chaplain to the King in 1912. He was a writer (especially, as Nicholson mentions, of sonnets) who befriended Beatrice Potter. He was also the first published author she had met and he later encouraged her to publish her first book, *The Tale of Peter Rabbit*.

sonnet every day before breakfast) with an unsurpassed knowledge of his beloved lakes and mountains — to go for a tramp with him was an education in itself; full of original ideas which he carried out with the zest of a schoolboy, he was quite unlike anyone else.

The first time I ever saw him was at a May-Day Festival which he had inaugurated at Keswick: he was leading the May Queen, seated on a donkey, round the town in pouring rain, himself with one hand on the bridle and the other supporting an umbrella. When the donkey somehow managed to deposit the May Queen in the mud he was not in the least disconcerted, but set her on her steed again and continued to lead the procession quite serenely.

He would send his friends most amusing postcards in rhyme, and he certainly had a most ready wit. I remember how in later years when he was staying with me in Manchester Leslie Heward[23], who was then one of my choristers, asked him to write in his autograph book. Leslie had hurt his finger and could not play, but had been singing; and Rawnsley, without a moment's hesitation wrote:

> "Little boys who cut their fingers
> Can't be players, must be singers!"

He loved a good story; I remember one in particular that delighted him. At the Keswick Convention a very earnest speaker had been urging the need for missionaries to go to some distant outpost where cannibals were still to be found. Next morning the town was decorated with large placards: — "Cannibals ask for Missionaries. Who will go?"

Almost the last time I saw him was when he came to stay with me at Westminster while I was living in Grosvenor Road, overlooking the river. He had been planning a vast series of bonfires to take place simultaneously all over the country to celebrate the end of the [Great] War, and he hit on the happy idea of using up the stock of army flares which would no longer be required. He had managed to interest some MPs and permission was obtained for a test to be made on the terrace opposite the Houses of Parliament. We waited anxiously for the moment, and then suddenly the whole sky and river were illuminated with a terrific blaze. Passers-by thought that here was yet another air-raid: fire-engines dashed up from all directions, and Westminster was thrown into an uproar. But the illumination soon died down, and left the solitary figure of the Canon, the author of it all, fairly chuckling with delight at the success of his great experiment.

In spite of all his eccentricity he was a very far-seeing man, and it should never be forgotten that he was the prime mover in the inauguration of the National Trust. Though laughed at, at first, as only the latest of Rawnsley's fads, everyone now recognises what this dream of his

---

23 For further information and photographs of Leslie Heward see Chapter IV and Appendix H.

has accomplished, and the thousands of acres of beauty spots which have been preserved for ever for the use of the Nation are a wonderful memorial to him who, from his own deep love of nature, conceived the idea of preserving it for future generations.

Of the other Canons the most remarkable was Archdeacon Prescott[24], who was also Chancellor of the Diocese (the last I believe of the clerical Chancellors). This extraordinary old man could be most exasperating, with the bitterest tongue, the most provoking conservatism, the most violent prejudices and the kindest heart imaginable. He ruled the Chapter with a rod of iron, and no one dared resist him: to the clergy who came before him whether as Archdeacon or Chancellor, he was a terror, and his Consistory Courts were notorious. He would get outrageous Chapter Orders passed just to suit his own whims: for instance there was actually an Order issued that the Te Deum on Sunday mornings must not last more than five and a half minutes; he rigorously timed each setting, and if it exceeded the limit the Precentor and I were hauled over the coals. We retaliated by having the Te Deum on Sunday mornings sung to one single chant throughout, till the protests from the congregation brought about a better state of things. The Precentor stood up to him splendidly, but he always got the last word. I remember the following dialogue:

> "Mr Precentor, the Te Deum on Sunday morning lasted 6 minutes 15 seconds: are you aware that this is a violation of the Chapter Order?"
>
> "Yes, Mr Archdeacon, but I judge music not by its length but by its value. If you want to shorten the service there is only one way; — shorten your sermon."
>
> "I never preach for more than 20 minutes!"
>
> "Well, last Sunday your sermon lasted 25, for I timed it."
>
> "Then your watch was wrong!"

Though an extreme protestant, yet he was (in his own way) a strong ritualist; he would ordinarily attend service in a surplice showing about a yard of trousers, but Sundays and special occasions he would mark by the addition of his cassock. His method of celebrating was entirely his own, but most punctiliously carried out. Any suggested change he always opposed on principle, unless he could be brought to think that it came from himself! He was a tremendously keen fisherman, and he managed to keep the splendid salmon-fishing in the Eden at Wetheral in the hands of the Dean and Chapter, or rather in his own hands. Like everyone else I had one or two tremendous rows with him, but after a while he came to regard me with some measure of approval and would on occasion support the very things that

---

[24] The Ven Archdeacon John Eustace Prescott DD (1832–1890) was an enthusiastic and, at times, controversial historian who specialised in the ecclesiastical history of Carlisle and its environs. He also published the book *Christian Hymns and Hymn Writers* in 1883. The Font in Carlisle Cathedral was a gift from him in 1891.

I hesitated to propose because of his probable opposition. He was extremely generous but most of his kindnesses were done in strict secrecy.

It is interesting to compare the Cathedral life of those days with the present. I suppose Carlisle was generally considered to be about the most backward and unprogressive of the English Cathedrals. Under the reigns of Dean Tait and especially Dean Close it had come to be associated with extreme Low Church traditions. The Altar, for instance, was entirely devoid of any ornament: such a thing as a choral Celebration was never even thought of: and though, when I came, there was a weekly celebration at 8 o'clock on Sundays, this was more or less of an innovation. Yet the opus Dei, the regular maintenance of the two daily choral services as prescribed by Statute, was regarded as all-important. One half-day was grudgingly allowed together with three weeks' holiday for the choir in the summer; otherwise the two daily choral services were maintained with unfailing regularity throughout the year. Of outside congregation on weekdays there was often none, or at the best a mere handful, but the Canons (not only the Canon in Residence) were nearly always present, so much so that if anyone was absent it was naturally assumed that he was either unwell or away from the city. On Sundays there were excellent congregations, especially in the afternoon when we had a long anthem and the choir would often be crowded. But all the services were very carefully rendered and in spite of the small weekday congregations no such question was ever raised as to whether it was worth while maintaining them; the possibility of doing otherwise never occurred to those who were clearly their guardians.

The result of all this was that there was much more corporate spirit than appears to be usual in these days. The Canons, for instance, needed to take a personal interest in the choirmen and choirboys, and, though there was perhaps a certain amount of condescension, they were made to feel that they were a real part of the Cathedral Body. The Custom was kept up by which twice a year a roll-call was held in the Fratry[25], when everyone from the Dean down to the youngest Chorister had to answer his name, and received (I believe in lieu of commons) a small sum varying from half-a-crown for the Dean to sixpence for the Choristers. Then on Saturday mornings the Choristers accompanied by their Master and the Precentor had to proceed into the Canon's Vestry after service: the Canon in Residence would make any comments he wished: he would then ask the masters if they had any complaints to make of the boys, and the same question would be asked of the boys as regards their masters: the answers in both cases being invariably "No, sir!" the little ceremony came to an end. I have not heard of this custom elsewhere, and I think that in such a remote place as Carlisle it may have been a relic of the old monastic 'Children's Chapter'. I am sorry to hear that it has

---

25 The Fratry was the dining hall for the monks of the mediæval Priory.

been given up since my time, for it brought the dignitaries into direct contact with the boys and rather caused them to 'magnify their office' accordingly.

Boys of the Voluntary Choir in their new cassocks and surplices 1905.

I cannot say that the Cathedral was popular in the city: indeed the ordinary access to "The Abbey" was barred by a heavy iron railing with a locked gate: and though many efforts were made at least to get the gate left open, the Archdeacon resisted to the last ditch. The society of "The Abbey," too, was somewhat exclusive, though it was very pleasant for those that had the entrée. But there was little attempt to make the Cathedral a real centre for the city, and the rather half-hearted popular Sunday evening services had little effect beyond reducing the congregations in the parish churches. They certainly were not attractive when I went to Carlisle, the singing being led by a perfectly appalling choir of elderly women and men. I did manage to improve matters by instituting a choir of voluntary boys and ex-choristers, and Prescott, after violently opposing the change, privately told me to buy them cassocks and surplices which he would pay for! But still the services, except on Sunday afternoons seemed to make little real appeal either to the city or the diocese, and neither were encouraged to make much use of them.

My aged predecessor, Henry Edmund Ford[26], who had been appointed as far back as 1842 and had been created Mus. Doc. by the Archbishop of Canterbury in recognition of his long service, was a very interesting link with the past. I suppose he was a fair specimen of the type of Cathedral organist of his day: he knew the style of rendering the old-fashioned Cathedral music and played regularly from the old scores with figured bass: his extempore playing was, however, very poor, I do not think he was ever known to tackle one of the major Bach fugues, and his general musicianship was not of a very high level; he was, for instance, quite unable to transpose and his compositions never went beyond a chant or two and, I believe, one anthem. True, there were several anthems ascribed to his name

Henry Edmund Ford

in the book of "Words of Anthems", but the music of these appeared to have remained in the composer's head! I should think he had taken to music more as a profession than an art, and he used regularly to speak of his 'teaching practice' which in old days had been very lucrative and was carried out mainly by visiting the big houses in the neighbourhood on horseback.

He had, however, done very good work in his time and had introduced a fairly wide repertory of the older music, not venturing much beyond Wesley and one or two of the earlier Stanford services, with of course a good sprinkling of the Victorians. But he told me that when he came to Carlisle the repertory consisted of only 12 Services and 20 Anthems, on which the changes were rung: there were no lights in the Cathedral, and on a dark winter's afternoon his predecessor would sometimes, when the anthem was announced, lean over the organ-loft and exclaim "Can't see to play!" and the Minor Canon would accordingly proceed with the prayers. When he was appointed he had to travel over Shap Fell in a stage coach, as the railway was not made. The then Dean was also Rector of St George's, Hanover Square, and was never seen except when the Deanery was opened for a few weeks for his summer holiday; most of the Canons held livings elsewhere and their houses were normally occupied by caretakers unless they chose to come into Residence.

---

26   Dr Henry Edmund Ford (1821-1909) played for his first service on 12th February 1842, and, even after his 'retirement', he remained the official Organist of Carlisle Cathedral until his death.

Dean Close[27] seems to have tightened things up a bit; he was evidently a great martinet. As most of the livings in the City are in the gift of the Dean and Chapter, when any of them fell vacant he would appoint himself, pending the time when he could find some suitable person of his own way of thinking whom he could plant there. Each week on Monday mornings there was a meeting of the city clergy at the Deanery, so that the Dean might discuss and approve their discourses for the following Sunday. No doubt he ruled his Chapter in similar fashion!

Ford was a friend of S S Wesley. He had been staying with him at Winchester, and Wesley (who was of course a great fisherman) said, "Here am I in this wretched hole with only a ditch to fish in, while you at Carlisle have one of the finest salmon rivers in the country and you don't care a bit about it. Will you exchange?" Ford laughed this off as a joke, but sure enough a few weeks later Dean Close summoned him and said:

> "I have a letter from Dr Wesley suggesting that you and he change places: what have you to say about it?"
>
> "Well, Mr Dean," said Ford, "it is surely a question of what **you** have to say about it."
>
> "What I have to say, Mr Ford, is this: if Wesley were to pay me his salary instead of my paying him I would not have him near the place!"

On another occasion at a Three Choirs Festival Wesley had continued his voluntary too long and kept the preacher waiting. After the service Ford found him raging up and down the Cloisters followed by a Minor Canon who was attempting to pacify him. Turning round on Ford he cried, "What do you think this insolent puppy did? He told me to stop playing! And he sent a message by a wretched choirboy!"

Ford's resignation had been brought about with great difficulty, as he was extremely full of vigour and naturally pointed out that if the bed-ridden Dean could retain his office, the Organist "who had never played better in his life" was deserving of equal consideration. The climax, I believe, was reached when one Sunday morning a terrifying and continuous roar resounded from the organ loft, and on an anxious Minor Canon ascending to see what was the matter, the poor old gentleman was found to have slipped off the organ-stool and on to the pedals, of which all the stops were drawn, unable to move as he had had some sort of seizure. Anyhow, he had been brought to resign with a great deal of resentment on his part and a very inadequate pension, considering his length of service (mostly drawn from his successor's stipend).

He [Ford] was an entertaining old man, very conceited and with an everlasting grievance against the Dean and Chapter, but he became very friendly with me and I saw a good deal of

---

27   The Rev Frances Close (1797-1882) was Rector of Cheltenham (1826-1856) and Dean of Carlisle from 1856 until 1881. Dean Close School in Cheltenham is named after him.

him and extracted many interesting reminiscences about old times in Cathedrals. It is of course from these that above stories of Dean Close and others are garnered. I always used to dine with the Fords about Christmas time, when the old gentleman would produce a bottle of [18]47 port, which he had laid down in '47 and never moved since. He outlived my time at Carlisle by a few years, and was actually organist for 67 years, which I think must be the record[28].

Another link with the past was James Walter Brown[29], who had been a chorister under Ford in the 50's and, starting life as a very poor boy, had risen to a good position through his own ability. He knew more of Carlisle in olden days than any other living person, and contributed interesting articles to the local papers for many years. His literary gifts were considerable, and he was a great authority on the Cumberland dialect, which he could speak to perfection. In collaboration with him I wrote several children's cantatas which were sung at the Carlisle and other musical festivals. He was devoted to everything connected with the Cathedral and its choir, though the most bitter critic of the Dean and Chapter, to whom he acted as a sort of gad-fly.

James Walter Brown

Then there was William Metcalfe[30], who had just retired from the choir when I came: he had been a bass singer for many years and was a well-known figure in Cumberland musical life, for he was actually the composer of the famous 'John Peel' which he partially adapted from an old Border tune to the words by John Woodcock Graves[31]. He was one of the old race of lay-clerks who were, even in provincial Cathedrals, reckoned as musicians of

William Metcalfe

---

28 "In conjunction with this it is interesting to note that Dr Ford's master, Ralph Banks, was organist of Rochester Cathedral from 1791 to 1841; master and pupil having thus been consecutively organists of two Cathedrals for a practically unbroken period of 118 years.' (*Chorister Life in the Early Sixties* J W Brown)

29 James Walter Brown (1850/1851-1930) was a chorister of Carlisle Cathedral from 1860 until 1865 and continued as a member of the choir for over half a century. A noted local historian and author, amongst his publications is *Chorister Life in the Early Sixties* 1910. It is from his account of this period that Nicholson drew some of his information regarding the customs of the Cathedral.

30 William Metcalfe (1830-1909) was a local piano teacher and composer as well as serving as lay-clerk in the choir for 50 years.

31 John Woodcock Graves (1795-1886) was actually the author of the song which he set to a Scottish tune he had heard his mother sing. It was published in *Songs and Ballads of Cumberland* in 1866. Metcalfe made an arrangement published in 1868 which made the song famous. Graves became penurious and moved to Hobart Tasmania, remaining there for the rest of his (very long) life.

considerable importance, and he did a lot of concert singing, teaching and conducting. He was a fine and most courteous old man as I remember him.

Plate from J W Brown's *Chorister Life in the Early Sixties*.
The central portrait without caption is J W Brown as a chorister.

One other link with the past I cannot refrain from mentioning. I was taken to see a very old woman living in one of the queer old alleys by which the centre of Carlisle is intersected. She told me she remembered her grandmother telling her how she stood in a hedge outside the City to watch [Bonnie] Prince Charlie's army go by in 1745.

No description of Carlisle Cathedral would be complete without reference to the Verger, ex-Sergeant-Major Windeler[32]. He was a wonderful character, trying to rule everyone from the Chapter downwards with military discipline. He was very loquacious and full of stories about his brilliant repartees to American visitors whom he detested, and about his innumerable conflicts with "'im", in other words his arch-enemy the Archdeacon. As a verger he was intolerably rude and it is wonderful that he was borne with so long, and he would certainly have been ejected but for his sterling worth and many excellent qualities. I could recall many stories about Windeler, but must content myself with one.

> One day a shabby sort of man, who proclaimed himself to be a rat-catcher, came into the Cathedral. "'Ave you got any rats in 'ere, guv'nor?"
>
> "No," said Windeler, "we haven't got any rats here, thank you."
>
> "Well then, you soon will have," replied the enterprising visitor, releasing a pair into the darkening church where they were soon lost sight of.

A few weeks after, we were quietly singing Evensong in the choir when the service was interrupted by a violent commotion in the aisle. After the service I asked Windeler what was the matter. "It was them rats," he replied; "I heard a bit of a scuffling, and I tip-toed out into the aisle, and there I saw a big fat fellow going along as bold as brass. So I up and after him, and I got him too — with an 'ymnbook!"

Another day I happened to come into the Cathedral in the afternoon (it was a half-holiday) and there I saw several of my choristers seated on a form in the Nave, under Windeler's eagle eye. I asked him what the matter was and what the boys were doing. "It was like this," he told me: "Them boys come to me for the key of their school-room and said their master had told them to come and do some extra lessons. But there was no fire and I wasn't going to let them stop there in the cold, so I says to 'em, "No, my boys, you come along with me, I'll set you a task: so I brought 'em in 'ere and I give 'em prayer-books, and I set 'em to learn the thirty-nine articles: and I heard 'em too!"

The old-fashioned vergers were a remarkable class of men, and many good stories have been told about them and their sayings.

I remember once, many years ago, visiting a Cathedral in the days when a charge was made for seeing the various 'sights': there were also large placards saying that the Vergers were

---

32   Daniel Henry Windeler (d 1931)

not allowed to receive gratuities. We were shown round by a very frowsy old gentleman, and after he had finished his tour he led us into a sort of cubby-hole under the organ screen and blandly remarked, "Well, gentlemen, if you wish to make any acknowledgment to the Sub-Sacristan now is your opportunity!" I suppose the old gentleman was a pluralist and could accept in one capacity what was unlawful in another.

It was before my day that the [Westminster] Abbey Vergers were reputed to be in the habit of calling out in stentorian tones to the visitors before Evensong, "Now then you must all go out – there's a service coming on!"

I remember once over-hearing a Verger who was showing a clergyman round the Cathedral and pointing out the empty niches, explaining that they were once filled with statues: "What a pity", said the cleric, "that they haven't put them back." "Oh, no, sir", was the reply, "We don't have anything Romanesque here!"

In Carlisle Diocese were many curious specimens among the country clergy. One dear old Honorary Canon used to tramp in to Cathedral in breeches and large hob-nail boots, carrying under his arm a brown paper parcel; from this he would undo a very aged and dirty surplice which reached about to his knees and, with it flying open in front, march into the choir. His delight was to be asked to read the lessons and if they happened to be of a dramatic nature the effect was remarkable. I remember how he would declaim such passages as, "Shall I smite them, O my father, shall I smite them?" or impersonate the three characters in the Judgment of Solomon, though perhaps not quite so realistically as another famous Canon who would read the parts of the two women in falsetto and that of the king in a stentorian bass.

It was not at Carlisle, though it might well have been, that two elderly Canons were standing at the two ends of the Holy Table; one who was reading the Ten Commandments unfortunately lost his place. Not in the least upset, however, he appealed to his colleague, "could you kindly tell me which Commandment I last rehearsed?" to which the reply came, equally undisturbed, " I am afraid I cannot tell you, I was not paying attention."

Another quaint story is of a Canon who accidentally dropped his false teeth in his stall during service. After the Vestry prayer, he beckoned a choirboy and addressed him thus: "Boy, you will go into my stall and search on the floor: there you will find a small ivory ornament; — bring it to me!"

At a certain Cathedral, where the Dean was rather absent-minded, it was the custom for him to say a Vestry prayer before the service. On one occasion he began, "For what we are about to receive, etc.," and it is said that at a subsequent dinner party when the assembled guests stood for Grace, the words chosen were "O Lord, open thou our lips."

An honorary Canon of Carlisle who was a great entomologist was preaching on a Sunday immediately before Bank holiday, and exhorted his congregation to spend it in a sensible manner and not in debauch: "As for myself," he explained, "I propose to spend the day in pursuing 'painted ladies' [i.e. butterflies] over the fells."

But I think perhaps the choicest clerical story that I can remember is of an ardent young curate who was preaching on the parable of the wise and foolish virgins, and concluded with this magnificent peroration; — "Grant, O Lord, that at the last great day we may be found waking with the wise virgins and not sleeping with the foolish ones!"

One cannot be a cathedral organist for 25 years without coming across some curiosities in the clerical world.

I found my work at the Cathedral very difficult at first. The organ copies of all the old music were in open score with figured basses and often in bad condition: it was as much as I could do to read them at all, and I often had to make manuscript short scores until I got used to the old books. A great deal of the choir music was in manuscript volumes in a terrible condition and quite often with several bars missing which the choir had to learn by heart: some of these books were of great age and there was one which had a drawing of some kilted Highlanders and a note "Prince Charles' army passed today. 1745."

The organ was a fine old instrument, one of the first (if not the first[33]) Cathedral organs built by Willis, and it was designed and opened by W T Best who was a native of Carlisle[34]. It was, however, very difficult to control and the action was terribly noisy[35], so that a rebuild was a necessity which could not be postponded[36].

The 1907 organ from the nave

---

33 Built in 1856, it was the first organ by Willis to be designed and built especially for a cathedral space. It was, however, Willis's second cathedral project. The large organ he had exhibited at the Crystal Palace Great Exhibition in 1851 was admired by S S Wesley, then organist of Winchester Cathedral, who recommended to his Dean and Chapter that it should be purchased. It was reduced in size and reconfigured to be installed in Winchester in 1854.

34 And former chorister of the cathedral.

35 Not only was Willis's original mechanism worn out and unreliable but the main-frame was deemed unsafe.

36 For Specifications and other information about the cathedral organ see Appendix E.

I think, as in all the other Cathedrals where I have been, I found my greatest interest in my work with the choir-boys. I found a very nice set to begin with, due to the excellent influence of their schoolmaster, The Precentor. I was, however, always recognised as the statutory Master of the Choristers, and as such was responsible for their well-being and discipline in the Cathedral and at any such times as they were not actually in school. They had hitherto had little in the way of corporate life or joint amusements or games, and I set myself to remedy this at once. In those days one could get cheap tickets for a shilling on a half-holiday afternoon to almost any of the lovely places within reach of Carlisle, and many were the outings and expeditions that were arranged. The boys were put into "Etons and Mortarboards" for Sundays and generally smartened up. A Choir Club was started for the older boys, in which they remained when they left the choir, and this did a good deal to foster a spirit of enthusiasm. So the boys began to get an excellent reputation in the city, and were always able to obtain good positions when they left the choir. All this of course reacted very favourably on their singing, and they soon reached a very good standard.

[Here follows a general discourse on the importance, role and discipline of choristers, which can be found in Appendix C.]

Beyond keeping up a pretty good standard in the singing and gradually improving the repertory, we were not able to do much as long as old Dean Henderson lived. But his successor, the Rev C J Ridgeway[37], who came from Christ Church, Lancaster Gate, immediately brought a great access of life and enthusiasm to the Cathedral: even [Archdeacon] Prescott had almost found his master! For his installation, the new Dean actually dared to ask for a Choral Celebration. Such a thing had not been heard of for generations and was strongly opposed: but nevertheless it took place and was a beautiful service, in spite of the fact that after the Church Militant prayer, the Archdeacon stalked out of the Cathedral, followed by his wife and family.

The era of change had come and improvements were gradually effected and resistance gradually weakened. I was able to form an association of the church choirs of the city and to hold choral festivals in the Cathedral, as well as to gather the choirboys from all the different churches for a delightful service on Innocents' Day, with a fine procession. The Bach *St Matthew Passion* became an established event in Lent. The complete rebuilding of the organ was taken in hand, and within a year of the inception of the scheme the funds had been collected and the lovely instrument completed by Messrs Harrison and Harrison and opened by Sir Walter Parratt[38]. It was in the week of the opening that our little Cathedral

---

[37] Charles John Ridgeway DD (1841-1927) studied at St Paul's School and Trinity College, Cambridge. Ordained in 1866, his Curacy was at Christ Church in Tunbridge Wells (where his father was Vicar), before appointment as Vicar of North Malvern. After serving as Rector of Buckhurst Hill and Rural Dean of Paddington, he became Dean of Carlisle in 1906.

[38] See Appendix E.

choir actually sang the whole of Brahms' Requiem without omission and without outside assistance or a conductor.

Dean Ridgeway's reign was a time of most happy progress, but it was only too short; for after less than two years he was promoted to the Bishopric of Chichester.

**C J Ridgeway
as Bishop of Chichester
on leaving Carlisle**

[Here follows a general discourse on the state of Cathedral worship, which can be found in Appendix D.]

Outside Cathedral circles life at Carlisle was most pleasant. There were a great number of delightful people living in the neighbourhood whose acquaintance I soon made. There were the Choral Society and the Cumberland Orchestra which I conducted and much enjoyed. Amongst my youthful indiscretions produced at Carlisle was a cantata for choir and orchestra called *Ivry*, which I thought very fine at the time. One of the good results of the Great War was that, [the music] being published by a German firm, the plates were melted down to make bullets; so it fortunately went out of print of its own accord. Then there was the Carlisle and District Musical Festival which was of immense interest and grew very rapidly during my time. Its President was Lady Mabel Howard[39], of Greystoke Castle, one of the most remarkable and versatile women I have ever known, and through the Festival I became very intimate with her and often went to her lovely home near Penrith both in the lifetime of her husband Harry Howard and afterwards.

---

39 Lady Mabel Harriet Howard (1858-1942) was the daughter of Mark McDonnell, 5th Earl of Antrim. In 1878 she married Henry Charles Howard (1850-1914) who was briefly MP for Penrith in 1885/86. She was appointed a CBE in 1920.

Above and below: Nicholson directing a Carlisle Choral Society Concert at Carlisle Castle in 1905

During my time at Carlisle I became increasingly interested in the Competitive Festival movement, being often brought into touch with my distant relative Mary Wakefield[40] who was practically its founder; in fact I was actually with her talking over festival problems on the day of her death at Grange-over-Sands. I was soon engaged to judge at Morecambe, which was then probably the chief competitive Festival in England, and, under the chairmanship of Canon Gorton the Rector, attracted the most splendid choirs from all over the northern counties. I judged there regularly for many years, and this led to similar engagements in many other parts of the country, so that I got as much of this work as I could undertake.

But when my beloved Dean Ridgeway left Carlisle I felt it was time to make a move, and in 1908 I applied for the vacant post of organist at Canterbury Cathedral and was duly appointed[41]. Immediately on my return to Carlisle, however, I received a letter from the Dean of Manchester, Bishop Welldon, offering me a similar post at Manchester Cathedral if I would go there instead of Canterbury. The decision between the two was very difficult, but I felt that the opportunities at Manchester were so much greater that, in spite of my mother's urgent wish that I should stick to Canterbury[42]; I decided to ask the Dean and Chapter to release me and to go once more to the north. As events proved I never regretted this decision. I was appointed to Manchester in the summer so I was in the curious position of being technically organist of three cathedrals at the same time. I was not required to take up duties for six months, so I decided to leave Carlisle in July and to make a long continental tour while I had the chance.

> Nicholson stayed with his old family friend Baroness Deichmann in Bendeleben near Sondershausen in Germany. On Sunday 20th Sept 1908 he attended the church and played Mendelssohn's 6th Sonata before the service. He noted:
>
> The service is very odd. The congregation sit the whole time (including the hymns), only standing when the Bible is read. The people do not join in anything except the singing which consists of Chorales and simple responses. Even during the Creed and Lord's Prayer they are silent. The whole service was over in an hour & about half of it consists of preaching.

---

40 Mary Wakefield (1853-1910) was born in Kendal to a local banker. She was a talented contralto and pianist who studied in London with Randegger, Henschel and Blumenthal and in Rome with pianist Sgambati. She sang at the Gloucester Three Choirs Festival in 1880. She founded and trained a number of choirs in the villages around Kendal and, in 1885, brought them together for the first time to take part in a 'Singing Competition' to raise money for Crosscrake Church. This was to be one of the earliest competitive music festivals and certainly the earliest to focus on choral music. The idea of competitive festivals took off from this point and her festival became known as the "Westmorland Music Festival". It still flourishes today.

In Nicholson's account of his family history in Appendix A he says: "One of my grandfather's nephews married Margaret Wakefield, of Kendal, the aunt of the Mary Wakefield who founded the Westmorland Musical Festival".

41 This appointment was announced in the press on 30th March 1908 and he received several letters of congratulation before it was changed.

42 Lady Nicholson noted in a letter that Sir Walter Parratt had advised him to take the Manchester post.

Bendeleben Church, Thuringia, Germany painted by SHN on 24th Sept 1908

I left home in August, and after spending a short time in Germany my brother Archie joined me and we made our way by Vienna to Trieste and thence by a succession of steamers along the Dalmatian coast, calling not only at the chief towns but at many of the islands. It is most interesting now to recall this visit to countries whose names have since disappeared from the map, and to have been there, I suppose, at the very beginning of the troubles that eventually gave rise to the Great War. For it was while we were at Ragusa that news came that the neighbouring states of Bosnia and Herzegovina had been annexed by Austria. There was great indignation, as the Austrian rule was by no means popular, but as England was supposed to favour Turkey it meant that Englishmen were well received everywhere. Consequently we had a most delightful and interesting trip along that most wonderful coast. Ragusa [now Dubrovnik] must surely be one of the most beautiful places in the world and Spalato [now Split], built mostly within the remains of the ancient Palace of Diocletian, one of the most interesting. But we were quite as much attracted by the smaller and more out-of-the-way places, particularly some of the enchanting islands. At Trau [now Trogir] we saw the manufacture of the local wine, and nearly turned teetotal in consequence. The grapes were brought in huge panniers hung across the backs of donkeys and were emptied into big vats standing on the quay. Into these jumped

Spalato (Split) October 1908: painting by SHN

children, stark naked, with their skins stained dark purple by the juice: they danced on the grapes till tired, and then they would jump out of the vats and have a game on the quay-side (where the donkeys had left plenty of 'visiting-cards') and then jump back again to their duties! The juice meanwhile trickled out from the bottom of the vat and was collected into pig-skins from which the pig had been so skilfully extracted that its contour remained, — head, trotters and all. A 'pig-full' of wine was then slung on each side of a donkey and driven off by a gaily dressed native, I suppose for further treatment. In spite of all this the wine tasted very good, which was fortunate as water was almost unprocurable.

From Cattaro [now Kotor], at the end of its wonderful 'fiord', we drove up the great zigzag road which climbs 4000 feet up the mountain side and over the top into a sort of volcanic crater which is (or was) the Kingdom of Montenegro. We stopped for lunch at the only village on the way, where the menu, consisted of dried goat's flesh, raw eggs and hard black bread, and in the evening reached the capital city Cettinje. This was the oddest little place, scarcely more than a village except for the somewhat pretentious "Embassies." Everyone was wearing the picturesque national costume, the men with rows of knives and pistols in their sashes, and the small round cap embroidered with the letter N, the initial of their beloved King Nicholas. The men looked very magnificent, but the women poorly clad and evidently mere drudges, pulling carts or carrying heavy loads while their lords and masters swaggered along by their side. Unfortunately we missed seeing the King who lived in a sort of patriarchal relation to his people, and could be visited personally by anyone who required justice. The country seemed a miserable place with hardly a blade of vegetation except in small patches between the boulders with which it is strewn; perhaps there may have been more fertile parts that we did not see.

After returning to Cattaro we made our way to Corfu and thence to Athens. From there my brother had to return home, while I continued my journey to Alexandria, and after a glimpse at Cairo and the Great Pyramid returned to Port Said and took steamer (there was no railway then) to Jaffa. Fortunately I travelled by a Turkish steamer; for the boat before, belonging to an Austrian line, met with some adventures: owing to the friction with Turkey the watermen at Jaffa refused to land any passengers, so they were taken on to Haifa only to meet a similar reception, then to Constantinople and finally back to Trieste whence they had started! I only had to put up with a somewhat dirty ship and 24 hours' delay for quarantine and was then duly landed at Jaffa in a surf-boat to receive a most warm welcome from my Aunt, Mary Keightley[43], whom I had come to visit.

She, with her friend Miss Chaplyn, had lived for many years at Jerusalem, in a regular oriental house made extremely comfortable by European additions. The situation, on a hill

---

43   See Chapter I

outside the Jaffa gate, commanded a wonderful view of the Holy City, and with such a splendid guide as my aunt, who knew every inch of the City and had been all over the country, I made the most of my short visit. It is a great satisfaction to have seen Jerusalem before it had become 'westernized', when it was still under Turkish rule and extraordinarily primitive: no artificial light or water supply laid on in the houses: shopkeepers plying their trades in the bazaar, the potters with their wheels, the water-carriers and so on: the gathering of all nations in their varying costumes at the Jaffa Gate. Then there was the Church of the Holy Sepulchre with the Turkish soldiers on guard to prevent the different Christian sects from cutting one another's throats; and the Temple area with the marvellous Dome of the Rock and the wailing place of the Jews.

Outside the city everything had to be done either in a carriage or on a donkey, as there were no railways except that to Jaffa and most of the roads were little better than tracks, while such things as motors or even bicycles were quite unknown. Through the kindness of my aunt and her friends I was enabled to see much that the ordinary tourist would have missed, and after about a fortnight in Jerusalem I made my way up country to Haifa, Damascus and Beirut whence I took steamer to Constantinople.

It was just at this time that the Young Turk party had come into power and some sort of democratic government was attained. Whilst I was at Jerusalem the election was held for the first members of the first Turkish Parliament, and on leaving Beirut I found myself on the same ship with the newly elected MPs.

The approach to Constantinople from the sea must, I think, be one of the most wonderful sights in the world: anyhow as I saw it on a clear evening with the sunset lighting up the snow-sprinkled hills and reflected in the water, with the towers and minarets in silhouette, it is one I shall never forget. We found Constantinople very full and in a great state of excitement over the conveyance of the parliamentary ballot-boxes to the Sublime Porte. This meant densely packed streets, dresses of all nationalities, sword dancers, howling dervishes, and Turkish bands of incredible cacophony. On arrival we heard that the Sultan Abdul Hamid, who had been in hiding for several months, intended to resume the 'Selamlik', his weekly visit to the Mosque, on the Friday morning, on which day I was due to return home.

On the ship I had made friends with a young English doctor who was also on his travels, and we decided to hunt in couples. In order to see the Selamlik it was necessary to secure a Pass from the British Embassy, but it was much too late to get one and no one seemed able to help us. So we went to Cook's and asked them to let us have the best possible guide, under whom to try our luck. At his advice we hired a carriage and drove up to the Palace, just as if we were invited guests. We were stopped at the gate by a very smart and polite Turkish officer, and explained through our interpreter that we were two Englishmen just arrived and knowing nothing about Embassy passes, yet most anxious to see the ceremony. Hearing we were English and taking our cards, the officer retired for a moment and then conducted us to front seats in the enclosure reserved for the most favoured guests; at least I concluded this to be the case from the uniforms and smart clothes around us, making us, in our shabby travelling kit, feel very much out of place. However that did not worry us much for we saw everything to perfection, the old Sultan driving in his carriage accompanied by his ladies to do his devotions in the Mosque and returning shortly to the Palace. He looked a terrible old creature, and I shall never forget those piercing eyes, with a look of intense suspicion as he seemed to be watching everyone. This was, I believe, the last time he ever appeared in public.

The scene was indescribably wonderful: brilliant sunlight, a sprinkling of snow on the ground, the glittering sea in the background and white mountains beyond in the distance: near at hand hosts of troops in most brilliant uniforms of all colours, the Arab regiments in all their war-paint galloping up on their superb horses, and in the midst of it all the beady-eyed old man, in obvious fear of his life, venturing out of his hiding place to meet those who had overthrown his power.

This was my last impression of a wonderful tour and I left Constantinople by the Orient express, travelling across Bulgaria and Servia[44] straight through to Ostend and arriving home for Christmas.

---

44 An old spelling of Serbia.

Alice in Wonderland

In this chapter Nicholson refers, somewhat disparagingly, to his cantata *Ivry*, but he does not mention that, whilst in Carlisle, he also composed two musical items for the cathedral choristers to perform, both of which were published.

Alice in Wonderland accompanied by string quintet, piano and percussion was published in 1905 by Dinham Blyth & Co – a London publisher who specialised in musical materials for schools. The words were adapted from *Alice in Wonderland* and *Through the Looking Glass* by Lewis Carroll.

The first performance of *Alice in Wonderland* in 1905

Two further performances of 'Alice' were given on 3rd Oct 1907 as part of the fund-raising for the new Carlisle organ. The choir raised £50 to add a Cornopean to the Choir manual. The organ was opened two months later[45].

The following year (1906) he composed *The Luck of Edenhall*[46], a cantata for treble voices with string orchestra. It was written for the Carlisle & District Musical Festival of 1907 and published by J Curwen & Sons in London in both staff and tonic sol-fa editions. The text was from *Northumberland and the Border* by Walter White (1811–1893).

---

45   See Appendix E

46   The 'Luck of Edenhall' is a 14C Syrian decorated goblet and legend has it that this ancient vessel embodied the continuing prosperity of its owners.

Chapter IV
Manchester 1909-1918

I began work at Manchester Cathedral on 1st January 1909. Manchester, though not strictly an 'old' Cathedral, had been a Collegiate Church with a charter from Queen Elizabeth, and had always maintained a small choral establishment with a Warden and Fellows, four singing Priests and six Choristers. When the Bishopric of Manchester was created in 1847, the Warden and Fellows became Dean and Canons and the choral foundation continued. The Cathedral, being also the ancient parish church of Manchester, was richly endowed, and in this respect provided a great contrast to Carlisle with its attenuated resources. The Dean was Bishop Welldon (former Headmaster of Harrow, Bishop of Calcutta and Canon of Westminster); he had recently been appointed[1]. The Chapter consisted of Canon Kelly[2], an aristocratic old gentleman who preached very long sermons, and the father of the founder of Kelham[3] [College]; Canon Wright[4], who soon left to become Archbishop of Sydney; Canon Hicks[5], who became Bishop of Lincoln, and Canon J J Scott[6], who devoted his whole life to the interests of the Cathedral.

Bishop Edward Hicks

They were a distinguished lot of men and I think that Bishop Welldon was the most efficient Dean that I ever served under. He was determined to bring the Cathedral services to the highest degree of excellence in every way and he spared no trouble or expense to secure this. Perhaps his chief care was for the great Sunday evening services, to which he invited every distinguished preacher of the day, making his plans a year ahead: but he was constant in his attendance at the regular daily services, and a keen critic of anything that he felt might be improved. He would say in his characteristic way, "I know nothing about the music, but everything about the musicians."

---

1   See p.97 for biography and photograph.

2   The Rev James Davenport Kelly MA was a former Scholar of Manchester Grammar School, a graduate of Wadham College in Oxford and served as Vicar of Christ Church in Ashton-under-Lyne from 1865 until appointment (in 1884) as Canon Residentiary of Manchester Cathedral and Rector of St Matthew's, Campfield.

3   The Rev Herbert Kelly (1860-1950) founded the religious order The Society of the Sacred Mission in 1893. They moved to Kelham Hall in Nottinghamshire in 1903 and ran it as a theological college.

4   The Rev John Charles Wright (1861-1933), son of a Bolton vicar (who founded Bolton Wanderers football club), studied at Manchester Grammar School and Merton College, Oxford. Appointed a Canon of Manchester Cathedral in 1904, he was chaplain to the Bishop of Manchester and in 1909 he was appointed Archdeacon of Manchester. Later in 1909 Wright accepted the archbishopric of Sydney in Australia. He was known for reducing the influence of Anglo-Catholicism in the diocese of Sydney including banning the chasuble from use in churches.

5   The Rt Rev Edward Lee Hicks (1843-1919) was educated at Magdalen College School and Brasenose College in Oxford and ordained in 1886. After serving as a Fellow and Tutor at Corpus Christi College in Oxford, he served as Rector of Fenny Compton before becoming the first Principal of Hulme Hall in Manchester, now part of the University. He was a Canon Residentiary of Manchester Cathedral and Rural Dean of Salford before appointment as Bishop of Lincoln in 1910.

6   The Rev Joseph John Scott (c 1847-1930), a graduate of Trinity College, Cambridge, was ordained Priest in 1871. He was Rector of St Andrew's, Ancoats and then Canon Residentiary of Manchester. He also served as Rural Dean of Salford and Subdean of Manchester.

My predecessor was Dr J Kendrick Pyne[7], a musician of some distinction and a very eccentric character; he had been a pupil of S S Wesley and was a remarkable organist and something of a genius, but not such a good choir-trainer. Consequently the choir, though containing some good material, was in an unsatisfactory state. The Precentor, my old Oxford friend the Rev Hubert Marsh, had greatly extended the repertoire and done much to introduce new ideas; but this meant that much new music was attempted with little or no rehearsal.

Canon Hubert Marsh

The first thing, clearly, was to tackle the choir, and in this Bishop Welldon proved a wonderful supporter. In a short time he found funds to increase the number of men to twelve and to pay them good salaries, and with the help of the Rev R M Tuke[8], the headmaster of the choir-school, the boys, who had been disorderly and out-of-hand, were soon licked into shape; so that in about two years we had an extremely good choir.

Manchester Cathedral Choir in 1910

---

7   See page 87.

8   Whilst at Manchester the Rev Ray Melville Tuke (b 1881) became a founder member of the National Federation of Cathedral Old Choristers' Associations in 1910. He served at St Paul's in Northampton from 1929 to 1940 and then at Gt Catworth in Huntingdonshire until retirement in 1959.

The organ was rebuilt by Hill and Son, and subsequently by Harrison and Harrison, and converted from an utter wreck into a very fine instrument[9].

The Manchester Diocesan Church Music Society[10] was soon formed, after meetings had been held in all the large towns, and a very strong organization was brought into being, each member (boys and men alike) paying an annual subscription of 1/- and getting in return a badge [see right] and the year's music as well as travelling expenses to the Cathedral Festivals. These were held at the Cathedral each year for one third of the Diocese with local Festivals for the remainder. In a short time there were 4000 members and about 7 or 8 active branches. As most of them were town choirs, many of them very good ones, we were able to do some really fine music, such as Bach's unaccompanied motets, with a choir of 1200 filling the Cathedral Nave.

I had soon made friends with the boys, and gradually an Old Boys' Association was formed, who used to meet in a cellar at my house[11].

Manchester Cathedral Choristers' Union 1912

---

9   See Appendix E.

10 First Festival Service 22nd Nov 1910.

11 Nicholson lived at 6 Wilton Polygon in Crumpsall. It was a large and expensive residence (letters to his mother indicate they were asking £65 p/a rent but that he hoped to obtain a better rate). He needed a large house for his two-manual Speechley organ. See Photographs on a subsequent page.

   Wilton Polygon was also the site of the offices of the long-established Manchester Jews School. The site has been redeveloped but the St David's Primary School for Jewish children is still there.

I started a Scout Troop for the choristers, which they took up very keenly, and I got hold of the deck-cabin of an old Channel steamer, the 'Normandy'[12], and had it placed on a field on the sea-shore near Rhyl[13]. Here I took the boys every year for a fortnight's camp.

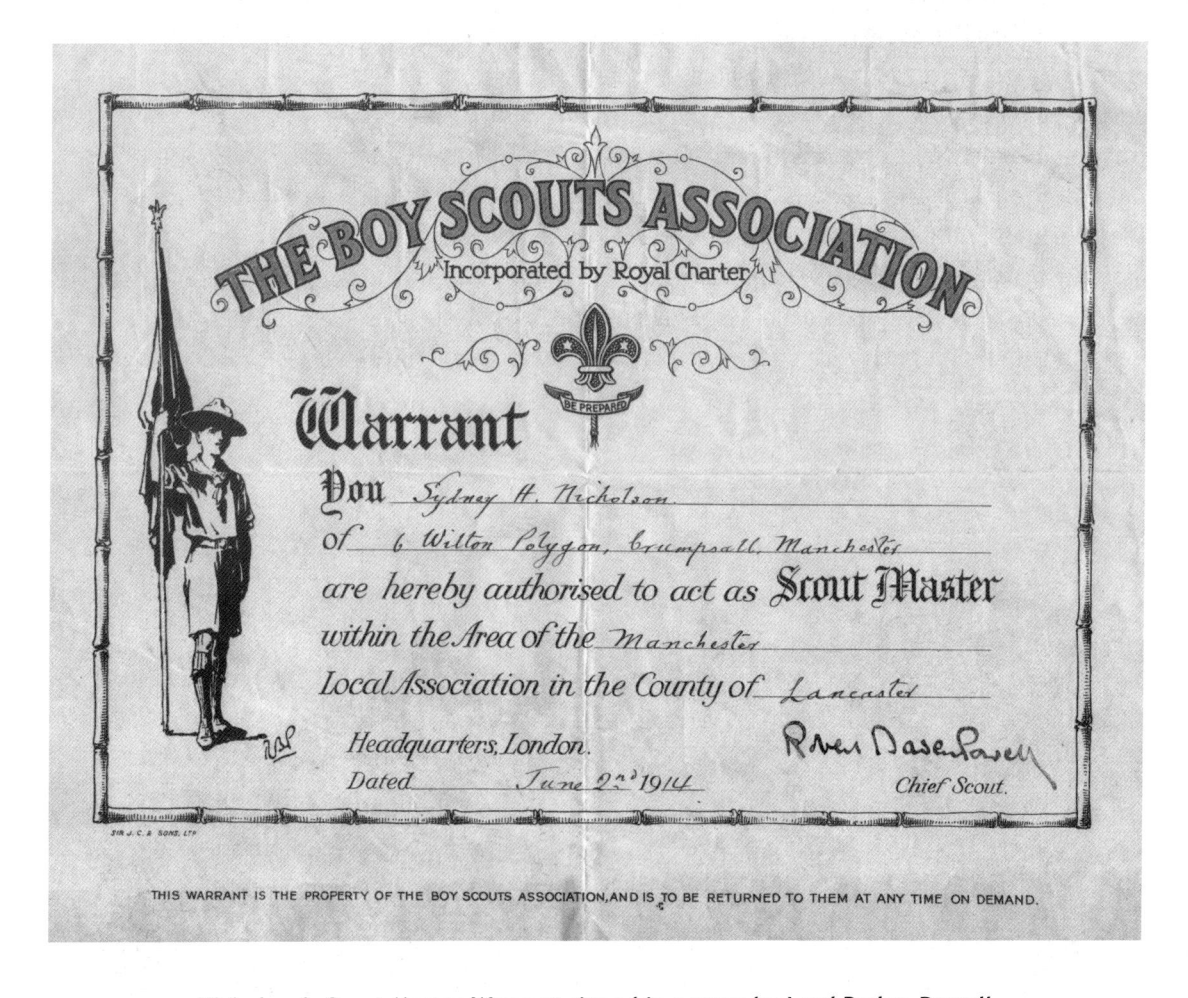

Nicholson's Scout Master Warrant signed in person by Lord Baden-Powell

---

12 The PS Normandy (PS = Paddle Steamer), built in Govan, Scotland in 1882, was fitted with Stroudley's patented feathering paddle wheels, which improved efficiency and speed without any increase in engine power. This enabled Normandy to make the crossing from Newhaven to Dieppe in less than three and a half hours. After passing through various hands, she was sold to Mr Richards, a solicitor, for operation out of Swansea. He sailed her under The Normandy Steamship Co colours of red funnels with black tops. She ran in competition with Pockett's PS Brighton, whom she regularly raced across the Bristol Channel. The Normandy Steamship Co lasted until 1907 and Normandy was finally broken up at Rhyl in 1909.

13 Nicholson had the deck cabin from PS Normandy placed on a farm by the sea some two miles from Rhyl, so that he could give his choristers a fortnight's break each summer. An annual feature of these breaks was the cricket match against the choristers of St Asaph cathedral. As well as taking the Manchester choristers there each year, he also made it available to other choirs at a modest charge of 10/- per boy, per week. The camp was able to accommodate a maximum of 20. These camps were run on scouting lines, each day starting with a bugle call at 6.30am and roll call and inspection at 7.00am. This was followed by drill or swimming and prayers and then breakfast.

He noted on one postcard that "By 1913 about 500 boys from various choirs had been accommodated - about 150 a year".

The cabin was moved to Fox Covert Lane in Lower Peover, Cheshire for the 1916-1918 camps, see painting on p.101.

P S Normandy (date unknown)

The Choristers at Scout Camp in Rhyl 1911

The Choristers at Scout Camp in Rhyl 1911

A postcard on which Nicholson has marked his house with an x

Dr James Kendrick Pyne (1852-1938)

Three Manchester Cathedral Organists (L to R: J K Pyne, J F Bridge, S H Nicholson)
On the appointment of Nicholson to Westminster Abbey September 1918

James Kendrick Pyne (1852-1938) was born in Bath. His father, also James Kendrick Pyne (1810-1893) was organist at Bath Abbey for 53 years and his grandfather, also James Kendrick Pyne (1788-1857) was a celebrated tenor. A pupil (at the age of 12) of S S Wesley in Winchester, Pyne was appointed organist of Chichester Cathedral in 1873, but in the following year he went to the USA as organist of St Mark's in Philadelphia. His two brothers (Minton Pyne and Ernest Pyne, both musicians) also emigrated to the USA. A year later Pyne returned to succeed (Sir) Frederick Bridge as organist of Manchester Cathedral. Pyne also became a professor at the Royal Manchester College of Music in 1893 and organist to Manchester Town Hall where he gave many recitals. When Nicholson took over the Cathedral post, Pyne continued to teach at the College until retirement to Essex in 1926. He died in Ilford.

The Manchester (and Salford) Whit Processions

The Whit Monday Procession c 1910 with Bishop Welldon[14] behind the mace-bearer. Behind him to the left are Nicholson (far left) with the Rev B Dennis Jones (Precentor).

The annual Whit[15] Monday Protestant Processions in Manchester were an important feature of the city year. The procession passed through the city to finish at the cathedral where they were met by the clergy for a special service. They were organised by a committee representing 40 Church of England Sunday Schools in Salford and Manchester. First organised in 1801 and suspended from 1916 to 1918, attendance peaked at about 25,000[16]. The procession still continues today on a smaller scale as the 'Manchester and Salford Church of England Procession of Witness'. With the disappearance of "Whit" activities in modern times, the procession is now held on Pentecost Sunday.

There was also a Catholic Whit-Walk on Whit Friday which ran from 1844 until 1939. Originally there was some rivalry, but the sectarianism so sadly seen in Liverpool and Glasgow did not evolve quite so aggressively in Manchester and Salford. For many years the Catholics undoubtedly put on a more spectacular showing than the Anglicans.

In the mid 1870's the Unitarians also organised their own walk to Cross Street Chapel on Whit Sunday.

---

14 Bishop Welldon is wearing his Doctor of Divinity robes
15 Most of the children wore white (Whit-Sunday = White Sunday)
16 They even published their own hymn book for the procession in 1899.

Leslie Heward

It was, I think, in 1911 that Leslie Heward[17] joined our ranks, and the story of how he came to Manchester is rather remarkable. I was judging at the Morecambe Festival, and in one class for 'Ear Tests' a small, delicate-looking boy presented himself, whom I simply could not 'stump': every test I devised he answered perfectly: the same with 'Reading at sight' on the piano: — I had brought a set of variations of graded difficulty: — he read them all! I then took him into the church:

> "Can you sing?"
>
> "Not much, sir."
>
> "Do you play the organ?"
>
> "Yes, a little, sir."
>
> "What can you play?"
>
> "I don't know any pieces, sir, but I think I could make up something."

Leslie Heward in Manchester 1911

Then followed a most remarkable extempore, I think on the theme of Mendelssohn's "Hear my prayer." I went back to Manchester full of this wonderful boy and asked Bishop Welldon whether we could not bring him there as a chorister. "Anything for a genius," was his characteristic answer. So Leslie came. At first he lived with a succession of elderly ladies who undertook to 'mother' him: but he was so delicate and so naughty that no one would keep him: so at last I determined to take him myself and, as I had a large house, two other boys were imported from outside to strengthen the choir and keep him company. He made amazing progress with his music. I disclaim any credit for teaching him; — the utmost I could do was to guide him; but he always maintains that the groundwork he received in the Cathedral music had much to do with his after success. He developed a good, though not a remarkable, voice and of course his musicianship was of immense value to the choir. He soon began to attract attention outside the Cathedral and Stanford, Parry, Arthur Somervell, Brodsky and others were greatly impressed with his powers. I should think he must be the only choirboy who has ever played a Mozart Concerto in an Eton suit at an orchestral concert, as he did in Manchester Town Hall with the 'Beethoven Society'. Of course he was a constant attendant with me at the Halle Concerts under Richter and later at the splendid series of operas run by Beecham; and in this way, I think, his ambition to become a conductor was fostered; I had the pleasure of taking him to his first orchestral concert!

---

17 For further information and photographs of Leslie Heward see Appendix H

Arthur Gayford at Barnet (above)
Harry Coleman at Carlisle (right)

I have always been most fortunate in my assistants. When I came to Manchester Dr Frank Radcliffe[18], who had been assistant to Dr Pyne, remained as Sub-organist and I brought with me two articled pupils from Carlisle, Arthur Gayford[19], who had been one of my choir-boys at Barnet, and who soon won the Keble Organ Scholarship, and Harry Coleman[20], who remained with me for some time and became my assistant, till he left to become organist of Blackburn Parish Church (now the Cathedral), and subsequently of Londonderry and Peterborough Cathedrals. When he [Coleman] left, Leslie Heward became Sub-organist at the age of 17: he had developed into a splendid player and was often left in full charge of the whole choir. He gained a Scholarship for composition at The Royal College of Music and was at the same time appointed an assistant music master at Eton under Basil Johnson. His successor was Ernest Bullock[21], fresh from Bairstow and Leeds Parish Church, aged about 18 and a most brilliant

---

18 Frank Radcliffe Mus Doc FRCO (1883-1922) later served at St Wulfram's Church in Grantham and went to St Mary's in Nottingham in 1914, remaining there until his death.

19 Went to Dulwich College as assistant organist in 1915. Nicholson's visitor's book shows that they stayed in contact for many years.

20 Richard Henry (k/a Harry) Pinwell Coleman (1888-1965) was born in and died in Dartmouth, Devon. He was an articled pupil of Nicholson's at Carlisle, and then transferred his articles to Manchester where, after two years, he became Sub-Organist (from 1909 to 1912). He claimed to be SHN's first articled pupil and went to him on the advice of Sir Walter Parratt, who described Nicholson as "the coming man". He then moved to Blackburn Parish Church as organist for two years and this was followed by four years at St Columb's Cathedral in Londonderry, before returning to England in 1921 as Organist and Master of the Choristers at Peterborough Cathedral. On retiring from Peterborough in 1944 he was at Hatfield Parish Church and then All Saints' in Eastbourne. He was the author of *The Amateur Choir Trainer* 1932 (re-issued as *The Church Choir-Trainer* in 1964) and *The Amateur Organist* 1955 (re-issued as *The Church Organist* in 1968) both of which were very popular. He also published a handbook of *Hymn Tune Voluntaries for the Organ* 1930 which listed some 225 hymn tune voluntaries composed by British composers. All his books were published by the Oxford University Press.

21 Sir Ernest Bullock (1890-1979) was born in Wigan, Lancashire, and was a chorister at Wigan Parish Church. He studied with, and was

musician. When war broke out he joined the army and was succeeded by Arnold Goldsbrough[22] who, as he was unfit for military service, stayed with me till I went to Westminster and accompanied me there.

Arnold Goldsbrough

Captain Ernest Bullock in WWI

A year or so before the Great War the choir had reached its apex and was undoubtedly the best choir I have ever had to deal with: — twelve men, all good and none of them old, the boys magnificent and a splendid organ. Among the boys, besides Leslie Heward, were three others who had taken prominent places in the musical world, all, curiously, as conductors with the BBC: these were Eric Fogg[23], Crawford McNair[24] and Eric Warr[25]: all these were in

---

assistant to, Edward Bairstow, at Leeds Parish Church, and assistant to SHN in Manchester from 1912 until called up for war service. He obtained a D Mus at Durham University in 1914 and, after a spell at Exeter Cathedral, he took over from Nicholson at Westminster Abbey in 1928, serving until the choir was disbanded in WWII. He was appointed in 1935 as Director of Studies for the SECM at St Nicolas College. Sadly his home at the Abbey and all his music were destroyed by a bomb in May 1941. He left life as a cathedral musician to become Professor of Music in Glasgow and then became Director of the RCM from 1952. Knighted in 1951, he was also Chair of the RSCM Council from 1949 to 1952.

22 Arnold Wainwright Goldsbrough (1892-1964) was the founder of what became the English Chamber Orchestra. Born in Gomersal, near Bradford, his father was a cabinet-maker and cellist. Arnold's musical ability was recognized at an early age, and he was discouraged from playing games, in order to preserve his hands. At the age of 12 he began study with Bradford organist Charles Stott and took his first post as a church organist in that year. He took his FRCO in 1915 before appointment to Manchester. He was not called up for war service because of a heart condition. On following Nicholson to Westminster in 1919, he enrolled to study composition, double bass and conducting at the Royal College of Music. He then taught there, as a professor of organ, from 1924-1941. He also taught at Westminster School and succeeded Gustav Holst as Director of Morley College. He resigned from Westminster Abbey in 1929.

23 Charles William Eric Fogg (1903-1939), son of Charles H Fogg the organist for the Hallé Orchestra in Manchester, went on to study with Granville Bantock in Birmingham. He was a prolific composer as a young man with 57 works completed (and many performed) by the age of 18. He moved to London and became musical director of the BBC's Empire Service in 1934.

24 Crawford McNair was deputy conductor of the BBC Northern Orchestra and later worked for the BBC in Palestine.

25 Eric Warr (b 1905) went on to work for the BBC as producer, arranger and composer. He was also Assistant Chief Censor at the BBC during the WWII and had a special telephone line to the Cabinet War Office and a bed in the basement of Broadcasting House.

the choir together as boys, — no wonder they were a musicianly lot! Besides a big and varied repertory of all the best Cathedral music we sang regularly once a month some Cantata at the Sunday afternoon service, in place of a sermon. Lunch-hour recitals were given by all the best organists of the day. The annual performance of the Bach *St Matthew Passion* by the Cathedral choir with a section of the Halle orchestra filled every corner of the Cathedral. In connection with the Manchester choir there happened a curious coincidence which seems worth recording. On April 29th 1906 the anthem was Henry Smart's *O be joyful*, and the quartet *O come hither and hearken* was sung by three men and a boy: quite accidentally it was discovered that it was the birthday of each of them: and the same quartet was actually sung by the same 'birthday party' on the same day in four successive years.

The Cathedral certainly fulfilled its duties splendidly under Bishop Welldon. The services were all well attended; a congregation of fifty, mostly business men, at week-day Mattins was by no means uncommon; the Sunday services and particularly the popular evening services brought crowded congregations. Life in Manchester was most pleasant and full of interest of every kind. The place itself was detestable, hideously ugly and frightfully dirty: but the people were most keen and ready to support one as soon as they had given their confidence. This took a little time to win, but once gained it was worth having. Of general society I did not see a great deal: there were some nice people connected with the University and some musical folks, such as the Behrens family who were great benefactors to music, and one or two others. But the Cathedral, though of course there is no Close (the Dean and Canons all living some miles away), had its own very pleasant circle. There was the Dean, with his boundless hospitality, and constant invitations to impromptu suppers on Sunday evenings, at which all sorts of people would be assembled, from actresses to non-conformist Divines. Wonderful were the powers of "Edward," his faithful servant and friend, in being able to provide on the spur of the moment for any who might chance to be invited — they might easily amount to fifteen or twenty! Then there were the Scotts. The Canon simply lived for the Cathedral, which he quite honestly believed to be the finest building in England (if not in the world), and to be a model for all others. He and Mrs Scott again were unstinted in their hospitality and in their kindness to all connected with the place. Then there was Dr Boutflower[26], a strong Anglo-Catholic, and devoted to the Cathedral and all its staff though intensely critical of its services; he hated what he called 'modern music', in which he included Bach, Byrd and Gibbons, and pleaded for the real 'old masters', Mendelssohn, Gounod, Sterndale Bennett and Rossini! He was the devoted friend and honorary doctor of generations of choirboys, and he entertained lavishly in the 'grand old style': his dinner parties would run to seventeen courses!

---

26 Dr Andrew Boutflower (1844-1932), surgeon to Manchester Prison and Physician to Chetham's School, was the author of *Personal reminiscences of Manchester Cathedral: 1845-1912*, London, Faith Press, 1914

Then there was the general music of the place. First the wonderful series of Halle concerts on Thursday evenings, conducted by Richter till the war, when he went to Austria. Richter was in some ways the perfect conductor: he gave an impression of finality in his performances that I do not think anyone else has quite achieved: one felt that, whether one liked it or not, he was certainly right. This of course applied chiefly to the classics, — the Beethoven Symphonies or those of Brahms, or in Wagner, or the B minor Mass, of which one performance remains in my memory as the nearest [to] perfection I ever heard.

The wonderful series of operas produced by Thomas Beecham belong to the period of the war; they were marvellously interesting. All sorts of then unfamiliar works were produced, such as Boris Godunov, Prince Igor, Falstaff, Otello, Louise, besides the whole range of Wagner and Mozart. Never, even abroad, have I had such a feast of opera.

At the Gaiety Theatre we had a wonderful series of productions by the famous Miss Horniman's Repertory Company and all sorts of interesting pieces were performed.

The Free Trade Hall Manchester, where Nicholson's Cantata *1914* was performed

The Cathedral Quarterly 1913-1916

In 1912 Sydney Nicholson and the Precentor of Manchester, The Rev B Dennis Jones[27], launched a new journal – *The Cathedral Quarterly* with the rather grand sub-title "A record of the work at, and in connection with the Cathedral Churches in Communion with the See of Canterbury." The first issue in January 1913 featured a foreword by Walford Davies, ironically a non-cathedral musician, and the stated aims of the journal were to present "facts rather than theories". In addition to a section of Cathedral News relating to services, concerts, choristers, lay-clerks, music lists and Diocesan Choral Associations, there were substantial articles about cathedrals and their organs, including information and photographs of clergy and musicians. There were also articles about choir schools and the usual obituaries, reviews and correspondence sections together with articles on liturgy. The journal was first published in Leighton Buzzard, and subsequently in London, by the Faith Press, with which Nicholson had a very close relationship. Nicholson and Dennis Jones together with the Rev C E Douglas, the Bursar of the Society of Faith, steered the journal through its first two years.

The first year ended, not unexpectedly for a new publication, with a financial deficit and at the end of the second year they reported that every issue was still making a loss. They established a management committee with Walford Davies as Chairman. The Rev W H Frere[28], the Rev Henry Dams[29] and Gregorian chant enthusiast Francis Burgess[30] joined the committee and all wrote articles for the journal as well as trying encourage subscribers. The journal was a high quality product on good paper with many photographs and the cost of this, together with the exigencies of wartime, resulted in the last issue being March 1916 – a grand total of 12 issues (there was no Christmas 1915 issue).

THE EDITOR,
THE REV. B. DENNIS JONES, M.A.

---

27 The Rev Basil Dennis Jones (1883-1968) was conscripted as an Army Chaplain in November 1914. In 1920, by which time he had been awarded the OBE, he went on to be Precentor of Trinity College, Cambridge. In 1926 he published *The Conduct of Public Worship*, in 1927 he published a *Passion* 'for small choirs' and the following year he changed his name by deed poll to the hyphenated Dennis-Jones.

28 See Chapter V. At this point Frere was still at the Community of the Resurrection in Mirfield, of which he was co-founder.

29 See Chapter III

30 The Rev Francis Henry Burgess (1879-1948) was organist of St Mary's in Primrose Hill from 1901, St Mark's in Marylebone Road from 1902, and then of St Columb's in North Kensington from 1904. A professor at Trinity College London, he was also briefly editor of the journal Organist and Choirmaster in 1917. Composer of much church music, he was Director of Music of the Gregorian Association (founded in 1870) from 1910 until his death. At the age of 65 he was ordained priest.

The Great War

So life at Manchester was very full[31], very varied and very prosperous. And then like a thunderbolt came the Great War. I was in camp with my choristers [at Rhyl] on 4th August 1914. Manoeuvres had been going on at Conway and all through the day and night a succession of trains passed along the main line nearby. Ordinary train services were suspended and it was with some difficulty that we got home. All was excitement, of course; talks of German spies, Russian troops in passing trains complete with long beards and snow, the rush for enlistment, and so on. Our Scout Troop was promptly 'mobilized' for national duty as messengers and working in conjunction with the police. All the bigger boys did a good deal of this service and stuck to it very well while the first emergency lasted, doing so many hours 'duty' each day in addition to their Cathedral work. Even the regulation dress of 'Etons and Mortar-boards', which they had to wear daily in those days, was relaxed in favour of Scout uniform, — though rather to the horror of the Dean who was most punctilious in such matters. Soon after the 'Derby' scheme[32] came into being, and I of course enlisted at once and got my 'armlet'. But I was just over age and was never called up.

The younger choir men began to go off to the war, and it was obvious that it would be difficult to maintain the full round of choral services. However the Dean and I talked things over and we decided that it was our job to keep things going somehow. He said then, "If we once let the services go, we shall never get them back again:' — a prophecy of which the wisdom has proved only too true in the majority of Cathedrals. So somehow we managed to keep two choral services going every day throughout the whole of the ten years I was at Manchester (including the whole of the war period), by various expedients — often 'boys only', or 'men only', or 'half-choir', or by the use of deputies; but still the continuity was not broken, and this is an achievement that I look back to with great satisfaction. It could never have been accomplished but for the unfailing support of Bishop Welldon[33].

War-time Concerts

One effect of the war was to throw many musicians entirely out of employment. A "Committee for Music in War-time" had been started in London[34], largely through the energy

---

31   Nicholson does not mention that in Jan 1914 the Royal College of Organists elected him a Fellow (without examination).

32   The Derby scheme was a voluntary recruitment policy created by the Earl of Derby in 1915. The scheme proved unsuccessful, and was abandoned at the end of the same year, being superseded by the Military Service Act of 1916.

33   The *Cathedral Quarterly* for July 1915 (Vol III, No 10) made the point that at Manchester two choral services (Matins and Evensong), complete with setting and anthem, 'are sung on every day of the year without exception.' This was achieved by making services 'men's voices' only during the boys' holidays and vice versa. The article goes on to say: "It is much to be wished that other cathedrals would adopt it [the plan] more largely, to save the disappointment which so many visitors experience at finding non-choral services during the summer."

34   A Committee for Music in War-time was formed of the Principals of the four music colleges in London, Sir Alexander Mackenzie, Sir Hubert Parry, Landon Ronald and Sir Frederick Bridge, together with Granville Bantock (Director of the Birmingham Institute) and with Walter Willson Cobbett (author of the famous Cobbett's *Cyclopedic Survey of Chamber Music*) as its Honorary Secretary. It compiled a register of "competent artists requiring work, and willing to accept such fees as either the Committee or the Society engaging them is able to offer. It

of Miss Mary Maud Paget, the idea being to give small paid engagements to approved artists in providing music in Hospitals, Camps, etc. We decided to establish a branch of this work in Manchester which had become the centre of a large number of hospitals, and I was soon put in charge of the entertainments in all of them. The organization developed to something big, and at one time we were giving over a hundred concerts each week. This meant first of all testing individuals and concert parties that wished to receive engagements, making arrangements with the Sisters-in-charge and receiving their reports, and often altering the destination or cancelling the engagement of parties at the last minute. This sort of thing, especially when it involved driving a car to outlying hospitals through darkened streets and at times a Manchester fog, was certainly no light task: but it was greatly appreciated and I was thankful to find a bit of war work that I was really qualified to do.

The high-class musicians of Manchester all volunteered to help; but classical concerts proved to be hardly suitable for hospitals and I soon had to stop them. Then the happy idea was suggested of getting these fine artists to give their services in a series of Tuesday Mid-day Concerts, and by their association with the scheme to give the assurance that they would be such as to appeal to a critical Manchester audience. The leading musicians often played themselves, giving their services most generously, but it was also possible to provide engagements for promising young artists as well as to raise considerable funds for financing the hospital entertainments. The concerts were held at the Houldsworth Hall, Deansgate, during the luncheon hour, and as soon as they became known were very well attended. Finances were greatly helped by the contributions of the wealthier Manchester citizens, many of whom gave the scheme their generous support. In the planning of these concerts I was greatly helped by Mr William Eller, who became their virtual organizer. On his death the administration was taken on by Mr Edward Isaacs[35], the well-known pianist, and by the end of the war they had become such a feature in the musical life of Manchester that it was decided to continue them. After 25 years, still under the most able direction of Mr Isaacs, they have achieved such a reputation that it is considered an honour for any young musician to appear at them: they are familiar to many people outside Manchester through their frequent inclusion in the broadcast programmes, but few probably remember that they began purely as a war-time venture.

In connection with these concerts, I was brought into touch with many of the leading Manchester musicians outside the Cathedral circle. Chief amongst these was dear old Dr

---

will collaborate with local musical societies anxious to continue their work, but debarred from doing so by the departure of active helpers, or by lack of sufficient funds to meet expenses."

35 Edward Isaacs (1881-1953) was educated at Manchester Grammar School, at the Manchester College of Music, in Germany and Austria, making his Berlin debut in 1904. Though referred to as a blind pianist, Isaacs was in fact not blinded until an accident in 1924 at the age of 43. Despite this, he continued his career as a pianist, teacher and lecturer. He broadcast frequently for the BBC and became Head of Music for the Third Programme in 1950.

Brodsky[36], the famous Russian violinist who had succeeded Charles Halle as Principal of the Royal Manchester College of Music. Though advanced in years he was still an incomparable player of classical chamber music. He was exceedingly kind to me and did me the great honour of playing (with his quartet and Miss Lucy Pierce[37]) a pianoforte quintet which I wrote for him. Miss Marie Brema[38], Mr Arthur Caterall[39], and Mr Frederic Dawson[40] were others who frequently gave their services, while my dear friend R H Wilson, the chorus master of the Halle concerts, was always ready to get together an excellent body of singers for choral concerts. The Cathedral choir, too, was much to the fore, and their Christmas Carol Concerts were among the most popular.

At this time I wrote a short Cantata for chorus and orchestra called *1914*[41], the words being taken from Rupert Brooke's sonnets. This was performed at a Halle concert, being splendidly conducted by Eugene Goossens, in the absence of Sir Thomas Beecham through illness.

Bishop Welldon

Bishop Welldon

It was, I think, in 1917[42] that Bishop Welldon[43] left Manchester to become Dean of Durham,

---

36 Violinist Adolph Brodsky (1851-1929), born into a family of violinists, studied in Vienna and taught in at the conservatory in Moscow from 1875, where he met and worked with Tchaikovsky. In 1884 in Leipzig he formed the Brodsky Quartet, before relocating to New York City in 1891. On returning to Europe, he settled in Manchester where he taught at the Royal Manchester College of Music, directed the Hallé Orchestra and founded a second Brodsky Quartet in 1895.

37 Pianist Lucy Eleanor Pierce (1886-1968) taught at the Royal Manchester College of Music. She retired in 1963 after 50 years service. The College (now the Royal Northern College of Music) still offer a Lucy Pierce Award to pianists.

38 Dramatic mezzo-soprano Marie Brema (1856-1925) was born in Liverpool of German father and American mother. After a very successful international career in opera she retired from the stage in 1912. She then became director of the opera class at the Royal Manchester College of Music.

39 Violinist Arthur Catterall (1883-1943) studied at and then taught at Royal Manchester College of Music. He became leader of the Henry Wood 'Promenade' Concerts at London's Queen's Hall in 1909 and subsequently taught at the Royal Academy of Music.

40 English pianist Frederick Dawson (1868-1940) studied with his father, and also with Sir C Hallé and E Dannreuther. By the age 10 he could play Bach's "48" from memory. After further study with Anton Rubinstein, he pursued a successful solo career. He taught at the Royal Manchester College of Music from 1893 and at the Royal College of Music in London. Nicholson appears to have mis-spelled Frederic, and this is not surprising as the RSCM Library contains a postcard from FD to SHN on which Dawson signs himself Frederic. There are several theories to explain this: 1 it was common practice to use the variant spelling; 2 it was an artistic whim; 3 During WWI the spelling was more popular and considered as being 'less German'.

41 This was very well received by the press and published in 1917 by J. Curwen & Sons, London.

42 Actually it was 1918

43 The Right Rev James Edward Cowell Welldon (1854-1937) was ordained priest in 1885 and appointed that same year as Headmaster of Harrow School, serving until 1898. It was Welldon who admitted the young Winston Churchill to Harrow, in spite of his poor showing in the entrance exam (he actually wrote nothing on the paper except his name). Churchill later wrote "It showed that he was a man capable of looking beneath the surface of things: a man not dependant on paper manifestations. I have always had the greatest regard for him". Welldon also wrote a public school story, *Gerald Eversley's Friendship* 1895, which achieved a certain notoriety as being considered the

97

and was succeeded by the Rev W S Swayne[44], who shortly after became Bishop of Lincoln on the death of Bishop Hicks. Bishop Welldon's time at Manchester was probably the most successful period of his life. Not only was he devoted to the interests of the Cathedral which he always put first, but he threw himself into every interest of civic life with unstinted energy. He was, I suppose, the best known figure of his day in Manchester, for his burly form could never escape notice: he always travelled backwards and forwards from the Deanery to the City by tram-car, and would talk readily with everyone he met, whether he knew them or not: he loved popularity and liked to be known as the 'Tram-Dean'.

There was an Episcopal Dean with a countenance ruddy & clean / He sat in a tram and observed "well I am" / "A most democratic old dean"

An illustrated limerick about the 'Tram-Dean by SHN's elder brother Charles[45].

---

epitomy of heavy and mawkish sentimentality. Welldon left Harrow to become Bishop of Calcutta briefly until 1902. He became Dean of Manchester Cathedral, serving from 1906 to 1918. Nicholson and Welldon became life-long friends and often dined together at the Athenæum Club. After leaving Manchester, Welldon became Dean of Durham, serving from 1918. Welldon retired to Sevenoaks in 1933, after suffering a severe fall in the cathedral which left him permanently crippled.

44 The Rt Rev William Shuckburgh Swayne DD (1862-1941) studied at New College in Oxford and was ordained in 1886. He served in Lyndhurst, Stalbridge, Lichfield, Walsall and at St Peter's, Cranley Gardens in Kensington before appointment as Dean of Manchester.

45 Sir Charles Nicholson left a whole book of illustrated (mostly original) limericks which he had drawn as a Christmas present for his mother.

Manchester Cathedral (with trams!) in 1903

In the Cathedral he was, on his day, a splendid preacher, and he was, I think, the most impressive reader of the Bible that I ever heard, and that in spite of a definitely ugly voice. Of his care for every detail of the services I have already spoken: in many ways he was the ideal Dean. But the jovial and rather over-hearty manner which he affected, partly I suspect because he thought it suited the warm-hearted Lancashire folks, rather tended to disguise the real man, with his immense learning and his great wisdom. This I came to realize more in later years when, in old age, he settled in Sevenoaks and I was often able to visit him and enjoy long and intimate talks. Considering the brilliance of his attainments in early years, his life must have been to some extent a disappointment. But although his time in India was generally accounted a failure, I believe that it was to this he looked back as his most important piece of work, and it is significant that many of the views which he had expressed in his characteristically blunt way and which were, no doubt, responsible for his resignation, were proved in the long run to have been right. In old age he acquired a somewhat detached attitude to life, and his observations on men and affairs were wonderfully shrewd and illuminating. He was a really great man though he never quite achieved the distinction he might have attained had he been less outspoken; for certainly he was no 'courtier'.

Lower Peover Camp with the choristers July 1918
(left) Nicholson with war-time rations;
(right) The only known image of Nicholson in Scouting uniform

In the summer of 1918 I was at Camp with my choristers; this had been moved to Lower Peover near Knutsford, as the sea-wall at Rhyl had given way and the former site of the camp had become liable to inundation. I was cooking for the party (with war-time rations) when a letter was brought me from the Dean of Westminster saying that Sir Frederick Bridge was leaving the Abbey at the end of the year, that my name had been suggested as a successor[46], and that he wished to see me. As soon as I could be spared from the camp I went up to London and the appointment was offered me.

It is rather curious that I have only twice in my life 'applied' for a post, as a young man at Winchester College and later at Canterbury Cathedral. In the first case I was not appointed and in the second I was appointed but did not go. For none of the posts that I have actually filled have I ever made application. There is some satisfaction in this, for whatever may have been my short-comings I could never be blamed for having thrust myself into an appointment!

---

46 Bishop Ryle (see Chapter V) wrote to Nicholson on July 14th indicating that he had made a short list of three candidates. He also warned that the Abbey "is not at all a bed of roses"! Nicholson was offered £300 per annum with £100 for 'habitation'. Nicholson replied by telegram that he could not leave the boys at the camp. Ryle replied to say that was understandable and invited SHN to The Abbey the following week. Negotiations did not take long and Nicholson sent a telegram to his mother on 30th July "All settled no need for secrecy". *The Times* formally reported his appointment on 3rd August 1918.

Two of Nicholson's paintings.

Left: St Oswald's Church, Lower Peover, an unusual timber building with a stone tower.

Painted in July 1916

Below: The Lower Peover Scout Camp. The ship's cabin on the left of the picture was moved from Rhyl after the summer of 1915.

Painted in July 1917

Soon after I was appointed to Westminster it became evident that the war was nearing its close, and I was still at Manchester when the Armistice was declared[47]. Almost immediately after 11 o'clock the Cathedral began to fill with a vast concourse of people and a service was extemporized at which I played well-known hymns which were sung with a fervour and emotion I shall never forget. It was a wonderful and spontaneous act of thanksgiving for a great deliverance. I played my last service at Manchester Cathedral on 31st December 1918, exactly ten years after my appointment.

Nicholson during his Manchester years

Nicholson's appointment to Westminster Abbey was generally well received, even by the press. A large number of congratulatory letters from his musical peers and from senior Anglican clergy are extant, both to himself and also to his mother.

The Bishop of Manchester wrote "We shall miss you very sorely. But I shall always reckon it a real privilege to have known you" and the Bishop of Carlisle was effusive in his delight. Several former Carlisle colleagues sent him a gift and there were also letters from Barnet.

---

47   11th Nov 1918

Sir Charles Stanford wrote his letter of congratulation in Greek! Percy Buck (then at Harrow School) also wrote in classical vein to say: "It's an Augean Stable which wants a Hercules, which I expect you find inciting."[48]

There was, however, one rather sad collateral to the appointment. Walter Alcock[49] had left Westminster for Salisbury in 1916 and it has been suggested that this move was precipitated by the Dean and Chapter of Westminster deciding in advance that he would not be in the running as Sir Frederick Bridge's successor. Two letters from Alcock to Nicholson add weight to this theory.

The first letter, reproduced on the right, is from Alcock to congratulate Nicholson on his appointment.

---

48 "Augean stable" refers to the fifth of the Twelve Labours of Hercules. In current parlance the phrase "clean the Augean stable" generally means "clear away corruption" or "perform a large and unpleasant task that has long called for attention", see Chapter V.

49 Sir Walter Galpin Alcock (1861–1947), knighted in 1933, was assistant organist of Westminster Abbey from 1896 (he had been unofficial assistant to J F Bridge for some 10 years before this). He was concurrently organist of the Chapels Royal from 1902 until his appointment to Salisbury Cathedral in 1916. Alcock played the organ for three Coronations, 1902, 1911 and (at the personal request of King George VI) 1937. His departure from the Abbey suggested that not all was well between the Dean and Chapter and Alcock, and perhaps the letters above confirm this. He remained a close friend of Nicholson, supported the work of the SECM and was elected Chairman of SECM Council in 1937. He diligently chaired Council meetings until June 1946, but after a period of ill-health he resigned in June 1947, shortly before his death.

> The second letter, was written a year later in response to an invitation to attend the first Cathedral Organist's Conference (see Chapter V) at the Abbey.
>
> On 1st April 1919 Alcock wrote:
>
>> I really cannot bring myself to face the Abbey again, at all events while the present Dean is there. He brushed my undoubted claim to sober consideration aside so brusquely & unkindly that I will not if I can help it, ever look him in the face again.
>
> Later he comments:
>
>> I believe my age to have been against me, but that should have been all the greater argument in favour of a gentle and kind attitude, that the Dean certainly did not show me.
>
> All this is rather surprising as Dean Ryle had a reputation for being a kind and gentle man.

It was interesting that for the second time an organist from Manchester had been chosen to succeed to Westminster Abbey, and I was duly photographed[50] with my two predecessors Sir Frederick Bridge and Dr Pyne. But still more curious was it that in the same year, 1875:

> Bridge went from Manchester to Westminster;
> Pyne was appointed to Manchester;
> and I was born.

The connection between Manchester and the Abbey has been continued by my successor, Ernest Bullock, who had been my assistant at Manchester. I was succeeded at Manchester by my old friend Dr A W Wilson[51] from Ely Cathedral, who has kept up the fine tradition of choral singing to the present time [1940].

---

50 See page 87.

51 Archibald Wayett Wilson (1869-1950) was organ scholar at Keble College in Oxford and initially read history rather than music. He graduated with a D Mus in 1897. He taught at Nicholson's junior alma mater Temple Grove School (see Chapter II) after it had moved to Eastbourne. He was organist at St Asaph Cathedral from 1898, at Ely from 1901 and at Manchester from 1919 until retirement in 1943.

Chapter V

Westminster 1919-1928

I played my first service at Westminster Abbey on 1st January 1919. It was of course a great delight as well as a great responsibility to have been chosen for such a post, and I was not unprepared for difficulties; indeed Bishop Ryle[1] had warned me what to expect.

It may be well to attempt, without any animosity but simply as a matter of history, to set down the position as I found it.

First, as regards the choir men: There were twelve regular 'Lay-Vicars' and six 'Assistants'. The former were only required to attend for half the year, in alternate months, both morning and evening services; so that there would be six of them at each service, augmented by the six Assistants in the afternoons. This meant that the personnel of the choir was constantly changing, and by interchange of duty a man could be absent for several months on end: as the deputy system was also rife and the men were allowed to make their own arrangements provided the requisite number were present, it followed that one never knew what sort of a choir one would have on any occasion. This might conceivably have worked pretty well except in the matter of rehearsals; but these were not provided for in the Lay Vicars' duties and were in fact only occasionally called, a special fee of 10/- [ten shillings] being paid for each occasion. Naturally my first requirement was that there should be at least one full rehearsal each week; but the sort of thing that would happen would be that, say at the end of the month, music would be rehearsed by one choir and performed by quite a different one. Or if a man could not conveniently come to a rehearsal in person he would send a deputy (probably paying him about 5/-) [five shillings] and the deputy would rehearse for him and then he himself would sing at the service!

I was almost in despair at first, for things like responses or psalms were never rehearsed, and so I suggested to the Precentor that on one Friday (unaccompanied day) we should call a rehearsal before Evensong and devote the whole of it to the details of the particular service. All went well, and we rehearsed everything, including the 'verses' in the Anthem and Service: when we had finished I was full of hope that we should at last have one decently rendered service. Imagine my feelings when, after the rehearsal 6 or 7 of the men walked out and another lot came to sing instead!

Further, the Lay-Vicars claimed rights to sing solos or verses quite irrespective of my arrangements or even of the fact of their having attended rehearsal. A curious example of the state of things may be given. One of my first big services was the marriage of H R H Princess Patricia, the daughter of the Duke of Connaught, the first 'Royal wedding' in

---

[1] The Right Rev Herbert Edward Ryle (1856-1925), whose father had been the first Bishop of Liverpool, studied at and was then a Fellow of King's College, Cambridge. An Old Testament scholar and author, he was ordained priest in 1883 and, after 20 years of teaching and academia was made Bishop of Exeter in 1901. Two years later he became Bishop of Winchester and then Dean of Westminster Abbey in 1911. He remained in office until his death.

the Abbey for hundreds of years and the first 'cheerful' State service since the war. All details had of course been carefully settled and rehearsed, including a quartet in the Anthem. On the actual day there was a short rehearsal just before the service. A Lay-Vicar whom I had never seen took his place with the rest and when the quartet came began singing the tenor part. I pointed out politely that this had already been allotted to another man, whereat the stranger said:

> "But I am going to sing it."
>
> "And who are you?" I asked.
>
> "X is my name and I am on duty."
>
> "Well, I have heard your name but I have never seen you before, and I am afraid the matter is settled."
>
> "It is my right to sing it and I intend to do so!"
>
> "Very well, then, I shall go to the Dean now and tell him that I cannot be responsible for the music unless my decision is upheld."
>
> He gave in and I suppose did not sing a note in the service.

When re-organisation was suggested two other men actually came to me and said that they quite saw that things would have to be altered and that if I would agree to their taking **two years** leave of absence to go round the world with a concert party, they would then settle down!

Such a state of things may seem almost incredible to those who know Cathedrals at the present time, it was just the remnant of an old and thoroughly bad system by which the choir was practically independent of the Organist or Precentor. It was not a question of incompetence for many of the Lay-Vicars were exceedingly good (though some were not). But it was quite obvious to the Dean and Chapter as well as to all others concerned that some serious steps must be taken to re-organize the conditions under which they served.

The difficulty of dealing with the situation was increased by the fact that the Lay-Vicars were 'on the foundation' and could not be dismissed except for serious moral fault. They were fulfilling their duties hitherto expected of them, and as the salary they were paid was quite inadequate for a full-time job, there was no real ground for complaint. So a scheme was worked out by which the number of Lay Vicars should be reduced to 6 full-time men with the duty of weekly rehearsals and only limited use of approved deputies, at double the previous salary. The place of the 'Assistants' (who were mostly 'past their best') was to be taken by Choral Clerks who should, as far as possible, be young men studying at one of the Colleges of Music, and only required for afternoon services and rehearsals. Each of the Lay Vicars was given the alternative of accepting the new conditions or taking a pension at his existing salary. Most of them chose the latter, and the Assistants were given small pensions or gratuities. So practically a new choir was formed, 14 out of the original 18 vacating their places and the choir being made up to 12 efficient men. With weekly rehearsals and a 'constant' choir it became possible to improve matters and considerable progress was made[2].

With regard to the boys the position was not so bad. The Choir School had recently been rebuilt[3] at great cost and the plan had been adopted of admitting 'non-singers' as well as choristers, all of whom were boarders. For many reasons the plan did not work well, and though there were some good singers among them the general attitude of the boys to their work was somewhat listless and uninterested. Later on the Choir School was reconstituted on better lines: non-singers were eliminated and additional choristers, including some day-boys, appointed, so that a sufficient number should be available to maintain full choral services throughout the year[4].

Unfortunately, however, this ideal was never realized. Certain morning services had been made non-choral as a 'war-time necessity', and we were never able to get them restored, though the re-arrangement of the choir would have made it perfectly feasible. In this respect it is impossible to free the Dean and Chapter from criticism. It is perfectly clear that every Cathedral Church (and the Abbey has a similar obligation) is bound by its ancient Statutes or 'Customs' to maintain two choral services each day throughout the year. This may seem a counsel of perfection, but given the necessary equipment and funds to maintain it, it can be done. That the central Church of the Empire should fall short in this respect cannot but be a matter for deep regret to all who value the history and tradition of Cathedral music.

In all these reforms my chief supporter was the Precentor, the Rev L H Nixon[5], with whom I worked in the closest co-operation: he was, to my mind, the perfect Precentor, except that perhaps he was too kind! Dean Ryle was of course most sympathetic and helpful, but amongst the Canons the forceful person who really got things done and helped me most was Canon

---

2   Frederick Bridge, when he arrived at the Abbey in 1875, experienced similar problems. In his memoir (*A Westminster Pilgrim*, London, 1918) he wrote "... the chief difficulties which operated against a good choral service were lack of discipline and the erratic attendances of the Lay-Vicars. There were some excellent singers among them, but also some old and very inferior ones. In one case the Lay-Vicar, on account of illness, never attended, but was represented by a deputy, and a very poor representative he was. Others attended apparently when they liked, having made special arrangements when they were appointed many years before to enable them to be absent very frequently. ... Another thing which seems incredible was the entire absence of full-choir rehearsals. The boys were practised daily, but there was no practice for men and boys combined." Bridge was only partially successful in bringing about any changes to the status quo. Such was Nicholson's inheritance.

3   The new choir house in Dean's Yard was opened in October 1915.

4   Nicholson, with the support of the Precentor, was instrumental in the reorganisation of the choir school. In a chapter of *A Joyous Adventure* [See later in this chapter - The Canadian Tour] entitled 'The Choirboys' he wrote: 'we are fortunate at the Abbey in having a double shift of boys, fifty in all. This plan was instituted some years ago in order that the strain of constant services might be lessened for the individuals, and, as a consequence, that they might have more time for their general education; and also in order that the choir might never be without boys even in the holidays.' An advertisement for prospective choristers was placed in *The Times* on 11th May 1922. In his unpublished autobiography, Abbey chorister Harry Abbott (whom SHN called 'Little Abbey') notes that there were 350 applications (hearsay), that 100 boys were auditioned and took a school examination and 16 were accepted. This was at the time that Nicholson increased the number of boys to form a Choir A and a Choir B to allow year-round choral services. The fifty choristers were made up of 30 boarders in the choir school and 20 day boys.

5   The Rev Leigh Hunter Nixon, M A, (1871-1941) was Precentor and Librarian of Westminster. He was Priest-in-Ordinary to H M The King until 1934 when he resigned and became Honorary Priest to H M. He was present at the opening service of the College of St Nicolas in Chislehurst in 1929.

Barnes[6] (now Bishop of Birmingham). He threw himself whole-heartedly into every project to improve matters and without his help I do not think the reforms would ever have been accomplished.

The Precentor of Westminster Abbey, Rev L H Nixon with Nicholson in 1922

---

6   The Right Rev Ernest William Barnes FRS (1874-1953) was a mathematician and scientist who became a theologian and bishop. Educated at Trinity College in Cambridge, he became a Fellow there and was elected to FRS in 1909. Ordained priest in 1903, he abandoned his career as a professional mathematician and became Master of the Temple in London in 1915. He was made a canon of Westminster Abbey in 1918 and in 1924 was elevated to the Episcopate of Birmingham, retiring shortly before his death.

It is curious that in all the posts I have held I have had my predecessor 'on my door-step'. At Barnet he remained as a valued member of the choir: at Carlisle he survived me by several years, and the same was the case at Manchester. When I arrived at Westminster Sir Frederick Bridge still retained his house [Litlyngton Tower] in the Little Cloister as "Emeritus Organist" and was a constant attendant at the Abbey services. I think my predecessors must all have been exceptionally forbearing and tactful people, for it has always been my lot to introduce innovations, and I have never had to suffer the slightest unfriendly criticism from any of them: indeed all of them have been my excellent friends and have given me every encouragement. Bridge was a great character and most amusing with his ready wit (of which I have already given examples elsewhere); but he was also a most kindly man and had done very good work (against untold difficulties) in his early days. I am glad to be permitted to quote from an interesting letter which I received on my appointment from Dr T B Strong[7] (afterwards Bishop of Oxford), as it does justice to the memory of one to whom the Abbey owes much.

> I remember well the arrival of Bridge and the disturbance it made in the Turle regime. You will have a much more sympathetic and intelligent Dean and Chapter than he had. The old organ was one of the oddest I have ever seen: it had been put together in a casual sort of way and was very hard to play. The pedals only went up to D: there were 3 composition pedals for the Great and no others of any kind: and the manuals were of different compass. But they would not hear of any alteration, and Bridge struggled along with this thing until 1885. The Precentor had complete control over the music, and I remember Bridge telling me that after a terrific battle for a somewhat enlarged repertoire he only succeeded in getting *Tours in F*. I always think that this lack of interest turned his attention to other lines of business, and is the reason why he has occupied himself so much with things in London outside the Abbey. He is much criticized for this now and it certainly is the wrong policy but I always think the Abbey people were largely responsible. (SHN: He might have added that the princely salary was then only £300 a year!).

> It will not be a very easy post to fill: you will almost certainly want to make changes, and I expect this will not be easy. I don't think Bridge will make difficulties, but the situation is a difficult one. Turle retained his house after Bridge was appointed, and used to trot smiling about, occasionally playing voluntaries in the Abbey — usually choruses of Handel's arranged for the organ.

In spite of all these difficulties Bridge did manage to effect great reforms and at a time when such composers' works were hardly to be heard anywhere, the names of Byrd, Gibbons,

---

[7] The Right Rev Thomas Banks Strong CBE (1861-1944) was educated at Westminster School and at Christ Church in Oxford. Ordained priest in 1886, he stayed on at Christ Church and served as Dean from 1901 to 1920. He then served as Bishop of Ripon (1920-1925) and Bishop of Oxford (1925-1937).

Purcell, Blow, Palestrina, Vittoria and other classics regularly appeared on the Abbey Service lists; and as a pioneer in 're-discovering' old music, and particularly the works of Dering, he deserves honoured remembrance.

When Bridge died in 1924 I moved from the house I had taken in Grosvenor Road to my official quarters in Litlyngton Tower in the Little Cloister. This was in many ways a delightful old house though hardly to be described as very convenient: one unique feature of which I was very proud was the 'lavatory' dating from the time of Edward the Confessor!

Litlyngton Tower c 1918

Westminster Abbey Special Choir

One great happiness of my work at the Abbey was the formation of the Westminster Abbey Special Choir. This body gave its first performance (*Israel in Egypt*) in 1919. It consisted of 100 men and 100 boys (including the Abbey Choristers): all alike gave their services without remuneration and worked together in the most happy spirit. Rehearsals were held weekly at St John's Church[8], except during the summer months, and three performances were given annually, — a series of Motets or sometimes an oratorio in Advent, the *St Matthew Passion* in Passion Week, and a special service illustrative of the work of some composer connected with the Abbey in the Octave of St Peter's Day. The work of the Special Choir continues

---

8 Probably St John's, Smith Square, now de-consecrated and a major concert venue.

happily[9] and efficiently under my successor and has established itself as a regular and valued feature of the musical life of London.

Special Services

To attempt to describe or even to make a list of the many important special services with which I was associated during my time at The Abbey would be quite impossible, and I must be content with mentioning a few of the most important. It is these special services which, like Funerals or Memorial Services, often have to be arranged at very short notice, that make the work of the Abbey Organist and Choir so exacting. The services themselves are generally simple enough to arrange: the difficulty is with the officials and friends concerned who generally seem to assume that a similar service has never been held in The Abbey before!

In my first year there was a constant stream of such services, besides the Royal Wedding already referred to. One of the most interesting of these was the Funeral of Nurse Edith Cavell on 15th May 1919. About a year later, in May 1920, there was a grand ceremony of the Installation of Knights of the Most Honourable Order of the Bath. This is one of the most picturesque functions that take place in The Abbey, the Knights of the Order attending in their gaily coloured robes and the Clergy also being furnished with special Mantles. On this particular occasion, being the first after the war, the King himself attended, which is not usual. A considerable portion of the ceremony takes place in Henry VII's Chapel, the Chapel of the Order, so is not visible to the general congregation: consequently a good deal of music is required, chiefly consisting of an extremely long and rather dull anthem by Battishill, *Behold how good and joyful*, and a number of marches and similar pageant music. It was not on this occasion but at a 'Bath Service' a few years later that a very amusing incident occurred. It was arranged that after the ceremony the Knights should pass in procession round the Cloisters, headed by the choir, while a military band played in the Cloister Garth. I, of course, had to approve of all the music to be played on such occasions within the Abbey, but for this outside function I left it to the bandmaster to choose some suitable march. This he certainly managed to do: the feelings may be imagined of those who, on emerging from the Abbey, recognised the strains of the 'March of the Peers' from *Iolanthe*, "Bow down, ye lower middle classes!" Could anything have been more appropriate? The Duke of Connaught spotted it at once.

Burial of the Unknown Warrior

At the end of 1920 came what was, perhaps, the most thrilling of the many great occasions when I was responsible for the music, — the 'Funeral Service of a British Warrior' on the second anniversary of the signing of the Armistice, on 11th November. As this service has become historic it may be well to give some account of what actually happened.

---

9   The Westminster Abbey Special Choir, founded by Nicholson, gave three concerts a year, two of which were church music. It was eventually disbanded in 1982. Nicholson's last concert with them before he retired included the 16 part unaccompanied *Mass* by Eduardo Grell. The men and boys were drawn from choirs in and around London.

The idea of burying the body of some unidentified British soldier in the Abbey had been suggested to Dean Ryle about a year before: he at once took up the suggestion and began to work out plans[10]. The Abbey was of course filled from end to end with what was probably the most representative congregation ever collected, from the King and Royal Family, Parliament, the Armed Forces of the Crown, and all classes of civilians to the humblest of his Majesty's subjects. The order of service was as follows:

The Choir and Clergy assembled in the Nave and proceeded to the High Altar singing the hymn *O valiant hearts*[11]. It was probably its use on this occasion that gave to this fine hymn its wide popularity, and I take this opportunity of recording that it was not sung on that occasion nor on any other occasion in the Abbey to the specially composed tune[12] with which the words are published, but always to the tune 'Ellers' by E J Hopkins. After this the congregation joined in singing *O God help in ages past* and after The Lord's Prayer the two minutes' silence was observed. This was followed by the singing of the Russian *Contakion of the Faithful Departed*, and then, after three Collects, the choir moved to the North Porch singing the hymn *Brief life is here our portion*. The *Burial Sentences* to Croft's music were then sung in procession from the North Porch to the Grave at the West end of the Nave. Beethoven's *Equali* for trombones were played and the 23rd Psalm sung at the Grave-side. Then came the Lesson, the hymn *Lead kindly Light* and the Committal, when earth from the soil of France was strewn on the Coffin. Then followed the hymn *Abide with me*, and after two final prayers all joined in singing Kipling's *Recessional* to the tune 'Melita'; then came the Blessing and Reveille[13]. Of the many wonderful services in which I took part while at the Abbey, this was I think the most impressive: the scene, as we stood at the open grave while the unknown body was committed to the earth must live for ever in the memory of all who were privileged to be present. It was after this service that the never-ending procession passed by the grave and established a custom which has been maintained ever since.

> The Times of 12th Nov 1920 noted that "Mr Nicholson and his choir must be warmly congratulated on the beauty of the music at this wholly beautiful service"

---

10. The idea of honouring an unknown soldier in this way came originally from the Rev David Railton (1884-1955), a young army chaplain who had the idea whilst serving on the Western Front in 1918. He first wrote to Lord Haig with the idea but there was no response. After the war, whilst vicar of St John the Baptist in Margate, Railton decided to write (as late as August 1920) to Bishop Ryle who liked the idea. Events moved very rapidly indeed for, in just two months, the whole complex logistical operation of choosing and transporting the unknown body with due ceremony and dignity was put in place by Lord Curzon's committee together with The Abbey arranging a major service at which the King and many others with busy diaries would attend.

11. This was sung unaccompanied.

12. The tune referred to was composed by Rev Dr Charles Harris, Vicar of Colwall in Herefordshire from 1909 to 1929. Despite attempts by Ralph Vaughan Williams and Gustav Holst to introduce further tunes, it is Harris's tune that seems to have stood the test of time and is commonly used today.

13. Nicholson does not mention a magic moment which impressed *The Times*. "The Dean spoke the Blessing. For a moment, to those at the West end of the Abbey it seemed as if this perfect ceremony were not, after all, to pass without a hitch. In a moment the keener ears among us realized the truth. From somewhere far away in the great church a scarcely audible whisper began to steal upon us. It swelled, with absolute smoothness, until we knew it for the roll of drums. Then the whole Abbey was full of the reverberating roar; and then it began to die away, and died into a whisper so soft that no one could say for certain when it stopped. Into the silence broke the Réveille..."

The procession at the Tomb of the unknown Warrior 1920

At first the Grave was covered by a simple stone[14] which merely recorded that it was the resting-place of an Unknown British Warrior, with the plain inscription (suggested I believe by my old friend Canon Richardson of Manchester) "They buried him among the kings.[15]" Later on a much longer and more elaborate inscription was substituted.

---

14 The simple stone was a slab of polished limestone from Tournai in Belgium inscribed in gilt:
   A BRITISH WARRIOR WHO FELL IN
   THE GREAT WAR 1914-1918 FOR KING AND COUNTRY.
   GREATER LOVE HATH NO MAN THAN THIS.
   It is recorded that over 200,000 people passed by the open tomb on that day. The grave was finally closed a week later on 18 November by which time a further one million people had paid their respects.

15 Nicholson was mistaken, it was the later stone which contained these words. Unveiled the following year on Armistice Day 1921, the present stone was supplied and lettered by Mr Tomes of Acton using black marble from Namur in Belgium and the brass for the inscription supplied by Nash & Hull from melted down ammunition. Dean Ryle composed the inscription. At this service the Padre's Flag, the Rev David Railton's personal 'war flag' was also formerly dedicated and installed on a pillar near the grave.

The Tomb of the unknown Warrior today

Nicholson's first Royal Wedding at The Abbey in 1922

Royal Weddings

On 28th February 1922 was the Marriage of H R H Princess Mary with the Viscount Lascelles. This, of course, was a very grand occasion. Beforehand the Bride and Bridegroom both came to meet me in the organ-loft to discuss the music, — rather a ticklish business. The only wish that the Bridegroom expressed was that I should play the Bridal March from Gounod's *Romeo and Juliet* at the end, and this was easily complied with. But when it came to the hymns it was more difficult. Needless to say 'O perfect love' was suggested, and I was asked by a Lady-in-waiting to play a certain tune for it which she produced. This I did, without comment, and H R H asked me whether I liked it. As politely as possible I said I did not, and she most kindly said that in that case we would not have the hymn at all. For the occasion I wrote a special anthem *Beloved, let us love one another*, to words suggested by Dean Ryle. Before the service I played a selection of, almost entirely, English music, and included (I think I may say re-discovered) the now famous *Trumpet tune* by Purcell[16].

The Marriage of H R H the Duke of York[17] with The Lady Elizabeth Bowes-Lyon (the present King and Queen) took place on 26th April, 1923, and was very similar in character. Again I had the honour of discussing the music with the Bride and Bridegroom at her parents' London house, but on this occasion everything was as easy as possible, for the whole matter left to me, except that they were kind enough to say that they would like my anthem [*Beloved, let us love one another*] to be repeated.

(Left to Right) Lord and Lady Strathmore, Lady Elizabeth Bowes-Lyon, the Duke of York, Queen Mary, King George V.

---

16 Published (arr H G Ley) in 1926 by Stainer & Bell. Although this *Trumpet Tune* is still generally described as "Purcell's", it is now, like the famous 'Trumpet Voluntary', known to be a composition of Jeremiah Clarke rather than by Henry Purcell. It is found in *The Island Princess*, a joint musical production in 1699 by Jeremiah Clarke and Daniel Purcell, Henry Purcell's younger brother; this latter association perhaps accounting for the confusion. It is listed as ZS124 in Zimmerman's Purcell catalogue.

17 Nicholson later claimed that this wedding was the only 'great occasion' in his career when he felt nervous.

Feb 23rd 1923
17 Bruton Street W1

Dear Mr Nicholson

Thank you so very much for your letter about the music for my wedding. I wonder whether you could come and see me on Tuesday at about 5 o'clock, or lunch on Friday? It would be so nice to talk about it all; or if you would prefer it, I would come & see you

Yours sincerely
Elizabeth Lyon

May 7th 1923
17 Bruton Street W1

Dear Mr Nicholson

I must write one time to tell you how <u>wonderful</u> the music was at my wedding. Even through my nervousness, I realized how perfect it was, and simply cannot thank you enough for having made it so beautiful.

Thank you also a thousand times for the Anthem you sent me – it was so kind of you, and I am so glad to have it.

Would it do a little later on, if we signed our names for the boys? We would love them to have some memento, and if they would like our signatures we should be delighted to do this.

I wish I could tell you how divine I thought the music, & so did everyone else – thank you <u>so</u> much Mr Nicholson.

I am, Yours sincerely <u>Elizabeth</u>

C V Stanford

The next service that I wish to mention was the Funeral of Sir Charles Stanford on 3rd April, 1924. Except for the Croft and Purcell *Burial Sentences* the whole of the music was taken from Stanford's works and included his lovely anthem *The Lord is my Shepherd*. It was a great satisfaction to me that I was enabled to suggest that Stanford should be so honoured and that the suggestion was accepted by the Dean. No composer ever did more for Church music and it is fitting that he should rest beside Purcell, Blow and Croft in the North Choir aisle, — the 'Musicians' Corner' of the Abbey. At St Peter's-tide in the same year was held a Festival service in commemoration of Stanford, sung by the Abbey choir and the Abbey Special choir. I refrain from quoting the many letters I have received after special services, but the following from Stanford's devoted friend[18] Plunket Greene[19] is of special interest:

---

18   Both friend and biographer: *Charles Villiers Stanford*, London, E Arnold, 1935.
19   Harry Plunket Greene (1865-1936) was a baritone singer on the concert platform and of oratorio. Also one of the earliest recording artists,

July 9th 1924

My dear Nicholson,

At last I'm able to sit down and thank you for that lovely service for C V S the other day. It was indescribably beautiful and touching — just like the funeral service. I did not know the Magnificat and Nunc Dimittis, and they and 'I saw another angel' were almost too much for me. It was all splendidly done and had a lovely spirit about it. I hope he heard it all. I felt as though he did. Thank you for it and all you have done and are doing to keep his memory green.

Yours ever,

H P Greene

One other little recollection of Stanford in connection with the Abbey may be of interest. Quite often he would attend service, coming to the organ loft. The music to be sung was regularly published in *The Times*: one Sunday morning the telephone rang and I heard the well-known voice at the other end saying, in irascible tones, "What the ____ do you mean by announcing an anthem by me that I never wrote?" (*O for a closer walk with God* it was). I replied that he certainly had written it, and he answered that he certainly had not. "Well," I said, "you had better come and hear it." He duly came and was very pleased; — he had entirely forgotten its existence! This is interesting as showing his extraordinary facility: one of the most charming and finished of his smaller works, and he had forgotten all about it!

We were in fact able to give him a 'first hearing' of quite a number of his works, and it always seemed to give him pleasure: but he told me that he never would go to a service if he knew that his *Te Deum in B flat* was to be sung, for "people always ruined it by taking it too fast."

Further Special Services

On 7th July 1924 was held the first Festival of Cathedral and Collegiate Choirs in aid of King Edward's Hospital Fund for London. Choirs within 100 miles of London had been invited and came from the Chapel Royal; St George's, Windsor; St Paul's Cathedral; Canterbury; Chelmsford; Chichester; Ely; Eton; Magdalene; New College and Christ Church, Oxford; Peterborough; Rochester; St Albans; St John's, Cambridge; Salisbury; Southwark and Winchester. This magnificent chorus filled the choir and a large portion of the Transept. The music included three short anthems by the three prominent Church musicians who had died in the early part of the year, Sir Walter Parratt, Sir Frederick Bridge and Sir Charles Stanford. It also included S. S. Wesley's *Ascribe unto the Lord*, S. Wesley's 'In exitu Israel', and Byrd's *Sing joyfully*, together with Psalm LXVIII sung in Procession and ending with Parry's *I was glad*[20].

---

he was the author of *Where the Bright Waters Meet*, London, 1924, a classic book in angling literature.

20 Nicholson does not mention a problem they had this service. In his unpublished autobiography, Abbey chorister Harry Abbott recalls that "A procession was led by the Abyssinian Cross of gold and very intricate filigree work carried by John Cruft who was a boy in the choir with me. Across the choir was a wire suspending a BBC microphone, the service being broadcast. The cross being held aloft caught the wire and

An interesting service was that on St Peter's Day 1925 in commemoration of the 16th centenary of the Council of Nicaea. This was attended by many of the Eastern Orthodox Prelates in their gorgeous robes. The service consisted of The Eucharist and the setting was Palestrina's *Missa Aeterna Christi Munera*. The Creed was recited in Greek by His Beatitude the Patriarch of Alexandria.

In November of the same year came the Funeral of Queen Alexandra, and this day was also marked by the tragically sudden death of Minor Canon H F Westlake[21]. He had attended to all the details of the arrangements for the service with his accustomed efficiency, and when it was all over he took some of the choristers into the Abbey to see the military guard that surrounded the coffin till its removal: within half-an-hour we heard that he had fallen dead in his house.

The Eastern Patriarchs Service at Petertide 1925
Cathedrals are constantly under repair. Here a banner fails miserably to conceal a ladder!

Life at The Abbey was not, however, confined to a continuous round of services, and there were many other interests, though the uncertainty of 'Special services' being called for at short notice made it difficult to accept many engagements outside London. Still I did manage to fit in a good deal of judging at Competitive Festivals in which I was greatly interested, always undertaking them on condition that The Abbey had the first claim on my time in the

---

became entangled in it. The whole thing had to be pulled down and the wire disentangled before the procession could proceed."
21 See Chapter II, Footnote 70.

event of conflicting calls; and sometimes this involved hectic journeys back to town from some distant place. As time went on I found it necessary to give up all but a very little of this work, confining myself to a few country festivals, which I always preferred, mainly those of the non-competitive type or at least without prizes.

An interesting experience was when the Bishops of the Anglican Communion assembled at The Abbey for the opening service of the Lambeth Conference in 1920, and I was allowed to rehearse them in the Chapter House before the service in the singing of Merbecke's Creed. Few musicians can have had a more distinguished choir to conduct, but I cannot say that their vocal ability was commensurate with their eminence in other directions.

Outdoor Services

At the opening of the Empire Exhibition at Wembley [1924] I was asked to help in the organization of a vast choir to sing in the Stadium, and was in charge of the processional singing. The main choir was conducted by Walford Davies, but the conditions of seating and the acoustics were too hopeless for a good effect to be produced. Towards the end rain began to fall, and after it was over I had to pioneer a section of the Abbey choir in their cassocks and surplices through the grounds to find a church which the Bishop of London was to open. No one could tell us where it was; the rain fell faster and faster, and the ground got muddier and muddier: when at last we arrived at our destination the service was all over, and we had to make our way back to our robing tents only to find that all the food that had been provided for the choir had been consumed and no more could be obtained!

Rehearsal for Empire Day 1925.

The next year [1925] we had a similar experience, though this time the chief enemy was the wind: the ex-choristers who had been detailed to carry enormous banners in the procession were carried off their feet by their unruly burdens and mostly had to abandon them to the elements. Charles Macpherson conducted the great choir on this occasion and made the immortal remark that the experience was like 'taking a jelly-fish out for a walk on an elastic lead!'[22]

One is terribly dependent on the elements for some big ecclesiastical occasions. After the unveiling of the Cenotaph, it became the custom to take the Abbey choir and Special choir (about 200 strong) to sing there on Whitsunday afternoon each year. If fine we were to proceed from the Abbey in our robes, if wet to robe in the Home Office and sing under shelter. And Whitsunday weather always seemed to be doubtful.

Procession Rehearsal for Empire Day 1925, Nicholson, as always, with his camera.

---

22   Nicholson originally typed 'elephant' and changed this in pencil to 'jelly-fish'. Nicholson himself used this phrase when conducting the 1930 Festival of English Church Music choir and it is commonly ascribed to him. It is also sometimes ascribed to Sir Malcolm Sargent who used it to the press after conducting the *Hallelujah Chorus* for the post WWII Olympic Games in London. It seems that perhaps Macpherson may have been the first to use it in 1925.

(Above and below) Empire Day Service 1925

One year it seemed safe enough and Dean Ryle said we would march from the Abbey in our robes. No sooner had we got into the street than a storm broke and the rain descended in deluges: soon the surplices began to turn red or blue, according to the colour of the underlying cassocks. Then I nearly did the bravest deed of my life – but I must confess that I 'funked it'. I nearly led the whole company into the underground lavatory at the bottom of Whitehall! We got home soaked to the skin, and we had to heat the choir-school furnace seven times hotter and literally to bake the cassocks so that they might be ready to wear again for the evening service.

On the whole I think outdoor ecclesiastical functions are not to be recommended in our climate.

First Conference of Cathedral Organists
Soon after I came to London my old friend Charles Macpherson, the Organist of St Paul's, and I decided to call a conference of Cathedral organists, similar to the annual meeting of Deans. The first of these Conferences was held at the Abbey on 24th April 1919 and they have continued annually (and later biennially) ever since. The attendance on the first occasion was most representative[23]. Unfortunately the distinguished organist of York Minster was not able to be present, but he wrote me a letter that so splendidly sets out the case for Cathedral music that, with his permission, I quote it in full.

1, Minster Court,
York.
April 20th, 1919.

My dear Nicholson,

It is very disappointing to me to be absent from the meeting of Cathedral organists on the 24th. I am prevented by an engagement of long standing from which it is impossible for me to obtain release.

I hope the conference will take a firm and unanimous stand against any action coming from whatever source which might result in the impairing of the efficiency of Cathedral or College Chapel choirs, and the consequent lowering of the standard of Church Music that will surely result from such action.

It might take the form of an attempt to do away with daily choral services on the ground of the small congregations attending them and the expenses they incur. But I am quite sure that if the quality of church music and the time and manner of its performance is to be governed by the taste and desires of congregations, then its fate

---

23 Amongst those who declined to attend were Walter Alcock (see letter on p 104) and Conrad Eden.

is surely sealed. The lowest forms of music are to be found in places of worship where only the effect on the hearers is considered. The noblest where music is offered with the same spirit that prompted the woman to offer the alabaster box of precious ointment. The Disciples said that this "might have been sold for much and given to the poor." Now we are told cathedral expenses must be curtailed and the money distributed amongst the poor clergy. There certainly are cathedral expenses that we wot [sic] of that might very easily be curtailed, but music is not one of them. I have heard of no one who proposes to allow the fabric to suffer, but I see no reason for putting architecture before music, nor can I think of any reason why God should be pleased that we should offer Him our best in buildings and their furniture, and yet desire us to offer Him second rate music which we musicians know full well is designed only to stimulate sentimental emotions that ignorant people mistake for religious feeling. I am quite sure that one of the reasons why the repertoire at the average Cathedral is better than at the average parish church is that, in the Cathedral, the main idea is to find the best music to sing, while in the parish church it is to find music which people like. Even a Sunday service in a Cathedral is very often spoiled by what are called 'popular hymns', so that one might truly say that the daily service is the best influence in English Church music to-day.

The threatened danger to the daily service through the new Education Bill can, I feel sure, be overcome by an influential deputation approaching Mr Fisher[24]. Both he and the Premier[25] are sympathetic to music, and both of them understand the good to be derived in this material age from a choir-school education which is bound to stimulate the spiritual, poetic and imaginative side of a boy's character far more than that of an ordinary school. It is a special training for a particular object, and is therefore good: but even to boys who are not making music their profession it is good, for in these days it is just those who have vision and initiative and who are not wholly selfish and material who succeed. Moreover there is a tremendous lot of self-consciousness about, most detrimental to children, and, as there is no success in music unless self-consciousness is conquered, a musical training is a splendid antidote to this evil.

All these remarks fail in their purpose when applied to Cathedrals where the service is sung — and the musical education given — in a mechanical, perfunctory way. Unless music is sincere expression it is so much useless sound — perhaps beautiful as such, but meaningless. It is to be feared that much of the talk one hears against Cathedrals and their music is due to places where the music is dead sound, not living expression. How musicians can spend their time teaching and performing such soul-less sounds is an

---

[24] Herbert Fisher (1865-1940) was President of the Board of Education and the bill referred to was the Education Act 1918, often known as the 'Fisher Act'. This Act of Parliament raised the school leaving age to fourteen and planned to expand tertiary education, what we now term 'further education'. The Act also included the provision of ancillary services such as medical inspection, nursery schools and education for pupils with special needs. The act is still in force in 2012, with many amendments of course.

[25] David Lloyd George (1863-1945) was Prime Minister from 1916 until 1922.

enigma I cannot solve. Would anyone but a child spend time in splashing formless daubs of colour — even beautiful colour — on a canvas?

There are a few other things I should have liked to touch upon, but this letter is too long already. Of one thing I am convinced: the Church is supposed to be setting her house in order, but most of the suggested remedies seem to me to be purely technical, when the man in the street is fully aware that it is enthusiasm, inspiration and vision — in fact spirituality that is lacking. If we are to make out a case for Cathedral music then we should above all things make sure that no such argument can ever be advanced against us. If the right sort of music is sung in the right spirit it will not be interfered with.

Yours sincerely,
Edward C Bairstow

The first Cathedral Organists' Conference 24th April 1919, In The Abbey Cloisters,

Attendees at the 1919 Cathedral Organists' Conference (less Harry Goss-Custard of Liverpool, who signed his name on the back).

Church Music Society

I had been an original member of the Church Music Society and when I came to London was asked to be its Chairman. Through this I was brought into contact with many kindred spirits, and especially with the founders The Lady Mary Trefusis and Miss Eleanor Gregory[26]. Hitherto the work of the Society had been mainly concerned with the choice of music, and much had been accomplished in the way of reform. Now it seemed that the time had come to pay more attention to the question of performance. With this object in view a small 'Demonstration Choir' of boys and men from the Westminster Abbey Special choir volunteered their services and we visited churches within reach of London about once a fortnight, rendering a simple Evensong with an address explaining our ideas. Such practical help was greatly appreciated [and] the success of the experiment was destined to bear fruit later on.

The Church Music Society had been doing quiet and useful work for about 20 years. At first it was generally regarded as a tiresome collection of cranks — 'people who wanted to prevent other people from singing the hymns they liked' was one description. No doubt in its early days it was, like many other reforming institutions, a 'trifle precious'; but its views gradually widened and won respect and a wide measure of acceptance; so that when the two Archbishops decided to appoint a 'Committee on Music in Worship', it was to the Church Music Society that they looked first of all for members.

This committee held many meetings, and though it was composed of people holding the most diverse views, it was found possible to issue a unanimous report which is generally recognised as the most authoritative document on the subject[27].

At the end of 1924 I was invited by Archbishop Davidson[28] to become a member of the Commission appointed by the National Assembly of the Church to consider problems connected with our Cathedrals. This involved many meetings in town and a number of visits on Sub-Commissions to various provincial Cathedrals in order to collect statistics with a view to future legislation. It was extremely interesting work, throwing much light on the state of Cathedral life. A valuable report was drawn up, and out of this arose the permanent Cathedrals Commission. Whether the practical result of the ensuing legislation, and the revision of Statutes, has done much to improve the efficiency and the spiritual influence of

---

26 The Lady Mary Trefusis (née Lygon) (1869-1927) lived at Madresfield Court near Malvern. She was a neighbour and lifelong friend of Edward Elgar who dedicated the 13th of his Enigma Variations to her. She served as Lady-in-Waiting (of the Bedchamber) to HM Queen Mary from 1901 until her death.

Eleanor Gregory (1862-1943), daughter of Robert Gregory, the Dean of St Paul's Cathedral was co-founder with Lady Mary Trefusis, of the Church Music Society on 20th March 1906 and they acted as Joint Secretaries. Failing health caused her to resign from the CMS and on her retirement in 1940, Archbishop Lang, President of CMS, suggested that she be made a Vice-President. H C Colles wrote in her obituary 'She handled Bishops and Deans and Musical Knights with unfailing tact. She could reduce an irritable committee to laughter with a flash of her wit, and best of all, unlike many secretaries, honorary or otherwise, her silences were masterly'. For further biographical information and photographs see *SNCSN*.

27 The report was entitled *Music in Worship: Report of the Archbishops' Committee* published in 1923, revised in 1938 and re-issued in 1947. The next Archbishops' Committee was appointed in 1948 and reported in 1951.

28 The Most Rev Randall Thomas Davidson, 1st Baron Davidson of Lambeth GCVO, PC (1848-1930) served as Archbishop of Canterbury from 1903 to 1928.

the Cathedrals remains to be seen, but it has undoubtedly put their affairs on a more business-like footing.

Hymns Ancient and Modern

Of work outside the Abbey perhaps the most interesting to me has been my connection with *Hymns Ancient and Modern*. This had begun as long ago as 1904 when I was asked to contribute two tunes to the new edition which appeared in that year[29]. The 1904 book was in advance of its time and its issue was greeted with a perfect storm of protest in newspapers which voiced in no measured language the feelings of those who felt themselves outraged by the omission or alteration of their 'old favourites'. Many of those who condemned the book did not even take the trouble to find out what it contained, so that it never came into general use, though it provided a rich store-house of good things on which the editors of subsequent hymnals were very ready to draw; while the *Historical Edition* compiled by Dr W H Frere condensed into one volume more expert knowledge of the subject than had ever before been made available.

But my real work in connection with the book began in 1913 when I was invited to meet the Proprietors and consult with them about the provision of a new Supplement to the old book which they had in mind. I was asked to undertake the Editorship of the music under the direction of Dr Frere, and thus a very happy connection began. One of the main joys of this work was that it resulted in much close collaboration with one of the most remarkable and versatile men of his day, and resulted in an intimacy which continued and ripened until his death. The Second Supplement was actually published during the war, in 1916, an unfortunate time for such a venture; but it was well received and gradually became an integral part of the old book, forming with it what came to be known later on as *The Standard Edition* [1922].

All this took place while I was at Manchester, and I was able to be in fairly close touch with Dr Frere who was then Superior of the Community of The Resurrection at Mirfield. But when I came to Westminster the editorial work still continued and various editions had to be seen through the press, the 'Transposed' edition prepared, and work begun on what was first intended to be a Plainsong Appendix but which ultimately took shape as the *Plainsong Hymnbook* and did not actually appear until 1932. In 1926 I was invited to become an Assessor and in 1928 was elected a Proprietor: to complete the history of my connexion with the book, I continued my Editorship and was responsible for the music of the *Shortened Music Edition* [1939] as well as of the Plainsong Book and certain other subsidiary publications, and on the death of Bishop Frere in 1938 I was chosen to succeed him as Chairman.

---

[29] Hymn 329: *Lord God! Our praise we give* — Tune 'Cosmos' and Hymn 531: *O living God, whose voice of old* — Tune 'Barnet'. A complete listing of Nicholson's original hymn tunes can be found in Appendix G.

The Proprietors of *Hymns Ancient and Modern*

This is perhaps the best place to explain something of the peculiar nature of the Proprietorship in *Hymns A and M*[30]. When the book was originally published in 1861 it represented an amalgamation of interests in various other hymnals that had recently been issued. The original body of Proprietors mutually agreed that any profits of the undertaking should be devoted to Church work, at the discretion of the individual members. In later years, under the Chairmanship of Bishop Frere, the proprietors agreed to enter into a voluntary Trust, by which the profits should be distributed by corporate grants to specified branches of Church work, including a percentage to the Central Board of Finance of the Church Assembly. So that the valuable property in the book is not and cannot be used for private enrichment, but after the deduction of ordinary expenses the income is all devoted to some form of Church work, such as missions, education, church music and similar objects. It was largely my election to a proprietorship that enabled the School of English Church Music to be founded and its College of St Nicolas to be maintained, and without this source of help it is very doubtful whether such an undertaking would have been practicable.

Hymns A and M. has had plenty of critics, from the earliest times when it was regarded with the greatest suspicion as 'High Church', to later years when it has been held up to ridicule as the embodiment of Victorian sentimentality. But in spite of all it is still by far the most widely used of any hymnal and its effect on the religious life of the country has been profound. It has, like all hymn-books, plenty of faults, (many of them those of arrangement, owing to the way in which it has grown by the addition of Supplements in preference to re-numbering); but it also contains many splendid things not to be found elsewhere, and when one considers the number of hymns which have now become classics and which first saw light in its pages, it is no matter for wonder that it has stood the test of time and still retains the affection of the great majority of church-goers.

Bishop Walter Frere

Bishop Frere[31] will probably be remembered in ecclesiastical circles mainly as a saint and a scholar; but I like to think of him rather as a delightful friend and companion. For as well as the ascetic side of his nature there was a very human one: no one enjoyed a good dinner or a theatre or an amusing story more than he, and he loved congenial company: in fact almost the only relaxation he did not enjoy was reading novels, which simply 'bored him stiff'! But in spite of all this he allowed himself the minimum of comfort, to other people he was most generous, but to himself positively mean. When travelling he would always choose the most

---

30 Hymns Ancient & Modern has always been spelled with an ampersand until recent years. Throughout his manuscript Nicholson uses 'and' and the editors have allowed this spelling to stand.

31 The Right Rev Walter Howard Frere (1863-1938), co-founder of the Community of the Resurrection in Mirfield, served as Bishop of Truro from 1923 to 1935. He returned to Mirfield on resigning his bishopric. As both a musicologist and liturgist, he contributed to Alcuin Club and PMMS publications. He was a long-standing member of the PMMS Council and the Briggs and Frere *Manual of Plainsong* of 1902 has remained in regular use and is still in print 110 years later.

miserable hotel he could find, and only travelled third class when there was no fourth[32]; and he allowed himself for 'spending money' about half what ordinary people would have thought economical. His familiar cassock had seen many years' good service, and more vulnerable points like the elbows had long been patched with leather. His holiday attire of a prehistoric grey flannel suit was even more remarkable, especially when combined with a purple-trimmed felt hat of which he was rather proud. Yet however clad, whether in Cope and Mitre or in his holiday suit he was always the most dignified and striking figure in any company. In many ways his outlook was medieval and yet he took the greatest interest in modern developments of art or science: he remained an aristocrat throughout his life yet he was, I suppose, a socialist by conviction: his choice was the monastic vocation, yet he was by no means apart from the world which, on the whole, he found a very pleasant place.

I treasure a little book of his devotions, given me after his death[33] by the Community, with favourite extracts and prayers written in his wonderful and microscopic handwriting in Latin, Greek and Hebrew and often with musical notation: this, I believe, he always carried with him. Most of his notes and directions for work on the hymns were written in the tiniest and most perfect script on minute scraps of paper, — occasionally rising to a post-card: as he made free use of abbreviations, as well as of different coloured pencils to indicate different significances, it required a certain technique to understand what was meant: but never once did I find him out in an inaccuracy. The plainsong Hymnbook, in which he was particularly interested, represented his gleanings (all entered in one minute note book) from libraries which he had visited in all parts of Europe, and many of the beautiful melodies he collected would probably otherwise have been left unnoticed in their obscurity. Of his work as a theologian I am not qualified to speak, though as a liturgical scholar I imagine he was un-rivalled. As a musician he was immensely gifted and had a very wide knowledge. He knew his Wagner inside out and few people had made a more complete study of Russian music, especially opera. His interest in Church music was certainly secondary to this; but his knowledge of hymnology and of plainsong was encyclopaedic, and he was one of the greatest authorities of his day on both these subjects. Though never attaining much technical skill he would 'play' anything at sight on the piano, — with marvellous results! No difficulties daunted him. He would sing any part required (generally the highest tenor) with the utmost 'verve' and assurance. With him it was always the music that counted rather than the performance. In later years he greatly enjoyed the wireless and the gramophone. When he was appointed Bishop of Truro some of his friends wished to give him a present, and a nice little sum of money was collected with the idea of helping the furnishing of 'Lis Escop'[34] and

---

32 Perhaps this is stretching a point on SHN's part. In the UK, following the 1844 Regulation of Railways Act, third class carriages were required to be 'enclosed'. Apparently some railways briefly introduced fourth class, using their old open third class coaches. There cannot have been many of these and probably none in the 20th C. In Germany, however, fourth class continued until 1928.

33 Sadly this has not passed into the RSCM Archives.

34 Lis Escop ("Bishop's House" in Cornish) was formerly the Kenwyn Vicarage and became the Bishop of Truro's palace on the establishment of the Diocese of Truro in 1876. The vicarage had been built in 1780 and John Wesley described it as "a house fit for a nobleman, a most

perhaps providing some comforts that he would have thought quite unnecessary: they were a little dismayed to find that everything had been expended on purchasing a Pianola and a Dictaphone!

He was never tired of sight-seeing, as I well remember during a short holiday spent with him in Germany: never have I seen so many different things in so short a time. Part of his last summer holiday was spent at my cottage in [Woodchurch] Kent, and I think that in five days we visited 28 churches!

His help and his wise counsel in the foundation of the School of English Church Music and especially in the work of the College of St Nicolas cannot be over-estimated: he thoroughly believed in the scheme and he did his utmost for it.

When his bodily powers began to fail and his eyes gave him trouble he was a model of patience and cheerfulness: I think he suffered a good deal, but he would never admit it and when asked how he was would say, with a smile, "Fading out quite nicely, thank you." And so he 'faded out' quietly at his beloved Community House, and surely the Church lost one of its greatest sons.

Bishop Walter Frere (left)
with Rev C S Phillips (right)
at Nicholson's cottage in Woodchurch c 1937

---

beautiful situation of any I have seen in the Country." It is still in use as a conference centre.

The death of Lady Nicholson

Considering their close relationship, it is perhaps surprising that there is no mention in Nicholson's 'Musings' of his mother's death on 2nd December 1923. Neither is there any mention of her health or final illness. The two corresponded weekly by post and he often went to see her, but the considerable archive of this correspondence seems to end around July 1923 and perhaps her death was preceeded by an episode of final illness. 1923 had been a busy year for him at the Abbey with Royal Weddings and several publications but his *Visitor's Book* (see following two pages), which he kept throughout the Carlisle, Manchester and Westminster years and which was normally so full of familiar names of the church music world's great and good, suddenly became empty. Sir Frederick Bridge was still alive and so Nicholson had not yet moved into the official organists' lodgings at The Abbey. He was lodging in 42 Grosvenor Road SW1, a short way from The Abbey along the Thames Embankment just past Millbank. It would appear from the Visitor's Book that his brother Archie moved in with him on 7th Dec 1923 and stayed for four months until the middle of April 1924, leaving the weekend before Easter.

It was at this time that Nicholson finished and published his Passiontide cantata *The Saviour of the World*, and, although the work bears no formal printed dedication, one might speculate that his personal grief found some outlet in this work.

DATE	NAME
Jan 2. 16	Charles V. & Miss Stanford / Lord & Lady Puff. / Jeni Stanford
July 8-20	S E Nicholson
Aug 5th - 9th	Archibald K. Nicholson
Aug 19th	Herbert A. Oliver
"	William H. Oliver
" 29th	C.M. Ritson
Sep. 3rd	Frederic Mansolen
Sept. 13th	May Coleman
"	Harry Coleman
Oct 31st	Ernest Bullock
Nov 2	W H Lere

Nicholson's *Visitor's Book* (1904-1927)
A (Manchester) page from 1916

Date	Name	
June 2 [19]16	Charles Villiers Stanford	Sir Charles Stanford made the only musical entry in SHN's book – the significance of the trill is not clear.
	Lord & Lady Puff	Perhaps the Stanford's pets?
	Jeni Stanford	Stanford's wife Jane Wetton was a singer who used the name Jennie but here is signed in by her husband as Jeni.
June 8-20	S E Nicholson	Nicholson's mother.
Aug 5th-9th	Archibald K Nicholson	Nicholson's brother.
Aug 19th	Herbert A Olivier	The eminent painter – see Chapter II: footnote 65.
	William H Olivier	Olivier's 12 year-old son, later Col William Herbert Olivier – cousin of Sir Lawrence Olivier.
Aug 29	C H Kitson	Charles Herbert Kitson, pedagogue, composer and organist of Christ Church Cathedral in Dublin.
Sep 3rd	Frederic J Ramsden	Chairman, Furness Railway Company.
Sep 13th	May Coleman	Harry Coleman's wife
	Harry Coleman	R H P Coleman – see Chapter IV: footnote 20
Oct 31st	Ernest Bullock	see Chapter IV: footnote 21
Nov 2nd	W H Frere	Bishop Walter Frere – see p 128 and also Chapter VI

Apart from family members and some of those mentioned above, the most frequent visitors in Nicholson's book are his protégé Leslie Heward, former assistant organists, organ-builder Arthur Harrison and his wife, organists Walter Alcock and Charles Hylton Stewart, and numerous Bishops. The French organist Joseph Bonnet also stayed for a week in June 1921.

Scouting – and Bow Brickhill

As to other activities: I had long been interested in Scouting, and after settling in London I was asked to become Commissioner for Music for the Boy Scouts' Association. This led to the issue of leaflets of Scout songs for which I also provided accompaniments recorded on gramophone discs for use in camp: and after a year or two the Scouts' Musical Competition was started. The Chief Scout [Lord Baden-Powell] was greatly interested in the scheme and warmly backed my efforts to improve the standard of Scout singing and to encourage choirboys to become Scouts. A very flourishing troop was soon formed at the Abbey[35], and when I took a country cottage at Bow Brickhill, in Buckinghamshire, I purchased a suitable field and planted on it three old railway carriages to form a permanent camp[36]. Each summer the boys would go there, half the choir at a time, and on Sundays they would sing at the village church or others in the neighbourhood, thus starting a kind of work which was to develop later into an important part of the movement for helping Church music. The Camp is now the property of the Abbey and is still regularly used by the Choristers and Ex-choristers. In connection with Scout work I was brought into touch with many interesting people including the Chief Scout, one of the most remarkable men of the day and surely one of the most fortunate in having lived to see his great ideal so wonderfully fulfilled. Another whose friendship began with the Scouts was Col Alfred D Acland, the Treasurer, who later on became one of my greatest friends and one of the keenest and most generous supporters of the School of English Church Music.

The railway carriages at Bow Brickhill in Open Square formation.

---

35 The 30th Westminster Troop – it was compulsory for choristers to join this!

36 Nicholson inherited a cottage – Harley House, 7 Church Road, Bow Brickhill. Three redundant railway carriages purchased by Nicholson were delivered to Bow Brickhill station and then hauled up a steep hill by a team of six shire horses to a site on rising ground just outside the village (about a mile away). The site was bounded at the rear by the forest of the Woburn Estate and adjacent to a farm and orchard. The three carriages were arranged to form an 'open square', with the open side facing a view over open countryside. Each compartment was fitted out with bunks sleeping 2-4 boys, with one carriage opened out to provide a dining and cooking area. A lady from the village (Mrs Ruby Burton) would act as camp cook. In addition to the Westminster Abbey choristers, other choirs from London and its environs (including St Albans Cathedral) were invited to use the camp. No trace of the camp remains today.

The Mermaid, Comic Opera

It was in 1921 that I wrote to Canon Hannay ("George A Birmingham")[37], whose books I had always greatly admired, and suggested that we should collaborate in writing a comic opera.

"Your proposal is a most amazing one, but, I must also add, singularly attractive," he replied, and, after pointing out certain difficulties, ended "I quite agree with you that a comic opera written by two men occupying our two positions ought to make a good start in life. The very collaboration of two cathedral officials in such a work would be in itself Gilbertian." Next came the idea of a 'plot' which I quote in the writer's own words:

An old fisherman in Clew Bay told me the following story. A certain young man, an inhabitant of Clare Island, once saw a number of mermaids sitting on rocks combing their hair and singing. He fell passionately in love with one of them. A wise old woman on the island told him that if he could lay hands on the cloak of a mermaid and carry it off that particular mermaid would be obliged by the law of her nature to follow him wherever he went and do his bidding whatever it was. Mermaids, it appears, wear these cloaks when under water and throw them off when they sit on the rooks combing their hair. The young man crept out on the rocks one moonlight night and succeeded in seizing the cloak of the mermaid he loved. She followed to the village where he lived and became his wife. She bore him seven sons, minded his house, cooked and washed for him like any mortal woman. The one thing strange about her was her shrinking from any association with Christianity, especially with the sign of the Cross. This, my friend explained to me, was because 'them ones has no souls'. When he was an old man and she apparently an old woman it happened that a neighbour was mending the thatch of their cottage one day. Thrusting his hand into the rotten straw he drew forth what he thought was a bundle of rags and flung it down to the mermaid in the kitchen underneath. She picked up the bundle and shook it out. It turned out to be her own cloak which the man had hidden in the thatch years before. She flung it round her shoulders, became instantly a young woman again and fled from her husband and children back to the sea.

Round this story, with necessary modifications, *The Mermaid* was duly written, and the collaboration involved much pleasant intercourse with the author who had meanwhile become Rector of Mells in Somerset. It was produced by one of the Abbey Lay-Vicars, Mr W H Bullock, with his Bermondsey Operatic Society, at the Guildhall School of Music theatre in 1927. It has had several performances since, and it has taught me a lesson — never again to score a work for orchestra which is destined to be performed by an amateur band. The singing on these occasions is nearly always good, the production often excellent, but the orchestra -----! Still it was great fun and brought me to intimacy with one of my greatest friends.

---

[37] George A Birmingham was the pen name of the Irish novelist and Anglican priest James Owen Hannay (1865-1950). Of his many books, *The Hymn Tune Mystery* (1930) is of whimsical interest, revolving around life at a fictitious provincial cathedral of the period.

The first production of *The Mermaid* 18th May 1927

War Memorial Carillon, Sydney University

Speaking of composition, one of the most curious requests I ever had was to compose 'Quarter chimes' and an 'Hour tune' for the War Memorial Carillon[38] in Sydney University. Naturally I was delighted to have the chance of this connexion with a place so closely associated with my father, but to attempt a composition of so permanent a nature and in such an unusual medium was somewhat daunting. However I had written a tune for use in The Abbey to a Sequence for St Edward's Day, taken from the Litlyngton Missal and translated by Minor Canon Westlake. This tune seemed to lend itself for the purpose, and I thought, too, that there would be a certain appropriateness in a connexion between the War Memorial at Sydney and the place where the Unknown Warrior was buried at home. The 'Quarter chimes' were made from phrases of the melody which appears in its complete form as the 'Hour tune'[39]. When the Carillon had been set up Professor Todd[40], of the University, wrote fresh words to the melody in the form of a memorial hymn under the title *Campanorum Canticum*, and as such it has become the regular hymn to be sung at the Anzac Day Commemorations.

Sydney University Clock Tower containing the Carillon

Many years after it was written, when visiting Sydney I found that the tune was played in full at each hour, much to the disturbance of Lecturers who were too kind to protest. I think there was a general sigh of relief when I said I thought it would be much better if it came only at considerably longer intervals. After all no tune could stand being heard every hour of one's life!

---

38 The University of Sydney War Memorial Carillon commemorates the 197 undergraduates, graduates and staff who died in the WWI. Paid for by private subscription, it was dedicated on Anzac Day, 25th April 1928, by English carillonist, Mr Bryan Barker. Originally the Carillon consisted of 62 bells giving 49 notes, the top octave bells being in duplicate. The bells were cast by John Taylor & Co of Loughborough, Leicestershire. The instrument was played at a keyboard of manual and pedal levers. For a short time a pneumatic keyboard was also used.

39 The tune is printed in Appendix G.

40 Frederick Augustus Todd (1880-1944) was a distinguished classical scholar who graduated from Sydney University in 1901. He also graduated from the University of Jena in 1903. Todd was appointed as a lecturer in Latin from the beginning of 1904, and became Acting Professor of Classics in 1920. He was appointed to the Chair in Latin in 1922, and held this position until his death. There is a photograph of him in Chapter VI at the presentation of an Hon MA to SHN in 1934.

Sydney University Carillon 2013.

Sydney University Carillon 2013 (54 bells in total).

Bishop Ryle

In August 1925 Bishop Ryle[41], the beloved Dean of the Abbey, passed away. To his inspiring leadership is largely due that awakening of the Abbey which, during his tenure of office, brought so much fresh life to the services. Himself by upbringing and conviction an Evangelical, he nevertheless felt the value, in such a glorious setting, of dignified ceremonial. The stately processions, which have since become such a popular feature of the Abbey services, were inaugurated by him originally in connexion with the Carol Service on Innocents' Day, with the enthusiastic help and expert knowledge of the Sacrist, Dr Jocelyn Perkins[42]: and other changes, such as more frequent Sung Eucharists and the revived use of Copes, were made under his regime. He gave the greatest encouragement to the revival of the Old Choristers' Association and its members became the recognised helpers in the Abbey processions, carrying banners etc., and thus retaining an active connexion with the place where they had served as boys. He never failed in his interest in and kindness to the choristers, and his Christmas parties were eagerly looked forward to year by year. The last letter I ever received from him, written during his last illness from Bournemouth, is so characteristic of his thought for everyone that I cannot refrain from quoting it.

The Dean: Bishop Herbert Ryle
Caricature in *Vanity Fair*
27th March 1912

Bournemouth Dec 23rd 1924

My dear Nicholson,
Will you most kindly find the best way by which the boys may obtain an additional ray of happiness at the present season? I should make a mistake if I sent some **thing**. But whether it is books for their library, or crackers for their feasts, or chocolates for their "tummies", you must please decide. Give the boys and the whole staff from me an

---

41 See also Footnote 1 in this chapter.
42 The Rev Jocelyn Henry Temple Perkins MVO MA DCL (1870-1962), ordained priest in 1895, was appointed a minor canon of Westminster Abbey in 1899 and served as Sacrist from 1900 until retirement in 1958. He was involved in four Coronations and his numerous books include accounts of the liturgy and ceremonial involved at each ranging from *The Coronation Book; Or, the Hallowing of the Sovereigns of England* in 1902 through to *The Crowning of the Sovereign of Great Britain and the Dominions Overseas: A Handbook to the Coronation 1953*. His career (documented in *Sixty Years at Westminster Abbey* 1960) was long enough to encompass numerous Deans and Canons such that his word on ceremonial and ornament almost become 'law'. He is accredited with repairing the liturgical neglect of the 18C and 19C which he inherited.

affectionate Christmas greeting! I hate not being with you. God bless you in the new home![43] I hear the house warmings were a splendid success.

Yours affectionately, Herbert Ryle (Bp)

To work under such a Dean was felt by everyone to be a real privilege, and he inspired the utmost loyalty from the whole staff. His kindness and consideration knew no bounds: if some big and important service had taken place in the Abbey, nearly always before the day was out would come a charming little note of appreciation. Such thoughtful acts do almost more than anything to encourage those who have heavy and responsible tasks committed to them. No one in such a position wants a lot of fulsome praise, but to go on year after year with no comment at all is a deadly experience[44].

Dean Ryle was succeeded by Dr Foxley-Norris[45]. It is a curious thing that just at the time I was leaving Oxford Dr Norris had asked me to be his organist at Barnsley in Yorkshire. When I found I could not accept his offer we little thought that we should work together in such different surroundings thirty years later. He was installed just before Christmas 1925.

---

43 ` Sir Frederick Bridge was dead and SHN had moved into the organist's lodging of Litlyngton Tower.

44 Sir Frederick Bridge, like Nicholson, was also fulsome in his praise for Bishop Ryle. In his Memoir *A Westminster Pilgrim*, London, 1918, he wrote: 'During the later years of my activities at the Abbey I have indeed been more than fortunate in the constant encouragement and recognition which I have found from Bishop Ryle, the present Dean of Westminster. The letters that he has kindly written to me after many of our great services speak for themselves, but I cannot withhold my special thanks to him for his letter written on the day when I laid down my charge of the Abbey music. At such a moment and crisis in my life it had a moving effect, and for this kindly act of affectionate consideration I am exceedingly thankful.'

45 The Very Rev Dr William Foxley-Norris (1859-1937) was educated at Charterhouse and at Trinity College, Oxford. After ordination he served curacies in Eton and Chatham and incumbencies in Oxfordshire and Yorkshire before his career moved towards ecclesiastical administration. He was Dean of York from 1917 to 1925 and then Dean of Westminster until his death. He is buried in Westminster Abbey. Foxley-Norris was also a respected painter in watercolours. Foxley-Norris was very supportive of Nicholson at the Abbey and indeed spoke in glowing terms of him at the inaugural meeting of the *School of English Church Music* on St Nicolas' Day in 1927. The suggestion that they became slightly estranged around the time of Nicholson's resignation from the Abbey might be judged from the resignation letters at the end of this chapter.

The Boy Bishop[46]

In January 1926 the Choristers gave the first performance of an opera which I had written for them on the subject of 'The Boy Bishop'. It was performed in the old Abbot's Dining Hall where it is quite possible that the Boy Bishop may have held his court in ancient times. And thereby hangs a curious tale. In memory of our parents my two brothers and I had undertaken to place certain memorials in the parish church of South Benfleet, Essex, near their old home at Hadleigh[47]. My eldest brother, Charles, restored the South aisle[48], Archibald designed and made the windows, and I had the little organ rebuilt[49]. These memorials were dedicated by the new Dean of Westminster on the Feast of the Epiphany under very interesting circumstances.

Charles A Nicholson's drawing for the South Porch of St Mary's, South Benfleet

The connexion between Westminster Abbey and South Benfleet had been long and intimate. Amongst the Abbey muniments are a large number of documents referring to the parish from the 12th century onwards, one or two of which are of special interest.

In 1360 there was made "a grant from Simon (Langham) Abbat and the Convent of Westminster to Frater Nicholas de Litlyngton Prior of Westminster, that on his decease they will celebrate his anniversary on St Nicolas Day each year, also that from the outgoings of the marshland at Southbenflet, all of which property the above Prior at his own charges united to the above Abbey, he distributed to the poor 6s. and 8d., and 3s. and 4d. for the recreation of the Boy Bishop and his companions."

---

46   The origins of a Boy Bishop certainly date back to the 10th C, when mention was made of a Boy Bishop at Rouen, but the custom may have existed earlier. Many mediæval cathedrals, churches and monasteries observed the custom which varied slightly from place to place, and indeed between countries across Europe. The general pattern was as follows: the Boy Bishop was elected by his fellow choristers on the eve of, or on the Feast of, St Nicolas (6th December), and he 'ruled' until Holy Innocent's Day (28th December). He would be habited in Episcopal robes complete with mitre and crozier, and would perform at the various offices of the church (except mass) including preaching a sermon, and would appoint his fellow choristers to assist him. It is more likely that he would only take an elevated position at services on either or both of these two feast days. The custom in England was suppressed by Henry VIII in 1541, but the ceremony has enjoyed a 20th century revival in some places, notably Salisbury Cathedral.

    For the libretto of *The Boy Bishop*, Nicholson used information drawn from *Historical Notices of the Office of Choristers* by Rev J E Millard (1848) and *The Mediæval Stage Vol 1* by E K Chambers, supplemented by the Westminster Abbey Inventory of 1388, which gives a detailed account of the vestments and ornaments provided for the Boy Bishop ceremony.

47   Sir Charles and Lady Evelyn are buried in the churchyard of South Benfleet Church. Curiously the boundary between the two parishes of Hadleigh and South Benfleet actually passed through the middle of Hadleigh House, former home of Sir Charles Nicholson Senior.

48   And the magnificent 15C timber South Porch.

49   The organ loft in South Benfleet Church, designed in 1925 by Sir Charles Nicholson Jnr, is adorned with paintings by Lady Nicholson executed in 1897 when a new organ by H Jones of Kensington was installed in the Chancel. This organ (two manuals and pedals, 7 stops) was rebuilt and enlarged by Harrison & Harrison of Durham in 1925 to a specification of SHN, and placed in the new organ gallery at the west end.

In the Treasurer's accounts for 1386 is the following record: — "....*et dat duobus pueris ludentibus in Misericordia praecepto domini Prioris iii^s. iv^d.*" (....and he gives to two boys playing in the Misericord by command of the Lord Prior 3s. and 4d); no doubt the lucky boys were the Boy Bishop and his mate.

The next entry provides a curious coincidence of name where it is recorded in the Treasurer's accounts for 1388 "*et cuidam Nich. ludenti ad organa xxvi^s. viii^d.*" (to a certain Nicholas for playing the organ 26s. and 8d.) This is the earliest mention of an organist in the Abbey records.

Laurence de Benflet was appointed to the office of Precentor in 1297, and his effigy appears on the earliest example of the Precentor's seal. But the connexion between the Abbey and South Benfleet does not end here; the living is still in the patronage of the Dean and Chapter, and it is probable that the land which was held by Sir Charles Nicholson may have been the 'marshland at Southbenflet' presented to the Abbey by Prior Litlyngton.

On the occasion of the dedication of the memorials all the Abbey officials mentioned in these early records were represented by their present-day successors who took part in the service.

Abbat Litlyngton was represented by the Dean of Westminster who dedicated the memorials; Laurence de Benflet by his successor as Precentor, the Rev L H Nixon, who took the service; Nicholas who played the organ in 1388 by myself; and the '*duobus pueris*' by the two Abbey Choristers who had performed the parts of the 'Boy Bishop and his mate' in the recent opera[50].

Wilfred Chappell:
Boy Bishop 1926

---

50 "An inventory of 1388 gives a minute description of the vestments and ornaments provided for the use of the Westminster Boy Bishop. These include a mitre with silvered and gilt plates and gems, and the inscription 'Sancte Nicholae ora pro nobis' set in pearls. There was a pastoral staff with images of St Peter and St Edward the Confessor upon thrones; two pairs of cheveril gloves to match the mitre: an amice, rochet and surplice: two albs, and a cope of blue colour worked with gryphons and other beasts and cisterns spouting water. Several of the vestments are again inventoried in 1540." — from Nicholson's introduction to *The Boy Bishop*.

The Boy Bishop's entourage 1926.

Ideas had been gradually forming in my mind that the time was approaching when I should turn my thoughts and energies away from Cathedral work to other branches of Church music. I had always been greatly interested in the music of parish churches, and my connexion with the Church Music Society had increased that interest, and shown me how much was waiting to be done. Then the Report of the Archbishops' Committee on Music in Worship had been issued and received with wide approval, and the question "What next?" seemed to be demanding an answer. But it was clear that to organize such work on a scale that would be necessary if anything worth-while was to be accomplished would be a whole-time job; and if I was to undertake it, it would mean a great change in my life. However these thoughts were only simmering and had not yet taken definite shape when they had to be set aside by a most unexpected call.

The Canadian Tour

The Chapel of St George's, Windsor, was closed for restoration, and an invitation had been accepted for the choir to make a tour through Canada under the auspices of the Canadian National Council of Education under the management of its indefatigable Secretary, Major F J Ney[51]. Almost at the last minute it was decided that the Windsor boys could not be allowed to go and there was danger of the whole scheme falling through. My old friend Dr E H Fellowes, who was then in charge of the Windsor choir, came to me almost in despair to ask whether, as the Abbey had a double shift of boys, 12 of them could be spared to go with the Windsor men and whether I could go with them and take charge of the music. A decision had to be reached quickly and the Dean and Chapter of Westminster readily fell in with the proposal, and so we left in January 1927, travelled right across Canada from St John's to Vancouver and back and were home for Easter Sunday[52].

Toronto 5th March 1927,
The Dean of Windsor Dr A V Baillie (left) and Dr E H Fellowes (right) both to the fore.

51　Major Frederick James Ney (1884-1973), born in England, emigrated to Canada in 1909 to be Headmaster of Russell High School in Manitoba. He became Chief Secretary of Manitoba's Department of Education in the following year and began arranging exchange visits between British and Canadian schoolteachers. After war service, in which he was seriously wounded, he became founder and vice-president of the Overseas Education League, receiving a medal of service from the Governor General of Canada in 1968.

52　The trip took place during winter. The Canadian authorities provided much equipment including leather motor-cycle style outer clothing, hats, gloves, boots and even ice-skates.

Leaving Dean's Yard, Westminster, for Euston 21st Jan 1927

L. TITCHENER. J. CRUFT E. H. BARNES H. V. ABBOTT H. A. WALLACE J. V. HAYWARD P. HOPKINS
B.G. PILLER W. G. CHAPPELL S.H.N. L. MITCHENER E. DAVY
P. KING W. F. KNIGHT

Abbey Choristers

Dr Nicholson, Harry Barnes (robed in an alb)
and the choristers
A press photograph for the Canada trip

145

The Canadian Pacific Railway Pullman Dining Car
Nicholson and Dean Baillie at the back and Harry Barnes front right

The Canadian Pacific Railway organised the tour itinerary providing the party with Pullman Cars in which they lived and ate for the entire six week trip. The choristers lived in the sleeping Pullman Car "Plaisance" and the men in the slightly more luxurious compartment car "Glen Major". Each car was provided with an attendant. There was also a dining car for meals (see photograph above) and a lounge car for lessons and an observation car. Dean Baillie noted that the strenuousness of the tour was greatly alleviated by the quiet interludes in the trains were there was relative privacy away from the crowds which met them at every stop.

Of this wonderful tour a full account has been given in the book which was compiled as a record, under the title *A Joyous Adventure*[53]. At that time the singing of boys was almost unknown in Canada: it aroused the greatest enthusiasm and indeed set an example which

---

53 *A Joyous Adventure in the Dominion of Canada*, London and Toronto, Dent & Sons, 1928, was in the nature of a travelogue, and included articles by the Dean of Windsor, Edmund Fellowes, Major Ney and Nicholson.

was readily taken up, so that whereas at the time of our visit hardly any boys' choirs existed, nowadays they are to be heard in most places. We also gave several 'Scout concerts': — the Scouts in Canada were very flourishing, but singing was considered 'sissy': we were able to show them that there was something in it, and the admirable *Canadian Book of Scout Songs* was a direct result of our visit. So we did some useful work, though it was a pretty strenuous business. Not only was I responsible for looking after the boys with the invaluable help of my former chorister Harry Barnes[54], but, being the only one of the party who could play a keyed instrument, I had to play at every service and accompany at every concert throughout the tour[55]. So I was not sorry when we saw Southampton pier and arrived home none the worse for our adventure.

The Rev Dr Fellowes and the Windsor Gentlemen before the Canada trip.

---

54 Ernest Henry (k/a Harry) Barnes (1909-1985), an important person in Nicholson's life, was a chorister at Westminster Abbey under Nicholson from Jan 1922 to Aug 1924. He went on to study the violin and organ at the Royal College of Music at Nicholson's suggestion (SHN also paid his fees). Nicholson asked Barnes, then aged 18, to accompany him on the Canada tour, not as a singer, but to help look after the boys. Barnes, with difficulty, obtained a term's leave of absence from the RCM to make the trip. He was then employed by Nicholson at the College of St Nicolas in Chislehurst from 1928 and he remained there until the College closed at the outbreak of WWII, concurrently holding a Lay Vicar post at Westminster Abbey from 1936. By 1973, Barnes was Senior Lay Vicar at Westminster Abbey and in that year was awarded an Hon RSCM. In 1977 he was awarded the MBE in recognition of his services to church music. After his death in 1985, a memorial tablet inscribed with the words 'To the glory of God and in grateful memory of Harry Barnes, 1909-85, who for more than forty years faithfully served this collegiate church as chorister and lay vicar' was placed beside the door leading to the choir school in the Westminster Abbey cloisters. Much further information and photographs can be found in *SNCSN*.

55 Nicholson and Harry Barnes also had to teach the children for their general education continued throughout the tour with lessons prepared by the choir school headmaster. Nicholson taught Latin and French amongst other things.

During the long journeys I had plenty of time to think about future plans and to discuss ideas with the Dean of Windsor and Dr Fellowes, and on my return to the Abbey, having seen the effect of a little 'missionary work', the call seemed to become even more urgent. I had been a Cathedral organist for nearly a quarter of a century, and if I was to do anything else with my life it was high time to make a change. So, after very full consideration and many talks with those whose advice I valued, I decided to resign my office at the end of 1927[56].

Nicholson's letter of resignation from The Abbey, written whilst at Scout Camp

Abbey Cottage,
Bow Brickhill,
Bletchley, Bucks, July 19th 1927

Dear Mr. Dean.

I have definitely come to the conclusion that I must resign the office of Organist and Master of the Choristers at the Abbey. You will not be altogether surprised at this decision after our conversation a week ago, I have thought very carefully over the matter and consulted two or three friends whose opinion I value, and now I see my way clear to decide on this important question.

After twenty three years work at Cathedrals I am anxious to be able to devote myself to musical work of a more diverse kind, and I feel that this is not compatible with retaining my post at The Abbey. I need hardly say that I shall give it up with the deepest regret, but I feel that there is other work that I can do when I am free from the heavy responsibility of the office, which will not be without value to the Church.

I should wish to give up after Christmas and I think this should allow you plenty of time to find a successor. It is obvious that the changes you have in view had better be worked out with the new man, so that you will be glad to get the matter settled as soon as you can; but of course I do not wish to hurry you or place you in any difficulty.

On personal grounds this decision has been hard to reach, for I have made many friends at The Abbey; and I can only trust that this valued friendship will continue when I cease to be a member of the Body, and that I shall have their good-will and interest in the work that I hope to undertake. My great desire is that you should find a successor who will carry my work at The Abbey further than I have been able to do.

Believe me,
Yours sincerely

---

[56] Nicholson's resignation evidently did not pass without some hint of mischief - see letters on the following two pages.

Nicholson's second letter to Dean Foxley-Norris

Abbey Cottage,
Bow Brickhill,
Bletchley, Bucks,   *Aug 3rd[57]. [1927]*

Dear Mr. Dean.

    Thanks so much for your letter, and forgive me answering on the type writer, as it will save you trouble in deciphering my scrawl. I am so sorry your daughter is ill, and of course understand you must go to her; but I hope I shall see you here some time, for I fully intend that the boys shall continue to have use of the camp[58] in the future, whenever it is wanted, and I trust their Scouting will go on. One of the worst things is leaving them, and it is too dreadful to bear thinking about.

    You will have probably got the hasty note I sent you yesterday. I don't know who has been talking at The Abbey, but I fear there is some mischief-maker; for two papers sent down interviewers here [Bow Brickhill] yesterday, and others have rung up asking if it is true that we have had a row, and asking lots of questions about the Choir School and the decision not to take any more boarders[59]. Of course I have said nothing, and have done my best to knock anything of the kind on the head; I have said, what I believe to be perfectly true, that there is simply no question of any quarrel and that our relations have been most friendly always. I have refused to express an opinion about the changes to the Choir School, so if they attribute anything to me you will know it is a lie. As you know I do not approve of abolishing the boarders, but I am certainly not going to be dragged into a controversy: it is for you and the Chapter to decide, and as I have decided to give up (quite independently of this consideration), it is really no further business of mine, and it would be most improper to express any opinion publicly so long as I am at The Abbey. At the same time this kind of tittle-tattle is most mischievous and exasperating, and must be as annoying to you as it is to me; yet I don't see how it can be stopped. No doubt these abominable interviewers get hold of people like Vergers and others and try and get them to talk, and very likely make it worth their while to do so, and we are powerless to control their "mischievous imaginations". But one step I have taken; I have telephoned a letter to the Press Association which they will circulate to all the papers[60], as follows:

---

57 *The Times* printed notice of his resignation on this day.
58 The Dean's letter to Nicholson has not been located, but it must have referred to the Bow Brickhill camp site.
59 It seems likely that the Dean and Chapter wanted to make economies. By recruiting two sets of boy choristers Nicholson had thereby increased the costs of the Abbey music.
60 Quotes from this press release were used in *The Times* on 4th Aug 1927.

Dear Sir,

With reference to my resignation of the post of Organist and Master of the Choristers of Westminster Abbey, I should be grateful if you would allow me to state the reasons which have led me to take this step.

After 23 years work at Cathedrals I wish to be free to devote myself to musical work of a more diverse kind, and in particular to the accomplishment of the scheme for the foundation of a School of Church Music, for the benefit of the music in Parish Churches, which was outlined in an article in *The Times* on April 30th last. The work which this is likely to entail would not be compatible with the heavy responsibilities of the Office which I now hold, so that I have regretfully felt bound to relinquish it.

Yours faithfully

S H N

I hope this may do something to stop silly gossip, but if I come across anything in the press which needs contradicting I will send it to you at once. If only the papers would cease to mind other people's business what a lot of trouble would be saved! To the interviewers I have simply concentrated on the School of Music scheme, and tried to turn their inquisitiveness into a channel of useful publicity. If you do have to write to the papers I think it would be a good thing for you to express what I know is your own feeling and that of several members of the Chapter (probably all) that this is a piece of work that wants doing and will be of great value to the Church; for you know that I tremendously want the support advice and help of The Abbey in the undertaking; it would be an enormous asset in the public eye, at anyrate; and I should in a way like it to be felt that I am going out of the Abbey to do this piece of work, if it can be done, and that is what makes any gossip about disagreements so hateful and harmful.

Hoping you will find your invalid better and with kindest remembrances to Mrs Norris.

Ever yours sincerely

Presented to

Sydney Hugo Nicholson Esq.

M.V.O., MUS. DOC., M.A., F.R.C.O.,

Organist of Westminster Abbey,

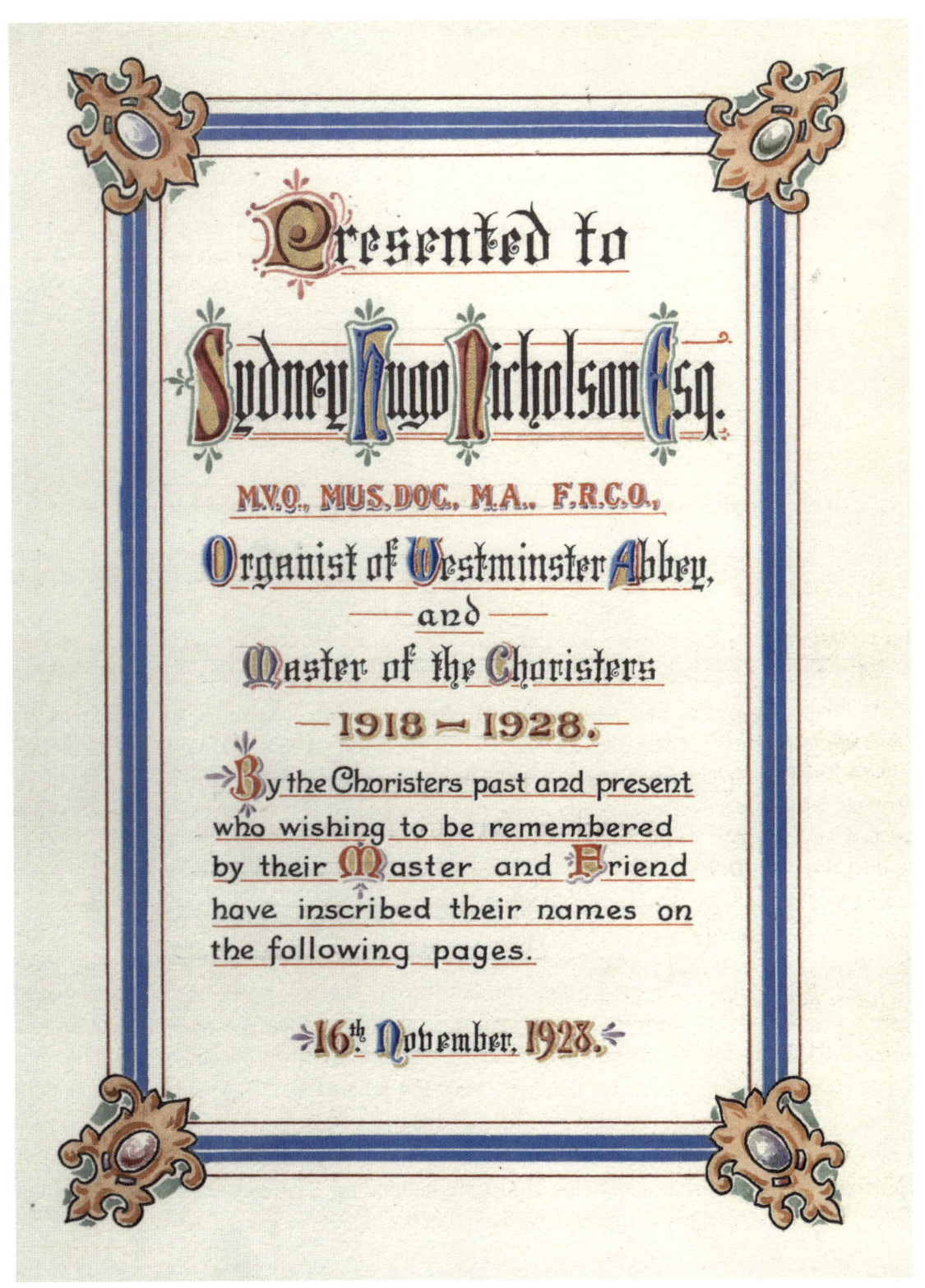

— and —

Master of the Choristers

— 1918 – 1928. —

By the Choristers past and present who wishing to be remembered by their Master and Friend have inscribed their names on the following pages.

16th November, 1928.

On leaving The Abbey, Nicholson was presented with a leather-bound book containing the signatures (and dates served) of 108 of his choristers.

Nicholson at the Westminster Abbey Organ[61]

The Inaugural Meeting of the School of English Church Music

On December 6th of that year an inaugural meeting[62] was held under the Chairmanship of the Dean of Westminster, whose counsels had been of the greatest value to me, in the Jerusalem Chamber, when I explained my ideas and plans and it was decided, on the proposition of Sir Walford Davies seconded by Sir Hugh Allen, that a Society to be called "The School of English Church Music" should be founded then and there.

The main object was defined: — to put into practice some of the chief recommendations of the Archbishops' Committee on Music in Worship by (a) giving direct help to existing choirs, and (b) providing practical training for Church musicians by the foundation of a College devoted to that purpose. It was pointed out that the day chosen for the meeting happened to be the Festival of St Nicolas, the Patron Saint of students and choirboys (as well as other less reputable members of the community): so it was decided that the College when it came into being must be called "St Nicolas College". Thus the scheme was launched and the unborn infant already christened. I handed over my work at the Abbey early in 1928 to my successor, Ernest Bullock, who since leaving Manchester for war service had been organist of Exeter Cathedral; and, on my relinquishing the post, Archbishop Davidson exercised his ancient prerogative in honouring me with the degree of Doctor of Music.

---

61 This rather poor quality photograph is the only known image of SHN at the Westminster organ. It probably dates from 1919 or 1920.
62 A full account of this meeting can be found in *SNCSN*.

Chapter VI

The School of English Church Music 1928-1939

It was a new experience to be 'without a job', or rather with a job yet to be made; but it certainly did not mean idleness. It was rather like starting a voyage on an uncharted sea: one had to find the way as best one could and it was exceedingly easy to get off the tracks that led anywhere. Even the nature of the problem had to be studied before one could discover the directions from which it could be tackled, for there were really no **data** to go upon.

The Church of England (in England alone) has some 13,000 churches. In the great majority of these there is musical activity of some sort, ranging from the parish church in a large town with a skilled choir and organist to the tiny, remote village with its harmonium and a few rustics to lead the singing. Every one of these musical organizations is a more or less self-contained unit: taken together they represent an enormous body of musical energy and enthusiasm. Further, each little unit is, by the nature of the case, working largely in isolation and more often than not under considerable difficulties. The need for some sort of help was apparent if this great mass of heterogeneous material were to be turned to the best use of the Church as a whole: yet how to tackle the problem had still to be discovered.

The answer, so far as one could be given, was supplied by the decision of the inaugural meeting: some definite organization must be created to deal with the whole question of Church music on a large scale and, as far as possible, from every angle. So a temporary Council was formed, a temporary office lent at my brother's studio in Gower Street, the temporary services of an Appeal Secretary were engaged and an appeal for funds was launched. The permanent staff then consisted of myself and my young friend and former Abbey Chorister Harry Barnes[1], who after a period of study at the Royal College of Music had decided to throw in his lot with the new venture.

First of all the problem had to be studied in more detail than had hitherto been possible, and to this end I spent as many Sundays as I could in visiting churches of different types in all parts of the country and taking careful note of what I saw and heard. It was clearly necessary to understand from first-hand observation what the real difficulties were before making plans to deal with them: one had to be careful to avoid the pitfall of attempting to set things right before getting a clear idea of what was wrong.

It soon became evident that consideration would have to be given to two main questions; — the **choice** of music and its **performance**; and that each would have to be examined in relation to Choirs, Organists, Congregations and Clergy. For though, ideally all these should be working in harmony to the same end, — the promotion of the best in worship, — it was quite evident that there is and always will be a certain conflict of outlook.

---

1   See Chapter V: Footnote 54.

It may be well, at this point, to give some conclusions at which I have arrived after ten years' pretty close study of the matter and personal visits to many hundreds of choirs in their own churches, though at the time when the work of the SECM was beginning I had still to gain the experience which has led me to them.

The state of music in Parish Churches – problems and solutions

First of all regarding **Choice** of music: In Choirs there is a very natural ambition, especially in the keenest ones, to tackle a good deal, — broadly speaking as much as they are allowed to. The more they are asked to do the keener they are; but if the music is difficult or in an unaccustomed idiom, they are apt to lose heart; and it is not easy to get them to see beauty which is not at once obvious. There is an undoubted affection for music that is not difficult either to grasp or to perform, and not much critical sense is exercised as to its merit so long as it makes an effect. So the old favourites in anthems (preferably containing solos for some of the men), or showy settings of the Canticles still persist and it is difficult to persuade a choir that the wish to substitute something better is not mere 'crankiness':— the real truth is that they cannot see what is wrong with the 'good old stuff' they 'always used to sing'. Choirs are very conservative and do not readily take to 'new-fangled ideas'.

The taste of the **Organist** (and in this term I include the Choirmaster) is generally in advance of that of his choir, as is right and to be expected. Many, however, are quite content to go on in the old ways, while others who would like something better, give up the struggle for the sake of peace and quiet. But there are plenty who carry conviction and do manage to get their choirs to support them whole-heartedly. It may, however, be taken as axiomatic that unless the choirmaster gives the lead to his choir, improvement in the matter of choice is almost impossible.

Now this brings us to one great difficulty which must be mentioned in no censorious spirit but with genuine sympathy. Take the case of an organist who has occupied a leading musical position in his town for a number of years. Generations of choirboys and choirmen have relied on his judgment; the congregation is proud of him and of the services. Suddenly he is told that the kind of thing he has been performing all this time is poor stuff, and it is suggested that he should make a change in deference to some outsider's opinion. It is difficult for him to do so even if he should be convinced, without appearing to admit that he has been mistaken in the past, — in other words that he did not really know his job. Of course this is an erroneous view, for music is always progressing and no true musician ever feels that he has ceased to be a learner. All the same it is very natural that a man in such a position should feel a little resentful of any criticism that might seem to undermine his position. So that very often suggestions for change are not welcomed or even seriously considered because they cannot be wholly divorced from criticism of an existing state of things. It takes a really big man to put his pride in his pocket and to be ready to revise his own standards. That so many are willing to do this speaks very highly for the profession as a whole.

The attitude of the **Congregation** in the matter of choice is generally a simple one. The majority, or at any rate those who express their opinion, are almost solidly against change of any kind. To their mind anything new is objectionable, and in country places at any rate change is, for some strange reason, almost synonymous with 'High-Church': and whatever Anglo-Catholics may say, this suggestion is alone sufficient to arouse suspicion. As to anthems, some of the congregation actively dislike them and consider them a mere waste of time; a good many accept them with passive tolerance now that the custom of sitting during their performance has become general[2]; a minority really appreciate them and some few definitely prefer the good to the bad. As to hymns, new ones are generally resented, especially new tunes to old favourites: musical merit hardly enters into the question; the fact that a tune is new is enough to condemn it. This may all sound rather bitter, but I do not think it is an exaggeration of the normal state of things. Yet I hasten to add that the taste of a congregation may be improved and that they can be brought to look on anthems and even new hymns as a real source of edification and help to the worship. But this change of attitude will come only gradually and long after the improvement has begun, — in other words people will get to like the newer methods when they have got used to them. But there is no real demand for improvement and ordinary folks are quite content to go on in the old ways.

As to Service-settings of the Canticles or the Communion Office, the congregation generally actively dislike them. It is not so much that they dislike the music: but they wish to have the opportunity of joining in, and Service-settings make this difficult or sometimes impossible. I believe that this one main reason why Choral Communions are seldom popular, at any rate at first: simply because people do not know the music. It is not so much that the congregation usually has a very strong desire to sing; when they get the chance they very often do not avail themselves of it. There certainly are some genuine 'die-hards' for congregational singing, but more often it is mixed up with a less worthy feeling: it is not so much that they want to sing themselves as that they object to other people singing for them.

Such an attitude can only be countered by teaching: but it must be remembered that most people do not like being educated, or at any rate the suggestion that they need education. It is very difficult to get a congregation to see that it is their duty to make their worship as good as possible; they are far too apt to regard it as something that ought to be arranged to please their own taste; and to hint that their taste is not perfect is an outrage.

This brings us to a consideration of the position of **Clergy**. The clergy are too often blamed for everything. Where the music is bad they are reproached for not insisting that it should be better: at least they have the ultimate control over the service and cannot entirely evade

---

2   The custom of standing for the anthem existed in some cathedrals. In the case of Exeter, it applied to those members of the congregation who occupied the back or top rows of the Quire stalls (the seats with names), and there used to be a notice in the stall informing the occupant that they were required to stand for the anthem. If you chose to sit elsewhere, this ruling didn't apply. The reason for this ruling was that the anthem was usually a setting of a Biblical text and was regarded as a canticle, like the Magnificat. The custom had fallen into disuse by the turn of the 19C in many places and as late as the 1960's in Exeter.

responsibility. But if, perhaps spurred on by a zealous organist, they try to make changes; they are immediately up against the congregation: "You spoil my enjoyment of the service by your new-fangled ways" is not an uncommon complaint, the objector quite forgetting that the object of the service is not his personal enjoyment but the glory of God. In the matter of choice a serious responsibility falls upon the clergy with regard to the hymns. Yet how seldom do they seem to be chosen with real care or thought. It is, I suppose, true to say that in the majority of churches the hymn-book in use is never thoroughly explored: the parson will often make out his hymn-list for the ensuing month as a rather tiresome duty that has to be got through in the least possible time. He will turn through the pages and say 'we know this', perhaps giving a hasty glance at the words, but thinking mainly of the popularity rather than the merit of the tune. So many good things remain untried while indifferent ones are repeated again and again. Contrast this with the more rare cases when the hymns are chosen with thought and care, the new being carefully explored along with the old. Surely the clergy should know something of hymnology and learn to choose their hymns on some definite principle, considering the important position they occupy in our services today. One wonders how many of them even keep a record of what has been sung during the year.

There are some clergy who are frankly 'philistine': they prefer, or say they prefer, the bad to the good, and they use such specious arguments as "if I find that a hymn which you call 'bad' saves souls, why should I not use it?" But are they so sure that it does 'save souls', or does anything more than arouse a transient emotion which soon passes away? Others say that it is all very well for musicians to talk, but they are not primarily concerned with the religious side and therefore their views as to what is desirable do not really count. Others frankly say, 'I don't know anything about music, but I know what I like', and they act on this principle.

But there are a great many, too, who would dearly love to have the best music and who cannot get their choirmaster or choir to perform it or their congregation to accept it. Their case is hard indeed and it is by no means uncommon: they badly need every help and encouragement that can be given to them. For the main difficulty that confronts those who are anxious for improvement is summed up concisely in the words of the Psalmist, — "Whereas thou hatest to be reformed", a text that might well adorn the walls of many a church: it might even be a **pendant** to one which the Archbishop of Canterbury saw emblazoned above certain choir-stalls which were occupied by a particularly flamboyant choir (not in this country) – "When thou hearest, Lord, forgive".

There is one other thing to be said about this matter of choice. It is not always easy for those who wish to improve to know what to substitute for that which they feel to be unworthy. And here the guidance of some responsible authority which understands the conditions under which they work can be of enormous help. It is no use for reform to be merely destructive: the reformer must be prepared to suggest a remedy that is not only an improvement but is practical.

This leads on to the even more difficult question of **Performance**. **Choirs** vary greatly in that essential quality of keenness which is the very key-note of efficiency. Most of them have at any rate a few keen members: but unfortunately these are not always the most competent singers, and it sometimes happens that the best singers are not the most regular in attendance because they quite genuinely feel that they 'know the stuff' all right. It has to be admitted that many if not most choirs lack the quality of self-criticism. In other words, so long as a thing 'goes pretty well' in their estimation, they do not see the need for much careful finish in detail. They feel that the practice of simple things like psalms and hymns does not really matter; — it is at best a fad of the choirmaster or the parson: what really counts is the set music, the Service or Anthem. It is only the exceptional choir that sees that the most difficult task that is set before it is to chant properly, and that familiar things normally need more care than novelties. It is hard for them to understand that a liturgical choir is something quite different from a choral society.

The boys are a far easier problem as a rule than the adults (and this includes women as well as men): in the hands of a competent choirmaster they are nearly always keen and generally efficient. But here again there is a curious difficulty. Owing to the decline in population and other causes, boys in many places are becoming scarce; there are many more counter-attractions for their spare time than was the case a few years ago, and on the whole parents do not urge their boys to join a choir as they used, nor back up the choirmaster in the matter of regularity. This means that choirboys are fewer, but on the other hand it often means that they are of better quality, for it is only the boys who are keen and musical that will join a choir at all. But in most places there are still plenty of boys available and it is very largely dependent on the choirmaster whether they will join and, still more, whether they will stick to the choir. If they do not find it interesting they will certainly not bother about it. The boys naturally are much more ready to learn than their elders; but they are also more dependent on their teachers.

Here should be mentioned a tendency which has increased much in recent years. Partly owing to the difficulty of getting choirboys the policy is being adopted on all sides of introducing women into Church choirs. It may be noted in passing that this tendency is very much more pronounced in the south of England than in the north and is quite as prevalent in 'high' churches as in 'low'. In some cases the boys are discarded altogether, in others women are introduced to help them though they often, in fact, succeed in silencing them. It is interesting to note that exactly the opposite tendency is shewing itself in the Dominions and the United States, where 'boy-choirs' are on the increase.

Now there can be no reason why women should not be employed in the choir if it is really a gain to the worship. But is it? Too often the clergy adopt this expedient in the hope of solving all difficulties, only to find that it creates fresh ones. Without going into these it is well to look at the question from the opposite angle, and to ask not whether the presence of women in a choir is a gain but whether the absence of boys is a loss. And surely there can be but one answer. The singing of boys is the most characteristic feature of the music of the Church of England: our choirboys are superior to those of any other country: we have an age-long tradition behind their singing and it would be a disaster if this were lost. Then again, with the many outside attractions of modern life, it is not easy to get young men to go to church at all, much less to join a choir; and such as are forthcoming are nearly always those who have begun as choirboys. So that if this source of supply were to dry up it is likely that in a few years' time there would be no fresh choirmen forthcoming, and choirs would become (as they are in some parts of the English-speaking world where choirboys are still uncommon) the prerogative of the elderly. Now the Church, or at any rate Church music cannot live without the invigorating power of youth, and the choir is the one opportunity of gaining a real and practical interest in church life and church work that is open to a boy. To deprive him of it is a suicidal policy.

As to the employment of women altos the case is quite different. There is a real scarcity of men altos, and boys (though they may well be employed to sing alto when their voices begin to change) are often not certain enough to carry the part by themselves. Many choirs are dependent on good women altos and many more would be the better for including them.

However good the material, it is true to say that in the matter of performance the main responsibility must rest upon the Choirmaster. Now it is one thing to understand the 'tricks of the trade', — voice production, discipline, power to arouse enthusiasm, and so on; but, essential as these matters are for a good choir, they will not in themselves assure a good performance. To achieve this, the choirmaster needs personal equipment. First he needs a trained ear, accurate and quick enough to detect faults and if possible to point out exactly what they are and where they occur. Then he needs a sensitive mind, (by 'sensitive' I do not, of course, mean 'ready to take offence'!) he has got to be able to see the possibilities in the matter of interpretation before he can pass them on to his choir. It very often happens that a really good choir fails in the matter of interpretation because the point of the music and the words has not been grasped by the choirmaster. That is why so many church choirs that are quite competent, fail to give any message in their singing. What they produce is just so much sound, — attractive perhaps, but almost meaningless. In the case of Church music, where more than anywhere each word counts, the need for sensitiveness in the choirmaster is proportionately great. Many of the words that a choir has to sing, as in the psalms, are archaic and the sentiments expressed are not those of everyday life. A choir cannot be expected to grasp these things unless they are interpreted to them; a soloist may perhaps be able to give individual expression to a phrase, but choral expression is corporate and the suggestion must come from the leader.

A very great number of the smaller choirs are in the hands of people who have had little serious musical training, and it is remarkable how well they do on the whole. But many professional musicians, who may be excellent organists and conductors and teachers, have not studied the peculiar work of training a Church choir simply because they have not had opportunity of doing so; they have had to find out as they went along. But it is highly specialised work involving, for success, a great variety of qualities, some of them not musical ones at all.

Generalizations are always dangerous, but it seems true to say that, considering the material available and the technical standard often attained, our Church choirs as a whole fall short of what they might attain in the matter of interpretation. The reason for this is partly that good models are not very numerous or easily to be heard; and partly that choirmasters either are not sufficiently sensitive to be able to see the inner meaning of what they have to teach, or are unable to put their ideas across to their choirs. Yet how hard it is for any man to get fresh ideas when he is tied to his organ bench for practically every Sunday in the year: how would the clergy like it if they had to fill their own pulpits with equal regularity?

In the matter of performance **Congregations** are generally apathetic: it is difficult to make them see that they have any actual responsibility for making their part in the music a real contribution to the worship: it is nearly always regarded as something provided for their enjoyment or edification. Congregational practices, if well directed, may do something to help their efforts and to give them a truer perspective of their duties: but it is usually difficult to arouse sufficient interest to make them very effective. So it happens that so-called 'heartiness' is taken as the criterion of congregation singing, and little serious attempt is made to go beyond this. Yet with the present state of musical education much more might be done if congregations could only be mobilised into more serious and united effort.

In the matter of performance, taking this to include their responsibility for the whole ordering of the service including the music and the choir, the Clergy have a most important part. If a clergyman is sufficiently musical, his criticism of the work of his choir may be invaluable: but even those who are not musical can often help by explanation of the meaning and purpose of what has to be sung, so that the choir at least understands what it is all about; though if a man can not only explain things but can appreciate efforts to interpret them through music it is an enormous gain.

But in any case the clergyman is supreme in the ordering of the service, and it is for him to see that the music really contributes to the worship and is not merely tacked on to it as a sort of attraction or trimming. So that the place of music in the service should be regarded as an essential part of liturgical training in order that a parson may be qualified to exercise the duty which will ultimately fall upon him.

Unfortunately many of the clergy do not realise their responsibility in this matter. Some of them leave the music severely alone, regarding it as a department with which they are not really concerned except in general policy: others exercise supervision mainly to curb the ambition of the choir and to try and keep the congregation happy: others, again, particularly elderly men in small places, seem to have given up all attempt to improve matters; they just acquiesce in what they have, admitting its feebleness but having lost any hope they once had of improving matters; they have really come to believe that in their own particular parish the difficulties are too great to make improvement anything more than a dream: others seem to feel that the music does not really matter unless it is so bad as to arouse violent complaint.

But there are many, and an increasing number, who do take the matter very seriously, and it is in their churches, when they have the help of a competent and sensitive choirmaster, that we get that feeling of 'atmosphere' which is so conducive to the spirit of worship. Amongst those who really care, some have the necessary knowledge to enable them to achieve, at least in some measure, their aims: but others have not that knowledge and would be only too thankful to receive help and advice if they knew where to turn for it.

In the matter of the technical performance of their own part in the service the clergy vary greatly. Some are able to render it most adequately: some of course are not musical enough to sing the priest's part; others attempt it when they had better not. But all could at least **read** the service properly, and if only it were more generally realised how much depends upon good reading an enormous advance could be made. How can a parson expect his choir to bring out the meaning of the words, say, in the psalms, if his reading of the lessons and the prayers is inexpressive or, as is sometimes the case, almost inaudible? It is abundantly clear that the efficient performance of their own part by the clergy is essential to an adequate rendering of the service, and without this the efforts of the best choir or organist are in vain.

Such seemed to be some of the main problems with which the SECM would have to deal:

- It would have to get into touch with actual choirs and actual services so that advice and help could be given on the spot.
- It would have to influence opinion by the dissemination of sound ideas.
- It would have to provide serious teaching and not mere general advice for those who were ready to learn, and this must include all concerned in the rendering of the service, choirs, organists, choirmasters, congregations and clergy.
- And if it could give practical examples of the methods which it advocated, so much the better.

It was a big programme! It was obvious from the first that the work would fall into two main divisions:

(a) Direct contact with choirs and parishes through publications, advice, instruction and, as far as possible, personal visits; and

(b) Provision for courses of teaching and for the full-time training of Church musicians at a central institution, where also the principles advocated could be demonstrated.

With regard to outside contacts it was early realised that little would be achieved if an attempt were made to give promiscuous help, and that the best chance of doing anything worthwhile was to get choirs and parishes keen enough to ask for it. So a system of affiliation was adopted under which any church choir could join the SECM so long as it was ready to accept the principles enunciated in the *Report of the Archbishops' Committee on Music in Worship*[3], summarised on the 'affiliation form'. Each choir must also take its share in the general expenses by subscribing at least £1 a year to the central funds, and it was recommended that wherever possible the actual members of the choir should make their personal subscriptions towards the Affiliation fee.

The announcement of this plan at first aroused a good deal of criticism, — choirs could not afford it, and so on: but feeling that choirs would value what was being done for them all the more if they had to contribute to the cost, besides being unwilling to pander to the prevalent desire to 'get something for nothing', the Council adhered to the original plan, and subsequent events have proved their wisdom in doing so.

My first duty was to address meetings, conferences etc. in all parts of the country, taking advantage of every possible opening for making the ideas and plans widely known. During the year 1928 I must have addressed some hundreds of such meetings[4]. Bishops and Clergy were most sympathetic and helpful and I was given every opportunity for explaining matters, while the press gave any amount of publicity. Indeed I do not know how the SECM would ever have got under way, still less how it would have continued to grow had it not been for the unfailing and generous support that has always been given to it by the press.

Not being endowed with gifts as a convincing speaker I found this work trying and, perhaps in consequence of my lack of oratorical power, I have come to the conclusion that big meetings are of very little use for getting anything done. I have addressed many of them; my audiences have always seemed sympathetically interested; but very little has happened in the way of direct results. Far more has been achieved by personal visits to choirs or congregations that asked for them; but of course this is a slow business and could only be undertaken very gradually.

A very pleasant little episode occurred to break this long routine of talking. During the last part of my time at The Abbey arrangements had been made to broadcast Evensong on one day each week[5] (I am bound to add against my wishes): of course many letters were received and amongst them was one from a French priest, M. L'Abbé Busson[6], of Mortagne in Normandy, expressing much interest in the music and especially in the English method of chanting the psalms with which of course he was entirely unfamiliar, as well as in the singing of the boys which again was unlike anything to which he was accustomed. We got into correspondence and I told him something of my ideas and plans for the SECM; he replied that a similar movement for the improvement of Church music was beginning in France and suggested that I should come over and see something of it for myself.

---

3   See p 126.
4   There is a fairly comprehensive list of these in the *RSCM* Archives.
5   The first BBC live broadcast of Evensong from Westminster Abbey was on Thursday 7th October 1926.
6   Abbé Maurice Busson, who had been a missionary in the Congo in the early 1890's, was also a composer. During Nicholson's 1928 visit he wrote a *Berceuse* for organ dedicated to Nicholson which is unpublished. Marcel Dupré's *Ave verum* Op.34/1 is dedicated to him.

So just before Easter I made a little tour, visiting various 'Maîtrises' (Choir-Schools), and found it a most interesting and amusing experience.

Visit to France, Easter 1928[7]

My first visit was to Rouen, where I found a very nice resident Maîtrise connected with the Cathedral. There were about 25 boys and I heard them practising Beethoven's *Mass in C* — very accurate and rhythmical but with rather hard and shrill voices. I saw them at supper, the smaller ones drinking beer from large 'carafes' and the monitors each with half a bottle of 'vin blanc': they were not allowed to talk at meals except on Sundays and Fêtes, but it seemed a nice cheerful place and the boys looked very happy. Their picturesque dress, in which they were thrilled to pose for snap-shots, consisted of white albs with girdles over a red cassock, large red capes with a hood which they sometimes wore over their heads, and red boots going right up the ankles. From Rouen I went to Paris, where I was taken in hand by M Nizan and met his daughter Renée[8], who was then little more than a child; yet she was able to play several of the big works of Bach from memory on the small organ in her father's house: she has since become a most brilliant organist and has given recitals all over the world.

After a hectic two days in Paris which included attendance at many services in different churches — High Mass at Nôtre Dame, a grand wedding, and an even grander funeral with 'Pompes funèbres', at which the 'Dead March' was the first movement of the *Moonlight Sonata* arranged for organ, violin and harp, I went on to Bourges. There I stayed some days in the Maîtrise, with its most delightful Directeur M. L'Abbé Signargout[9], and found a large choir of excellently trained boys and the services most beautifully ordered and efficient in every way. He told me that this care about boys' singing was a new thing in France and that nothing of the kind had been attempted twenty years ago. Certainly wonders had been accomplished, and if it did not seem to me that they sang quite so well as English Cathedral boys, it is probably because the kind of tone that is liked in France, as shown by their organs, is not the same as that which we admire. On

L'Abbé Camille Signargout

---

7 On his return, Nicholson wrote an article entitled *A Musical Tour: The French Cathedrals* published in *The Times* 21st April 1928.
8 Renée Nizan (1913-1945) initially learned the organ from her father Henri Nizan, organist of Notre-Dame in Boulogne. She went to Paris as a pupil of Henri Dallier and Louis Vierne, giving the first performance of the latter's 6th Organ Symphony. She became an international organ recitalist. She was 15 when Nicholson met her and had recently made her Paris debut giving a recital at the Salle Gaveau.
9 L'Abbé Camille Signargout, ordained priest in 1910, was maître de chapelle of the cathedral in Bourges from 1913.

Maundy Thursday I was present at a magnificent ceremony, the Blessing of the Sacred Oils by the Archbishop: I was given a special seat in the Choir close to the Archbishop's throne, and in that glorious building it was certainly one of the most magnificent functions I have ever witnessed; and it was splendidly carried through in every detail.

From Bourges I went on to Nantes and attended the Cathedral for the Mass of the Presanctified, rather poorly sung by a choir of men to plainsong. It is curious how some French church musicians seem to regard their prescribed liturgical chant, — almost as if it were a necessary evil. I was several times advised not to bother about a particular service; — "Pas de musique — seulement le plainchant!" They were quite surprised that I was interested in it. I lunched at the Maîtrise and though it was Good Friday we had an excellent meal — no meat of course but plenty of good wine and liqueurs with our coffee. Then at 1.30 came a grand full rehearsal of the music for Easter: the choir was formed of boys and seminarists, with a scratch orchestra in which I particularly remember one portly priest who played the trombone with great vigour. It seemed strange to be listening to a rehearsal of Easter music just at the time when most Churches in England would be in the middle of the Three Hours service. But they don't seem to be very particular about such things in France, and I have more than a suspicion that the rehearsal was put forward in order that I might hear what they could do before I had to leave!

From Nantes I went on to Angers and there found a delightful choir, nearly though not quite as good as at Bourges. The choir was placed in the Apse behind the High Altar and the singing was mostly done from huge books placed on lofty lecterns, at the foot of which small boys in full robes turned the pages with long canes. The words in these books had been written out in beautiful and very large script by old choirboys 'for love', their Director adding the notes. Quite elaborate polyphonic work was set out in this way — an immense labour. This seemed a wonderful choir-school: the Abbé Turpault told me that there were 80 boys, all voluntary, (of course they are not boarders), and that they came to practice every day: each summer he took them to a seaside camp. There had been an appeal for funds, for it was 'very expensive' and last year had cost (reckoned in English money) £176 — but this included their robes and the camp! For the High Mass on Easter Day they sang Palestrina's *Missa Papae Marcelli*. After Vêpres [Vespers] there was a sermon and the choir went out; thinking the service was over I went round to the Maîtrise: but all were in their full robes, for there was still to be a Procession: — my friend the Director, in a richly embroidered cope, was distributing to the boys from a window a large parcel of sweets which I had bought them, and which they were eagerly munching in the courtyard in their red cassocks and surplices and little skull caps; presently a couple of acolytes came hurrying in from the church with a warning that the sermon was drawing to a close; there were excited cries from the Abbé "O, la, la, la! — depechez vous, la, la!"; in less than a minute all were in order with their hands folded and most pious expressions on their faces, and filed off into church to finish the service!

I went on by Le Mans and Chartres, where the music was disappointing, to Mortagne, to make the acquaintance of my correspondence-friend Abbé Busson. Here I had a most delightful time comparing notes and seeing a good deal of French clerical life. The Abbé had by this time introduced quite a lot of English music into his services, and it was very curious to hear our own tunes "Richmond" and Smart's "Rex Gloriae" (a special favourite) sung to French hymns, and still more to find Anglican Double Chants used as settings for the Antiphons to psalms sung to the 'Parisian tones'.

L'Abbé Maurice Busson with his housekeeper and her son.

A painting by Nicholson of the Porte Saint-Denis in Mortagne

I attended a village wedding and subsequent déjeuner at the house of the Archiprêtre, — a most sumptuous repast, myself the only layman present, with every kind of wine and liqueur brought up — the bottles covered with fungus — from the 'cave' under his front hall into which he descended through a trap-door. On another day I played at the First Mass of a young priest (the music was again very 'Anglican'); when it was over and everyone had congratulated him on the way he had performed his duties, marking the occasion with suitable gifts, we adjourned to a large marquee that covered in the whole of the back garden of his parents' house, for déjeuner at which 86 people sat down. We started eating at about 1.30. At 3 o'clock I went off with a company of priests to listen to the broadcast of The [Westminster] Abbey Evensong, which I duly explained to them: and it certainly was an odd experience in the middle of this extremely French function to hear the first psalm sung to the very chant we had been singing in the morning at the Mass. After the broadcast was finished we returned to the marquee where the meal was still going on: it ended about 4.30!

Nothing could exceed the kindness and hospitality of these French priests: I found them all most charming and cultivated men with a deep interest in, and sympathy for the English Church and most anxious to know more about our ways. Since then Abbé Busson has been a frequent and most popular guest at the College of St Nicolas, making a most careful study of our services and their music. He has done much excellent work with his own choir, now at Flers de L'Orne, training his boys on English lines, and having translated several English works and performed them in his church: these include Charles Wood's *Passion according to St Mark* and Arthur Somervell's *Christmas*. Last time I saw him he was engaged in writing music for a production of T S Eliot's *Murder in the Cathedral* of which he had made a French translation.

The Advent of the SECM

This delightful little adventure had necessarily to be brief for there was much to be done at home. A real start had been made and a few choirs gradually began to affiliate: the first was that from the village of Childe Okeford In Dorset[10].

Meanwhile a permanent Secretary, Mr H L A Green[11], had been appointed and the work of organization had begun in earnest. The most urgent matter was the appeal for funds; though we had but few big subscriptions the smaller amounts came in a fairly steady stream, so that it could be felt that the work was at least going forward, though the financial position through the whole of the history of the SECM has been one of anxiety.

But there was general agreement that the scheme could not be considered as being fully launched until the projected "College of St Nicolas" became an accomplished fact. So far the SECM had little practical existence except on paper and a permanent centre of work and teaching seemed to be essential.

Yet how was such an ambitious scheme to be realised? Well, it was realised, and after many possible places had been inspected it was finally decided to secure a property known as 'Buller's Wood' at Chislehurst, and there to establish the College of St Nicolas. The house was eminently adaptable for its new purpose: the original building had been largely added to, the latest and most important additions having been designed by Ernest Newton with decorations by William Morris. The situation was ideal, in about ten acres of beautiful grounds. Some criticism was passed on the Council's decision to plant their College outside the London area. But a convenient service of trains made access to all parts of London quite easy, and it was

---

10   The date of their affiliation is given as 21st July 1928.

11   (Herbert) Leslie (Arnold) Green (1903-1995), a former chorister at Durham Cathedral with the Rev Arnold Culley, was the first Registrar of the College of St Nicolas and was appointed Secretary of the *SECM* from 1st Jan 1931 having been 'Shorthand Typist Secretary' from 1st Aug 1928. On that first appointment Nicholson described him as 'a TOC H man, aged 25, musical and very much interested in the School'. His initial salary was £200 per annum. Much of his work, especially dealing with affiliated choirs, courses and festivals, was done in the London office rather than at Chislehurst though he sang Alto in the choir on many occasions. In 1940 he assisted Nicholson in moving the *SECM*'s effects to Tenbury and later to Leamington and Canterbury, though he was commissioned into the Royal Navy during WWII. Green also planned and executed the *RSCM*'s move to Addington Palace, Croydon, in 1954. He retired to Canterbury in July 1964 to a house which he and his wife had purchased when the *RSCM* was based in Canterbury. In 1986 he was honoured with an FRSCM. At a memorial service in Canterbury Cathedral on 6th Feb 1995 Harry Bramma, Director of the *RSCM*, summed up his appreciation of Green by saying 'It is no exaggeration to say that, without Leslie Green, the *RSCM* would not exist in its present form today'.

felt that any inconvenience caused by distance from the centre of things would be more than compensated by the advantage to the work of the students, in the quiet surroundings and absence of the counter-attractions of town life.

The freehold was secured and a few necessary alterations were made, the chief being the conversion of the drawing-room to a temporary Chapel and the transformation of the garage and stables to a Students' Hostel.

A generous benefaction of Mrs Wright[12], of Chester, in memory of her husband who had been Precentor of the Cathedral encouraged the Council to venture on the establishment of a small Choir-school which was felt to be essential in order that regular choral services might be established from the first. It happened that, on the death of the 7th Duke of Newcastle[13] about this time, the private Choir-school at Clumber Park had been closed, and it was ascertained that several of the boys would be available as Choristers. So arrangements were made by which ten boys could live in the College and receive their general education at Bickley Hall Preparatory School, which was fortunately within a few minutes' walk. Six boys came from Clumber and the rest were appointed after a trial. The first Chorister to be appointed was Ian Dolan, whose mother[14] is now the indefatigable Hon Secretary of the "Friends of the College".

The opening of the College of St Nicolas[15]

The College actually started to function on 15th January 1929, when the first student and the ten choristers arrived. The 'staff' consisted of myself as Warden, Harry Barnes as Master of the Choristers, and The Rev G H Salter[16], Precentor of Winchester Cathedral, who was allowed by the Cathedral authorities to act as our temporary Chaplain in so far as his Cathedral duties permitted. It was at first only possible to provide accommodation for three resident students who, with the Secretary of the SECM were housed in a cottage on the property until the Hostel should be ready for occupation.

The first service was held in the Chapel on 16th January when the Bishop of Truro (Dr Frere) dedicated the various gifts that had been made. Among these were the Cross and Candlesticks presented by "those who served Westminster Abbey as Choristers from 1918 to 1928", and the Silver Chalice and Paten as well as the Processional Cross (which had been carried by Harry Barnes during the Canadian tour), [donated] by The Society of the Faith.

---

12 Ethel Beatrice Wright, widow of Rev Harold Hall Wright who had been Precentor of Chester Cathedral, donated £500 towards the setting up of a choir school in memory of her husband.
13 Henry Pelham-Clinton, 7th Duke of Newcastle-under-Lyne (1864-1928) was a staunch Anglo-Catholic and addressed the House of Lords on Ecclesiastical matters. He was Deputy Lieutenant of Nottinghamshire. On his family estate at Clumber Park in Nottinghamshire (now owned by the National Trust) the Duke built a fine parish church, St Mary the Virgin in 1886 and he established the Clumber Choir School in 1893.
14 Ethel M Dolan (Mrs H J Dolan), mother of Chislehurst chorister Ian Dolan, was Hon Sec to the Friends of the College of St Nicolas and Chair of the Ladies Committee from their inception. She was elected to *SECM* Council in 1935 and served diligently until 1941.
15 A full description of this is in *SNCSN*.
16 The Rev George Henry Salter (1884-1969) had been a minor canon at Manchester Cathedral (when Nicholson was there) before moving to Winchester. In 1929 he was appointed Vicar of St Sepulchre's, Holborn, a post he was to occupy until 1962.

The opening service of the College of St Nicolas, Chislehurst, 16th Jan 1929

The choir consisted of the ten newly arrived Choristers, resplendent in their new surplices and bright [more accurately, light] blue cassocks (which had been chosen as the 'College colour') assisted by the staff and a few ex-choristers from The Abbey. The company assembled in the hall in readiness for the service which was timed to begin at 8.30 pm. It was a bitter night, and as the ancient 'central heating' refused to function and no fires (except one gas stove) were available, conditions were not exactly cheerful: and our spirits sank lower and lower when we heard that the arrival of the party of special friends who were coming from London would be delayed, as their train had been cancelled on account of a 'fog service'. So we waited, shivering, till at last they came and the choir moved into Chapel singing the beautiful hymn "Christ is our corner-stone". This was the first piece of music to be sung in the College Chapel and it has found a place in every subsequent 'special service'. Nothing could better express the hopes of those met together than the words: —

> On His great love our hopes we place
> Of present grace and joys above.
> ---------------------------
> Here, gracious God, do Thou for evermore draw nigh;
> Accept each faithful vow, and mark each suppliant sigh;
> In copious shower on all who pray
> Each holy day Thy blessings pour.
> ---------------------------
> Here may we gain from Heaven the grace which we implore;
> And may that grace, once given, be with us evermore.

After the Dedication of the gifts and a short address by the Bishop, the company proceeded to the part of the building which had been set apart as a Choir-school and here prayer was offered for 'Our Benefactors' and a short service was held in the dormitory.

And so 'The College of St Nicolas' started on its way. Regular choral services, morning and evening, were begun at once, invariably including the "College prayer" which had been composed by Bishop Frere.

> Bless, O Lord, our College, and grant that the indwelling grace of thy Holy Spirit may direct our learning and sanctify our lives in loyalty, zeal, and purity of heart, for the sake of Jesus Christ our Saviour. Amen.

The choir gradually began to take shape. At first the boys sang on Sunday mornings with the choir at Bickley Parish Church, but on 16th May the Rev G H Salter was instituted and inducted as Vicar of St Sepulchre's Church, Holborn. Through this connexion a centre was supplied for the practical work of the SECM in one of the finest of the City Churches, and the College choir began to sing there on each Sunday during term time. For the service of Institution by the Bishop of London, the affiliated choirs In the London area were invited to take part and nearly 400 singers attended; this was the first of many gatherings of choirs that have since been held at St Sepulchre's.

The dingy and derelict condition of the Church when Salter took it over baffles description. I had previously paid a 'visit of inspection' on a Sunday morning, when the total congregation numbered five; — but this was an exceptional number, for a Charity was to be distributed which involved the attendance at Divine Service of all who wished to participate in it! Many articles of furniture were ready to collapse at a touch: there was a dangerous hole in the flooring in one corner, and the floor of the pulpit collapsed when I went into it to conduct the assembled choirs: the beautiful Jacobean Altar was 'camouflaged' by a large 'frontal' of mouldy red material hung in front of it on a long framework; the fine old Renatus Harris organ[17] was a complete ruin, the keys being piled up anyhow and the pipes leaning at all sorts of angles: a thick layer of dust covered everything from floor to ceiling. The marvellous transformation that has been effected, converting this 'barn' into one of the most lovely churches in London, can only be realised by those who knew St Sepulchre's as it was before 1929.

The formal opening and Dedication of the College took place on 3rd July 1929, and the Archbishop of Canterbury [Cosmo Gordon Lang], as President of the SECM, himself officiated. A large number of guests had been invited and about 600 attended. The ceremony was most impressive and the perfect weather and beauty of the grounds formed a wonderful background for it. In addition to the College choir there were contingents of men and boys from Westminster Abbey, Rochester Cathedral, and the Westminster Abbey Special Choir. These, together with several Doctors of Music in their robes and the Clergy and Archbishop

---

17 See Appendix E.

with his attendants, formed an imposing procession, which first of all assembled in the courtyard outside the main entrance to the College. As the Archbishop approached, the hymn "Christ is our corner-stone" was sung, and the Archbishop performed the ceremony of Dedication. The procession then moved to the Hostel singing psalms, and after the Blessing of the Hostel, moved through the Chapel to the lower terrace, where a short service was held. The Archbishop addressed the people and declared the College open, saying that the Blessing he had pronounced that day on the place and on the work to be undertaken therein might be held to be the blessing of the Church. The anthem was Stanford's *Glorious and powerful God* and the service concluded with Gibbons' *Te Deum in F*. After the service the Archbishop dedicated the memorial tablet in the Chapel to The Lady Mary Trefusis[18] (who was also commemorated by a scholarship founded in her name) and unveiled the memorial in the Choir school to the Rev Harold Hall Wright.

Almost immediately after the Dedication of the College came a Festival of Cathedral Choirs[19] held under the conductorship of Dr Bullock at Westminster Abbey. Sixteen Cathedral and Collegiate choirs took part in this magnificent service and the collection made a valuable contribution to the funds of the SECM.

At the end of the summer term came the first Summer School to be held at the College, arranged by the Church Music Society: and this (but under the auspices of the SECM) became an annual event. Its main purpose was to gather people interested in church music for a few days' social intercourse, interspersed with lectures and discussions: the Chapel, in which every type of service was as far as possible represented, has always been regarded as the centre of the work.

During the holidays the choirboys enjoyed the first of their annual "Singing-scouting" tours[20], visiting various places (mostly villages) in the west country, camping in a schoolroom or 'any old place', doing scout-work, during the day and singing a 'model' service each evening in the church. These tours, lasting a week or ten days, were continued for several years until more urgent calls compelled their abandonment.

It is only fair to say how much of the success of the College and the outside work of the SECM has been due to the unfailing response of the choristers to all demands made on them, and to their keenness and efficiency.

Nicholson's Summer Holiday in 1929

In the summer of 1929 I had another little holiday of a rather unusual kind, this time with my brother Archie. Being fond of places off the beaten track we first made our way to the island of Gottland in the Baltic, staying at Wisby where there are the ruins of I forget how many ancient Cathedrals. We found the island most attractive and after exploring it we made our

---

18 See Chapter V: Footnote 26.
19 These festivals were begun by SHN in 1924. See p 117.
20 For further information about these tours and photographs see *SNCSN*.

way across Sweden and Denmark by means of local trains and small lake and river steamers to Schleswig and eventually to Hamburg. There we embarked on a liner bound for Southampton arriving late at night. My brother had to return home but I wanted to go on to France. It was too late to land in the ordinary way, but I persuaded the authorities to smuggle me off the ship somehow and took a taxi to the cross-channel quay, only to see the lights of the Havre steamer disappearing in the distance. However there was still time to catch the Channel Island boat, so I thought I might as well go there and pick up another for France. All went well till we ran into a fog between Guernsey and Jersey and arrived to see the St Malo boat just going out of the harbour: - and there was nothing else for two days! However, I heard rumours of a motor-boat that ran to Cartaret, and that it was a possible trip for a good sailor; so I thought I might as well risk it. I found a sort of life-boat on which I and two or three other venturous people seated ourselves. There was no cabin and we were tucked in beneath large tarpaulin sheets, up to the neck. The sea was extremely rough and I never experienced a worse two hours. Still I survived without 'evacuation' and since then the sea has no terrors for me! I put up at a charming little Café at Cartaret, where Madame provided me with an excellent meal and bed, called me at 4 the next morning and only charged me 2/6 [two Shillings and sixpence]; and from there I made my way, with numerous changes, to Flers to meet Harry Barnes who had been staying with Abbé Busson to improve his French. Our going home was more normal.

I remember how much amused Bishop Frere was when he visited Flers a little later on, to hear of the visit and doings of "Aribans", [Harry Barnes!] and it was some time before he could imagine who this mysterious visitor had been.

At home there was plenty of activity. The affiliated choirs were steadily growing in numbers and an organization of area and local representatives had been created and a "Guild of St Nicolas" was established to deal with the religious and social sides of choir work.

In 1930 two important events happened. A property known as 'Hydeswood', adjacent to the original 'Buller's Wood', came into the market and after much consideration it was decided to acquire it and to accommodate the Choristers and their Master together with the Warden in the house, using the Lodge for a sanatorium. The new buildings provided a welcome addition to the space available in the College which had become so restricted as to be almost unworkable. At the same time an outlying portion of the original property was sold.

The first *Festival of English Church Music* 1930

The other event was connected with external work and happened thus. One day the Editor of the *Daily Mail* rang me up and asked me to call and see him. He told me that the paper had been following the progress of the SECM with much interest and would like to do some big thing to help us, asking for suggestions. These resulted in a most generous offer to finance a big Festival of English Church Music to be sung by representatives of affiliated choirs in the Albert Hall, the *Daily Mail* undertaking the whole cost of transport and music and providing accommodation at hotels for those who could not return home the same night. Such a wonderful and unexpected offer of help gave the SECM exactly the impetus it needed, and for which it can never cease to be grateful.

Needless to say a very large number of choirs wished to avail themselves of this opportunity of a visit to London to take part in such an inspiring gathering, and the representatives from each choir had to be limited in most cases to six. Actually over 180 choirs were represented amongst the 1000 singers and they came from as far away as Scotland, Wales and Cornwall. The Festival took the form of Evensong with additional anthems, all the choirs attending in surplices and cassocks and producing a striking and unaccustomed effect in the Albert Hall. Our idea, however, was not merely to give a grand performance of Church music but to try to create the atmosphere of a regular religious service ordered on proper liturgical lines, and at the same time to try and demonstrate the methods we were constantly advocating.

The question of the psalms was one of obvious difficulty. 'Speech-rhythm', as it is called, — that is the enunciation of the words with natural emphasis and a complete freedom from the shackles of 'strict time' — had always been a prominent feature of SECM propaganda. But the method had not by this time become at all general and it seemed a risky business to attempt it with a miscellaneous collection of 1000 singers and only one full combined rehearsal.

However the risk was taken and, to meet the needs of all, one psalm was sung to an Anglican chant and one to plainsong. In order to help choirs in their preparation gramophone records had been prepared beforehand by the College choir to act as a guide to what was wanted. As to the results I quote from the *Musical Times*:

> The singing of the psalms proved that Anglican chanting need not be stiff and that plainsong can be very far from free. No doubt the bulk of the choir were new to plainsong, — anyway the Anglican chanting was far better. In such phrases as "To/ keep thee in/ all thy/ ways", for example, the ease with which the vast choir stepped lightly from 'to' to 'keep' (instead of the conventional 'toooooo') was as surprising as it was delightful. .....The chanting was one of the best features of the Festival, and no better augury for the success of the present forward movement can be desired than the fact that such pains had been spent, and spent successfully, on 'mere' chanting.

Looking back on the anxiety with which I faced the prospect of having to pilot this big choir through the unaccustomed 'speech-rhythm', I am amazed to think how simple it has since become, and how little trouble it now is to get unanimity as well as natural emphasis from gatherings of combined choirs not only on great occasions but even when the music is of the simplest and the choirs the least expert. I cannot help feeling that if the SECM has done no more than help to effect the revolution in chanting that has characterised the ten years of its existence, its work has not been in vain.

Origins of *The Parish Psalter*

The pointing always used by the SECM in its publications is that of *The Parish Psalter*, and a few words as to the origin of that book may be appropriate at this point. The idea of 'speech-rhythm' chanting originated (at any rate in its modern form) with the late Dr Robert Bridges[21]: at all events it was he who formulated the main principles on which so many others have built. Combining in himself the qualities of a most eminent man of letters with those of a keen musician, he was exceptionally well equipped to deal with the problem: and he laid it down as a principle that, whatever kind of musical setting was employed for the Psalter it must be so elastic as not to obscure the natural rhythm or emphasis of its matchless language. The music, in short, must be adapted to fit the words, and the words not distorted to fit the music.

A large committee had been formed to produce a psalter pointed on these lines, and I well remember its meetings: they generally ended with several people simultaneously singing certain verses to their favourite pointing at the tops of their voices, when the meetings would break up in confusion: I do not think that the committee ever got beyond the end of the psalms for the first evening of the month! So it was eventually dissolved and a few of us were left to bring out *The Psalter Newly Pointed*[22], on the lines which had been generally agreed. But the work had been long delayed and other psalters had begun to appear in the field.

At The Abbey we were using a very 'stiff' old book and the Precentor and I were anxious to make a change. We tried one or two of the new psalters but found that none of them provided exactly what we wanted, and considered that simplicity of marking would produce better and more natural results than a multiplicity of signs. We also realised that there is in many cases no 'best pointing' for a particular verse, so much depending upon the particular chant to which it is sung; and we did not want to make big changes in our Abbey chants. So we hit on the expedient of enlisting the interest and help of the choir, and through the generosity of the Lay Vicars in attending a short practice before service each day for a month, armed with pencils with which to make alterations in the existing books, we gradually made our own new pointing by modifying the old, naturally only introducing changes when we felt that they were a real improvement. The great advantage of this plan was that we made no important changes without testing the effect with the particular chant to be used: we would often try one verse in several different ways before deciding which 'sang best'.

It was as a result of this practical experimenting that *The Parish Psalter*, with its companion *St Nicolas Chant Book* (largely based on the old Abbey selection) was produced during the

---

[21] Robert Bridges (1844-1930), a medical doctor, was a poet and hymn writer, becoming Poet Laureate in 1913 until his death. He moved to Yattendon near Newbury in 1896. There he published the *Yattendon Psalter* (and a book of chants to go with it) in 1897 and the *Yattendon Hymnal* 1899.

[22] Published 1925 and reprinted 1956.

period between my leaving the Abbey and the opening of the College. The SECM has never claimed that *The Parish Psalter* is better than any other: but at least it is simple to understand and, when thoughtfully used, can produce satisfactory results: and I think its success is the result of its being based on the experimental work of an actual choir rather than the deliberations of a committee.

Choir Festivals at the Crystal Palace[23]

The success of the first big Festival was so great and the experience for the choir so thrilling, that there was immediately a clamorous questioning "When will the next one be?" "Never again on the same lines", was my answer: for though the generosity of the *Daily Mail* had given the whole movement an enormous impetus, it was not healthy that SECM choirs should be beholden to any outside body (even assuming that they would have repeated their kindness) for something which they ought to be doing for themselves. But I told the choirs that if they would save funds to meet their own expenses, I would try to arrange another festival in three years' time.

Crystal Palace Exterior in 1854

---

23 The Crystal Palace was a cast-iron and plate-glass building originally erected in Hyde Park to house the Great Exhibition of 1851. More than 14,000 exhibitors from around the world gathered in the Palace's 990,000 square feet (92,000 m2) of exhibition space to display examples of the latest technology developed in the Industrial Revolution. Designed by Sir Joseph Paxton, the Great Exhibition building was 1,851 feet (564 m) long, with an interior height of 128 feet (39 m). Because of the recent invention of the cast plate glass method in 1848, which allowed for large sheets of cheap but strong glass, it was at the time the largest amount of glass ever seen in a building and astonished visitors with its clear walls and ceilings that did not require interior lights, thus a "Crystal Palace". After the exhibition, the building was rebuilt in an enlarged form on Penge Common next to Sydenham Hill, an affluent South London suburb full of large villas. It stood there

Crystal Palace Festival Rehearsal 1933

The response was so ready that the numbers that wished to come far exceeded the space available in the Albert Hall, and the outcome of this enthusiasm has been the triennial Festivals of English Church Music with 4000 voices at the Crystal Palace in 1933 and 1936; and when the Palace was no longer available owing to the disastrous fire just after the 1936 Festival[24], at the Albert Hall in 1939, preceded by a series of Regional Festivals at different Cathedrals. The festivals at the Crystal Palace were unique and it is never likely that such a setting will be available again, unless the Palace should ever be rebuilt on its former scale. The long processions of surpliced singers converging from five different points on to the orchestra, singing hymns without accompaniment in alternating sections, provided a most striking piece of pageantry as well as an unusually beautiful musical effect, and the acoustics of the great central transept proved to be so excellent that it was possible to get complete unanimity from the huge chorus massed on the only orchestra that would contain them. Indeed so unanimous was the singing that it is possible easily to follow the words in the gramophone records which were taken during the 1933 festival.

---

from 1854 until its destruction by fire in 1936. (Information from Wikipedia.)

24   On the night of 30th November 1936.

I must confess that I was somewhat alarmed at the prospect of conducting this vast choir for the first time, and I could not come across anyone who could tell me what the experience would be like. But owing to the wonderful planning of the orchestra and the way the singers knew their work (so that books were hardly needed), it was as easy as conducting an ordinary choral society. One felt the whole time that they were 'at the end of one's stick'[25]. I think that of all the varied musical experiences of my life I have enjoyed conducting those two great festivals more than any, especially that of 1936 when I no longer felt the same anxiety as on the first occasion. But in speaking of these later festivals I am anticipating, for many other important events had been happening in the meantime.

In 1930 the SECM became incorporated as "A Company limited by guarantee and not having a share capital". I have never been quite sure what this meant, but in the opinion of those qualified to judge it was a great step towards solidarity. A regular Council was appointed and Articles of Association drawn up, and in the following year Sir Arthur Somervell became the first Chairman.

In 1931 the quarterly magazine *English Church Music* made its appearance, taking the place of a less ambitious *News-sheet*. The first of a series of *Choir Books* was also issued, being made possible by the ready co-operation of various music publishers: the object was to help affiliated choirs to build up a library of first-rate music suitable to their own needs, at a very low price. *Choir Book No. 1* has been followed by five others.

In the same year the College staff was strengthened by the addition of the Rev Dr C S Phillips[26] as Resident Chaplain and Mr (now Dr) C H Phillips[27] as Senior Tutor. On St Nicolas Day the beautiful new organ presented for the Chapel by Mrs Man Stuart[28], in memory of her husband[29], was dedicated by the

Arthur Harrison (1868-1936) Organ Builder

---

25 Quite a contrast to the 'taking a jelly-fish out for a walk on an elastic lead" comment at the 1930 Festival.
26 Rev Charles Stanley Phillips (1883-1949) studied at King's College, Cambridge, and was ordained priest in 1908. A Fellow of Selwyn College, Cambridge, he served as a priest in Radley, Halifax, Buckingham, and was then Rector of All Saints' Milton near Cambridge from 1927 before appointment as Resident Chaplain to St Nicolas College in 1931. He became Sub-Warden in 1933 and resigned at Easter 1939. Following College closure he was Vicar of Stalisfield from 1941 and of Sturry in Kent from 1947. Author of *Hymnody Past and Present* 1937, he worked with Nicholson on *Hymns A&M (Revised)*, but, like Nicholson, he did not live to see its publication. There is a photograph of him in Chapter V p 130.
27 Dr Charles Henry Phillips (d 1947) studied at the College of St Nicolas and then served as a tutor, senior tutor (from 1934) and briefly in 1939 as Sub-Warden in succession to Dr C S Phillips. In 1936 he was appointed Organist and Choirmaster to St Peter's, Eaton Square, in London. He was awarded his D Mus from Durham University in 1939. He went on to King's School, Canterbury, as music master and subsequently taught at Merchant Taylor's School (1944) and Glasgow University from 1945 until his premature death. He was editor of *English Church Music* from 1938 to 1940 and again from 1943 to 1947. His popular book *The Singing Church* (1945, Faber, London, reprinted many times) was the end result of lectures given at the College of St Nicolas.
28 Mrs Man Stuart (1857-1955), a longstanding benefactress of the *SECM* and *RSCM*, had known Sydney Nicholson (and his brothers) from childhood and was a close friend of his mother Lady Nicholson.
29 Col John Alexander Man Stuart (1841-1908).

Bishop of Rochester. This lovely little instrument[30] was built by Messrs Harrison and Harrison and every pipe was finished in the Chapel by Mr Arthur Harrison himself.

All the while the work [of the SECM] was expanding both within the College and outside; for the greater convenience of visitors the office of the SECM was moved from the College to London in 1933 and thus brought into closer relations with the S P C K in whose building it became domiciled.

The College was quietly growing. The influx of new students was somewhat disappointing at first, but gradually increased: 'short courses' for choirmasters, clergy, ordination candidates and others were found to meet a real need, especially those for choirboys from affiliated churches. Visitors from every part of the country and from all parts of the world found their way to the College in a fairly constant stream, so that its work as the centre of SECM activities became more and more valuable as time went on and its influence gradually spread outside its own walls.

Domestic upheavals were at first only too common, but at last a happy solution was found with a male staff of Steward and Cook, assisted by a number of houseboys, for whom the essential qualification – surely unique – was that they must have been choirboys in some affiliated church. Thus everyone in the College, whatever form his work took, came to feel that he had an important share in making it fulfil the purpose with which it had been founded.

Not only was activity increasing at home but choirs were becoming affiliated in distant parts of the world. Such a development had never been contemplated when the SECM was started, or some other less insular title might have been chosen: — for the word 'English' is not always very acceptable outside our own borders and even the Scottish Episcopal Church found a little difficulty over the title though they have always backed the work of the SECM whole-heartedly. However incorporation had been effected and it was too late to change.

Several requests had come that I should make an extended tour amongst the affiliated choirs overseas, and at last it seemed possible to get away for six months. So I left home at the end of July 1934, visited Australia, New Zealand, and Canada, spending also a short time in the United States, and returned home early the next year.

This was a most wonderful experience but a description of the long round of visits to choirs, choral festivals, lectures and broadcast talks would be tedious. It is not easy to give general impressions in a few words but it was most interesting to compare the state of Church music in the Dominions with that at home.

---

30   For the specification, photographs and description of this organ, see *SNCSN*.

One great difference I found to be in the constitution of the choirs. It is not generally 'the fashion' outside the United Kingdom for boys to sing in choirs, though there are a number of churches in the larger places which employ them. But on the whole it is considered 'sissy', — in other words a girl's job. Consequently there is little tradition behind it. Yet many of the boys, particularly in Australia, have excellent voices and where they are well trained produce fine results: such is the case in the Cathedrals at Adelaide, Melbourne (where a daily full choral service is maintained) and Sydney.

(Right) Nicholson seems to have taken the *SECM* Banner with him on this trip. Here it is in Adelaide at a choir festival in 1934. The RSCM still has this original banner, albeit in need of considerable restoration work.

(Left) Sydney Cathedral Choristers 1934

But the music in ordinary parish churches is mainly in the hands of large mixed choirs of ladies and gentlemen. Almost all the women are robed in cassock, surplice and mortar board; the vestry (which not infrequently also serves as a 'beauty parlour') is, if possible, at the west end of the church, so that there may always be a 'Processional' and 'Recessional'; quantity is evidently reckoned as of more importance than quality in the singing and the choir often seems to outnumber the congregation. The organs are generally too large for the churches and the common desire is that they should be played as loudly as possible: I heard of the case of a man who had been appointed to a church in Australia where one of these organs had recently been installed: he liked to play softly sometimes; but the church officers objected and finally he was told that they had spent a great deal of money on the organ and that they expected to hear it: if he couldn't make more sound come out of it they would have to find someone else who could! I am not sure if this is the same church as had a Carillon stop fitted to its organ: feeling that they were not getting their money's worth by its occasional use, the Church officers instructed the organist that the 'bells' were to be used in his voluntary on every Sunday till further notice! But of course such conditions were by no means general, and in many churches I found excellent work going on and people were very ready to listen to ideas, some of which were quite new to them. So many choirs became affiliated that, before I left Australia, I was able to advise the formation of an Australian Branch of the SECM, and was asked by the General Synod to make recommendations as to their future policy, on SECM lines in the matter of their music.

SHN about to receive his Honorary MA in the Great Hall of Sydney University on 25th Sept 1934. Professor F A Todd (left), Dean of the Arts Faculty, outlines Nicholson's achievements to Sir William Portus Cullen KCMG (right), University Chancellor. Behind SHN is his father's portrait and behind the Chancellor is a large French tapestry given to the University by Sir Charles and which still hangs there today.

From a personal point of view the high light of my time in Australia was my visit to Sydney. It was of course deeply interesting to visit my father's various homes and to see for myself the University of which I had heard so much, with the Museum that bears his name — a name held in the highest honour as recalling one of the great pioneers of education. It was a moving experience for me when I was given an MA degree in the Great Hall which my father had seen built, standing beneath his portrait while the honour was conferred upon me by his successor as Chancellor.

In New Zealand the absence of choirboys was even more noticeable than in Australia, though in the Cathedral of Christ Church I was delighted to find a regular endowed choir with a daily choral Evensong sung in the best English tradition.

Christ Church Cathedral Choristers in 1934. The man on the left, with the outward appearance of a workman, is Dr J C Bradshaw[31], the eminent cathedral organist.

To speak of the absence of choirboys is perhaps hardly accurate, unless one places the emphasis on the first syllable of their title, for there generally are some boys in surplices though there seems little idea that it might be desirable for them to sing. On my last Sunday I went to a large town church and in the vestry I found perhaps twenty very smartly dressed boys, some of them in scarlet cassocks, being titivated by the "choir-mother", who seems to be a great institution in the Antipodes. Being rather tired of the usual type of choir, I looked forward with pleasure to something out of the ordinary, especially as the boys looked promising. However they were soon merged with the usual large number of women and men, who proceeded into the chancel, of course singing the inevitable hymn: but these cherubic boys, in spite of all their lovely clothes, not only took no part in the singing but actually were not even provided with books or music of any kind, and during the anthem remained seated in complete boredom! When I asked what was the idea I was told that 'of course the boys were purely ornamental'. Ornamental choirboys! What a mockery! I am afraid I must have given some offence in my last broadcast from the Southern hemisphere, just after this

---

31 John Christopher Bradshaw (1876-1950) studied at Victoria College in Manchester and was organist of All Saints' in Scarborough and assistant organist of Manchester Cathedral (before Nicholson's time) prior to moving to New Zealand. He graduated with the degree of Mus D at the age of 25 and was said at that time to be the youngest doctorate in music in the British Empire. He served at Christ Church Cathedral for many years, was city organist from 1908 to 1917 and also taught at Christ Church university.

experience, when I finished my remarks on Church music in the Dominion with the words "You don't deserve to have good choirs if you treat your choirboys as no better than animated clothes-pegs!"

In Canada I found that the seed sown at the time of the visit of the Westminster–Windsor choir had borne fruit. Many more boys' choirs had come into being and much improvement in the general ordering of services had been effected. Certain little episodes stick in one's mind. I think of a wintry day in one of the big prairie towns with the temperature about 30 degrees below zero, and how a set of choirboys in their fur caps and long snow boots came to meet me at their church. They wanted to sing to me but they could not find the key of their music cupboard; so it seemed hopeless till I asked them if they could do anything by heart. Yes, they thought they could manage "Let the bright seraphim"; so we got the organ going and together gave a terrific performance from memory! In Toronto, where on my first visit I was told that there were only three boy-choirs, I spent a happy day with representatives from over 30 churches who assembled for a 'Choirboys' School and Festival'.

My visit to the USA was very short, but I got my first glimpse of New York and spent Christmas with the choristers of the noble Cathedral of St John the Divine, at their delightful choir-school; I also "enjoyed" one or two motor drives on ice-bound roads at 65 miles an hour; and I experienced a Chicago blizzard.

Everywhere during my long journey I met with the most wonderful kindness and hospitality, and it seemed as if people were very much interested in what I had to tell them. There was no sort of opposition or resentment, so far as I could see, at an Englishman coming more or less as a critic, and indeed I was rather humiliated to find the almost legendary excellence attributed to English choirs. When people expatiated on the subject I felt inclined to say "wait till you come home and I will show you a thing or two!"

On the whole I thought the signs were very hopeful: I sensed a growing discontent with what was unworthy and a definite desire for something better. The difficulties are often very great, but there is abundant enthusiasm especially among the younger organists and members of choirs; and the bishops and clergy are, as a rule, anxious to encourage this spirit. On a journey like this, being brought into contact with all kinds of people and institutions, one cannot fail to learn much: indeed I feel, looking back on it all, that I learned a great deal more than I was able to teach.

- I learnt to respect the wonderful devotion of those who are often working in distant places under almost unimaginable difficulties with hardly any help or encouragement.
- I learnt that there are other ways of looking at many problems which we are apt to consider as settled at home.
- I realised as never before the value of an established church when reform is contemplated and the parson is not financially dependent on his congregation.

- I realised as never before the almost frightening readiness to look to England as a model for all that is best in the Church and its music.

During my long journeys by sea and rail I whiled away the time by writing an opera for boys, *The Children of the Chapel*, which was produced by the St Nicolas choristers the following summer.

On my return home Dr Ernest Bullock, who had been keeping an eye on the work of the College during my absence, was appointed Director of Musical Studies, thus enabling me to be more free to attend to the growing demands for work among the choirs. An important step was also taken in the nomination of several eminent musicians as Fellows of the College, and by The Archbishop of Canterbury in inaugurating his Diploma in Church Music.

In May 1937 came the Coronation of Their Majesties King George VI and Queen Elizabeth. Six of the St Nicolas choristers were invited to sing in the choir, and we were glad to entertain at the College the four boys who had been chosen to represent the two Metropolitical Cathedrals during the previous weeks of rehearsal. I was enabled[32] to take a humble share in this wonderful ceremony by acting as Hon Secretary of the Coronation Choir, and in this capacity was responsible for its organization. It would be useless for me to attempt to describe the grandeur of the occasion, — by far the most magnificent of the many functions I have been privileged to attend.

In December 1937 was celebrated the tenth anniversary of the foundation of the SECM and the Archbishop conferred the first ACDCM diplomas in Lambeth Chapel.

The ACDCM

At the 62nd meeting of the Council of the SECM in February 1936 there was discussion about a diploma or certificate to be awarded "after a test of musical efficiency and liturgical knowledge" to those who completed courses at the College of St Nicolas. It was decided to consult the President (the Archbishop of Canterbury, Cosmo Lang). Archbishop Lang, after consultation with the Royal College of Organists and his own advisors, reported that he would like to make it the *Archbishop of Canterbury's Diploma in Church Music*. By the summer of 1936 the RCO and SECM had approved the musical syllabus and testing arrangements and Lambeth Palace had finalised the liturgical syllabus and assessment procedure.

---

32 The Abbey Precentor, Cyril Armitage (1900-1966) was to be choir secretary but was taken ill. Nicholson was asked to replace him and his plans for the 1937 Coronation were so successful that they were committed to paper and used as the basis for planning the 1953 Coronation Choir.

The *ACDCM (continued)*

The Archbishop issued a press-release on 4th June 1936:

<u>The Archbishop's Diploma in Church Music</u>

In order to emphasise the importance of music in the life and worship of the Church, the Archbishop of Canterbury has decided to institute a diploma in Church Music. Candidates will be required to show a knowledge of all branches of church music and of liturgical subjects, and a necessary preliminary is that they should be Fellows of the Royal College of Organists and have taken the RCO diploma in choir training. The examination will be conducted by the School of English Church Music. Particulars may be obtained from the Secretary, College of St Nicolas, Chislehurst, Kent. The requirements to enter the examination were stringent – the candidate had to be an FRCO holding the ChM (Choirmaster) diploma. The following September (1937) it was reported that seven Candidates had entered for the examination.

At this first examination in October 1937 the examiners were Dr William Harris for the SECM, Sir Ivor Atkins for the RCO and the Rev Canon J H Crawley for Lambeth Palace. One candidate failed and one did not attend – (Sir) Sydney Campbell, whose subsequent career did not appear to have been held back by not achieving this diploma! The five who passed were Gerald Hocken Knight, Leslie Alfred Lickfold, Charles Henry Phillips, Richard Francis Cutbush and Arthur Morgan Stacey[33]. They received their diplomas from the Archbishop at a special service in Lambeth Palace Chapel on St Nicolas Day (6th December) 1937.

The following year a formal constitution for the diploma was agreed by all three parties and it was requested of the Archbishop that the ACDCM be permanently established. In 1938 there were three entrants all who passed – John Eric Hunt (blind), Frederick Vernon Curtis and Philip Benjamin Tomblings.

Examinations were suspended during WWII but further examinations were then held in 1947[34]-49, 1951-53, 1956-76 and 1978-1990. The post-war regulations were amended to specify that candidates would be accepted from "any church which is a member of the World Council of Churches and to members of the Roman Catholic Church." The initial high pass rate was not maintained and notably, in 1967, only one candidate out of eight passed. It was possible to pass the three sections of the exam on separate occasions and so there were many 're-sits'. In total, 158 individual examinations were held between 1936 and 1990. 72 passed, 76 failed and there were 52 're-sits' – indeed one candidate sat on 10 occasions without success.

There have been no further candidates since 1990.

---

33 Biographical information about these musicians can be found in *SNCSN*.
34 From this time 'ACDCM' was shortened to 'ADCM'.

In May 1938 I again visited Canada and the USA. to try and consolidate some of the work that had been set in motion during my previous visit. I had a most pleasant time, confining most of my visits to 'boy-choirs' and taking part in a delightful American choirboys' camp on an island in Lake Erie. There we celebrated 'Independence Day' in a manner that was surely unique, by inviting a party of Canadian choirboys from the other side of the Lake to spend the day with us and join us in singing Evensong.

Choir Festival in Toronto 25th May 1938. Nicholson is seated immediately to the far side of the conductor's rostrum.

During my absence from home my name appeared among the King's Birthday Honours[35] as the recipient of a Knighthood. This meant far more to me than any personal honour, for it was clearly a recognition of the importance of Church music in the life of the nation.

---

35 Nicholson was participating in a Choirboys' Camp at Put-in-Bay, Ohio, when he received (by telegram from the British Embassy in Montréal) the news of his appointment as 'Knight Bachelor'. On his return from Canada he was prevented from receiving the Knighthood directly from the King by some prior engagement. It is clear in a letter from Buckingham Palace that if one cannot attend at the "King's pleasure" then one does not get another chance and so he received the award from an official at a later date.

> **G**EORGE THE SIXTH BY THE GRACE OF GOD OF GREAT BRITAIN IRELAND AND THE BRITISH DOMINIONS BEYOND THE SEAS KING DEFENDER OF THE FAITH To all to whom these Presents shall come Greeting Know Ye that We of Our especial grace certain knowledge and mere motion have given and granted and by these Presents do give and grant unto Our trusty and well-beloved SYDNEY HUGO NICHOLSON Esquire Member of the Fourth Class of Our Royal Victorian Order Doctor of Music Fellow of the Royal College of Organists the degree title honour and dignity of a KNIGHT BACHELOR together with all rights precedences privileges and advantages to the same degree title honour and dignity belonging or appertaining In Witness whereof We have caused these Our Letters to be made Patent Witness Ourself at Westminster the thirtieth day of July in the second year of Our Reign.
>
> By Warrant under The King's Sign Manual
>
> Schuster

Nicholson is somewhat modest in his memoirs by making little reference to his various honours. He does briefly mention the Lambeth D Mus (in Chapter V), the MA conferred on him in 1934 by Sydney University (earlier in this chapter) and also the knighthood but not his:

FRCO In Jan 1914 the Royal College of Organists elected him a Fellow (without examination).

MVO Member (Fourth Class) of the Royal Victorian Order 1925, almost certainly conferred in gratitude for the music arrangements he made for the two Royal weddings. The appointment letter is on the following page. Most major honours require parliament's consent, and so Queen Victoria established the Royal Victorian Order in 1896 as a junior and personal order of knighthood that allows the Sovereign to bestow direct honours for personal services. The first and second classes of the RVO were knighthoods, the third (Commander) and fourth (Member) were not.

ARAM An Honorary Associateship of the RAM was conferred on Nicholson in March 1928.

♛

BUCKINGHAM PALACE

23rd.December, 1925.

Sir,

I am commanded by the King to inform you that His Majesty has been pleased to announce his intention of appointing you a Member of the Fourth Class of the Royal Victorian Order on the occasion of the New Year.

I shall feel obliged if you will kindly complete and return the enclosed Form at your earliest convenience.

I am,

Sir,

Your obedient Servant,

F. Ponsonby

Secretary of the Royal Victorian Order.

S.H.Nicholson Esq.

Nicholson's invitation to join the Royal Victorian Order in 1925. Note that the Palace stationary has a black border. This indicates that the Court was currently in mourning – in this case for Queen Alexandra, for whose funeral SHN had directed the music a few weeks beforehand.

The Insignia of the Royal Victorian Order (Fourth Class) worn by Nicholson.

As on my previous journey I managed to write another opera, this time not for boys but for men. The writing of these operas (all of them continuous music) has been a great amusement and has passed the time for me far more pleasantly than in deck games or cocktail parties. It is good fun to be one's own librettist, as the attractiveness of tunes so much depends upon the metre and rhythm of the words, and if one is free in both directions one can think of them together. The first of these efforts was *The Boy Bishop*, written for The Abbey boys; [then came] *The Children of the Chapel* written for the St Nicolas boys, [which] deals with the Chapel Royal choir at the time of the Restoration of Charles II, the characters including Captain Cooke[36] and Mr [Samuel] Pepys, with [John] Blow and [Henry] Purcell and their contemporaries[37] as choristers. This was written during my journey round the world and each Act was completed without access to a piano. It is dangerous on board ship to let people find out that one can play at all, and it is most amusing to have to wait till a large chunk of manuscript is completed before hearing a note of it. Another effort was *Passionate Peter*, written for the St Nicolas students, which is about Pirates and Clergymen and Boy Scouts. This has been performed several times by old Choristers from The Abbey, St Paul's and The Temple, and for them also was written (during my last journey) *The Guggenheimer Emerald*. This, I think, must be unique as being the only Detective-opera in existence[38].

---

36 Henry Cooke, a former Chapel Royal chorister during the reign of Charles I, had been a captain in the Royalist army during the Civil War. He was Master of the Children of the Chapel Royal from 1660 until his death in 1672. He was also Composer to the King from 1664.

37 The Chapel Royal choristers at the time of the Restoration in 1660 under 'Captain' Cooke also included Pelham Humphrey, William Turner, Thomas Tudway and Michael Wise. Henry Purcell arrived a few years later.

38 Probably true at the time, but not today.

On my return from America I found everything in a very flourishing condition. The College was now full and several extremely gifted students were among its resident members. Short courses which had been announced were all filled and the demand for additional ones during term time had become so great that it was decided to increase the accommodation by 12 rooms. The choir had reached a higher standard than ever before, and, I am thankful to say were able to produce a splendid series of gramophone records as a permanent example of their work. So the tenth anniversary of the Dedication of the College in July 1939 was in every sense a real festival, for it seemed that at last the College was on its feet and that a long vista of years of useful work was opening out, while the SECM had so expanded that the affiliated choirs numbered over 1500. The Archbishop again visited the College and saw the progress that had been made since he had declared it open ten years before: the Abbey choir joined with that of the College in rendering the music of a memorable service: and the Processional Cross was carried (actually on his 20th birthday) by our first chorister, Ian Dolan[39]. After term was over a very happy Summer Camp for Church Singers was held at which sixty men and boys enjoyed a week's singing: thoughts of war seemed very remote and few could have imagined that this would prove to be the last activity at the College that they had come to love so well, for a considerable period.

Then, during the holidays, came the tragic events of the beginning of September. It was decided that the provisional decision of the Council must be put into operation at once and that the College must be closed for the duration of the war.

It was obvious that as the large majority of the students, actual or potential, were of military age, very few would be available as residents, while the practicability of arranging Special Courses in war-time seemed more than doubtful. To have gone on incurring heavy and probably increasing expense in such circumstances would have been a suicidal policy, so it was determined to act promptly and to take immediate steps to economize resources in the hope of being able to re-open on the conclusion of hostilities. With a view to effecting further economy the SECM Office was once more removed from London to the College Sanatorium: an Air Warden's post was established in the basement of the College in the former Vestry. The Students and Staff were dispersed and seven of the Choristers were accepted by the Dean and Chapter of Canterbury Cathedral as members of their Cathedral Choir and Choir-school. And thus the first chapter in the history of the College was closed. It was decided that the work of the SECM amongst the choirs must not be allowed to languish, but must be adapted to meet their altered needs at a time when they would want all the help that could be given to them.

---

[39] Ian Dolan also carried the processional cross at the Crystal Palace Festival Service in 1936. For biographical information and photographs see *SNCSN*.

As to the future, who can say? But, looking back on the past, one cannot but feel thankful that we were rash enough to embark on the College. When the idea was first mooted it was received with kindly sympathy, but with a good deal of misgiving: some regarded it as no more than the dream of an idealist, others as a crazy venture which could never succeed. At least it has proved to be neither the one or the other; and many of those who at first "shook their heads" have become amongst its most active supporters.

It has been a costly venture, and, but for the help of *Hymns Ancient and Modern*, it could never have been maintained, for such an institution, designed to provide help for those who are usually not greatly blessed with worldly goods, could never be 'made to pay' or even to cover the costs of its maintenance. Yet it may safely be said that the College has amply justified its foundation. The people who have been brought directly under its influence, numbering some thousands and drawn from all kinds of churches in all parts of the world, have almost all carried away some measure of inspiration from their contact with its daily life and work and, above all, from its Chapel services.

It was indeed grievous to have to cry 'Halt'. And yet it may be that this enforced interruption of the work of the College will not in the end prove the disaster that it might appear. In embarking on a new venture of this magnitude the process of discovering what will work and what will not work is bound to result in some disappointments as well as encouragements. Mistakes are sure to be made, even if the ultimate balance is largely on the side of success. But when an institution is in active operation and has to carry on from day to day and from term to term, it is not always easy to make changes or to foresee their practical effect if made. So it may well be that a period in which the work of the College during the ten years of its existence can be viewed as a whole, as it were in perspective, will enable it, when the time comes for re-opening, to be re-constituted on better lines than would otherwise have been possible.

The next chapter in its history has still to be written[40] but whatever the future may have in store, every one of those who have in their several ways contributed to make the College what it has been during its first decade may feel thankful that they have had a share in "something accomplished"; but equally they will refuse to regard their work as "something done", for they all look forward with confidence to the time when it will be possible to build something even better upon the foundations that have been so "well and truly laid".

---

40 But see the following chapter for his own thoughts. For the wartime and immediate post-war period in the life of the *SECM* see Chapter VIII and *SNCSN*.

Chapter VII

> At a later (unknown) date, Sir Sydney Nicholson typed a further essay about the future of church music. He may have used this as a lecture for it was discovered separate from the main autobiography and filed amongst his lectures. He did, however, begin this typescript with 'Musings of a Musician CHAPTER VII'. Unlike the other chapters, it is not strictly autobiographical, except in the sense that it draws upon his immense experience of the diversity of church music in the UK. There has probably been no person before or since (even in the latter days of RSCM Commissioners) who has personally visited, experienced and assessed as many church choirs as he did. Whilst making these church visits, several thousand in total, Nicholson would annotate notebooks or diaries with what the choir sung, the hymns, the quality of responses, chanting, choir tone and so on. These notebooks are so highly abbreviated and illegible that it is hard to identify the choirs — he often only indicated the date of the visit and not the church name.

The present and future of church music

It is always difficult and sometimes dangerous to dogmatize about things that are happening around us, while to attempt to look into the future and anticipate the course of events is in many ways a fruitless task. Yet unless we do try and see where we stand and consider what is likely to happen and prepare to meet it, surely we are to blame. Indeed unless we are mere fatalists few of us can be content merely to 'wait and see'. This is not lack of faith — it is just common sense.

Our country is at war[1]: that is the overwhelming fact that dominates all our thoughts. But a time will surely come when we shall be at peace again, and we talk rather vaguely of 'building a new world'. Those who have special interests at heart can hardly fail to give some thought as to what that new world will be like, how those interests may be affected, how to safeguard what is worth keeping, and how to strengthen and renew them when happier times come.

The present state of church music and its future developments - even its future existence - are so closely bound up with those of the Church and its public worship, that it is impossible to consider the one without the other: and this must be the excuse for a mere musician daring to express his opinions about highly controversial matters which many might say were none of his business. These at any rate have an easy remedy in their own hands by saving themselves the trouble of reading what follows.

---

1 This comment determines the date of this chapter to between 1940 and 1945.

As one looks back over a life-time spent mainly in the service of the Church and its music, one can hardly refrain from asking two questions: — 'What does it all amount to?' and 'What of the future?'

It must be admitted that, considered merely from an artistic standpoint, the career of a church musician, as such, must necessarily be somewhat circumscribed. Of course the average organist will seek and will almost certainly find some outlet for his energies and his artistic expression other than his church work: without this his whole musical outlook would inevitably suffer, and he would soon become nothing but a 'stuffy old organ-grinder'. And it is true to say that the best church musicians are those who also have other musical interests outside the Church. Nevertheless the work, especially in a Cathedral, is engrossing; if it is conscientiously done it takes up much of a man's time and makes additional work outside his own immediate sphere somewhat difficult. Some find their outlet in teaching, some in composition, [and] some in a certain amount of conducting. But all these activities are secondary to the main job, and it must be admitted that the main job is limited in scope by its very nature.

In the first place the organist is not his own master in the things that belong to his art. He is not supreme in his own department: he cannot entirely choose what he will perform and he may even have to perform music with which he is not in sympathy. Neither can he ordinarily choose his own performers nor dispense with the services of any whose performance is not to his liking. No doubt, if he knows his business, he can generally get his own way in the long run; but he often has to wait long and patiently for reforms which the ordinary musician could put into effect at once: and he can never be certain that his opinions, however well-grounded, may not be over-ridden by a superior authority. Unless he is exceptionally strong-minded he may be in constant danger of interference, often by someone who has far less musical knowledge than himself. By the very nature of his position he is a constant target for criticism, which is the more difficult to meet in that it is more often made behind his back than to his face, and is often unfair as it is based on circumstances over which he has no control.

Again, apart from the fact that he is never really 'master in his own house', the work of the church musician must be limited by its very nature. For it must be remembered that church music would not exist at all were it not for the church service. Therefore unless the music for which he is responsible is a real contribution to the worship it has no justification, however good it may be in itself. So that church music can never be regarded as 'absolute music', to be judged purely on aesthetic grounds; it is always 'music with a purpose': and the main criterion of excellence is how far it fulfils that purpose.

Now it might seem that these limitations would make the work of the church organist a very dull affair, if nothing worse. Yet there are and always have been many excellent, all-round musicians who do not find it so, and who, on the contrary, get more joy out of it than from any other form of musical activity.

What is it that makes this so?

Before seeking for an answer it should be stated plainly that the church musician, if he is to be happy and successful, must be a convinced churchman: unless this is so his music is bound to have some element of sham about it; and a sham thing never brings any permanent satisfaction. But he must not only be a believer; he must be interested and sympathetic to the services of which his music forms a part; otherwise his music is bound to be a misfit. Just as a conductor who had no knowledge of or sympathy with the stage could never give a satisfactory performance of opera, however successful he might be with a symphony, so the organist can never make his music take its proper place in the service unless he understands it and is in sympathy with all that it expresses.

The work of the church musician, then, is highly specialised. But artists are more or less specialists, — it may be in portraits or landscapes or architecture: and this means that these are the subjects with which they are most at home, though not necessarily that they can do nothing else. And it is so with musicians; some are mainly composers or conductors, or instrumentalists or singers: this does not mean that they can only do one form of music, but that there is one form in which they excel. It is in this form that they reach the highest expression of their art and from which they ultimately derive the greatest satisfaction. Given, then, the necessary religious background, the specialist in church music, whatever gifts he may possess in other directions, probably finds that this is his best medium for artistic expression.

The church musician works on a comparatively small canvas. To some people this would seem a severe disability: but to others it gives an added charm; — to the type of mind that delights in the perfection of finish rather than in big effects. The church musician has, normally, no huge chorus or orchestra at his command; only a handful of singers and those of a very special kind. The music they have to sing is mainly on a small scale, comparable to chamber-music rather than that of the concert hall. But the constant singing together of a good choir gives scope for unanimity and sensitiveness equalled only by the string quartet.

For the church musician, if he is interested in that side of human nature, there is the constant joy of intercourse with the young: to many men the greatest happiness of their work is the part of it that is concerned with the teaching of their choirboys. No other musician has a similar joy, and many might envy the wonderful responsiveness of these youngsters than whom, as has been truly said, there is no finer choral material in the world. There are, no doubt, some who are not successful with boys: a man must have special gifts and must keep fresh and interested himself if he is to get results. But how rich are his rewards when he gets the goodwill of his boys: they will do anything for him; and what more can a musician ask?

To many the feeling that they are helping to carry on a great and honourable tradition is in itself a never-ending source of satisfaction. To perform the works of Gibbons or Purcell in the very place where they may have first been heard under the direction of the composer, and to feel that something of the tradition of those first performances may have been handed down to the present time through the unbroken chain of choristers who have sung there ever since, (for choirboys learn far more from one another than they do from their masters), is a privilege that falls to few. But the wonderful heritage of our English church music is one in which all can take a share, and it is difficult not to find in it an incentive to hand on the tradition to the future, unimpaired and perhaps even enriched.

But probably the greatest attraction of all lies in the fact that the church musician whose work lies in a Cathedral or a fine church has by far the noblest setting for his music of any of his professional brethren. To one of artistic sensibility the mere sight of the architecture, to say nothing of the marvellous acoustical possibilities, — quite unrivalled in any concert, room or theatre ever built — or of the beauty of colour or ceremonial, must be a constant inspiration. So in spite of its limitations the work of the church musician is not such a dull business as many might suppose.

But we live in an age of hurry and noise and startling events: and in a world where so much happens every day most people need big thrills to make them 'sit up and take notice'. This applies not only to ordinary affairs but to music. Save for the few who find their joy in refined simplicity and sheer beauty whether of design or performance, the demand is for sensationalism: — new tone colours, — new harmonies (or discords), — orchestras ever bigger and bigger, — more and more noise, in fact, something startling. Plain dignity and restraint is boring, but emotionalism runs riot. If indication were needed we have only to listen to the ordinary wireless programmes, — not of course the serious things like symphony concerts or chamber music, — but the popular items: those miserable songs, simply chock full of unreal emotionalism - 'It's you I want, only you', and that kind of thing: how inferior to the old-fashioned music-hall ditty, vulgar though it may have been, that they have ousted! Then again that bastard instrument to be found in cinemas which is what the great public has been brought to think of as an organ! How can the noble cathedral instrument compete with the palpitating gurgles of this monstrosity among a public that wallows in sentiment? Or how can the pure singing of a choir of boys and men touch palates that are jaded by a glut of 'crooning'? If true emotion is to be judged by the amount of tremolo whether of voice or instrument, what chance has the singer who uses his voice properly or the organist who treats his instrument with respect?

And there is a further tendency which is not without danger to church music, whose proper function is to voice the aspirations of the many rather than the individual. Personal expression is rated higher than that artistic restraint which subordinates everything to the main purpose of so presenting the music that it may convey its own message. This tendency to personal expression has even invaded religious services, and it is so much admired by some people that there is a real danger of its finding its way from the BBC studios to church and cathedral choir-stalls[2].

In these circumstances the path of the church musician cannot be an easy one, for the musical taste of the general public is almost entirely indifferent, if not antipathetic to the very kind of thing by which the best church music is distinguished.

But there are other difficulties. Whether or not the world is growing less religious, it is perfectly clear that people of today sit more lightly than formerly to what used to be called their 'religious duties'. Amongst the younger folks church-going is definitely out of fashion, and even amongst older people it is no longer a regular habit or even a 'sign of respectability'. This may or may not be a good thing: it certainly does mean that the people who go to church, at any rate in most cases, go for a proper purpose. But it has certain very serious effects on church music.

In the ordinary parish church the supply of people ready to sing in the choir is diminishing: many of those that give their services do so partly because they like the work and partly from a sort of general good nature, but few from a sense of duty: indeed some seem rather to think that they are conferring a favour on the parson. Of course there are still many men, women and boys who are really in earnest and take their work most seriously: but that can hardly be said to be true of the majority, and the choirmaster has often to put up with casual ways and lack of serious effort in order to keep a choir alive. The clergy recognise this and equally have to accent a sort of compromise — the best they can get.

This indifference to church-going affects not only the supply of adults but that of boys: for whereas in the old days the parents were often church-goers and were proud to see their boys in the choir, nowadays the majority do not care. If they seldom darken the doors of the church from one year's end to another, even though they are nominally 'church people', is it to be wondered at that they do not encourage their boys to do other than follow their example?

Another result of this indifference is shown on the financial side. The payment of organists and choirmasters has always been scandalously inadequate, but with diminishing congregations it tends to grow worse. This means that the trained musician is less and less inclined to venture on a church appointment, however keen he may be on the work, because he knows that unless he secures one of the leading positions it will be difficult to make a livelihood, especially as the insecurity of his tenure makes the building up of a teaching connection a somewhat risky venture.

In cathedral and similar appointments the financial position is not so stringent, though it is seldom lucrative: there is at least some endowment apart from the contributions of the

---

2 He mentioned his antipathy to broadcast services in Chapter VI p 161.

congregation and a reasonable security of tenure for the musician, whether in the organ loft or the choir-stalls, so long as he does his job properly.

The main difficulties are of another kind. For these 'choral foundations' date from a time when men believed in the value of a worshipping community and the ideal of worship for its own sake — the '*opus Dei*' as it was called in monastic times. This ideal has largely been lost sight of at the present day. The average person thinks of church-going (if he thinks of it at all), in terms of big congregations, not small communities whose main business in life is worship. The test of a parson's success is 'does he draw a big crowd?' not 'is his church a home of worship?' So the case for the cathedral service is weakened in popular estimation. People are apt to ask what good are these services when so few people go? Even cathedral dignitaries may fall into the same snare. Some who are frankly unmusical think them rather a waste of time and a needless expense: some would even agree with a famous Dean who is reported to have said that he couldn't imagine that the Almighty wished to be serenaded twice every day! Of course there are many Deans and Canons who take an entirely proper view of their responsibilities and who value the community worship for its own sake. But the criticism remains, and efforts are being made everywhere to make Cathedrals justify themselves in the public esteem by putting them to uses for which they were never intended. The daily choral services are maintained more or less on sufferance and 'stunts' of various kinds are put on in the hope of attracting big crowds.

There was a danger some years ago of parish churches unwisely trying to imitate the cathedral service: now there is a danger of Cathedrals becoming little more than glorified parish churches. Yet, with all the difficulties by which we are surrounded, there are still many people to whom church-going of the unsensational type means much and who quite honestly feel that the old ways were better. And who can look at the world today and say they are wrong? Since England ceased to be a church-going country has she been a happier one? There are many people who feel that, not only in other countries but in England too, the disregard of what is due to God in the matter of worship may well be a reason for many of the troubles by which we are beset. And who shall say they are wrong?

Now music is and has always been regarded as one of the most natural of all adjuncts to worship: so much so that we can hardly think of public worship without music of some kind. And if a return to public worship should come to pass, music must be prepared to take its proper place in it. So it may be worthwhile to consider a few of those directions in which existing conditions need to be improved in order that it may function properly in the 'better world' to which we all look forward.

The greatest need of all is that music should be given its proper place as a definite part of public worship, — a true means of approach to God and not a mere attraction for the listener. Further the 'sacrificial' aspect must not be overlooked: it is something offered to the glory of God and must therefore be the best than can be given, even if it is costly. [*cf* 'precious ointment' comment quoted by Bairstow in a previous chapter]

In this respect music must be put on a level with the other arts contributory to worship. It is no longer easy for an ignorant parson or stubborn churchwardens to spoil their churches by injudicious 'restorations' or the insertion of bad stained glass or vulgar memorial tablets. Diocesan advisory committees and Chancellors' Courts have done much, though not everything, to check such abuses. But in music there is no protection. Any parson can order anything he likes to be sung in his church without let or hindrance, and the musician can only protest without the least authority to back him. Congregations, or influential members of them, can demand their special favourites, be they good or bad, and can make it so hot for the parson or organist if they don't get their way that they often throw up [in] the sponge for the sake of peace. The organist can run riot in his voluntary and the choir in the anthem.

The first requirement, without which all else would be useless, is that the importance and dignity of church music should be asserted and the need for the best accepted. And to bring this to pass certain reforms are needed.

First of all in parish churches:

1. The position of the organist must be improved and strengthened.

   At present he has no security of tenure. A man who does his work with entire competence may be dismissed by his parson without any other cause than personal inclination, and he has no redress whatever. Admittedly this power is not often exercised in an arbitrary manner: but the organist should have some measure of protection, such as a right of appeal to a higher authority. Exactly what form this protection might take would be a matter for consideration, but possibly there might be some sort of 'licence to a church' or 'licence to officiate in a diocese' similar to that which is given to duly accredited lay-readers.

   If the Bishop or other authority felt unable to investigate the fitness of an organist to hold such a licence, the aid of a duly appointed Musical Adviser in each diocese might be enlisted.

2. Organists should be paid a more adequate salary.

   If the importance of their work were more fully recognised this should not be difficult. Much money is spent in churches, often on luxuries like decoration or even organs, while the organist is paid a stipend that in any other profession would be considered quite ridiculous. It cannot be that funds will not permit of this. Statistics taken from the Official Year Book of the Church of England show that in the three years from 1936 to 1938 the total voluntary contributions from the English Dioceses have increased by over £270,000, while in the same period the net income of the Clergy has increased by over £51,000. Yet the salaries of organists have, generally speaking, remained stationary and in many cases have been reduced.

   As well as increased salaries there should be some sort of contributory pension scheme such as that provided for the clergy.

3. Additional funds are needed for the proper maintenance of the music.

   To meet the cost of such reforms, as has been indicated, and as an official recognition of its importance, some portion of the central revenues of the Church should be ear-marked for the purpose of church music. It is significant that at present the Central Board of Finance, while subsidising almost every other form of church work, does not contribute one penny piece to the support of church music. Yet what would be the effect on congregations if they had to do without it?

4. The choice of music should be regulated.

   Though the Incumbent must clearly remain supreme in ordering the service in his own church, there should be a Musical Adviser or even a Musical Director in each diocese, who would be engaged, as a whole time job, in visiting churches and giving advice or instruction. He should be appointed by the Bishop as his delegate in musical matters and his authority should be similar to that of an Archdeacon, so that even if he could not override the Incumbent he could at least advise him and mediate in cases of difficulty.

5. The position of the choir should be regularised.

   It should be regarded in each parish as a definite organization with definite membership and definite duties: the 'casual membership' which is so common should be terminated once and for all. No one should be allowed to sing in a choir unless he has been formally admitted as a member, and this admission might well take place at or in connection with a public service. This would tend to raise the status of the choir and enhance the dignity of an important office. A firm stand should be made to preserve the historic form of choir whenever possible, consisting of boys and men only. In the smaller places the help of women may be indispensable, but it should not be regarded as the ideal arrangement.

   It should be boldly stated by those in authority that the best form of choir for any church that can have it is the traditional one of boys and men. The Roman Church made this pronouncement some years ago: why not the Church of England which has a far more continuous and excellent tradition of male choirs than any other branch of the Church?

In Cathedrals the main needs would seem to be these:

1. The anomaly should be finally abolished by which the authority of the Director of the music is technically subordinate to that of a priest, other than the Dean and Chapter, who need not be a trained musician. The Director of the music should be subject to the authority of the Dean and Chapter in their corporate capacity and not to that of any individual.

2. A return to a fuller recognition of the need for a worshipping community in the Cathedral is essential. Those who cannot see the value of this regular community worship (not for the clergy alone but for the whole cathedral body including Lay Clerks and Choristers) should not be appointed to posts in Cathedrals where regular participation is part of their duty.

   Canonries should not be used to find salaries for Diocesan officials.

   Periods of 'Residence' should be abolished. Deans and Canons, like other members of the cathedral staff, should have regular holidays, but at other times they should be expected to attend to their duties and to provide proper deputies in enforced absence.

   Available funds would seldom suffice to allow a large number of such full-time canonries, but one or two whose sole duty was with the Cathedral and its services would be far better than a larger number of half-timers.

3. The social aspect of community life in a Cathedral should be restored, and it should be recognised that it is shared by laymen as well as clergy. Lay Clerks and Choristers should no longer be treated, as is sometimes the case, as if they were mere hirelings just brought in to sing and nothing more; they should be treated as honoured members of the same body as embraces the Dean and Canons, with their own special place in the community life.

But none of these reforms will produce any big result unless the Church can bring itself to give a more emphatic call to the nation for a return to public worship. There must be an end of the sort of apologetic attitude that has so long been taken in this matter. We need some plain speaking. Practically everyone, Christian or non-Christian, admits to the existence of some Supreme Power, which we call God, who is (a) Creator and (b) Omnipotent. Otherwise how can the mysteries of life and the wonders of the universe be explained? It is evident that the Power that created us gave us a certain measure of free will. Can we be surprised, when that free will is exercised to ignore or to slight the Power that gave it, that the Creator should show His displeasure?

An instinct for worship of some kind is ingrain[ed] in almost every human being. But it does not always take the same form: the heathen will worship stones or idols; civilized people will worship wealth, or power, or beauty, or patriotism. But if God is omnipotent it is to Him and Him alone that worship is due.

Are we not justified in believing that the tragic state in which the world finds itself today may be a direct sign of God's displeasure with a people that have 'hardened their hearts'? Or that a true and visible return to the acknowledgment of God's supremacy would not be the essential prelude to a new and better world? Now all this may appear somewhat crude and out of place in the mere 'musings of a musician'. Yet it goes to the very root of the matter, for if there is no reason for worshipping God why should we bother about how we do it?

Granted that the need exists, what indication have we as to how the duty of public worship may best be fulfilled?

We may at any rate turn to the expert for advice. It would be difficult to find a more comprehensive theory of worship than that given by the Psalmist:

> "Ascribe unto the Lord the honour due unto his name."

First of all we must admit that worship is due to God and to God alone.

> "Bring presents and come into his courts."

The place for public worship is God's house, and when we come to worship there we must not come empty-handed: we must bring a gift with us, —it may be of our time, or our money, or our art: it does not so much matter what we bring so long as it costs us something. The sacrificial element in worship must not be lost sight of.

> "O worship the Lord in the beauty of holiness."

Beauty is surely the expression of God's will on earth; ugliness is its negation. Therefore we should surround His worship with all that is beautiful in art, architecture, music, literature and ceremonial. But all that is beautiful in itself is not necessarily appropriate for the solemn business of the worship of God, for we must not forget the final injunction,

> "Let the whole earth stand in awe of Him."

There must be nothing flippant or unworthy in our worship. Surely there is no greater need in our services today than a renewal of this sense of awe. Those of us who do go to church so easily forget this when we talk of 'enjoying the service', or the 'nice hearty singing', or the intellectual treat of a good sermon.

It should be noticed that the psalmist says nothing whatever about the benefits we may expect to receive from 'coming into His courts': the whole stress is on our duty of giving to God, not on what we shall get for ourselves. Indeed in the many allusions to worship in the Bible it would be hard to find any answer to the question 'What good do we get by going to church?'

Surely, then, this is the great need of the day, that the Church should fearlessly proclaim to the world that it is the duty of all men to worship God, and that worship means activity and not merely a passive state. Not only must the clergy proclaim this truth boldly, but they must set the example themselves. If they believe in worship for its own sake how can they justify their frequent neglect of their prescribed duty: — 'All Priests and Deacons are to say daily the Morning and Evening Prayer, either privately or openly, not being let by sickness, or some other urgent cause. And the Curate that ministereth in every Parish Church or Chapel, being at home, and not being otherwise reasonably hindered, shall say the same in the Parish Church or Chapel where he ministereth, and shall cause a Bell to be tolled thereunto a convenient time before he begin, that the people may come to hear God's word, and to pray with him'.

It may be that congregations will be small or even nil, but that does not justify the Services not being held: to drop them because they are not well attended is as good as admitting that they serve no useful purpose. And if the clergy even seem to admit this how can they expect the laity to take their admonitions seriously?

In this matter either the rule of the Church ought to be kept, or if it is felt to be obsolete, should be relaxed by competent authority: to allow it to fall into neglect at the discretion of the individual is disastrous. But surely something might be done to make this daily worship more worthy of God's acceptance. True, the effort of the parson and the few who join him does mean 'bringing some gift'; but where is the 'beauty of holiness'? Do we, for example, really explore the musical possibilities of weekday services? In the Cathedrals there is no excuse for them to be bereft of the beauty of music, but even in parish churches something more might often be done. There are still a few churches, for instance, where a weekday choral Evensong is sung with a few choirboys and others where a few women can be got together in place of the regular choir. This sort of thing was more common 25 years ago than it is today, but it might well be renewed, and even if it did not draw big congregations it would at least be an effort to attain some measure of the 'beauty of holiness' which would not be without value.

If there is to be any real and permanent return to public worship it must include the young. Congregations are becoming more and more elderly, and the call to worship is failing to draw the rising generation. Young men, unless they are definitely engaged in some form of church work such as the choir or serving at the Altar, are in many churches conspicuous by their absence, and young women, though perhaps more plentiful, are still but few. Yet the youth of the day is not antagonistic to or even uninterested in religion: the reason for his not going to church is far more often that he does not see why he should go. And this is partly because the clergy do not put it before him as a clear duty. No doubt it is a help if a young man can be found a definite 'job' in the church; but all young men cannot sing in the choir or serve at the Altar, though a great many more could be employed in this way if it became more natural and less of a preserve for the favoured few. But the idea of service is one which appeals to the young; — witness the success of such movements as the Scouts, Rovers, Toc H, and the similar organizations for girls: the key-note of them all is service, — doing things for someone else. It is a challenge which appeals to the young, and if the idea of serving God by worshipping Him can be recaptured, it is at least probable that there would be a response. But what is never likely to succeed is an attempt to make church-going a sort of counter-attraction to other ways of spending free time on a Sunday. However 'bright and breezy' services are they will never compete with the charms of the motor-bike or the cinema.

Yet there are often great practical difficulties, and it may be that the Church will have to reconsider some of its accustomed ways. Services, for example, may have to be held at unaccustomed times or even duplicated; for under modern conditions young people ought to be able to enjoy Sunday as a day of rest and recreation as well as of worship. 11.00 am and 6.30pm break into a day terribly, and even 8 o'clock in the morning is not always possible.

But it is not only a question of reasonable facilities for recreation. Take the case of an agricultural parish. On leaving school nearly all the lads go into some sort of farm work. Even if they wish to attend church at the normal hours they cannot do so, except possibly in the evening, simply because they have to look after the milking, or attend to the feeding of the stock, or other such duties: if there is any leisure on Sundays it will not generally be for the junior farm-hands. It is really appalling to think that thousands of these lads have been brought up as churchmen and have been instructed and confirmed, but never have the chance of making their Communion. If the ordinary hours are impossible under present day conditions, what is the Church going to do about it? Would it not be better that these lads should make their Communion at mid-day or even in the evening (when most of them can come if it is late enough), than not at all? Is it right that a 'godly custom' of the Church should take precedence of its Master's express injunction?

Problems like these will have to be faced anew, and failure to face them leads to the almost complete alienation that too commonly exists. If something cannot be done the result, in a few years, when the present congregations have passed on, will be entirely empty churches. To suppose that young people will be brought back to church by giving them 'jolly hymns of a manly type' is sheer nonsense: but if he can be shown that a certain course of action is his duty, the young Englishman is not usually slow to respond. Most young people of today are kindly and well-disposed, and ready to take on social work. This is all to the good, and much of it no doubt is due to the influence of the Church which rightly takes a lead in all good works. There is a readiness amongst young and old to do their 'duty towards their neighbour': but it is sometimes forgotten that there is an even greater commandment — 'duty towards God.'

To tackle these various problems is going to make even bigger demands on the parish priest than at present. But it has got to be recognised that in the 'new and better world' after the war everyone has got to be prepared to work harder, even if there is no corresponding rise in wages.

It seems, somehow, alien to religion to talk of finance: but, for good or ill, money is a necessity for us all, not perhaps for its own sake but because it provides us with the necessities of life as well as most of its amenities. To take an obvious example; we cannot worship God in the appropriate 'beauty of holiness' unless we are prepared to spend some money on it. This may be an unpalatable truth, but nevertheless it cannot be controverted. And this problem of finance is one that is for ever pressing on the clergy, taking their thought and time from the things that are really their job. Men are ordained to lead the worship of the Church and to teach the truths of Christianity, not to be good men of business or to manage funds. Yet they are nearly always called upon to undertake this work, for which they have normally had no training and for which many of them are by nature quite unfitted.

The clergy cannot help it, as things are. But surely there is an obvious remedy — a very drastic one no doubt, and one that might cause a good deal of heart-burning; but one which would do almost more than anything else to relieve the clergy from an unsuitable duty and win for them that respect for their office which is so urgently needed. It is that the whole administration of finance should be taken out of their hands. Why should not all church funds be administered by a central authority, having representatives, of course, in each parish answerable to it and not to the Incumbent? The central authority would receive all income and would pay all salaries, not only to the clergy including Bishops, Deans and Canons as well as parish priests, but to organists, vergers, choir men, and in fact everyone who earns emoluments of any kind.

The machinery would be big and complicated, no doubt: but would it be bigger than that, say, of the Post Office or the Board of Education? Both of these function in every point and on a larger scale than the church. There can be no question that considerable economy as well as greater efficiency would be achieved as a result of such a change. But even more important than any financial gain would be the improvement of the position of the clergy in the eyes of the ordinary man in the street. The ordinary man eyes the position of the parson more or less with suspicion — witness the pitiful agitation over the matter of tithe: he commonly thinks that the parson has a 'soft job' and is well paid for it (he does not quite know how), and that somehow or other the money comes out of his own pocket. But if the parson and all who serve the Church were paid a definite salary from a central source, just as the schoolmaster, for example, is paid, all this financial difficulty would be at an end and the parson would be free to get on with his proper job, which is saving souls, not administering funds.

A central authority exists in the Ecclesiastical Commission, which already deals with a good many financial matters: why could not its operations be extended to cover the whole, and to take financial questions clean out of the province of the clergy?

It is hardly likely that such a change could be effected without great opposition. But if the Church is to gain ground and not go on losing it, something drastic will have to be done. Some may think that this is a wild idea and that its importance is exaggerated. But many years' close connection with the Church and its worship and an intimate acquaintance with hundreds of clergy of all degrees of standing surely justifies even a musician in forming his own conclusions. And these views are quite definite; that the two main needs for the Church today are a fresh realization of the duty of worship and a freedom from financial responsibility.

And what is to be the position of church music when the new era dawns, and what should we be doing about it now? Surely there is some cleaning up to be done if it is to be fit to take its rightful place in a return to worship. We must set our faces against the second-rate where the first-rate is attainable. We must have done with that sort of smug self-satisfaction which makes us say we are doing the best when we can, when that is simply not true. Why is bad music tolerated any more than bad architecture or bad art of other kinds? Only for one of two reasons: because people prefer it, or because they cannot get anything better.

Let us examine each of these briefly. Popular taste is surely not the proper criterion of fitness. In other things as well as music many people prefer the bad to the good; if it were not so what would be the use of sermons and exhortations? To admit bad music because people like it is to cut clean through the true theory of worship, because it is putting the idea of getting before that of giving. Can we seriously suppose that God is pleased if we give Him what we know and what He knows is not our best?

The other common excuse for bad music is that we can do no better. This, if were really true, would be a perfectly valid one: God cannot ask more than our best, and the humblest offering of praise in the tiniest village church, if it represents sincere effort, may be just as acceptable as the magnificent rendering of some superb anthem in a Cathedral. But is it often true that we are giving of our best, or rather that we could not do much better than we do? Too often again it is a question of finance: if we really want the best we must be prepared to pay for it.

Some years ago I went to visit a village choir. I was met by a Rolls Royce car and taken to a palatial house: after an excellent dinner I had a long talk with my hostess during which she told me, I am sure with complete sincerity, of her intense desire to make the music of the church more worthy. The great difficulty here was the lack of a competent choirmaster. "Of course" she said what can one expect? "The salary we can afford to offer is so small that no first-rate musician could possibly be secured". I could have replied, though I had not the courage, 'It is perfectly simple; if you really want this so much, lay up your Rolls Royce and run an Austin instead: then what you save will supply all that is needed to find your choirmaster and make the music what it should be.'

But the price demanded is very often not that of £.s.d. [Pounds, shillings and pence] but of honest work and loving care. We must get rid of all that is slip-shod in our church music and must see that it is efficient. There are no two standards of efficiency, one for the concert platform and one for the church. What is bad, — things like out of tune singing or ugly tone or careless diction, — is bad everywhere: and what is not good enough to offer to a concert audience or a festival adjudicator is not good enough to offer to God.

Calmly to say that we are giving our best, then, is very often quite untrue. We could nearly all do better if we really wanted to enough: the trouble is that we do not want the best sufficiently to be prepared to make the personal sacrifices that are needed in order to attain it.

So it is with our choice of music. It is little use to talk about our glorious heritage if we leave it unsung on publishers' shelves. When we have so much that is good, why are we content to put up with so much that is second-rate? It would be the height of absurdity to demand the unattainable: no one would expect or wish a village choir to tackle a Byrd *Mass*. But this does not excuse our common habit of being content with what we know is not the best of which we are capable. It is acquiescence in the second-rate that is the real mischief, — not failure to attain perfection.

In our choice of music we must get rid of all cant and prejudice: we must try and judge it by sound critical principles and not by personal likes or dislikes. The person who would reject all plainsong because he finds it dull is no more ridiculous than the person who would exclude the music of Wesley or Stanford, because he prefers that of the Tudor period. The Church has room for music of all styles and all periods provided that it is a sincere and artistic expression of religious emotion; and it must never be forgotten that the music which rouses a response from one man may leave another cold. Yet taste must and can be educated in music as in all other arts. This education of taste will be one of the problems that will have to be faced before Church music will be able to take its rightful place in the worship of the Church and the life of the nation.

Readers who have got so far in this chapter may feel that its tone is somewhat pessimistic. But that is not the writer's intention. There is every hope for a glorious future of a glorious art. It can hardly be that this particular kind of music which, more than any other, is characteristic of our country, and which has survived with almost unbroken continuity through a thousand years of our nation's history, will be allowed to collapse. Indeed, even as things are, it has far too much vitality for such a thing to be credible. But it is no use to shut our eyes to facts, and if church music is to take the place to which it is entitled in the new life which, it is hoped, is coming to the Church, then proper preparation will have to be made. And to realize our short- comings is the first step towards putting them right.

It is a big task but not a hopeless one, and surely it is one that is worth tackling.

Chapter VIII [by the editors]

The Final Years

1939-1940

At the outbreak of the Second World War on 3rd September 1939, Nicholson suddenly found himself without a College to run. Most of the choristers had been transferred to Canterbury Cathedral Choir, the Chislehurst College closed and the students dispersed — many of them to be called up for military service. It would seem that for the second time in his career, Nicholson found himself starting yet another voyage 'on an uncharted sea': although not entirely uncharted in this instance, because there was still the work of the *SECM* to carry forward. Free from the day-to-day concerns of running a residential college, and the attendant financial worries, he was able to divert all his attention to making sure that the *SECM* continued its mission.

Nicholson moved out of the College, and took up residence in his cottage at Woodchurch, a village near Ashford. Not one to remain idle, Nicholson set about writing his memoirs *Musings of a Musician* in the closing months of 1939. At the same time he was formulating ideas about how to carry on the work of the *SECM* in spite of all the war-time restrictions now being put in place. These problems included evacuation of children, call-up and petrol rationing, as well as general transport difficulties. He also lacked a base from which to operate. However, even with all these problems to contend with, Nicholson had managed to organise and direct a choirboys' course at Eastbourne College starting on 28th December 1939, followed by a second course at Wellingborough School starting on 3rd January 1940 and without a break in between!

He then turned his attention to the decline of boy choristers in choirs. This action was prompted by figures published in *The Official Year Book of the Church of England*, which showed a steady decline in the total number of choristers of all sorts during the pre-war years 1935-1938. In February 1940 he issued a memorandum entitled 'Bringing boys back to choirs' which had been endorsed not only by the Archbishops of Canterbury and York[1], Lord Halifax[2] and Sir Samuel Hoare[3], but also by many leading musicians of the day, including Walter Alcock, Edward Bairstow, Adrian Boult, John Dykes Bower and Walford Davies. Nicholson noted in his *Chronicle*:

> [it] had an excellent effect, and probably preventing the total extinction of many choirs.

In the same month he toured affiliated churches in East Anglia, visiting 54 choirs, where he met upwards of 600 choirboys and covered over 800 miles by car. In June 1940 he went north

---

1   During 1940 Archbishop Cosmo Lang (Cantuar) and Archbishop William Temple (Eboracum) were in post.
2   Lord Halifax (1881-1959) was British Foreign Secretary from 1938 to 1940.
3   Sir Samuel Hoare (1880-1959) was Lord Privy Seal during the early months of 1940, but resigned during the year and became Ambassador to Spain.

visiting churches and running festivals, culminating with a festival at Bedford, after which he took up residence at Tenbury.

The summer of 1940 saw him running festivals at Newbury and Weymouth before going on to Cornwall, where he was able to reunite with those St Nicolas College choristers who had been evacuated to St Blazey, together with the rest of Canterbury Cathedral boarder choristers (the cathedral day-boy choristers had remained in Canterbury to carry on the daily round of choral services). Whilst he was there, Gerald Knight had put on four performances of *The Children of the Chapel* using many of the original cast of boys from Chislehurst, including Harry Barnes as Captain Cooke. September saw Nicholson running a combined choirboys' course and adult summer school at Oxford where, for a week, he undertook the responsibility of providing all the music in Christ Church Cathedral, as well as being involved in holding lectures and discussions. In December Nicholson together with Leslie Green, the Secretary, visited central Wales, running choir gatherings at Brecon Cathedral and Merthyr Tydfil, where most of the boys were evacuees from churches in Kent.

St Nicolas Day was duly observed at a special festival held at St Nicholas' Church, Hereford, attended by 120 boys from affiliated churches in the area, including choristers from St Michael's Tenbury and Felsted School, which had been evacuated to Ross-on-Wye for the war. To round off the year there was a Christmas choirboys' course at Badminton, to where Betteshanger School had been evacuated for the duration. Queen Mary, who was staying at Badminton House, attended the service on Sunday evening, and met the boys afterwards. On the staff, as well as the Director and Dr C H Phillips[4], was a young Kenneth Jones[5], a former Chislehurst chorister now at King's School, Canterbury, who superintended the games and outdoor activities. A complete catalogue of Nicholson's war-time activities would provide material for a book on its own, but the above account of events in 1940 does at least demonstrate his total commitment, and his unflagging enthusiasm and energy.

Expansion

As we have seen, Nicholson was determined that the *SECM* should continue to grow and flourish in spite of all the war-time difficulties. And grow it did, from a membership of 1,500 affiliated churches in 1939 to 2,072 by 1945. Throughout the war residential courses for choirboys were held in many centres, including Christ Church Oxford, Betteshanger School, St Michael's Tenbury, Whalley Abbey, Barnard Castle, Godalming, Roslin, Leatherhead, Dumfries and Durham.

In addition, he started:

- Public Schools' Festivals, the first being held at Gloucester Cathedral in June 1941 with over 200 singers.
- Choirboys' Festivals, the first being held at Westminster Abbey in June 1942.

---

4   Dr C H Phillips: see Chapter VI: footnote 27.
5   For further information about Kenneth Jones see *SNCSN*.

- Cathedral Courses, the first being held at Gloucester in the same year, which started a tradition that carries on to this day.

Equally important to Nicholson was the continuing contact with affiliated churches up and down the country. With the help of the Archbishop of Canterbury, he had managed to secure an extra petrol allowance, which permitted him to carry on these visits. He even purchased an 'auto-bike' which he used for some journeys, in order to save petrol.

In his *Chronicle of the SECM*[6], Nicholson notes the following war-time statistics:

- Personal visits to choirs by the Director, and latterly by the Commissioner (Hubert Crook) totalled 908
- Number of boys attending courses 1270[7]
- 4 adult summer schools
- 554 new affiliated churches

Commenting on Nicholson's war-time work, which took him all over the country, Gerald Knight said:

> I can feel nothing but admiration for my predecessor. His spirit in face of adverse conditions was as irrepressible as it was infectious[8].

The Westminster Abbey Choirboys' Festivals

The Westminster Abbey Festivals were high-profile occasions, attracting considerable media attention at a time when good news was at a premium. The first of these Festivals in 1942, organised and conducted by Nicholson, was especially noteworthy, being held in a war-damaged London, with all the attendant transport difficulties, but still managing to draw 450 choristers. *The Musical Times* commented most favourably on the massed singing of Bach's *My heart, ever faithful*.

> Their management of the little turns and runs with suppleness was a wonderful experience[9].

The 1943 Festival was attended by 560 boys from about 100 affiliated choirs. Once again *The Musical Times* reported on the event:

> Their two-part singing was surprisingly well-balanced; a fine sense of climax was shown throughout ...and not once was there a hint of out-of-tuneness or of bad quality in the tone[10].

---

6 The *Chronicle of the School of English Church Music and the College of St Nicolas* (hereafter the *Chronicle*) was a personal hand-written notebook/diary of events kept by Sir Sydney Nicholson. It was divided into two parts (on facing pages within the book - *The Chronicle of the College of St Nicolas 1929-1939* (kept up-to-date until College closure in 1939) and *The Chronicle of the SECM 1928-1947* (this Nicholson continued until his death).

7 This figure of 1945 seems quite low but Nicholson made a distinction between 'instructional courses', to which this figure of 1270 refers and choir 'festivals'. The wartime attendance at the Westminster Abbey boys' festivals alone was 1560.

8 From a talk given at Church House, Westminster on 9th December 1967.

9 *The Musical Times* No. 214

The Westminster Abbey Festivals of Boys' Voices in 1942, 1943, 1945 and 1946 attracted 400, 560, 600 and 600 boys respectively. This photograph was taken in the Cloisters on 13th June 1942.

Cathedral Courses

The first of these Cathedral courses was held at Gloucester Cathedral in August 1942 and was as a direct result of the Dean, Dr Costley-White, asking Nicholson if he could provide a choir to sing the cathedral services for a fortnight. Nicholson readily agreed and took charge of the music, with Gerald Knight playing the organ. Attendance was by invitation, extended to boys and young men who had distinguished themselves at residential courses, or who were personally recommended by their Directors of Music. The course was housed at the College of Domestic Science in Gloucester.

In 1943, the course at Carlisle Cathedral mustered 50 singers from 30 different choirs, but with fewer men than at Gloucester, mainly through the call-up to National Service. The Dean of Carlisle, Cyril Mayne, wrote afterwards: 'Any cathedral that gets the opportunity of welcoming the *SECM* choristers will be well-advised to take it.'[11]

The 1944 Cathedral course was held at Durham, from 7th to 14th August[12]. The course was covered in some detail in an article entitled 'English Church Music Carries On' in the September issue of *Picture Post*. Boys from churches as far south as Yeovil, together with boys from Rugby, Haileybury and Merchant Taylor's schools formed the choir, with senior boys supplying the lower parts.

> We were able to sing two full choral services most days, besides putting in about 3 hours practice: however this was not enough to satisfy us, for most of the evenings after supper were spent in informal singing round the piano[13].

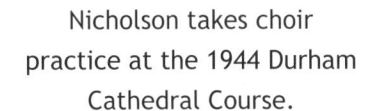

Nicholson takes choir practice at the 1944 Durham Cathedral Course.

---

11 *ECM* October 1943
12 This was the course for which John Ireland composed his beautiful *Ex ore innocentium*.
13 Anon: *Choristers' Leaflet* October 1944.

Durham Cathedral Course 1944.

Several photographs were published in the *Picture Post* article. This (rather grainy) example bore the caption:

'The day's work is over. The boys, on their way back to the school in which they are living, enjoy themselves by the river-side.'

The cathedral course at Norwich, held from 6th to 20th August 1945, coincided with the end of the war in the East, and the choir, who had broadcast evensong on Tuesday, suddenly found themselves contributing to a service of thanksgiving for victory, broadcast nationwide by the BBC at 9.30 the following Sunday morning. Among the trebles taking part on this course was a young Martin How[14]. Two days VJ holiday had been declared, but not for the choir, who carried on with the cathedral services. The October issue of *English Church Music* records:

> It was not easy to enjoy a well-earned rest at night as loudspeakers just outside the dormitories relayed music for dancing in the streets which went on until the early hours punctuated by frequent fireworks and accompanied by displays of lamp-post acrobatics.

---

14 Martin How (b. 1931) served as Headquarters Choirmaster from 1964 and as *RSCM* Commissioner for the South. He was responsible for the introduction of the *RSCM* Chorister Training Scheme in December 1965 and was founder of the *RSCM* Cathedral Singers in 1967.

Tenbury

As an expedient measure, the office of the *SECM* on the outbreak of war was moved from London to take up temporary quarters at the Chislehurst College. However, in August 1940 the *SECM* office moved again, as St Nicolas College had now been taken over by Kent County Council for the duration of the war, and there became an urgent need to clear the building of all furniture. When Maxwell Menzies[15], the Organist and Choirmaster at St Michael's, Tenbury was called up for military service, Nicholson volunteered to take over as Director of Music, which the Governors were delighted to accept. Nicholson almost certainly regarded this as his contribution to the war effort, and was, one may safely assume, offered for free, or at any rate in return for board and lodging. After he had taken up residence at the College, he discovered a nearby unoccupied rectory and proposed to Council that the *SECM* should rent it, initially for one year, in order that all the St Nicolas furniture could be stored there. In addition the *SECM* Secretary, Leslie Green, could move in so as to be in closer contact with the Director. The College furniture, after an event-filled journey, finally arrived at Tenbury. The total contents which filled four lorries and three railway trucks, also included livestock, namely chickens, a hive of bees, 'Jock' the Director's Scottish terrier, and 'Mignonette', the Secretary's goat! Thus Tenbury became the operating base for the *SECM*.

As well as running the St Michael's College choir during term, Nicholson set about recruiting a choir of local boys to sing in the holidays. He wrote:

> Another new development has been the 'village choir.' I found that there was little or no music at the church during the holidays, so that the services were very dreary. So I managed to collect a few boys from the village to form a choir, and they were soon able to sing fairly simple settings of the Eucharist ….and also an Evensong each Sunday[16].

> After so many years of telling people how to tackle the job I am trying to do it myself! Well, I find it great fun[17].

He also broadcast, at the invitation of the BBC, a series of four talks during the spring of 1943 entitled 'Quires and Places where they sing.' These talks covered the principles of voice control, breathing and enunciation. Not only did Nicholson use the Tenbury College choristers to provide musical examples, he also got his newly-formed 'village choir' to make a contribution.

---

15 Maxwell Menzies (1912-1988) had been a chorister at St Michael's College from 1923 to 1926 and studied at the College of St Nicolas in Chislehurst in 1931 where he was the 'Archbishop's Scholar'. He was Organ Scholar at St John's College in Oxford from 1932-1935 before returning to St Michael's College as organist from 1935. He later served at Maidstone Parish Church from 1952 and Portsmouth Cathedral from 1959 to 1964. He then taught at the Birmingham School of Music until retirement.

16 From an article in the College Magazine for 1942.

17 From *English Church Music* Vol. X, No.4.

More Moves and Appointments

Leslie Green had been called up for military service in the navy at the end of 1941 leaving Nicholson, assisted by A W Jackson who had been a member of the office staff since 1931, to run the *SECM* office. In February 1943 Alec Jackson was appointed Bursar, until he, too, was called up.

At a Council meeting on 20th January 1943 it was decided that the College of St Nicolas would be reopened as soon as conditions permitted, but at Canterbury rather than Chislehurst, and in a house to be rented from the Dean and Chapter. Given that the total income of the *SECM* for 1943 was only £2000, and bearing in mind that the Director was not drawing a salary, the restarting of the College was what Watkins Shaw described as 'a robust act of faith.'[18]

The *SECM* office was to move again in July 1943 to Leamington Spa, as Tenbury, situated as it was in the depths of Worcestershire, was found to be rather too remote! This was envisaged as an interim move before finally settling in Canterbury. This move did not pass without incident[19]. The house in Milverton Crescent, Leamington Spa, although reasonably large and conveniently placed for the town, was not ideal, described as old-fashioned without a telephone or even electricity. 'We find modern gas lighting not too bad,' Nicholson wryly comments.

Hubert Crook was appointed full-time Commissioner from the beginning of September 1944. Crook had resigned as Organist and Choirmaster of High Wycombe parish church, a post in which he had been highly successful, in order to take up this appointment. He was already well-known to countless choirboys on the many courses run by Nicholson, at which he had assisted. This appointment would greatly ease the pressure of work on the Director, who had in essence been battling on virtually single-handed for much of the war.

---

18 Harold Watkins Shaw, *Vocation and Endeavour: Sydney Nicholson and the early years of the Royal School of Church Music (School of English Church Music)* in manuscript and published 1990 by the Church Music Society.

19 For further information about this see *SNCSN*.

The Founder's 70th Birthday

Nicholson was resident at 13 Milverton Crescent, Leamington Spa at the time of his 70th Birthday on 9th February 1945. *The Times* of that day mentioned his birthday, and he was inundated with letters and telegrams of congratulation. These came from *SECM* choirs, individual singers, bishops, deans, organists, former pupils and of course numerous friends worldwide.

Many of the messages were very affectionate in tone, and Nicholson decided that he would reply to them all. He therefore duplicated a 'thank you' letter (reproduced on the following pages). The 'unique birthday present' mentioned on the second page of the letter took the form of a recital in Leamington Spa Parish Church on 10th February 1945. The combined choirs of Leamington (Parish Church, Holy Trinity and St Mark's) and Warwick (St Mary's and All Saints') sang a programme of Nicholson's music which included the *Magnificat in D flat*, the anthem *Teach us, good Lord*, the first performance of *Hymn of praise and thanksgiving after victory*[20], the *Gloria from Mass of St Nicolas* together with excerpts from his cantata *The Saviour of the World*. Alan Blackall of St Mary's, Warwick, directed the choirs, and Mr J W Martindale-Sidwell[21] played the organ in lieu of Sir Walter Alcock who was ill. After the concert, Hilary Chadwick-Healey[22] entertained the choirs to tea, and SHN was presented with a cheque from an anonymous donor towards the work of the *SECM*.

---

20 Nicholson's composition of this piece, dated 11th November 1944, shows optimism, for WWII had not yet ended.

21 John William Martindale Sidwell (1916-1998), a former chorister and assistant organist at Wells Cathedral, was one of the foremost choral conductors in the post-war years. His choir at Hampstead Parish Church, where he was organist from 1947 until retirement in 1992, was first rate. He taught at the *RSCM* from 1958 until 1966.

22 Businessman Hilary Chadwick-Healey (1888-1976) was a chorister under Nicholson at Chipping Barnet Church c.1900 and was a tenor in the choirs of St Sepulchre, Holborn, and of All Saints, Margaret Street. Co-director of the British Tabulating Machine Co. Ltd (retiring in 1956), he was very generous to the *SECM* with both time and money. Active from the inaugural meeting of the *SECM*, he was on the first Provisional Council and was appointed on 18th Sep 1930 as one of the first batch of SECM Council Members proper. He personally prepared and financed the first two years of the house journal *English Church Music*. He was active in visiting parishes and made the first ever parish visit, to Childe Okeford Church in Dorset, the first choir to affiliate to the *SECM*. He subsequently served as Hon Treasurer of the *SECM/RSCM* from August 1940 until 1955.

13, Milverton Crescent
Leamington Spa.

My dear Friend,

   I wish I could reply individually to all the letters and telegrams I have received bringing me good wishes on my 70th birthday, but it would be quite impossible so I can only ask you to let me use our 'duplicator' to thank you for your kind message and to tell you how happy I have been in all the expressions of good-will and affection that have come to me from my oldest as well as my youngest friends.

   I think I am unusually fortunate in that, as I grow older, my circle of friends, though sadly reduced among contemporaries, is almost daily being increased among the rising generation. I am proud to think that I can claim the distinction of knowing more choirboys than anyone else, and perhaps my greatest joy in life has been my work amongst them. In this I of course include my most happy association with choirmen, choirmasters and organists, for they are all members of that great fellowship which most of them entered in boyhood. It was the kindness of some of my newest friends, guided by some of my oldest, that led to the unique birthday present which they gave me in Leamington Parish Church and an experience I shall never forget; - indeed a red-letter day in my life.

I am thankful for the wonderful health I have been granted and that I still feel quite fit to devote a good deal of energy to stabilizing the foundations of the work I have been permitted to do for Church music, so that its future may be assured.

This is now my chief concern, and the delightful expressions of appreciation which you and so many others have sent me are the strongest possible encouragement to carry on, for the assurance they bring that, when the time comes for me to take a back seat, the support that has meant so much to me will surely be forthcoming for those who will take my place.

With warmest thanks for your friendship and all it means to me,

   Believe me yours very sincerely,

P.S. Let me tell you of a most practical 'birthday present', anxiously awaited for five years and more
THE S.E.C.M. is NOW ON THE TELEPHONE
   LEAMINGTON SPA 2434

Reopening of College of St Nicolas

Gerald Knight was appointed Warden of St Nicolas College, Canterbury, in February 1945. In an article entitled 'The Shape of Things to Come'[23], the editor reports the appointment of Dr John Dykes Bower as Associate Director[24] – to provide some alleviation of Nicholson's duties, but adds that he (the editor) doubts if the Director will avail himself of this opportunity. The other appointment announced was that Dr Alan Blackall to be Lecturer at the College. On 30th March 1945, by Royal command, the *SECM* became 'The Royal School of Church Music'[25]. On 20th November 1945 the *RSCM* office opened for business at Roper House in Canterbury.

The College of St Nicolas opened on 30th January 1946 at No. 17, The Precincts – a fine Georgian house, once the home of Dean Stanley when he was a residentiary canon at the cathedral. The opening service was held in the cathedral and sung by the newly-formed College Choir. Peter Carnes (b. 1930), one of the last remaining of the Chislehurst boys who came to Canterbury at the outbreak of war, carried the processional cross. The service was as far as possible the same as that held for the opening of the College in 1929. Nicholson notes that:

> Forming the choir and amongst the officials were several who had taken part in the original opening service including the Chaplain, the Rev G H Salter, and one of the first choirboys, Henry Wardell[26]. Our own organ from Chislehurst, which had been erected in the Eastern Crypt, was used for the service[27].

It had been decided not to pursue the idea of a residential choir school for the College choristers, which had proved a costly enterprise at Chislehurst. Instead, boys from affiliated churches in the area (as far as Whitstable six miles away in some cases) were recruited. The boys were formed into three choirs, with each choir singing twice a week – in addition to the practices and services at their own churches. This was quite a commitment on their part! So, once again, the College students would have a choir upon which to practise their choir-training skills, with the other students supplying the lower parts.

---

23 *ECM* April 1945

24 Dr John Dykes-Bower was appointed Associate Director at a salary of £250 p.a. in February 1945. He was originally asked to be Deputy-Director but felt that he could not commit to a post which might translate into becoming full-time director as he was not prepared to relinquish his post at St Paul's Cathedral. He then changed his mind, but decided not to accept any remuneration for his work, thus becoming 'Honorary'.

25 This honour/recognition was not a spontaneous gesture by King George. It is something that was 'applied for' by the *SECM* Council with the backing of the Archbishop of Canterbury.

26 Henry Wardell (1916-2010) was the first Secretary of the St Nicolas College Old Choristers' Association. He served in the RAF during WWII.

27 *ECM* April 1946

On 11th July 1946 The King and Queen, together with Princess Elizabeth, visited Canterbury, and the Warden and members of staff were presented. July also saw the first meeting of Fellows of the College since July 1939. Gradually the various strands of the organisation were being taken up again. One of the first students admitted, on an A & M Scholarship, was Michael Fleming[28].

One of the most important customs from Chislehurst days in Nicholson's eyes was resumed on 6th December 1946. This was the first St Nicolas' Day Festival to be held at Canterbury, and was marked by a Sung Eucharist in the Crypt of the Cathedral. The cathedral choristers joined with the College students to form the choir, but in the evening Evensong was sung by the College choristers and students, followed by the restarted tradition of the St Nicolas Feast, held at Roper House, attended by the Boy Bishop, with the Dean of Canterbury as guest of honour. In the *Chronicle* Nicholson records:

68 sat down to eat, Christmas tree in the conservatory, present for each boy, games organised by students, with a concert following.

The first St Nicolas Festival to be held in Canterbury in Dec 1946. Gerald Knight, Warden of the College, and organist of Canterbury Cathedral, is in the middle with SHN on his left and Sir Ernest Bullock on his right.

---

28 Michael Fleming (1928-2006) was organist of All Saints Margaret Street in London from 1958 and taught in the choir school there. In 1968, when the school closed he was appointed a tutor for the *RSCM* at Addington Palace, also serving as Warden there and as organist of Croydon Parish Church. He was subsequently organist of St Mary's, Primrose Hill, and of St Alban's, Holborn until 1998 when, at 70, he moved to St Michael's Croydon. He retired finally from the *RSCM* in 1993.

Farewell

Nicholson had always worked at full stretch, and was always happier doing so. Any regard for his own health seemed to be a secondary factor. In his Director's Letter in the *Choristers' Leaflet* of January 1942, he tells his young readers that he has spent some time in Birmingham Hospital where he underwent an unspecified operation. He writes 'this was pretty boring, but I am back again now at Tenbury and hope soon to be quite fit and able to "take the road again." However the years were starting to take their toll. The photo of him at Canterbury (on the previous page) shows a tired man, but he doesn't seem to have considered taking things at a slower pace. Gerald Knight wrote:

> As always, he drove himself hard, rushing hither and thither in the furtherance of church music. He in fact drove himself too hard[29].

The Chronicle of the SECM, which Nicholson had kept since the founding of the School, has one last entry dated 1st-2nd January 1947, which recorded the holding of the ADCM examination for the first time since 1938. There were six candidates. One can only speculate as to why the *Chronicle* was discontinued after this date, but perhaps it may be taken as a sign of some easing up on Nicholson's part.

At Easter 1947 he drove up to Rossall School, Fleetwood to direct the choristers' course there. It was an unrelenting week. After the course he motored back to Woodchurch in one day. This proved to be too much. On arriving back home, he suffered a slight stroke the following day. However this did not prevent him from attending two festival services for affiliated choirs at Canterbury Cathedral on 10th and 17th May, see photograph on the following page, but he had a further stroke the following week and was removed to hospital at his own request. The end came peacefully a week later, on 30th May 1947. He was 72.

The funeral service was held at Woodchurch on 3rd June, attended by the Warden and members of the College, together with the choir and congregation of the parish church, followed by cremation. The burial of ashes was held at Westminster Abbey on 6th June. The Abbey choir sang Croft's burial sentences, Stanford's *Beati quorum via* and the hymn *Blessed City* to Purcell's tune as arranged by Nicholson, and *Rise in the strength of God* to Nicholson's own tune 'Totteridge'.

English Church Music reported that:

> It was a most moving service, sung just as he would have wished it in the place where he served so many years[30].

His ashes were interred in the cloisters, and the spot is marked by a memorial stone. After the service, the Abbey bell ringers rang a half-muffled Peal.

---

29 From *RSCM: The First Forty Years* ed Gerald Knight, Croydon, RSCM, 1969.
30 *ECM* July 1947.

After his death he was also remembered by memorial services in Barnet and Chislehurst Parish Churches, and in Carlisle, Manchester and Canterbury Cathedrals.

In an article entitled 'Our Best Friend'[31] the editor of *English Church Music* wrote:

> In twenty years we have had the unhappy task of recording in these pages the passing of men and women whose service to the cause which is our cause has been notable — amongst them Walford Davies, Henry Colles, Eleanor Gregory, Hylton Stewart, Harvey Grace, Henry Phillips. But no loss can mean as much to the *RSCM* as does the death of its Founder and Director, Sydney Hugo Nicholson.

The last photograph including Sir Sydney Hugo Nicholson MVO, MA, D Mus, FRCO, ARAM
The *RSCM* Festival in Canterbury in May 1947

---

31 *ibid*

Appendix A: Nicholson's account of his ancestry

It is a curious fact that we know little or nothing of our ancestry on my father's side[1], except that he was born in 1808, the son of Charles Nicholson of London. We know no more of his father than this. [We do not know] what his profession was, whether he had [any] other children, or even when he died. My father used to say that he was born at Cockermouth (or thought so), and this was corroborated many years later when his reputed birth-place, an old house under the shadow of Cockermouth Castle, was shown to me. At the time of his birth this house was occupied by a firm of solicitors, *Nicholson and Bragg*, who were agents to the Earl of Egremont. I could find no record of his baptism in the Cockermouth Registers, and could get no more confirmation than the local belief that this 'Cockermouth worthy' was born there.

His mother was Barbara Ascough of Bedale, Yorkshire, a member of a well-known family in that place, and he *may* have been born there, as stated in the *Australian Encyclopaedia*, though again no record can be found in the Registers.

Both his parents died when he was a child, and he was brought up, together with his first cousin James Holmes, by his uncle William Ascough[2] and his aunt Mary Clink. William Ascough had been married in early life to a Miss Blashford, from whose family Queen Victoria bought the Osborne estate. She [Miss Blashford] died young, and he then seems to have begun a life of adventure. He sailed his own ships from Whitehaven and had six[3] of them, which used to trade to Australia and race home with a wool cargo in the hope of winning a bonus. I regret to say that the cargo outward-bound often consisted of convicts, — but the tradition remains that on these ships they were very kindly treated, and especially on the *Portland* which Ascough himself commanded.

After experiencing shipwreck, capture by Spanish pirates and other vicissitudes, but evidently having made a considerable fortune, he settled in Australia and, according to the census of 1828, he was the owner of 2700 acres at Mudgee, New South Wales. He soon sent for his two nephews, Charles Nicholson and James Holmes, to join him, with his sister Mary Clink to look after them. They came out in 1834.

---

1 Despite his best efforts Sir Sydney Nicholson was unable to unravel his paternal family history. He did not realise that his father had been vague and slightly dishonest in some of his assertions, probably to conceal the fact that he was an illegitimate child, indeed his original name was not even Charles but Isaac. **Much of the information given by Nicholson on these first few pages is now known to be false.** He was encouraged in his genealogical research by his mother, who was therefore probably unaware of her late husbands precise origins. See a subsequent page for the story as far as it is now known.

2 William Ascough (b 2nd October 1777, Iburndale, Yorkshire; d 11th June 1836, Borken Bay, NSW, Australia) married Susannah Blashford (or Blachford) at Windsor, NSW, in September 1823. They then sailed to England, with William in command of the *Competitor*. Susannah was one of the earliest young Australians to seek fame and fortune in London. An unusual match of a country girl aged 21 and a tough sea captain of convict ships aged 46, William returned to sea almost immediately with his next consignment of convicts bound for Australia. He had been very successful in his business, buying his own ships and retiring around 1835 to his estates in Hawkesbury and in Wellington. Whether he was still married to Susannah or whether she had died is unknown, but in 1835, after he had brought his remaining family to Australia, William Ascough made a new will. With the exception of annuities to his sister Mary and to his nephew James, he left the whole of his considerable fortune to his nephew Charles Nicholson MD of Sydney.

3 The *Malabar*, the *Competitor*, the *Ann and Amelia*, the *Marquis of Huntley*, the *Portland* and the *Mary*.

But he was not destined to enjoy family life for long. The following extract is quoted from an obituary in the 'Sydney Gazette' of June 25, 1836:

> On the 11th instant, whilst proceeding to his estate on the lower Hawkesbury, William Ascough Esq [died] aged 60 years, lamented by numerous friends. The melancholy event happened by the vessel on which he was a passenger being upset by a sudden gust of wind, by which all on board, to the number of eight persons, perished.

I have in my possession a 'memorial ring' containing a fragment of his hair, such as was customarily given to members of the family on these occasions. The ring states that he was 57 years of age. It was given to me by one of his descendants in another branch of the family, of whose existence I was unaware until I went to Australia in 1934 – exactly a hundred years after my father!

Evidently my father was the favourite of the two nephews, for the Captain left the bulk of his property to him. And that is how my father came to go to Australia and to settle there.

He used to tell us that he went to school at York, but we know no more details: he certainly went to Edinburgh University[4] to study medicine, and he took his MD degree there in 1833, being the first man of his year and the only one to write his thesis (on 'Asphyxia') in Latin. He was a contemporary of Simpson[5], who discovered anaesthetics, and a pupil of Dr Knox[6], who was associated with the notorious Burke and Hare, and is reputed to have employed 'Resurrection men'.

> The biographies of Sir Charles Nicholson found in the *Dictionary of Australian Biography* 1949 and *Australian Dictionary of Biography Vol 2* 1967 contain many of the same errors as Sir Sydney's personal account, probably all of this originating from disinformation spread by Sir Charles. It is perhaps not surprising that he kept his humble, illegitimate origins a secret, but it is extraordinary that he succeeded for so long and never revealed them to his wife of 38 years.

---

4 It is not known who paid for Nicholson's (very expensive) education in York and Edinburgh; possibly William Ascough or perhaps his absent father.

5 Scottish physician Sir James Young Simpson (1811-1870) discovered the anaesthetic property of chloroform and introduced it for medical use. He was also physician to Queen Victoria.

6 Robert Knox (1791-1862) ran an anatomy school in Edinburgh. He paid for cadavers from the body-snatchers and murderers Burke and Hare, but, unlike them, he was not prosecuted for his role in the affair.

Portrait, date unknown, by an unknown artist of Sir Charles Nicholson as Chancellor of the University of Sydney (1854-1862)

Sir Charles Nicholson's ancestors[7]

Sir Charles Nicholson's mother was Barbara Ascough (bap 15th November 1789, Ugglebarnby, Whitby, Yorkshire; d July 1814, Whitby), the sister of William Ascough[8]. In the parish baptismal register she is notated as 'Askwith' probably a phonetic spelling of Ascough. Her father John Ascough (1747-1813) was not a wealthy London Merchant but a labourer. Barbara died aged only 24, a year after her father and two years before her mother Elizabeth (1756-1816). Her illegitimate son was born on 23rd November 1808 and baptised in Ugglebarnby Chapel on 1st December 1808, not with the name Charles but as Isaac. The baptismal entry records "Isaac Ascough, the illegitimate son of Barbara Ascough (spinster)". In this register Barbara's name was correctly spelled Ascough and no father's name is recorded in the entry. It seems that illegitimate children in the Whitby area were commonly given Biblical names.

There is no certain evidence of the child's father or why Isaac Ascough was renamed Charles Nicholson. It is possible that the father was a 'Charles Nicholson', but research by Michael Turner, Senior Curator of the Nicholson Museum in Sydney, at the North Yorkshire Records Office showed that there was no Charles Nicholson born or bred in the local area. There was however a William Nicholson, chandlers' merchant, living in Whitby. His nephew, named Charles Nicholson, was a naval lieutenant whose ship had wintered in Whitby in early 1808, some nine months before Isaac's birth. A connection is possible but remains unproven. It is interesting to note also that a William Nicholson was a founding member of Whitby Museum and that William Ascough's wife and sister, who had long since left Whitby, later donated items to the museum.

Nicholson's grandparents John and Elizabeth, together with his mother Barabara are all buried together in a single grave in the churchyard of St John the Evangelist in the village of Sleights outside Whitby - there was no burial ground in Ugglebarnby.

On the death of his mother and grandparents, the young Charles was brought up by his uncle William Ascough and his aunt Mary Ascough. The latter eventually married an Australian Adam Clink to became Mary Clink and so Sir Charles's assertion that he was brought up "together with his first cousin James Holmes, by his uncle William Ascough and his aunt Mary Clink" are indeed correct although she was not to become Clink until much later.

Ugglebarnby Chapel, (before demolition in the 1860's)

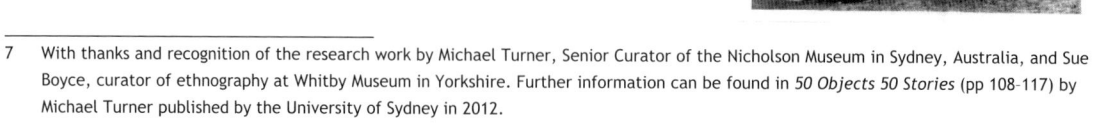

---

[7] With thanks and recognition of the research work by Michael Turner, Senior Curator of the Nicholson Museum in Sydney, Australia, and Sue Boyce, curator of ethnography at Whitby Museum in Yorkshire. Further information can be found in *50 Objects 50 Stories* (pp 108-117) by Michael Turner published by the University of Sydney in 2012.

[8] see the first page of this Appendix.

He went out to Australia in 1834, in a sailing ship, with his aunt and his cousin and a party of friends. Of course they went round the Cape, and the journey took about a year: they were six weeks getting out of the English Channel; they carried live-stock for food which was replenished at various points of call. But in spite of discomforts, my father used to say that he preferred the old sailing-ships to steamers.

At first he practised his profession as a doctor[9], but he soon entered into political life[10]. An Act 'for the Government of New South Wales and Van Diemen's Land' was passed by the New South Wales Parliament in 1842 . The Legislative Council was henceforth to consist of 36 members, 12 nominated by the Governor, the rest to be elected by owners of freehold. The Port Phillip District (which had in 1841 unsuccessfully petitioned for separation) returned five members, the town of Melbourne one, and the town of Sydney two.

The newly-constituted Legislative Council met for the first time on 1st August 1843. Charles Nicholson was returned to the first Legislative Council as one of the five members for the district of Port Phillip[11]. He was again returned in 1848 and, for the county of Argyle in 1851. He was Speaker three times between 1846 and 1856. He was a nominee member for the first Legislative Council of Queensland and became its first president in 1859, but resigned in 1860.

Meanwhile he had been closely associated with the cause of higher education and took a prominent part in the foundation of the University of Sydney, of which he was elected Vice-Provost in 1851, and delivered the inaugural address at the official opening in 1852. He became Chancellor in 1861[12].

During his Australian life he returned to England in 1856, chiefly in connection with the affairs of the newly founded University, for which he secured Arms from the College of Heralds and eventually a Royal Charter.

Writing from 20, King Street, St. James' [London], on August 29th, 1856 to his old friend Mr Thomas Barker[13], of Roslyn Hall, Darlinghurst, Sydney, chiefly with regard to the 'Steam Company that has obtained the contract for the Australian mails' (the P and O), he adds:

> After visiting Scotland and Ireland, I am thinking of joining a party that purpose going to Upper Egypt for the winter. I shall indeed be glad to escape the climate of England, which for alternations of heat and cold — for damp and fog, is worse than I ever dreamt it was. I shall be glad when the time arrives for retracing my steps to the colony, where I feel that I have friends whom l can never replace elsewhere, and a sphere of action such as no other part of the world can afford.

---

9   He set up his practice in Jamieson Street, Wynyard, Sydney.
10 And on receiving the inheritance from his uncle in 1835 he retired from medicine and invested in land, becaming a succesful businessman.
11 Nicholson's own footnote reads: These facts were communicated to me by the Secretary of the Lord Mayor of Melbourne in 1934.
12 This is an error, Sir Charles (Knighted 1852 with Baronetcy conferred in 1859) became Chancellor in 1854, serving until 1862.
13 Built in 1834 and described by a visitor as 'more like a palace than a private house', Roslyn Hall was the home of Thomas Barker (1799-1875) engineer, manufacturer, grazier and philanthropist.

Meanwhile he [my father] was busy collecting funds to insert stained-glass windows in the Great Hall of the newly opened University. An extract from his letter asking for support will perhaps serve better than anything else to show his outlook as to the proper functions of the institution for whose foundation he was so largely responsible.

> It is not, I trust, necessary to combat that mercenary view, which deprecates as unsuitable to the Colony every outlay on objects of a not strictly utilitarian character.
>
> Those who desire to make the Colony their permanent home, — who do not regard it as a place of mere temporary sojourn to be abandoned on the acquisition of a fortune to be spent in other countries, — will require no argument to induce them to enrich as much as possible the land of their choice with all those attributes and associations connected with art, which in so large a measure constitute the chief claim of older countries.
>
> In these often poorer communities large sums are systematically bestowed on objects of a purely aesthetic character, from the conviction that they tend to elevate and improve the moral tastes and habits of all classes.
>
> The same argument applies with infinitely greater weight in a new country, like ours, destitute of all historical monuments and traditions.
>
> It is my persuasion, however, that an impulse has already been given in the right direction — that the real Colonist, whether so by birth or adoption, will be influenced by a generous desire to emulate as far as possible the spirit so prevalent in Europe, and that it may be destined to many of us, — amidst the evidences of a material prosperity not to be paralleled in the history of the world, — to see our Metropolitan City and our chief provincial towns presenting those means for creating and gratifying a cultivated taste, which are so universally met with in older and less affluent communities.

The large sum of money needed for the complete series of windows was successfully collected, and the execution of the work was entrusted to Messrs Clayton and Bell, and was, I believe, their first important commission. My father had the honour of explaining them [the plans] to Queen Victoria and the Prince Consort, and they were for that purpose erected in St George's Hall at Windsor.

The projected journey to Egypt in the winter of 1856-57 resulted in a large and very fine collection of Egyptian antiquities which, together with a collection of Etruscan, Grecian and Roman objects, are now suitably housed in the Museum which bears my father's name in Sydney University.

I wish I could remember his many amusing stories of these journeys, though without the twinkle in the eye with which they were told they would lose much of their humour: but a few of them stick in the memory.

His travelling companions on the Nile found that his eagerness to secure specimens, which included several mummies, grew rather embarrassing; so they agreed that it must be limited, and he told his servant that on no account must any more be accumulated. On one occasion the party had left the boat for some expedition and on their return my father found, to his annoyance, that yet another mummy had made its appearance on the deck. His servant apologetically explained "A black fellow came, wanting to sell this: I told him we did not want it and to go away, but it was no use: so I threw an old blacking bottle at him. He picked up the bottle, extremely pleased, bolted with it and left the mummy behind!"

During this visit to the Old World besides travelling in Egypt he went to Italy and to Russia as well as other countries, with his old friends Sir Philip Rose[14] and Sir Drummond Wolff, He used to tell as how Sir Drummond Wolff's father had been captured by Algerian pirates and made a slave: he was subsequently exchanged for a blind donkey, and he finally escaped by swimming to the flag-ship after the bombardment of Algiers.

It would be deeply interesting to learn something more of the adventures of travellers to out-of-the-way places in those far-off days: but, alas, no records remain, for a reason to be explained later[15].

My father had received the honour of Knighthood in 1852 (no doubt in connection with the opening of the University). He returned to Australia in 1859 and the patent of Baronetcy followed him: he was, in fact, the first Australian to be so honoured. He received many other distinctions: Hon DCL Oxford 1857, when at the Encaenia he walked between Stephenson and Brunel, Hon LLD Cambridge 1868, Hon LLD of his old University of Edinburgh 1886.

His second sojourn in Australia was short. I fancy that he found the changing conditions of the Colony, caused by such events as the Gold rush, less congenial than those of its earlier days. Anyhow he came back to England in 1862 and settled in Portland Place, [London,] and in 1865 he was married to my mother, Sarah Elisabeth Keightley. Though at the time of his marriage he certainly contemplated a return to the Colony, this plan never matured: but his heart was always there. The following are extracts from three letters written about this time to his old friend Thomas Barker[16].

Sept 10 1867

My dear Mr Barker,
The birth of your son must have been a source of the greatest delight and happiness to you and Mrs B. I can the more readily sympathize with you from the fact of my wife having also presented me with a boy, (my eldest brother, Charles) a fine healthy little fellow, full of health and vigour. You would I dare say be, like some of my other friends, surprised at my entering into married life after waiting so many long years

---

14 Sir Philip Rose (1816-1883), solicitor, first 'agent' of the Conservative Party, was the founder of the Hospital for Consumption and Diseases of the Chest now known as the Royal Brompton Hospital.

15 They were lost in the 1899 fire which destroyed The Grange in Totteridge.

16 Nicholson's own footnote reads: This Mr Barker was born in London in 1799 and came to Sydney in 1814 to learn engineering and flour milling from John Dickson, who imported and erected the first flour-mill in Sydney.

before taking that step. I can only say that I have found every reason for congratulating myself in the choice I have made. I really feel my domestic happiness complete in the society of my dear wife and the endearments of our little boy.

We spend a great part of our time in the country, where we generally contrive to have one or two old (often Australian) friends staying with us. I should myself have no hesitation about returning to the Colony, and making it my last final resting place. My wife, however, although ready to conform to any step I may wish to take, is naturally unwilling to be separated from her family and the numerous and attached friends she possesses in England. All the accounts that reach us from Australia, representing the lawless state of society prevailing there, — the murders and wholesale brigandage — the floods and droughts which desolate the country year by year, — are all calculated to prejudice people against the Colony. For the present we therefore consider ourselves domiciled in England, — where no doubt all the resources of the highest civilization are to be found in the largest degree. I moreover find that I enjoy much more vigorous health in England than I did when last in the Colony. You should take a trip home with your wife and boy. The voyage and change of scene will add 10 years to your life.

April 10 1869

To the same.

There is really no joy in life comparable to that which springs from the parental tie. Our boy is within a few days of completing his second year; he is full of health and life and every day adds to his vocabulary some new word or phrase, the result of growing intelligence, the marked development of which it is most interesting to trace. There is but one cloud that casts a shadow over this treasure, and that is the feeling that I can hardly expect to live to see him come to years of discretion, or to be able to guide and direct him on the perilous outset of life, with all its pitfalls and countless temptations that await every young man on his entering the world. I can only hope to be spared sufficiently long to give his mind a right turn and to train him in the essence of those qualities which are to be his safeguard in after life.

.......I have a little place about 35 miles from Town, with a small old-fashioned house, where we find the greatest enjoyment after the excitement and fatigue of London life. In this little spot (Hadleigh) we are as much out of the world as if living in the Bush of Australia. Our nearest visiting neighbour (except the Clergyman) is 7 miles off, and I do not think that a gentleman's house has been erected in the neighbourhood within the last 300 years. Should you be tempted to revisit the old world again, I should be delighted to receive you in our Bush house.

Feb. 16. 1871

To the same.

Your son has the advantage of some 3 or 4 years in age over mine. I hope, however, that years hence, — when each of us has passed away, — our boys may have the opportunity of forming a friendship with each other, and that that friendship may be as long and sincere as that which existed between their respective Fathers.

That wish was partially fulfilled 63 years later, when I had the pleasure of meeting Mr T C Barker, the son referred to, of Maryland House, Bringelly, NSW. He gave me the letters written by my father to his, from which the above extracts are drawn, and he took me to see the site of my father's country house at Luddenham about 40 miles from Sydney.

Another letter of July 20th 1875 [from my father] to his old friend Mr W C Windeyer (afterwards Sir William Windeyer[17], Judge) whom he had befriended in boyhood and who was the first graduate of Sydney University, is worth quoting for its general interest as well as that part which is personal to the present writer.

> My dear Windeyer,
> .... I have not been able to see much of Mr. Russell beyond the occasion when he dined with me, chiefly in consequence of his being constantly on the move, and only in London at intervals. I am glad to renew my acquaintance with him, for he does credit to the Colony, and to the Institution to which he owes his training. I need not say how glad I shall be to see (and endeavour to show civility to) any friend of yours from the Colony, who may be visiting England. I always strive, as far as I can, to give a helping hand and to show any little attention in my power to **young Colonists** arriving for the first time in this great and bewildering Babel of London. I find many of them coming here, — intelligent and presentable men, — with ample means; but without any introductions to such society as it is desirable they should meet. Society in England is to most strangers cold and distant, and it must **in truth** be added that of late years so many people have returned to Europe, whose **sole** credential to consideration was their **wealth**, that there is a disposition on the part of the better classes to give the go-bye to all who hail from Australia.
>
> This feeling is of course easily overcome by a few friendly introductions. There is, however, really a want in London of someone **officially** to represent the Colonies, and who ought to be provided with a stipend that would enable him to show some little attention and some sort of (social) civility to people coming from the Colony for the first time: even if no more could be done than is practised by the American Minister who asks all his countrymen to tea.
>
> Each Colony ought to have its own House in a good part of London, where the public office of the Agent General might be established and apartments provided for residence, of sufficient extent for him to gather — on a few stated occasions — the Colonists, and introduce them to each other and to such of the leading statesmen as

---

17 Sir William Charles Windeyer (1834-1897), judge, educationalist, politician and Attorney-General in several administrations.

might, and would be willing to respond to his invitation. A liberal stipend ought to be attached to the office, which would in point of fact resemble that of a foreign Minister. Without saying anything to the disparagement of the present Agents for the Colonies, it may be sufficient to note that their pay is utterly inadequate to enable them to dispense anything in the shape of **hospitality**, or fairly to be considered as **representative** men.

It might be difficult to find men in the Colony who would combine in themselves all the requisites for such a post. Still, I have no doubt such men might be found. Do not imagine for a moment that I include **myself** in the list of those eligible for such a position as that which I have sketched. Do, however, think over the subject; it is one that affects you and every Colonist who has a family, and who is anxious that the Country of his adoption should stand well in the eyes of European society.

......I have little personal news to give you. My wife presented me with a third son about 6 months ago, whom, from association with the Colony, I have named 'Sydney'. If life has lost with me many, — nay most — of its illusions, it has not been without the compensation of substantial happiness in the **new** interests which have sprung up around me in my domestic relations. Were I a few years younger, I should return to the Colony, which I look forward to as likely to be the home of my boys. The tie of my wife's relations and the education of our eldest son will, I reckon, bind me to England for the rest of my days.

There came into my possession in recent years an interesting Memorandum dealing with my father's life in Australia. I have no idea who wrote it, nor of its date, but obviously it must have been about the time when his Australian life was coming to an end. It reads as follows:

SIR CHARLES NICHOLSON Bt.
MEMO.

This gentleman is an exemplary instance of one who, having attained colonial fortune and honours, devotes his means and position to the advancement of the land of his adoption, not in merely filling offices thereat and indirectly enhancing his own interests, but by visits to the land of his birth, and thence to every part of Europe, promulgating his experience to the encouragement of emigration and local enterprise on the one hand, and to stimulating commercial reciprocities and appreciation on the other.

As a discerning settler in Australia, with possessions discreetly selected, in various districts of New South Wales, he acquired that knowledge of the capabilities and requirements of a vast region whose phases and prosperity depended vitally upon profound **legislation**! Hence, for several years up to 1858, his solicitude and energies were directed to this object in the capacities of "Speaker" or "President" of the several forms of local Parliaments until Colonial responsible Government became fairly established.

In like spirit he infused a yearning for the more exalting and time-honouring institutions of his fatherland and his 'status' as a scholar and an accomplished beneficent man eventually distinguished him as the first Chancellor of the Sydney University — a perpetual monument of his taste, ability and munificence. Indeed, so richly has he endowed it — even to the produce of his extensive researches in Europe and Asia and especially by the collection of Egyptian and other antiquities, which he personally sought at a vast expense, that he will prove in the future of Australia what Sir Hans Sloane[18] is to us in reference to the British Museum! — while his wisdom, benevolence and amenities will be the leading star of her Society; and the numerous papers he has disseminated on her statistics and resources will be the handbook and text for our new world's elucidation and guide.

This somewhat pompous document suggests that my father was a very wealthy man. Whether that was actually the case when he was in Australia, I do not know: evidently his uncle left him well-off and he must have made a good deal to have been able to afford his large gifts to the University, But certainly when he settled in England he could not be described as 'very rich'; and it is my belief that he acted up to his convictions in this matter. He often spoke with indignation of people who went to the Colony purely to make money, and when they had accomplished their object of getting the utmost out of the country came away to spend it elsewhere. And I think it is probable that all or most of the money he made in Australia he left behind him in his magnificent gifts.

He retained his deep interest in Australia and all that concerned it to the end of his life, and nothing gave him greater satisfaction (in his 94th year) than the receipt of the following telegram dated September 30th, 1902[19].

> Senate and members of the Sydney University assembled to celebrate its jubilee recognise the goodness of Providence in prolonging your life to see this day and thank you for your good wishes and continued interest in the University whose first steps you guided with so much sagacity and foresight.
>
> MacLaurin, Chancellor.

---

18 Irish physician and collector Sir Hans Sloane (1660-1753), inventor of 'drinking chocolate' and founding governor of the Foundling Hospital in London, left his large house and vast collection of 'curiosities' to the nation: effectively the beginning of the British Museum.

19 And which arrived on 11th Oct 1902.

My mother was the eldest daughter of Archibald Keightley. He was born in 1795[20] and was one of a large family, mainly settled in Ireland; the most distinguished of them was the Right Hon. Thomas Keightley, who became Lord Treasurer of Ireland and married Frances, the youngest daughter of Edward Hyde, Earl of Clarendon: her elder sister was married to King James II and was the mother of Queen Anne. The family takes its name from the town of Keighley in Yorkshire.

In early life my grandfather set up as a solicitor in London and he became a great friend and the sole executor of Sir Thomas Lawrence[21], the artist. At Lawrence's death he had to deal with a vast accumulation of papers as well as with his complicated business and artistic affairs, and had to make all the arrangements for the State Funeral in St. Paul's Cathedral, He collected and had inserted in five large volumes a very large number of autograph letters from all the notabilities of the day, — artists of course, statesmen, soldiers, bishops, nobility and royalty, besides many beautiful sketches by Lawrence and others. These he arranged and catalogued in a most careful manner. The collection was handed down as a family heirloom and eventually came into my possession. But I have thought it best that it should be preserved among the archives of The Royal Academy of Arts, of which Lawrence was so distinguished a President, and it has been accepted by them.

Archibald Keightley

My grandfather subsequently became Registrar of the Charterhouse in 1838, and it fell to him to make the legal arrangements when the School (at which he himself had been educated) was moved to Godalming. As the Charterhouse was my mother's old home, it was in the Charterhouse Chapel that my parents were married[22] and their three sons baptised.

I think my parents became acquainted with one another through Admiral Sir Henry Denham[23], an old friend of both families. He became my godfather: all I know about him is that he was reputed to be the man who invented the plan of putting paddle-wheels at the sides of steamers instead of at their stern. My other godfather was George Salting[24], son of an old Australian friend[25], whose wonderful collections of artistic treasures are to be seen at the Victoria and Albert Museum.

---

20 In Liverpool. He died in 1877 in London. In addition to the four daughters mentioned in this book, he had a son Archibald Harry Keightley who died at the age of six in Dec 1847.
21 1769-1830
22 on 8th Aug 1865
23 Sir Henry Denham (1800-1877) charted the south-west Pacific Ocean and served as Commander-in-Chief of the Pacific Station from 1864-1866. On his return he was knighted for his hydrographical services.
24 Born in Australia and educated at Sydney University, George Salting(1835-1909) was a wealthy London art collector who also left paintings, bronzes, miniatures and china to the British Museum and National Gallery. The entire collection was worth over £10 million.
25 Severin Knud Salting (1805-1865) was a Danish immigrant to Australia and made his fortune in sheep-farming and sugar-growing. Another benefactor of Sydney University, he retired to England in 1858.

To return to the family: One of my grandfather's nephews married Margaret Wakefield, of Kendal, the aunt of the Mary Wakefield who founded the Westmorland Musical Festival[26], and did more than anyone to give the initial impetus to the Competitive Festival movement which has achieved such marvellous results throughout the country and all over the world. I am glad to be able to claim a connection, though a distant one, with such a gifted musician and with her extremely musical family whom I got to know well later on when I lived in the north.

My grandfather married (1836[27]) Sarah Elizabeth Yates[28]. The home of the Yates's was Sapperton Hall, near Uttoxeter, and it remained in the possession of the family until 1880. The original house was destroyed during the reign of Charles I but was rebuilt.

One of these Yates's, Christopher (born in 1677), compiled some most interesting Memorials of the family, including a complete pedigree from 1471. It would be impossible to quote this curious old document in full, but some of it is so quaint and gives such a picture of the times, that it seems worth while to give a few extracts.

> The family of Yates of Sapperton in the County of Derby, whereof I now intend to write is of ancient and gentle lineage as will plainly appear in these Memorials by me carefullie gathered together from divers sources as familie papers preserved of long time in the Muniment Chest at Sapperton, ...

> The Founder of the House, the Adam, as I may call him of the Race may have been a Chief of the tribe of the Corytani, or perchance of the Cornarji, which, as wee learne from J Caesar, his Commentaries, were the ancient British Inhabitants of the central parts of this Island, where they dwelled in huts made out of timber, or of mud and clay and were much given to fighting and hunting, wherein mostly they passed their lives. ..... And albeit the Emperor J C did consider these ancient Britons to be meer Barbarians, and, indeed, called 'em so, yet, methinks one need not be ashamed to reckon 'em amongst one's Forefathers; For by all accounts they were a brave, honest and generous race; and though they might not peradventure looke verie much like Gentlemen with their bodies painted in various colours and habited in skins of wild animals, with their long yellow hair streaming over their shoulders, and with thick mustachies on their upper lips, as J Caesar describes 'em, yet it must be truly allowed that they had good Blood in their veins as witness their love of Liberty and their brave defence thereof against the martial Romans in many fierce Battles and during many years. But since I cannot produce Testimonies; — "quia vates carent" that my ancestry flourish'd among the Britons I will pass 'em bye, yea, lett 'em pass with their yellowe Heads and their blewe posteriours, a trulie marvellous sight, sure, Solomon in all his glorye was never array'd like one of 'em.

---

26 See Chapter III
27 They married in Church Broughton, Derbyshire on 27th Dec 1836.
28 Born in 1812 in Sapperton, Derbyshire, died at 2 Ashburn Place, London in 1893.

The following is a copy of a letter, included in the same papers, from Christopher Yates to his brother Arthur:

Dearest Brother,

Tho' I have no business nor news to send you yet write I must, if it be only to plague you for your silence, but (to confess a truth), I myself take a vast pleasure in this sort of entertainment and this waie of enjoying you by ye strength of imagination is ye only consolation for ye want of real enjoyment. And since my fancy runs low, I shall supply ye defecte of it by telling you 2 or 3 idle stories which fly about town. T'other day (then to fall upon ye matter) one Mr. Evelyn, son to ye virtuoso Evelyn, and Mr Foster with another gentleman were all in a certain musick-club room after having drunke to a great pitch and it happen'd yt one of 'em finding himself disposed to be musical, took up a Violin and began to fumble upon it. Mr Evelyn, having likewise an harmonious soul was resolved to beare some part in ye musick and being able to doe nothing else kept time with a great heavy case knife yt laid very conveniently for ye purpose upon ye table; ye other gentleman Mr Foster while his two camerades were in ye heat of action, chanc'd by ill luck to lay his finger on yt part of ye table upon which his neighbour beat time, and whether it was yt ye man's ill genius guided his hand or how it came about, ad huc sub judice lis est, but he cut ye poor finger of with ye greatest dexterity imaginable, insomuch yt ye Surgeons do all admire ye Mans address in picking ye joint so critically; — however its a bad wind yt blows nobody profit and this ill accident is likely to make work for ye Lawyers, ye Man yt is maimed designing to bring his action of assault and battery against his companion."

The last of our branch of the Yates family was Arthur (born 1841[29]). He inherited the sporting instincts of his ancestors and was a celebrated trainer of horses: he himself rode no less than 460 winners, and is the hero of the famous incident at Croydon when, thrown in a race, he grabbed the horse's tail, pulled himself back into the saddle, and won. He trained 'Cloister' the winner of the Grand National in 1893. He only made one bet in his life, 1/- [One shilling], which he lost! I remember him as an old man at his home at Bishop's Sutton, Hants, surrounded by all sorts of animals, which he adored: he had only recently given up driving a four-in-hand of zebras!

So much for my forebears. If these records of the past have been somewhat lengthy it is mainly because I feel that they are too interesting to be entirely lost sight of amongst family papers. But I must confess to a special fondness for such links with the past. I like to think that my father was born in the reign of George III: he knew an old lady who used to drink tea with Dr. Johnson: he left England to begin his life's work when railways were newly invented, and he lived to ride in a motor-car. But my favourite link of all is that my father was alive with Haydn, Haydn with Handel, and Handel with Purcell: so that it needs only three lives to bridge over the time between the greatest organist of Westminster Abbey and myself.

---

[29] Arthur Scotland Yates (1841-1922) won over 450 races as a jockey and rode in the Grand National in 1870 and 1872, however he did not win that race as a jockey, but only as a trainer. He is said to have saddled 2955 winners.

Appendix B: Recollections of Sir Charles Nicholson

1) By Clara Lane[1]

Looking through the vista of years, almost the first recollection of my dear friend is the "little Sarah" — home from school, wearing a black frock (I think in mourning for kind Miss Croft), with her sunny brown hair falling upon it; and she and my father together examining our family sketches and portraits, with great sympathetic interest and the same disregard of age that drew her, later on, to become the warm-hearted friend of both my father and myself. For, in the bright home of the Charterhouse, with its old-world character and beauty, the genial hosts made many holiday meetings for us, in so informal and intimate a fashion that it was like a family circle. Paintings, music, charades, little recitations, were frequent and delightful pleasures for the days and evenings of some happy years.

The pursuit of art was ever more and more enjoyed in our homes; we were often together, daring every kind of subject, and nothing daunted by failures; we loved the Studio at Charterhouse, and the happiest hours passed in drawing flowers, faces, figures, corners of the Charterhouse, folds of drapery, and each other. Society was at a discount, but politeness was ingrain; so that when, one day, — the sunlight at its best, — leisure quite assured as we thought, the door opened to admit our dear hostess with a gentleman friend, there was only a well-repressed note of displeasure at the interruption. "Don't disturb yourselves", we were told, and Mrs Keightley and Sir Charles Nicholson sat down on a large restful sofa behind us. Momentous results followed shortly. One evening, in that pretty octagon drawing-room, packets were handed to Miss Keightley and her sister, clearly addressed, and found to contain turquoise jewellery, — necklace and brooch suggesting "forget-me-not" very gracefully and slyly. "Would they be accepted?" At my home, soon afterwards, my father and mother learned that Sir Charles had won the troth of her who was to be the most faithful and devoted of wives. My father was touched and delighted with Sir Charles' cordiality in meeting us, and a warm friendship began which has been like sunlight in our lives.

Long drives by day; happy evenings; every turn in that summer-time brought to light the rich stores of learning and memory in the mind of Sir Charles: — and his heart must have gladly thrilled when Sarah sang Ruth's words "Thy people shall be my people and thy God my God", — which she did very sweetly.

Then the day came when the guests arrived at hospitable Charterhouse for the marriage. No home could have been more suited for the occasion: all hearts were warm in kindly sympathy. All that taste and love could suggest was there. The Bride and Bridegroom were worthy of each other.

Their wedding trip was unfortunately cut short by the death of their good friend Mr Salting. Therefore the married life began at Hadleigh House; and there Miss Yates and I were soon privileged and proud visitors. There, life was an ideal experience of cheerful social duties

---

[1] See Chapter I, p 6.

and (in the home) bright and kindly intercourse and intellectual enjoyment.

The house in Devonshire Place looked at first almost a bachelor-like abode. The furnishing was solid and grave; but it was soon invested with taste and lightness by the lady's presence. And then old friends and new trooped into the kind influence of it; and the best society that England afforded gathered there, in literature and art, distinction in science, and in all professions; each one being sure of being understood in the discussions that called forth every kind of ability. Sir Charles and his wife always loved society; they brought out the best in everybody's nature. In Sir Charles' case this was sometimes effected by contradicting people, very likely by throwing a perfectly new light on a subject; for there was an alert freshness in his intellect that brooked no superficial plausibility; and he had a store of facts at his command, safe in his extraordinary memory and accuracy.

There was a very busy time for the master and mistress when they saw the house at Totteridge that struck them as suitable for them to live in fresh air, and yet keep in touch with London. The plan of removal ripened and became an accomplished fact, and The Grange was made a most comfortable house. Sir Charles never tired of developing and improving the modest estate, while the lady adorned and perfected the house with singularly happy success. It became an ideal home for the sons, however they might be away from it in manly business and studies.

The third little son will be oftenest thought of as at Totteridge, for there, in a world of charm for so quick a child, Sydney was thorough in all his tastes. I remember his father delighting in the child's bright presence, — asking me with beaming eyes "what do you think of that thing?"

The fine, lofty lime-trees, chestnuts, oaks and many other varieties of trees, with firs and azaleas, rhododendrons, cedar, laurel; — the boat on the pond; — the gay flowers — were all mysterious delights to the boy in a neat black velvet suit, who in the evening listened with a hush for the "High Barnet train" speeding on with a shrill whistle, as he nestled to sleep in his cot.

The Grange, too, was full of charms in its interior; it boasted a fortunate dining-hall for displaying the precious Flemish tapestry, that had crossed oceans and was yet as bright and fresh as ever; a picturesque staircase, adorned with many a portrait and picture by his mother; a flower-decked studio and drawing-room in which he found the greatest treasure in the whole list, the piano for his small fingers to test with delight.

The Grange was constantly visited (or filled) by friends from far and near, who met with the heartiest of welcomes from Sir Charles, who had been devoted to hospitality all his life, and whose resources for entertaining and interesting every receptive person, every intelligent listener, were inexhaustible and, moreover, most ably seconded by the good hostess: an unobtrusive old-world politeness placed every grade of persons at their ease. The life was healthy and good in every sense.

2) By Baroness von Deichmann (née Hilda de Bunsen)[2]

My recollections of Sir Charles Nicholson date from my early childhood, and I remember that he was classed as a man of letters and an Egyptologist, at Abbey Lodge, as one who shared my father's wide interests.

Sarah says she first remembers me when I was sixteen, when, soon after her marriage, Sir Charles brought her to a party at Abbey Lodge. She said that Sir Charles had told her that he thought she would like the de Bunsens, as they were unconventional. But I little thought then that a friendship of a lifetime would unite me to his wife. Now, as I recall old memories of Sir Charles, he is connected intimately with the bright years of my girlhood and the joys and sorrows of later years. He always received me in the same genial, kind manner, and his almost paternal interest was ever the same.

It must have been about 1870 that I went to Hadleigh, Sir Charles' place in Essex, and formed the beginning of our so happy intercourse, Sir Charles lending me books to read and telling me so much about his historical and archaeological interests. I particularly remember a long walk, during which he discussed the Moabite Stone and how wonderfully it proved the truth of ancient scripture history.

I do not think I ever saw anyone so kind as Sir Charles uniformly was, to what one usually terms "bores" or "hangers-on". He paid them just the same attention as he did the distinguished people in Science and Art who came to his house.

There was something old-fashioned about his courteous manner to all. Also, though he loved a joke and had a great sense of humour, his eyes twinkling when he told a funny story, I never heard him say an unkind word about anyone, or judge anyone. His nature had something childlike and guileless about it, and he did not seem to be 'of the world', but to think all were as he. His interest in the political affairs of the day was very keen, and remained so to the last. Australia, which he had done so much for in its early days as a Colony, was very near his heart.

In his London house, Devonshire Place, I spent such happy hours in almost daily intercourse with Sarah. And how many interesting people I met there! It was a most hospitable centre for so many, and Sir Charles seemed to have heart for it all.

The Grange suited him exactly for the beautiful evening of his life, for the planting of trees was his great pursuit and he had a great love of gardening, and The Grange became more and more [important] to him when he gave up the London house. He made it a country home to so many, and he received all with the same kindness.

The failure of his eyesight was a dreadful trial in his later years, and I often admired his patience and sweet temper under so great an affliction, and he once latterly told me how he clung more and more to the New Testament and the words of Our Lord. Indeed they seemed

---
2   See Chapter I, Footnote 13

to be the guide of his daily life, and how beautifully he repeated the Lord's Prayer at family prayers the last time I saw him there downstairs, a few weeks before he died. How bravely he bore the great disaster of destruction of the old Grange by fire and the loss of so much that could never be replaced. It was then that the journal of his life was burnt, which would have been such a valuable relic now.

I love to think that he had the pleasure of his little grand-daughter, and the last time I saw him out of doors was on Whit Monday in lovely weather, sitting under the magnificent lime-tree with the baby on his knee.

When I last saw him, about a week before he "passed over" he was on the sofa in his room and very weak; but a glance of recognition came into his face as he kissed my hand. How I love to think of it now!

He died, honoured and respected by all who knew him, and his long life seems to have been singularly happy and prosperous.

Appendix C: Nicholson's observations on the role of choristers

It is a great satisfaction to me to think how well most of my old choristers have done in after life and how few have turned out failures. I am certain that choristers gain something which other boys miss, and that any time that is lost from their general education is amply made up by that gain. But exactly what is the nature of the gain it is hard to say: I think, however, that two important elements in it are a sense of responsibility and a sense of reverence – I mean not only for things religious but for things beautiful. Certainly they are profoundly affected by the beauty of the music and the architecture by which they are surrounded, as well as by the stately services in which they take so important a part: so that they approach their duties with a greater seriousness than ordinary boys of their age. I have, for instance, known my choristers to be quite miserable if an anthem has gone badly, but I have not yet met a set of boys who were seriously disturbed if their arithmetic were not up to sample! Probably the secret lies in the high standard both in music and conduct that is expected from choristers.

In the days of which I am speaking a familiar piece of furniture in every Cathedral practice room, as familiar as the venerable grand piano, was the cane. This was still and, as history tells us, has been from time immemorial the recognised instrument for dealing with the delinquencies of choristers, whether in their behaviour or singing. I believe it has now gone out of fashion under more modern educational methods. No doubt in old days it was often abused, but I still think that, properly employed, it was the best form of correction, far better than such things as impositions, which seem to me a pure waste of time. Boys learnt to take their punishment manfully and without ill-temper, and it had the advantage of being soon over: to talk of humiliation or the lowering of a boy's self-respect seems to me sheer nonsense: I never saw a sign of such a thing. So most of my boys, though we have always been most friendly and happy together, have had to 'bend over the desk' at one time or another, and I think we have been all the better friends because they knew that they could never with impunity be disorderly or cheeky or slack in their work, but were, to use the old Monastic expression, 'children under the rod'.

I feel certain that the choirboys are the most important element in the music of any church or cathedral: their singing and their behaviour and their general outlook on their duties can do more to make or mar a service than anything else. I attribute nearly all such success as I have attained as a church musician to the wonderful support I have always received from my choristers, and I am proud to number some of my old boys among my best friends in after life.

Two criticisms are commonly expressed against the effect of a chorister's life on a boy, nearly always by those who have had nothing to do with choristers. The first is that their general education suffers in comparison with that of other boys of their age. The second is that they get so much church-going in boyhood that they never wish to go near a church again when they are released from the choir. If we mean by education only the state-made, conventional article, where the number of periods per week allotted to a schedule of subjects is the criterion of efficiency, then perhaps the chorister does suffer. But if we take a broader view of education, judging it largely by the results shown in after life, it will be found in actual experience that the music is not a hindrance to development but is in itself a very fine medium of mental training. There are certain choir schools where non-singing boys are admitted — in some of them the choristers are even in the minority. Yet, judged by the mere test of scholarships gained, the choristers almost invariably beat the non-singers. If it were possible to compile a list of those who began as choristers and have reached good positions and even distinction in later life (not only in the musical world), the results would be surprising. Of course there are some failures, but I question whether many men who have been choirboys look back to their experience in a good choir with anything but gratitude.

As to the idea that they get sickened of religion, one has only to consider the very large number of clergy who have been choirboys: amongst them are Deans, Bishops and Archbishops. And amongst the ranks of the men in Cathedral and parish church choirs such a large majority have been choirboys that were it not for their presence the choirs would hardly exist. The truth is exactly the opposite of what is so often stated. In most cases choirboys get such a love of the Church that they are miserable when the time comes for them to give up their singing, and in after years (especially where they are looked after and encouraged at the time of adolescence) they become among its most loyal members. This is not a matter of opinion but of actual fact, as any impartial enquiry would show.

I suppose I am one of those lucky people who have always found it easy to get a response from choirboys: there certainly seem to be some who do not find it so, and it is evidently more a matter of temperament than of training: but this response is absolutely necessary if good results are to be attained. The key to the situation is the relationship of the master to his boys: and the points (apart from musical matters) which I think are most likely to establish a good relationship are these — personal interest and acquaintanceship with the individual boy, his home, his interests, his ambitions: never to 'talk down' to a boy's supposed level or to treat him either as a fool or a knave, but always to assume that he is a sensible person wanting to do his job properly: an entire absence of any sentimental relationships between the master and the boy: an understanding of what can reasonably be expected of a boy, with strict discipline at the proper time, but no punishment unless the boy knows he deserves it, and above all no 'nagging' when it is over and done with. The greatest mistake, and one most commonly made, is when the boys of a choir are treated merely as a 'choral unit', without care for or knowledge of the individuality of each. You can never get the best out of boys by dealing with them 'in the lump': it is individual knowledge that counts every time.

Appendix D: Nicholson's observations on cathedral worship

It may be wondered why I should have given such a full account of Carlisle Cathedral as I knew it. My excuse is that I feel that there is a certain usefulness in putting on record some sort of a picture, however imperfect, of life in a rather remote and comparatively unimportant Cathedral, before Cathedrals had been 'improved', and as they were in the 'dead old days'. Comparing those days with the present there is certainly much cause for thankfulness: - for the greatly Increased use that is made of the Cathedrals; for the welcome that is extended to all who care to visit them; for the care bestowed on their fabric and adornment; for the vast improvement in the quality of the music sung by Cathedral choirs (I am not so sure about the quality of their actual singing). But I cannot help feeling that there is also something to regret in the peaceful way in which the whole Body, clergy and choir, did their duty as they saw it, with a complete absence of advertisement or 'stunts' of any kind.

One looks back on the days when the full morning and evening services were sung, as a matter of course, in every ancient Cathedral, on practically every day in the year: when the daily psalms were always sung in full, and even the Exhortation was not shortened or the State prayers curtailed at a statutory service. I suppose it was all a bit formal; but at least it did not give the impression that the main object of going to church was to get out of it as soon as possible!

Is there not some danger nowadays, with our care for fabrics and ornaments, the advance in ritual and ceremonial, the desire to draw thousands of visitors and to arrange special services of a popular character (of course with the proviso that they must not be too long), lest the true purpose of these ancient buildings should be forgotten? They were undoubtedly intended (as any of the ancient Statutes will show) to be noble shrines for the continual worship of a community, both of clergy and laymen: and who shall say that this faithful service was without value? Is the Church really stronger and the country more religious since the regularity of this community worship in the central church of each diocese has been so largely intermitted, and Deans and Canons have in so many cases apparently come to think that their presence is not required unless they are technically 'in residence'? I feel sure that if the main duty could be done without leaving the other things undone the gain, not only to Cathedral life but to the Church in general, would be great. In these bustling days surely there is a place for the calm of the daily Cathedral service, and even the rushing motorist might often be glad to pause at a Cathedral if he were reasonably sure that he would not strike a 'dumb day' or choir holidays!

There is a great and laudable desire to restore the fabrics of Cathedrals to their former glory, and to fill them with beauty and colour: but why should the choral worship so often be stinted and curtailed? "So few people attend," - but at the least 'two or three are gathered together'. "It is so costly," - but so was the alabaster box of precious ointment[1].

---

[1] Sir Edward Bairstow also uses the "alabaster box of precious ointment" analogy in his 1919 letter to Nicholson, see Chapter V.

Appendix E: The principal organs played by Sydney Nicholson

1. St Andrew's, Totteridge: Brindley & Foster, 1881
2. Rugby School Chapel: Bryceson, 1872
3. Rugby School Speech Room: Bryceson, 1890
4. Chipping Barnet Church: William Hill, 1884
5. Eton Lower Chapel: Lewis & Co, 1891
6. Carlisle Cathedral: Willis, 1856
7. Carlisle Cathedral: Harrison & Harrison, 1907
8. Manchester Cathedral: Hill, 1871
9. Manchester Cathedral: Hill, 1910
10. Nicholson's house organ: Henry Speechley, c 1900
11. Westminster Abbey: Hill, 1848 rebuilt 1884/1899/1908
12. St Sepulchre-without-Newgate, Holborn Viaduct: Harrison & Harrison, 1932
13. *St Nicolas College, Chislehurst, Hill c 1860 rebuilt Harrison & Harrison, 1928*[1]
14. *St Nicolas College, Chislehurst, Harrison & Harrison, 1931*[1]

---

[1] For photographs and specifications of the two organs at the College of St Nicolas, Chislehurst, see *SNCSN*.

St Andrew's, Totteridge: Brindley & Foster, 1881

Swell	Violin Diapason	8
	Lieblich Gedact	8
	Vox Angelica	8
	Salicet	4
	Oboe	8
Great	Open Diapason	8
	Dulciana	8
	Hohl Flute	8
	Principal	4
	Geigen	8
	Harmonic Flute	4
Pedal	Sub Bass	16
	Flute Bass	8

Manual compass CC to g^3, Pedal compass CCC to F
Tubular Pneumatic action throughout
Couplers: Sw/Gt, Sw/Ped, Gt/Ped, Gt Suboctave
Three composition pedals

This organ was rebuilt by Rest Cartwright (possibly a former employee of Brindley & Foster) in 1949 and then replaced in 1970 with a 'Positive' model pipe organ built by J W Walker.

Rugby School Chapel: Bryceson, 1872

Echo				Solo		
	Dulciana	8			Harmonic Diapason	8
	Voix Celestes	8			German Gamba	8
	Gemshorn	4			Flute	4
	Hohl Flute	4			Corno di Bassetto	8
	Euphone	8			prepared	
	Tremulant				Tuba	8
Swell	Bourdon & Double Dulciana	16		**Great**	Double Open Diapason	16
	Open Diapason	8			Open Diapason	8
	Flute	8			Rohr Flute	8
	Lieblich Gedact	8			Salicional	8
	Keraulophon	8			Principal	4
	Principal	4			Octave Gamba	4
	Harmonic Flute	4			Twelfth	2⅔
	Fifteenth	2			Fifteenth	2
	Cornet	III			Full Mixture	III
	Cymbale	II			Posaune	8
	Double Trumpet	16		**Choir**	Violin Diapason	8
	Cornopean	8			Lieblich Gedact	8
	Oboe	8			Cone Gamba	8
	Vox Humana	8			Spitz Flute	4
	Clarion	4			Clarinet	8
	Tremulant					
Pedal	Double Open Diapason	32			Bass Flute	8
	Open Diapason	16			Twelfth	6
	Violone	16			Fifteenth	4
	Bourdon	16			Trombone	16
	Violoncello	8			Bassoon	16

Five divisions on three manuals plus pedals. Electro-Pneumatic action and detached console.

Rugby School Speech Room: Bryceson, 1890

We have been unable to locate the specification of the 3-manual, 40 stop instrument by Bryceson, which was completed in the 'Speech Room' (i.e. school hall) in 1890. See photograph in Chapter II.

Chipping Barnet Church: William Hill, 1884

Swell	Bourdon	16
	Open Diapason	8
	Rohr Flute	8
	Salicional	8
	Voix Celeste	8
	Principal	4
	Octave Gamba	4
	Fifteenth	2
	Mixture	II
	Cornopean	8
	Oboe	8
Great	Double Diapason	16
	Open Diapason I	8
	Open Diapason II	8
	Hohl Flute	8
	Principal	4
	Wald Flute	4
	Twelfth	2⅔
	Fifteenth	2
	Mixture	III
	Posaune	8
Choir	Dulciana	8
	Lieblich Gedact	8
	Suabe Flute	4
	Flautina	2
	Clarinet	8
Pedal	Violoncello	8
	Open Diapason	16
	Bourdon	16

Manual compass CC to g^3, Pedal compass CC to f^1. Tracker and tubular pneumatic action, blowing hydraulic, three composition pedals to each manual, toe pedals for Gt/Ped and Tremulant. Couplers: Swell to Pedal, Swell to Great, Swell to Choir, Swell octave, Choir to Pedal, Great to Pedal.

The organ was rebuilt in 1924 by Rothwell, in 1939 by Hill, Norman & Beard and in 1967 and 1969 by N P Mander.

Eton Lower Chapel: Lewis & Co, 1891

Swell			Great		
	Lieblich Gedact	16		Bourdon	16
	Geigen Principal	8		Open Diapason No 1	8
	Rohr Flöte	8		Open Diapason No 2	8
	Viole da Gambe	8		Flute Harmonique	8
	Voix Celestes	8		Octave	4
	Geigen Principal	4		Flute Harmonique	4
	Flautina	2		Octave Quint	2⅔
	Horn	8		Super-Octave	2
	Oboe	8		Trumpet	8
Choir	Salicional	8	**Pedal**	Great Bass	16
	Dulciana	8		Sub-Bass	16
	Lieblich Gedact	8		Trombone	16
	Flauto traverso	8			
	Clarinet	8			

Manual compass CC to a^3, Pedal compass CC to f^1. Tracker (originally tubular pneumatic) action, blowing hydraulic, three composition pedals to Swell, four composition pedals to Great and Pedal, two pneumatic pistons to Great and Pedal.

The organ underwent a major rebuild in 1927 by Hunter and in 1970 by Harrison & Harrison.

Carlisle Cathedral: Willis, 1856

Swell							
	Double Diapason	16			Fourniture	III	
	Open Diapason	8			Trombone	8	
	Stopped Diapason	8			Trumpet	8	
	Vox Angelica	8	(1875)		Clarion	4	
	Principal	4		**Choir**	Open Diapason	8	
	Flageolet	2			Claribella	8	wood
	Echo Cornet	IV			Dulciana	8	
	Contra Fagotto	16			Gamba	8	
	Hautboy	8			Harmonic Flute	4	
	Trumpet	8			Clarinet	8	
	Clarion	4					
	Vox Humana (+ trem.)	8					
Great	Double Open Diapason	16		**Pedal**	Double Open Diapason	32	(1875)
	Open Diapason Large	8	(1875)		Open Diapason	16	wood
	Open Diapason	8			Violon	16	
	Stopped Diapason	8	wood		Octave	8	wood
	Principal	4			Principal	8	
	Twelfth	2⅔			Fifteenth	4	
	Fifteenth	2			Trombone	16	
	Sesquialtera	V			Bassoon	8	wood

Manual Compass CC to g^3, Pedal Compass CCC to F
Specification drawn up by Dr H E Ford and Mr W T Best.
Blowing gas engine driven cylinder air pumps (added 1893[2])
Couplers: Sw/Gt, Ch/Gt, Sw/Ped, Ch/Ped, Gt/Ped. Six thumb pistons on Great and Swell. Six pistons on Pedal, Three reversible pedals : Sw/Gt, Gt/Ped, Ch/Ped
Alleged to be the 3rd organ in the world to have thumb pistons

Notes

The Swell Echo Cornet was V ranks in 1856. The 1875 Vox Angelica was achieved by separating off the 8' wood rank from the cornet and revoicing it.
The Swell Trumpet 8' was named Horn until 1875.
The Pedal Octave 8' was originally a Bourdon 16' until 1875.
The Pedal Bassoon 8' was named Trumpet until 1875.
The organ was without case. It was tuned to equal temperament.

This organ was opened by Dr Ford on Sunday 22nd June 1856 with a *Service in D* especially composed for the occasion by W T Best. Best also gave an opening recital.

---

2   The blowing equipment was placed outside the cathedral in a small purpose designed structure. This is now the verger's vestry.

Carlisle Cathedral: Harrison & Harrison, 1907

Solo						
	Quintaton	16		Hohl Flote	8	wood
	Harmonic Flute	8		Principal	4	
	Concert Flute	4		Wald Flute	4	wood
	Harmonic Piccolo	2		Twelfth	2⅔	
	Viole d'Orchestre	8		Fifteenth	2	
	Viole Celeste	8 (FF)		Sesquialtera	17,19,22	
	Viole Octaviante	4		Trombone	16	
	Contra Fagotto	16		Tromba	8	
	Clarinet	8		Octave Tromba	4	
	Vox Humana	8				
	Tuba	8	**Choir**	Double Salicional	8	
	Tremulant			Open Diapason	8	
				Claribel Flute	8	
Swell	Lieblich Bordun	16		Viola da Gamba	8	
	Open Diapason	8		Dulciana	8	
	Lieblich Gedeckt	8		Spitz Flote	4	
	Echo Gamba	8		Flauto Traverso	4	
	Vox Angelica	8		Gemshorn	2	
	Octave	4		Cornopean	8	
	Lieblich Flote	4 wood				
	Flautina	2	**Pedal**	Double Open Diapason	32	
	Mixture	III		Open Diapason	16	
	12.19.22			Open Wood	16	
	Oboe	8		Sub Bass	16	
	Double Trumpet	16		Violone	16	
	Trumpet	8		Octave Wood	8	
	Clarion	4		Flute	8	
	Orchestral Hautboy	8		Ophicleide	16	
	Tremulant			Fagotto	16	
				(Encl. in Solo box)		
Great	Double Open Diapason	16		Posaune	8	
	Open Diapason Large	8		Bassoon	8	
	Open Diapason Small	8		(Encl. in Solo box)		
	Stopped Diapason	8 wood				

Blowing Electric, tubular pneumatic action except for manual to pedal couplers
Couplers: Sw/Ped, Sw/Gt, Sw/Ch, Sw Octave, Ch/Gt, Ch/Ped, Gt/Ped, Solo Octave, Solo Sub Octave, Solo Unison Off, So/Ped, So/Gt, So/Ch, Reeds on Solo
Balanced expression pedals to Swell and Solo
4 adjustable pistons each to Great and Solo
5 adjustable pistons to Swell, 3 adjustable pistons to Choir

Pistons for Gt/Pd and Sw/Gt
Great and Pedal combinations coupled, Pedal to Swell pistons coupled
Tremulants to the Swell and Solo each operated by pedals

Notes

Nicholson's initiative to rebuild the organ was financed by donations. At a public meeting on 26th Oct 1906, with Nicholson as Hon. Secretary and the Mayor of Carlisle (Mr W Crowder Jun.) as Treasurer, a "committee of ladies" was formed to undertake collection of funds.

The cost of the project was £2000 to Harrisons, £90 for the blower, £30 to alter the organ loft and around £60 for advertising and other committee expenses. By the time of the opening, the total sum raised through donations was £2075[3]. Two further additions were made to Harrisons original scheme. Major George Dixon (1870-1950, an influential organologist) gave the Solo Viole Octaviante and the choristers of the cathedral raised £50 for the Choir Cornopean by giving an entertainment. Virtually all of the Willis pipes were retained, though sometimes in a different octave.

The Bishop of Carlisle, in a testimonial letter for Nicholson to the Dean and Chapter of Manchester Cathedral the following year, commented that the whole project was a testament to Nicholson's enthusiasm and determination; it had been completed in under 14 months.

The 1907 Harrison & Harrison console.

---

[3] The largest single donor was American businessman, organ lover and philanthropist Andrew Carnegie, who donated £500 - a quarter of the total cost.

Opening Services and Recitals 1907

10th December

The organ was opened on Tuesday 10th with Evensong at 3.00pm followed by a recital given by Sir Walter Parratt, with a further recital by Parratt at 8.00pm.

EVENSONG
PROCESSIONAL HYMN	"Christ is our corner-stone"	(A&M 239)
SPECIAL PSALMS	CXXII (Chant by Dr C H Lloyd)	
	CXXIV (Chant by Rev T W Stephenson)	
MAGNIFICAT AND NUNC DIMITTIS	Basil Harwood in A-flat	
ANTHEM (unaccompanied)	*Hosanna to the Son of David* Orlando Gibbons	

Recital after Evensong by Sir Walter Parratt MVO, Mus Doc, &c (Master of the King's Music)

CHORALVORSPIEL "Ein feste Burg"	Max Reger
ANDANTE TRANQUILLO in F	Sir Charles Stanford
PRELUDE and FUGUE in C major	J S Bach
PRELUDE to "Parsifal"	Wagner
MARCHE DE COURONNEMENT	Saint-Saëns

Recital at 8.00pm by Sir Walter Parratt MVO, Mus Doc, &c (Master of the King's Music)

OVERTURE to "Tolomeo"	Handel
LARGO from the "New World" Symphony	Dvorak
TOCCATA in D minor	J S Bach
AIR "Let the bright Seraphim" (Samson) sung by the Cathedral Choristers	Handel
MARCHE AUX FLAMBEAUX	Guilmant
AVE MARIA	Henselt
"ITE MISSA EST"	Lemmens

12th December

On the following Thursday evening at 8.00pm, the Cathedral Choir performed Brahms' *German Requiem*[4] and a collection was made to pay for the electric blowing equipment.

15th December

The next Sunday was Nicholson's day, with several sung services and two recitals by Nicholson – as with Parratt, one following Evensong and another at 8.00pm. The full programme is reproduced on the following pages.

---

[4] Nicholson notes in Chapter III that this was "performed without omission and without outside assistance or a conductor"

Sunday, December 15th.

8 0 a.m.—LITANY.

8 15 a.m.—HOLY COMMUNION ... ... *Merbecke.*
    (Sung by Old Choristers of the Cathedral.)

11 0 a.m.—MATINS AND SERMON.

    PROCESSIONAL HYMN—228.

    SERVICE—Harwood in A flat.

    ANTHEM ... ... *Himmel.*

    "O come, let us worship and kneel before the Lord our Maker, for He is the Lord our God."

    HYMNS 550, 379.

    PREACHER—The Bishop of Barrow-in-Furness.

12 15 p.m.—HOLY COMMUNION.

---

3 0 p.m.—EVENSONG.

    PROCESSIONAL HYMN—546.

    SERVICE—Stanford in G.

    ANTHEM ... ... *Sir F. A. G. Ouseley.*

    "It came even to pass, as the trumpeters and singers were as one, to make one sound to be heard in praising and thanking the Lord; and when they lifted up their voice with the trumpets and cymbals, and with instruments of music, and praised the Lord, saying, for He is good, for His mercy endureth for ever; that then the house was filled with a cloud, even the house of the Lord; So that the priests could not stand to minister by reason of the cloud; for the glory of the Lord had filled the house of the Lord. Hallelujah. Amen."

    HYMN 396 PART 2.

THE 3 O'CLOCK EVENSONG WILL BE FOLLOWED BY A

RECITAL

BY

Mr. SYDNEY H. NICHOLSON.

1. SONATA in E minor ... ... *Rheinberger.*
2. PRELUDE and "Angel's Farewell" from "The Dream of Gerontius" ... ... *Elgar.*
3. PRELUDE in C sharp minor ... ... *Rachmaninoff.*

---

6 30 p.m.—EVENSONG AND SERMON.
(Voluntary Choir.)

PROCESSIONAL HYMN—50.

PSALMS 45, 46.

HYMNS 53, 225, 222.

Preacher—THE DEAN.

TO BE FOLLOWED BY A

RECITAL

BY

Mr. SYDNEY H. NICHOLSON.

1. PRELUDE AND FUGUE on the name B.A.C.H. ... *Liszt.*
2. PASTORALE from 1st Sonata ... ... *Guilmant.*
3. TOCCATA in F. ... ... *Widor.*

17th December
H W Richards of Christ Church, Lancaster Gate, London, played at 3.00pm (before Evensong).

PRELUDE and FUGUE in G	J S Bach
"SURSUM CORDA"	Elgar
OVERTURE "Athalie"	Mendelssohn
DUO	Bizet
TRAUMEREI	Strauss
ROMANZE AND SCHERZO	Schumann
HYMN 166 "All people that on earth do dwell"	
ANDANTE in F# minor	S S Wesley
NOCTURNE in C# minor	Tchaikovsky
OVERTURE "Meistersinger"	Wagner

19th December
Basil Harwood of Christ Church Cathedral, Oxford, played at 8.00pm.

PRELUDE and FUGUE in E-flat	J S Bach
ARIA in F	J S Bach
LARGHETTO from the Clarinet Quintet	Mozart
MARCHE RELIGIEUSE	Chauvet
CONCERTO in F (No 5)	Handel
MINUET AND TRIO from Symphony in G minor	Sterndale Bennett
HYMN 308 "O praise ye the Lord"	
FANTASIA IN E-flat	Saint-Saëns
ALLEGRO CANTABILE from 5th Organ Symphony	Widor
DITHYRAMB (by request)	Harwood

Manchester Cathedral: Hill, 1871

The 1871 console (note Wagner on console!)

This organ, the gift of Sir William Houldsworth[5], was placed on the Choir Screen in a case designed by Sir Gilbert Scott. The Swell and Pedal organs occupied spaces in the Choir Aisles.

> Four Manuals, 51 sounding stops, Manual Compass CC to g^3, Pedal Compass CCC to F
> Couplers: So/Ped, Sw/Ped, Gt/Ped, Ch/Ped, Sw/Gt, So/Gt, Sw/Ch
> 4 composition Pedals to Great
> 3 composition Pedals to Swell
> 1 Pedal for Gt/Ped
> Tremulant

---

5 Sir William Henry Houldsworth (1834-1917), knighted 1887, was a mill-owner in Reddish and Stockport. He served as Conservative MP for Manchester North West from 1883 to 1906. The City of Manchester made him a freeman in 1905 and the Victoria University of Manchester awarded him an honorary LLD. He also built and paid for St Elisabeth's Church in Reddish.

Solo	Harmonic Flute	8		Flautina	2
	Harmonic Flute	4		Clarionet	8
	Corno di Basetto	8		Harmonic Flute	4
	Orchestral Oboe	8		Principal	4
	Tuba	8		Twelfth	3
				Fifteenth	2
Swell	Lieblich Bourdon	16		Full Mixture	III
	Open Diapason	8		Sharp Mixture	IV
	Stopped Diapason	8		Posaune	8
	Dulciana	8		Clarion	4
	Keraulophon	8			
	Principal	4	**Choir**	Open Diapason	8
	Suabe Flute	4		Salicional	8
	Dulcet	4		Dulciana	8
	Flageolet	2		Clarabella	8
	Sharp Mixture	III		Principal	4
	Dulciana Mixture	II		Wald Flute	4
	Double Trumpet	16			
	Oboe	8	**Pedal**	Double Open Diapason	32
	Cornopean	8		Open Diapason (wood)	16
	Vox Humana	8		Open Diapason (metal)	16
	Clarion	4		Violon	16
				Bourdon	16
Great	Double Open & Bourdon	16		Principal	8
	Open Diapason	8		Violon	8
	Open Diapason No 2	8		Fifteenth	4
	Stopped Diapason	8		Trombone	16
	Gamba	8			

Manchester Cathedral: Hill, 1910

Nicholson noted that:

> The main part of the part of the [1871] organ was built upon the choir screen – a position excellent in its acoustic result [for solo playing] but subject to the drawback that, when the singers were seated in the choir, and their singing was accompanied by the organ, it was difficult to hear their voices in the nave. In the new organ the main part has been placed in the choir aisles; but for the purpose of accompanying the congregational services a small, though powerful section of the organ, under the control of a separate manual, remains on the choir screen.

Hill's retained as much original pipework as possible. The action was entirely new using tubular pneumatics and a new hydraulic blowing plant was installed. The new organ, which cost £4000 was again paid for by the original donor Sir William Houldsworth. The manual compass was extended up to C and the pedals to G.

The 1910 console, note the crescendo marking over the pedal combinations and lack of a balanced swell pedal

6 combination pistons to Great and Pedal,
6 combination pedals to Great and Pedal,
5 combination pistons to Swell + 1 variable piston, 4 combination pistons to Choir, 4 combination pistons to solo + 1 variable piston, 3 combination pistons to Screen Organ, Three Pistons for couplers,
Reversible pedal for Gt/Ped,
Swell and Solo Tremulants

Couplers: Ch/Ped, Gt/Ped, Sw/Ped, So/Ped, Screen organ/Ped;
So/Ch, Sw/Ch, Tuba Mirabilis to Ch;
Ch/Gt, Sw/Gt, So/Gt, Screen Organ/Gt;
Sw Octave, Solo Octave, Solo Sub-Octave, Solo Unison Off, Ped to Gt Pistons

Solo All Encl.	Quintäton	16
	Viole d'Orchestre	8
	Viole Céleste	8
	Harmonic Flute	8
	Concert Flute	4
	Piccolo	2
	Contra Fagotto	16
	Orchestral Oboe	8
	Clarinet	8
	Vox Humana	8
	Tuba	8

Swell	Bourdon	16
	Open Diapason	8
	Salicional	8
	Vox Angelica	8
	Lieblich Gedackt	8
	Principal	4
	Stopped Flute	4
	Flautina	2
	Fifteenth	2
	Mixture	V
	Double Trumpet	16
	Cornopean	8
	Oboe	8
	Clarion	4

Great	Double Open Diapason	16
	Open Diapason No 2	8
	Open Diapason No 3	8
	Clarabella	8
	Principal	4
	Wald Flöte	4
	Twelfth	2⅔
	Fifteenth	2
	Mixture	III
	Contra Posaune	16
	Posaune	8
	Clarion	4

Choir	Double Dulciana	16
	Geigen Principal	8
	Dulciana	8
	Keraulophon	8
	Stopped Diapason	8
	Octave Dulciana	4
	Suabe Flute	4
	Dulcet	2
	Dulciana Mixture	III

Screen Organ (top manual)

	Hohl Flöte	16
	Open Diapason No 1	8
	Open Diapason No 2	8
	Doppel Flöte	8
	Octave	4
	Fifteenth	2
	Tuba Mirabilis	8

Pedal	Double Open Diapason	32
	Open Diapason (wood)	16
	Open Diapason (metal)	16
	Violone	16
	Sub-Bass	16
	Octave	8
	Bass Flute	8
	Violoncello	8
	Contra Trombone	32
	Contra Fagotto (from solo)	16
	Trombone	16
	Trumpet	8

> The organ was rebuilt again and revoiced in 1918 by Harrison & Harrison when a Horn 8' stop was added to the Swell. The opening recital was given by Sir Walter Parratt.

Opening Services and Recitals

The organ was reopened on 12th Dec 1910 by the three successive organists of the cathedral, Sir Frederick Bridge (organist 1869-1875), Dr J Kendrick Pyne (organist 1875-1908) and Mr Sydney Nicholson (organist from 1909).

12th December

The organ was opened on Monday 12th with Evensong, accompanied by SHN, at 3.30pm followed by a recital at 4.30pm given by Sir Frederick Bridge and a further recital by Dr Pyne at 7.30pm.

Evensong

MAGNIFICAT AND NUNC DIMITTIS	Bridge in G	
ANTHEM	*Hear my words, ye people*	C H H Parry

Recital after Evensong by Sir Frederick Bridge MVO, Mus Doc, MA
(Organist at Westminster Abbey; King Edward Professor of Music, University of London)

LARGHETTO in F-Minor	S S Wesley
CHORAL MIT FUGE "Jesu meine zuversicht"	Merkel
THREE SKETCHES	Schumann
SOLEMN MARCH for the Funeral of Queen Mary 1694	Purcell
ANDANTE and FUGUE from Sonata	Sir F Bridge

(the theme of the Andante is taken from the anthem composed for the consecration of Bishop Fraser in Manchester Cathedral 1870.)

ELEGY in F	Merkel
FANTASIA in C	J S Bach
FUGUE in G	J S Bach
ANDANTE and FINALE	Silas

Recital at 7.30pm by Dr J Kendrick Pyne
(Organist to the Corporation of Manchester, to Manchester University and Professor, Royal Manchester College of Music)

ANDANTE with variations from a Concerto in B-flat	S Wesley
SICILIANO and FINALE from a Sonata	Arne
GRAND STUDY in C#-minor	S S Wesley
ADAGIO varied "Hymne Autrichien" arr.J K Pyne	Haydn
SUITE in C-minor	Joseph Bonnet

Andantino espressivo; Stella matutina; Andante con moto; Romance sans paroles; Caprice Héroïque (dedicated to J K P)

ANDANTE RELIGIOSO	Devred
TOCCATA and FUGUE in D-minor (Dorian)	J S Bach

CANON in B-minor	Schumann
IMPROMPTU ELEGIAC	J Kendrick Pyne
GRAND CHOEUR "Marche de Fete"	Henri Büsser

(It being the centenary of Arne, Schumann and S S Wesley, their compositions have been specially included in the programme.

18th December

On Sunday 18th the choir performed selections from *The Last Judgement* by Spohr following 3.30pm Evensong. There was a further Evensong at 7.00pm when the concluding voluntary was the *Toccata* from Widor's 5th symphony.

19th December

Nicholson's recital was given on Tuesday 19th at 7.30pm, with the programme below.

RECITAL
BY
Mr. SYDNEY H. NICHOLSON, M.A., Mus.Bac.
Organist of Manchester Cathedral.

1. Prelude and Fugue in B minor ... J. S. Bach.
2. Two Chorale-Preludes.
   (a) "Wachet auf" ... ... J. S. Bach.
   (b) "Es ist ein ros" ... ... Brahms.
3. Passacaglia in F minor (from Op. 63) Max Reger.
4. Ave Maria d'Arcadelt ... arranged by Liszt.
5. Dithyramb ... ... Basil Harwood.
6. (a) Impression.—"La Nuit" ... S Karg-Elert.
   (b) Menuetto from "Berenice" ... ... Handel.
7. Rhapsodie No. 3 (founded on Breton Carols) ...
                                        Saint-Saëns.
8. Grand Fantasia in F minor ... ... Mozart.

In 1911 and 1912 Nicholson arranged three series of recitals on the new organ played by himself and guest organists. Unfortunately the collections were not sufficient to cover expenses and the recitals were discontinued.

Nicholson's house organ: Henry Speechley, c 1900

Organ at 6 Wiltra Polygon.

Nicholson's house organ by Henry Speechley was purchased for him by his father on the rebuilding of the Grange at Totteridge in 1900. Nicholson took the instrument to Carlisle and Manchester. The exact specification is unknown, but it can be seen that there are six stops on the Swell, four stops on the Great, one Pedal stop and three couplers.

Westminster Abbey: Hill, 1848 rebuilt 1884/1899/1908

During Nicholson's tenure at Westminster Abbey a history and specification of the organ was published by the Rev Andrew Freeman in *The Organ*[6]. Much work has been done on the instrument since then but the specification quoted here is as presented by Freeman in 1923.

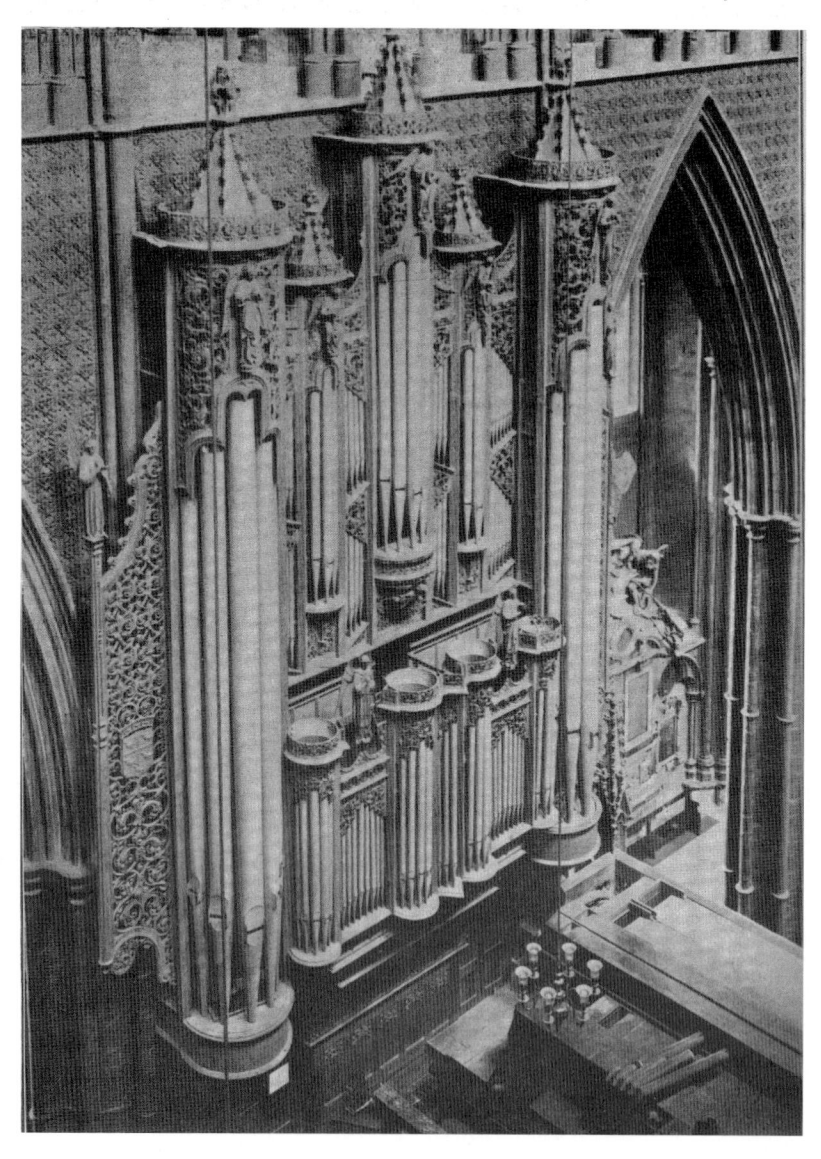

The South Case of Westminster Abbey viewed from the Triforium

---

6   Vol II, No. 7, Jan 1923. The Rev Andrew Freeman (1876–1947) studied music at Cambridge University, obtained the FRCO diploma and was an organist in Newbury, Guildford and Streatham Common before becoming ordained priest in 1916. He then served as priest/organist in Lambeth and, from 1922 until his death, as vicar of Standish-with-Hardwicke in Gloucestershire. He contributed many articles to the journals *The Organ* and *Musical Opinion* and he published a notable book on organ cases. The photograph above was taken by Freeman.

The 1848 Hill organ in The Abbey had 34 speaking stops on three manuals and pedals. A six stop solo organ was added in 1868 and further stops were added in 1871 before a major rebuilding by Hill in 1884 to provide an instrument with 56 speaking stops on four manuals and pedals. In 1894 three more stops were added to the Swell and the following year they added a Celestial Organ of 16 stops and a set of 36 brass gongs, which had been given as a gift. In 1908 there were further additions so that when Nicholson arrived in 1918 the specification was as follows:

Solo
Gamba	8
Stopped Diapason	8
Lieblich Flute	4
Harmonic Flute	4
Orchestral Oboe	8
Clarinet	8
Vox Humana	8
Tuba Mirabilis	8

Celestial Organ
(A = Organ Accompanimental Stops)
(B = Organ Solo Stops)

Double Dulciana Bass	16	A
Double Dulciana Treble	16	A
Flauto Traverso	8	A
Viola da Gamba	8	A
Lieblich Gedact	8	A
Höhl Flute	8	A
Voix Celeste	8	A
Dulciana Cornet	VI	A
Suabe Flute	4	B
Flageolet	2	B
Glockenspiel	III	B
Cor de Nuit	8	B
Harmonic Oboe	8	B
Harmonic Trumpet	8	B
Musette	8	B
Vox Humana	8	B
Gongs	36 brass gongs	

Swell
Double Diapason Bass	16
Double Diapason Treble	16
Open Diapason I	8
Open Diapason II	8
Höhl Flute	8
Röhr Flute	8
Dulciana	8
Salicional	8
Voix Celestes	8
Principal	4
Dulcet	4
Lieblich Flute	4
Fifteenth	2
Mixture	III
Double Trumpet	16
Cornopean	8
Oboe	8
Clarion	4

Great
Double Open Diapason	16
Open Diapason I	16
Open Diapason II	8
Open Diapason III	8
Open Diapason IV	8
Höhl Flute	8
Principal	4
Harmonic Flute	4
Twelfth	2⅔
Fifteenth	2
Mixture	IV
Double Trumpet	16
Posaune	8
Clarion	4

Choir			Pedal		
	Gedackt	16		Double Open Diapason	32
	Open Diapason	8		Open Diapason	16
	Keraulophon	8		Open Diapason	16
	Dulciana	8		Open Diapason	16
	Lieblich Gedacht	8		Bourdon	16
	Principal	4		Principal	8
	Nason Flute	4		Violoncello	8
	Suabe Flute	4		Bass Flute	8
	Harmonic Gemshorn	2		Contra Posaune	32
	Contra Fagotto	16		Posaune	16
	Cor Anglais	8		Trumpet	8

The compass was CC to a^3 on all manuals and CCC to F on the pedals. The action was tubular pneumatic throughout except for the Celestial Organ which had an electric action. Blowing was by gas.

Couplers: Sw/Ped, Sw/Gt, Sw/Ch, Swell octave, Swell suboctave, Swell unison off
Ch/Ped, Gt/Ped, So/Ped, So Octave/Ped, So/Gt,
Solo Octave, Solo Sub Octave, Solo Unison Off
Celestial to Pedal
Celestial A to Manual 4
Celestial A to Manual 5
Celestial B to Manual 4
Celestial B to Manual 5
Celestial Sub Octave to Manual 4
Celestial Sub Octave to Manual 5
Celestial Octave to Manual 4
Celestial Octave to Manual 5

6 (1 adjustable) thumb pistons each to of Great and Swell, 4 thumb pistons each to Choir and Solo, 3 thumb pistons to Celestial, Gt/Ped reversible thumb piston, 6 (1 adjustable) toe pedals each to Pedal and Swell, Reversible toe pedals for Gt/Ped, Sw/Gt, So/Gt 3 hitch down Swell pedals, Great and Pedal combinations

The organ case was designed by Gothic revival architect J L Pearson for the 1884 rebuild but the cases were not made through lack of funding. The north case was erected in 1896 in memory of Henry Purcell whose bicentenary had taken place the previous year when Hill made additions to the organ. The south case was finally put up in 1901 in time for the Coronation of King Edward VII.

The organ was further rebuilt in 1936 and first used for the Coronation of King George VI in 1937.

The celestial organ is still present in the Triforium but has not been in use for many years. It was not included in the rebuilding work of the 1980's.

St Sepulchre-without-Newgate, Holborn Viaduct: Harrison & Harrison, 1932

The organ has its origins in a one manual instrument built by Renatus Harris about 1676[7]. After a number of rebuilds and enlargements over the course of two centuries, it was moved from the West Gallery to St Stephen's Chapel in 1879. by Gray and Davison. The next rebuild before Nicholson encountered it in its ruinous state had been in 1891 by J W Walker and Sons. In 1928 Nicholson was appointed as organ advisor and Harrison & Harrison of Durham were given the contract. Unfortunately lack of money prevented a major project and the end result was an instrument at the East end of the church in the north choir aisle. Some of the existing pipework was re-usable and there a few additions were made. The necessary changes to the old Harris case[8] were planned by SHN's older brother Sir Charles Nicholson. This small 13-stop two manual organ[9] is unusual in having a 32' Double Open Wood on the pedal. This particular stop, one of the 1891 additions by Walker, was only restored because Nicholson generously paid for it out of his own pocket. The 1939 ROX series of recordings, made by Columbia for the School of English Church Music, were recorded in St Sepulchre using this organ.

Swell	Open Diapason	8	
	Lieblich Gedackt	8	
	Gemshorn	4	
	Fifteenth	2	
	Cornopean	8	[new stop 1932]
Great	Lieblich Bourdon	16	
	Open Diapason	8	
	Claribel Flute	8	[new stop 1932]
	Salicional	8	[new stop 1932]
	Octave	4	
Pedal	Double Open Wood	32	
	Open Wood	16	
	Sub Bass (from Gt)	16	

The compass was CC to a^3 on all manuals and CCC to F on the pedals.
The action was tubular pneumatic throughout from a detached console.
The blowing was electric.
Couplers: Sw/Ped, Sw/Gt, Swell octave, Swell suboctave, Swell unison off, Gt/Ped
Balanced Swell pedal, 3 pistons each to Swell, Great and Pedal.

Sadly the organ is again in a poor state and unusable.

---

[7] This is when the first organist was appointed.
[8] The most important change was the removal of the side towers.
[9] The 1891 Walker organ had 46 stops on three manuals and pedals, so the present instrument represents a considerable down-sizing.

Appendix F

Nicholson as composer

Although no-one would suggest that Nicholson was a great composer, (he, too, did not regard himself as such) he nevertheless wrote a considerable amount of very servicable music — in addition to the liturgical necessities required of any cathedral organist. The scope of his compositions was far-reaching, and most were composed for a particular need, be it for the choristers' entertainments, his choral societies or for special services in his various appointments. He has left us with a large catalogue of some 200 pieces which range from juvenilia kept by proud parents, through student exercises in composition and orchestration, his Oxford B Mus compositions, other less academic items composed for performance whilst at Oxford and pieces for his Chipping Barnet Parish Choir — to the more mature writing of part songs and church music. These include hymn tunes, organ voluntaries, anthems and settings of services, as well as lighter-veined compositions to accompany his many excursions into musical entertainments and light opera. Most of his output may be described as well-crafted, if not always inspired with originality. Some of the church music was printed privately for use in all his major posts, but much was also printed commercially by publishers such as Novello, Oxford University Press, Curwen, Cramer, The Faith Press and The Year Book Press.

In 1950 when Canon W K Lowther Clarke[1] was canvassing material for a proposed biography of SHN, Gerald Gay, the Managing Director of The Faith Press, provided information about the sales of Nicholson's music saying:

> Musicians generally seem to think little of Nicholson's musical ability and, except for one or two of the popular congregational settings, our sales[2] of his more serious attempts would confirm that general critisicm.

Henry Coleman, also in a reply to Lowther Clarke, made a similar comment concerning Nicholson's compositions:

> Compared with other church composers of his time, I should imagine that it was a great deal better than most, and, assuming that there will be church choirs in 50 years' time; I should say his music is more likely to be heard than most of such music.

---

1 Canon William Kemp Lowther Clarke (1879-1968) was a graduate of Jesus College, Cambridge. Ordained in 1904, he obtained his Doctorate of Divinity in 1926. The author of many books on ecclesiastical and theological matters, he also wrote two histories of the SPCK, of which he was Editorial Secretary from 1915 to 1944. He was Curate of All Saints' in Dulwich from 1921 to 1945, an Honorary Canon of Canterbury Cathedral 1942 and 1943, Bursalis Prebendary of Chichester Cathedral from 1943 to 1945 and thereafter Canon Residentiary of Chichester Cathedral unitl his death.

2 Gerald Gay reported that the *Communion Service in G* first published in 1917 had sold 41,000 up to 1942. It was reprinted in 1949 and sold a further 1000 copies in less than a year. It is still 'in print' in 2013. The *Communion Service in C* of 1923 sold over 33,000 copies "and is still in big demand". At the other end of the scale the *Missa Omnium Sanctorum* 1930 (mentioned on the next page) only sold 250 copies between 1930 and 1950. The Faith Press is the only publisher for which we have sales figures for Nicholson's music.

Harry Abbott, one of Nicholson's Westminster choristers[3], wrote to Lowther Clarke:

> He liked doing things and getting them done. Having done them he would set them aside and turn to something else. This I felt was the fault in his musical composition. It was full of ideas - but always like the Curate's Egg. It was a pity he never returned to a work to reconsider and re-write the weak parts. But no — by that time he had something else on hand and what was past was forgotten. He was the first to admit it. In fact I heard him say that he knew that he would not go down in history as a great organist or composer.

Watkins Shaw commented later:

> As a minor composer, well-skilled in the craft, he was gifted with a flow of attractive melody removed from the expected academic invention of the stock figure of a 'church composer.'[4]

Less generous is Christopher le Fleming, a student under Nicholson at Chislehurst, who is somewhat dismissive of SHN as lacking a characteristic idiom of his own. However he does go on to comment on Nicholson's flair for improvisation[5].

> 'His voluntaries by way of run-up to the liturgical wicket were unfailingly both apposite and masterly.'[6]

In his writing for boys' voices, Nicholson's compositions show a sure knowledge of what is effective for their range. To take just two examples, the stirring 2-part anthem *Be Strong in the Lord* has an immediate appeal, whilst the more elegiac *Cleanse us, O Lord* for 4-part trebles (undeservedly out-of-print) is not without its own stirring high-points. Both of these anthems score by being memorable, a real bonus for choir-trainers regarding rehearsal time. The 2-part *Teach us, good Lord*, however, continues to enjoy a place in anthem lists for treble voices.

Of his many settings of the Communion Service, the *Missa Omnium Sanctorum* (1930) written for the Choir of All Saint's, Margaret Street is on a more elaborate scale, being set (apart from the Kyrie) for double choir with a largely independent organ part. Nicholson had taken his student Christopher le Fleming along to Margaret Street to hear it performed. This student was to comment later in his autobiography:

> ...the impression that remains of the music is one of impeccable and even brilliant writing, though any hint of burgeoning individuality was invariably swept aside by intimations of other men's music.

He then, one suspects somewhat tongue-in-cheek, goes on to add:

---

3   See *SNCSN* for photographs and further information about Harry Abbott.

4   Harold Watkins Shaw (1911-1996), *Vocation and Endeavour: Sydney Nicholson and the early years of the Royal School of Church Music (School of English Church Music)* in manuscript and published 1990 by the Church Music Society.

5   David Willcocks, also a former Chislehurst student, made a similar observation regarding SHN's prowess in extemporisation.

6   Christopher Le Fleming (1908-1985) worked in musical education and was assistant director to the Rural Music Schools Association. A pupil of Vaughan Williams, he composed many songs and some church music. He was Director of Music at St Mary's School in Calne from 1943-1946 and his autobiography *Journey into Music by the Slow Train* was published in Bristol by the Redcliffe Press in 1982.

> ...it was as though a succession of familiar friends had dropped in for a chat and, while present, tended to monopolise the conversation.

Perhaps Nicholson was more successful with his settings for more modest resources. In complete contrast is his *Missa Choristarum* (1940), written for the choristers of All Saints', Warwick. The reviewer in *English Church Music* wrote[7]:

> ...simple canonic imitation in the Kyrie, conjunct passages in thirds in the Sanctus, short expressive solos answered by the chorus in the Benedictus and Agnus Dei, and some ringing top notes on the last page of the Gloria.

He goes on to say that any vocal difficulties which may arise at key changes, are helped out by the organ part which one might be inclined to call perfunctory:

> ..were it not so clearly intended to give the voices a maximum of support.

Another feature of the settings for more limited resources was versatility, for example, the earlier setting of *A Simple Communion Service in C, suitable for congregational singing* (1923) may be sung in unison or harmony, accompanied or unaccompanied, with optional descants. This setting was originally intended for performance by the local choir and congregation at Bow Brickhill Parish Church, whilst the Westminster Abbey choristers were on summer camp there, the boys supplying the descant part.

Turning to Nicholson's hymn tunes, most church musicians will be familiar with 'Bow Brickhill', set to the words *We sing the praise of Him who died* and 'Crucifer', set to the words *Lift high the cross*. Less familiar perhaps, and undeservedly so, is the tune 'Chislehurst', which Nicholson set to the Ascension hymn *Hail the day that sees him rise*, usually now sung to the tune 'Llanfair'. Of the 15 tunes by Nicholson included in *Hymns Ancient & Modern Revised* (1950), Kenneth Long in his review[8] wrote that for quality, there was little to choose between Nicholson's well-known processional 'Crucifer', the triumphant 'Hosanna in excelcis' and 'Feniton.' He goes on to comment on 'Airlie' as being an attractive tune for children, and finally he singles out 'Aethelwold', 'St Nicolas' and 'Woodchurch' as showing the many sidedness of his ability to write congregational hymns. Incidentally, in the introduction to *The Sydney Nicholson Commemoration Book*[9], the editors refer to 'Airlie' as being almost Nicholson's favourite, and that he had said on more than one occasion that he wished it to be sung at his funeral, as indeed it was[10]. The setting of the *Evening Canticles in D flat* continues to occupy a place in many of our cathedral and larger parish church music lists[11], as do the better-known of Nicholson's hymn tunes, whereas his cantata *The Saviour of the World*[12], along with many of his other compositions, has all but disappeared into

---

7   *ECM* Apr 1948

8   *ECM* July 1950. *Nicholson in D-flat* was published by Novello and, unlike the Faith Press, no sales figures are available.

9   The introduction to the *Commemoration Book*, dated "St Nicolas Day 1948", was signed by the three Honorary Assistant Directors who were appointed to replace Nicholson — John Dykes Bower, Gerald H Knight and William N Mckie.

10 'Airlie' is reproduced in Appendix G.

11 *A Century of Cathedral Music 1898-1998* by John Patton records that in 1998 19% of UK Cathedral still used the D-flat service and it remains in print, available from the RSCM. The *Two Communion Hymns (O Salutaris, Tantum Ergo)* also still had a cathedral presence in 1998 and are also still available.

12 Although the hymn tune 'Bow Brickhill' from *The Saviour of the World* is still widely known.

obscurity. It is worth noting that by February 1950, this cantata had sold over 10,000 copies and was about to be re-printed, showing that it once had significant popularity and is perhaps worthy of re-appraisal[13].

The opening page of Nicholson's Evening Canticles in D-flat

---

13 One of Nicholson's unpublished anthems is printed in Appendix I as an example of the kind of modest singable parish music which dominated his output. Copies are available from the RSCM at www.rscm.com.

Printed and published compositions

1) Liturgical and sacred choral music (for named hymn tunes see Appendix G)

A Babe Is Born 1918, SATB, published by the Faith Press, London. *The Faith Press Christmas Carols No I*, Text traditional.

A Grace for Choristers: Before Meat, After Meat (undated), SSS unaccompanied, privately printed on cards. Text: Before Meat – Benedictus benedicat; After Meat – Benedicto benedicatur.

A hymn of praise and thanksgiving after victory: From the Book of Common Prayer. Forms of Prayer to be used at sea 1944, SATB and organ, published 1945 by the SECM.

A Hymn on the Nativity of My Saviour: Christmas Carol ['I sing the birth was born tonight] 1900, SAATB, published by Charles Vincent, London. Text by Ben Jonson.

A Simple Communion Service in G for Choir and Congregation 1917, Unison congregation with SATB choir and organ, published by the Faith Press, London. Also a 2nd edition including the *9-fold Kyrie*. Later published as 'Communion Service in G', Croydon, RSCM, C141.

A Simple Te Deum on Tones VIII & VII 1939, Unison with SATB and organ, published by the SECM in *SECM Choir Book No 6* 1939, re-issued in 1944 at Leamington Spa, and later still as RSCM 106 with a congregation edition RSCM 107.

Above the Clear Blue Sky: Anthem for Boys' (or Female) Voices 1913, SS with organ, published by J Curwen & Sons, London. Curwen Edition 71399. Author of text not stated, but it is John Chandler (1806-1876), vicar of Witley, Surrey.

An Ode on the Birth of our Saviour ['In numbers, and but these few'] 1931, SATB with optional solo, published by H F W Deane & Sons The Year Book Press, *Anthems and Church Music A74*. 'By kind permission of the 'Daily Mail' for which it was specially composed.' Text by Robert Herrick. Re-issued in the *Sydney Nicholson Commemoration Book*, Canterbury, RSCM, 1948 and later published in RSCM A328.

And I heard a great voice out of Heaven: Introit 1918, SATB and organ, Privately printed, Composed for the Installation of the Very Rev W S Swayne, BD, as Dean of Manchester. 18th Oct 1918.

Angelus Ad Virginem 1936, SATB and organ, published by the Faith Press, London. Melody from Dublin Troper arranged by Sydney Nicholson. Text translated from the Latin by J M C Crum. Used in *Hymns A&M Revised* 1950 No 547. Republished, edited by Gerald Hocken Knight, as RSCM 347.

Anthem for Penitential Seasons 1928, SATB and organ, published by J B Cramer & Co, London. *Cramer's Library of Church Music No 18*. Text by J D Carlyle.

Be Strong in the Lord. Anthem for Boys' Voices 1919, SS and organ, published by J Curwen & Sons, London. Curwen Edition 71528, Biblical text, composed for the Lower Chapel Choir, Eton College. Later published as RSCM A4.

Beneath the Cross of Jesus: Anthem 1925, SATB and organ, An extract from **The Saviour of the World** 1924, issued separately by the Faith Press, London.

Beloved, let us love one another 1922, SATB and organ, Privately printed by Novello and Company. 'Composed for the marriage of H R H Princess Mary with the Viscount Lascelles, DSO in Westminster Abbey, 28th February 1922.'

Benedicite Domino ['Three shepherds lay in Bethlem's field'], SATB, Self-published 'Christmas 1925' and re-issued by Novello and Co, London. *Novello's Christmas Carols No 524*, 1938.

Benedicite omnia opera in G: Set according to the arrangement suggested in the Prayer Book as proposed in 1928. 1938, SATB unaccompanied, published by the Faith Press, London.

Cantemus Domino 1922, SATB unaccompanied, published by the Faith Press, London. *The Faith Press Christmas Carols* [series without number]. Text from Prymer of Salysbury adapted by H F Westlake.

Captains of the Saintly Band. Anthem for Festivals of Apostles or General use 1937, Boys and Men (both divisi) with organ, published by Oxford University Press, London. *Oxford Easy Anthems E30*, Based on an old French melody. Text by H W Baker. Also published in RSCM *Choral Service Book 3*, 1956.

Carol, Sirs, the Blessed Birth 1934, SATB, published by SPCK, London. *SPCK Church Music No. 65*. Text by M Howse.

Christ Was Born on Christmas Day 1918, SATB, published by the Faith Press, London. *The Faith Press Christmas Carols No II*, SHN also printed this carol on his 1913 Christmas Card.

Christmas Carol [As I rode out this enderes night] 1920, SATB, Self-printed. Used on his 1920 Christmas card 'With best wishes Xmas 1920 from Sydney H Nicholson.'

Cleanse us, O Lord Anthem for Boys' voices: Suitable for a confirmation 1939, SS [both divisi] and organ, published by Oxford University Press, London. *Oxford Modern Anthems A89*. Dedication: 'To Paul A Beymer and the Choirboys' Camp at Put-in-Bay, Ohio.' [The camp was in early 1938.]

Come, let us join our cheerful songs: Anthem for Easter 1929, SATB and organ, published by J B Cramer & Co, London. *Cramer's Library of Church Music No 6*. Text by Isaac Watts.

Commemoration Anthem. Let Us Now Praise Famous Men 1931, SATB and organ, published by the Faith Press, London. For the Tercentenary Service at St Sepulchre's Church, London 21st June 1931 – the 'Tercentenary of Captain John Smith. Sometime Governor of Virginia and Admiral of New England, who departed this life the 21st of June 1631.'

Communion Service for Men's Voices (in E) 1942, ATB with divisions and solos unaccompanied, Privately printed. Dated 14th January 1942, Bibury.

Communion Service in C suitable for Congregational Singing 1923, Unison congregation with SATB choir and organ, published by the Faith Press, London.

Evening Service for Boys' (or Female) Voices: Magnificat and Nunc Dimittis 1913, SS and organ, published by J Curwen & Sons London. Curwen edition 80554. 'Composed for, and dedicated to the Choristers of Manchester Cathedral.'

Evening Service (Plainsong in alto) with Fauxbourdons on Tones VI and III/4 1946, published in *Service Book No 5*, Canterbury, RSCM.

For God and St. George (undated), Unison voices and piano, Privately printed by Goose & Son, Norwich for the 'Primrose League'. Text by Lady Wingfield.

Hark, how all the welkin rings! Anthem for Christmastide 1928, SATB and organ, J B Cramer & Co, London. *Cramer's Library of Anthems No 4*. Text by Charles Wesley.

I will lift up mine eyes 1898, SATB with tenor solo and organ, Privately printed by Dinham Blyth & Co September 1898. 'The words selected from Psalm 121, Psalm 103, and a hymn by Rev F H Lyte.'

In memoriam A K N ['God said, Let there be light'] c 1937, SATB unaccompanied, Privately printed. Text Biblical.

Introit, Gradual, Offertory, and Communion together with Kyrie Eleison Proper for the Dedication Festival 1941, SATB divisi unaccompanied. Privately printed. Written for the Choir of St Michael's College, Tenbury.

Kyrie Eleison (Ninefold) (undated) SATB and organ, Novello & Co, London. This is an extra alternative movement to No 4 in *Nicholson in D-flat*.

Let Love Arise and Praise Him: Anthem for All Saints' Day 1935, SATB divisi with organ, Privately printed. Written for the Choir of All Saints', Margaret Street. Text by the Rev Canon J M C Crum.

Let Us With a Gladsome Mind: Anthem for harvest or other festivals 1936, SATB and organ, published by the School of English Church Music. Text by John Milton. Later published as RSCM 243 and in *Service Book One* S16.

Love Divine all loves excelling: Anthem for Quinquagesima or general use An extract from **The Saviour of the World** 1924, issued separately by the SECM 1944 and by the RSCM 1963 as edition 212. Also re-issued in the *Sydney Nicholson Commemoration Book*, Canterbury, RSCM, 1948.

Magnificat and Nunc dimittis for Men's Voices based on the Psalmtune "St Stephen" 1940 in *Four Evening Services for Men's Voices*. [By E Bullock, H P Chadwyck Healey, S H Nicholson, O H Peasgood], published by Stainer & Bell, London.

Magnificat and Nunc Dimittis in A-flat 1901, SATB divisi and organ, published by Novello and Co, London.

Magnificat and Nunc Dimittis in E-flat: St. Nicolas Service 1937, SATB unaccompanied, published by the Faith Press, London. 'The main themes used in this Service are based upon phrases of the composer's hymn for St. Nicolas Day.'

Magnificat and Nunc Dimittis in G 1923, SATB and organ, published by the Faith Press, London. Composed for the Rochester Diocesan Choral Association Festival 1923. Also an edition for unison singing.

Magnificat and Nunc Dimittis on 'Parisian Tones' for Boys' Voices 1940, SS with organ, published by Novello & Co, London. *Novello's Chorister Series No 81.*

Mass in E-flat 1928, SATB with divisions, SATTB soli and organ, printed facsimile of ms. For W S Vale, All Saints', Margaret Street 'In remembrance of April 18th to May 8th 1928'. The organ part is missing. Revised and published as *Missa Omnium Sanctorum.*

Missa Choristarum: Communion Service in F for Boys' Voices 1943, SS with organ, published by the Faith Press, London, 1947. Written at Leamington Spa for the Choristers of All Saints', Warwick.

Missa Omnium Sanctorum 1928, SATB divisi with organ, published by the Faith Press, London, in 1930. 'Written for the choir of All Saints' Church, Margaret Street.' [Kyrie Eleison, Responses to the Commandments, Credo, Sanctus, Benedictus, Agnus Dei, Gloria in Excelsis. This is a later version of the *Mass in E-flat*.]

Missa Sancti Magni: Simple Communion Service in F 1937, SATB and organ, published by the Faith Press, London. 'Founded on phrases from the hymn tune 'St. Magnus' by Jeremiah Clarke. (1670-1707).' [Kyrie Eleison, Responses to the Commandments, Sanctus, Benedictus Qui Venit, Agnus Dei, Gloria in Excelsis.] Included in *SECM Choir Book No 5* 1937.

Missa Sancti Nicolai: Communion Service in Polyphonic Style 1931, SATB unaccompanied, published by the Faith Press, London. 'Written for the Choir of St Nicolas College, Chislehurst'. [Responses to Commandments, Kyrie Eleison, Credo, Sanctus, Benedictus, Agnus Dei, Gloria in Excelsis.] 'The main themes used in this Service are based upon phrases of the composer's hymn for St. Nicolas Day.'

Morning and Evening Service together with the Office for the Holy Communion in D-flat 1913, SATB with organ, published by Novello and Co, London. To the Rev Canon Scott: Sub-Dean of Manchester Cathedral [No 1: Te Deum Laudamus, No 2: Benedictus, No 3: Jubilate, No 4: Kyrie Eleison, No 5: Kyrie Eleison (Alternative Setting), No 6: Credo, No 7: Sanctus, No 8: Benedictus Qui Venit, No: 9 Agnus Dei, No 10: Gloria, No 11: Magnificat, No 12: Nunc Dimittis]. No 11 & 12 published by the RSCM as edition E135.

Morning Service for Boys' (or Female) Voices: Te Deum Laudamus and Jubilate 1913, SS with organ, published by J Curwen & Sons London. Curwen Edition 80553. 'Composed for, and dedicated to the Choristers of Manchester Cathedral.'

Office for St Nicholas Day 1931, SATB unaccompanied. Private printing [Introit, Gradual, Alleluya, Offertory, Communion, and an Antiphon].

Processional Psalms set to Plainsong Tones (Ps. 121, 122, 124, 132) with fauxbourdons and organ interlude (undated), Privately printed facsimile edition of composer's ms.
The **Processional Psalms set to Plainsong Tones** (Ps. 121 & 122) from the above were typeset and re-issued by the RSCM as edition 331 in 1957.

Rock of Ages 1911, SAATTBB unaccompanied, published by Dinham Blyth & Co. Text by A M Toplady. [Facsimile of the composer's ms.]

Sequence for St Edward's Day: From the Missal of Abbot Litlyngton 1921, SATB and organ, Printed at Leipzig for Westminster Abbey.

Solemn Te Deum in B-flat. For Choir and Congregation in Unison with a Descant for Boys' Voices 1919, SS with organ, published by the Faith Press, London. Also a 'People's Part'.

Te Deum and Benedictus in E-flat: St Nicolas Service 1937, SATB and organ, published by the Faith Press, London. 'The main themes used in this Service are based upon phrases of the composer's hymn for St. Nicolas Day.'

Teach us, good Lord, to serve thee: Anthem for Choristers (undated, 'A Prayer of St. Ignatius Loyola.'), SS and organ, dedicated 'To the Choirboys of the SECM.' Published as RSCM 205.

The Saviour of the World: A Devotion on the Passion 1924, Tr, T, Ba soloists, SATB, narrator and organ, published by the Faith Press, London. The text arranged by the Rev C E Douglas. An edition in Dutch was published by Uitgave J J Lispet of Hilversum c.1963. [A version with string orchestra was also started but is incomplete].

The Supreme Sacrifice 1921, SSATTB unaccompanied, published by J Curwen & Sons, London. Curwen Edition 61123. Text by John S Arkwright. Dedication: 'In memory of THE UNKNOWN WARRIOR, Westminster Abbey, Nov. 11th, 1920.' Ms dated Dec 1920.

Three Introits for Xmas, Easter, and Whitsun 1901, SATB and organ, Privately printed by Dinham Blyth & Co, London. Written for Barnet Parish Church Choir.

Two Communion Hymns: 1. O Salutaris, 2. Tantum Ergo 1930, SATB (treble solo in No 1) and organ, published by the Faith Press, London. Later re-published as RSCM 255.

What Thanks and Praise: Anthem for St Luke's Day (undated), SATB and organ, Privately printed. SHN is not specifically named as the composer. Voice Parts only are extant.

Who Are These Like Stars Appearing? Anthem for Choral Festivals 1920, SATB and organ, published by the Faith Press, London. Text by Francis E Cox (from the German).

2) Secular vocal and choral music.

1914: Sonnets written by Rupert Brooke set to music 1917, Baritone solo, SATB Chorus and Orchestra, published by J Curwen & Sons, London. Curwen Edition 3592 [full score, vocal score, choral score, orchestral parts]. 'In memory of Rugbeians who have given their lives for their country.'

A June Night 1931, two equal voices and piano, published by H F W Deane & Sons: The Year Book Press, *Unison and Part-Songs No 351*. No 3 of the Cycle 'Nature Songs'. Text by William Wordsworth.

Alice in Wonderland: Musical Play 1905, SSS with solos accompanied by string quintet, piano and percussion. Privately printed by Dinham Blyth & Co, 'Written for the

Choristers of Carlisle Cathedral', The words adapted from "Alice in Wonderland" and "Through the Looking Glass" by Lewis Carroll by kind permission of Messrs. Macmillan & Co.

Butterfly 1920, two equal voices and piano, published by H F W Deane & Sons: The Year Book Press, *Unison and Part-Songs No 172*, Text by William Wordsworth. [This may have been No 2 of the cycle 'Nature Songs'.]

Cards and Kisses possibly 1927, ATTB unaccompanied — an arrangement of the SATB version, Privately printed. Text by John Lyly (1553-1606) 'Composed for and dedicated to the Gentlemen of the Choir of St George's Chapel, Windsor.' The arrangement may date from the Canadian Tour in 1927.

Cards and Kisses (undated) SATB unaccompanied. Privately printed. Text by John Lyly (1553-1606) with piano reduction 'for *Musical Times Competition*'. Motto: "Esse quam videri".

Childe Allen-a-Dale 1913, SA with two pianos, published by J Curwen & Sons, London. Curwen edition 3566. Text by James Walter Brown. Composed for the Morecombe Musical Festival. [Several versions — vocal score, full score for two pianos, Tonic Sol-fa edition and libretto.]

Foundations: Note-Against-Note 1937, Unison voices with piano, private printing for SECM by Novello & Co. This song was part of an SECM appeal for General Purposes and Endowment. Subscribers purchased notes in the score. The text is probably by SHN.

Four Songs 1901, voice and piano, published by Laudy & Co, London. No 1 To Amaryllis: No 2 Philiis and Damon: No 3 The Starlings (2 versions: in C and E-flat): No 4 Sing Heigh-Ho.

Golden Daffodils 1922, two equal voices and piano, published by H F W Deane & Sons: The Year Book Press. *Unison and Part-Songs No 196*. No 5 of the Cycle 'Nature Songs'. Text by William Wordsworth.

I hear along our street 1899, SATB, published by Novello and Co, London. *Novello's Christmas Carols No 285*. Text by Longfellow, adapted to a Breton Melody.

Ivry: A Song of the Hugenots: Choral Ballad 1905, SATB and orchestra, published by Breitkopf & Hartel, Leipzig. 'Composed for, and dedicated to the Carlisle Choral Society'. Text by Lord Macaulay. [Full score, vocal score and orchestral parts.]

Little Sir Hugh: A cantata for children's voices in two parts 1908, SA with piano and flute obligato. Published by J Curwen & Sons, London. Curwen edition 3522. Text by James Walter Brown. [Some of the melodies are derived from Cumbrian folk songs.]

Mother Goose's Rhymes: Song Cycle 1911, SATB and piano, published by Stainer & Bell, London. Composed for the 'Folk-Song Quartett' and dedicated to A Foxton Ferguson. Contents: 1. Prologue [Quartet: Old King Cole], 2. A Good Child [Soprano solo: I love little Pussy], 3. A Bad Child [Quartet, Ding, dong, bell], 4. Retribution [Bass solo: Dr Faustus], 5. A Warning [Contralto solo: Three children sliding on the ice], 6. A Bargain [Tenor solo: Curly-locks], 7. Prudence [Quartet: There was a little man], 8. Courtship [Soprano/Bass dialogue: Where are you going to my pretty maid?], 9. Epilogue [The cat and the fiddle].

Oh, the Month of May (undated), Tenor, Baritone, Bass. Privately printed at the Academic Copying Office, Oxford. Possibly From Nicholson's university years.

Phillida Flouts Me 1901, SSATB unaccompanied, published by Laudy & Co, London. *Part Songs by Modern Composers No 38.* "This Madrigal gained the Magpie Society's Prize in 1900." Dedication: To Basil Johnson. Text: Seventeenth Century.

Runilda's Chant 1921, SATB unaccompanied, published by H F W Deane & Sons: The Year Book Press, London. *Unison and Part-Songs No 185.* Text by George Darley.

Song of the Scythes 1911, SSC and piano, published by Stainer & Bell, London. *Part Songs for Treble and Alto Voices No 39.* Dedicated to Miss Emily Macfarlene. Text by Andrew Lang from 'Grass of Parnassus'.

The Boy Bishop: An Opera for Boys 1926, SS and solos with piano, published by the Faith Press, London. Full score, vocal score and libretto editions. Text also by SHN. 'Written and composed for the Choristers of Westminster Abbey.'

The Children of the Chapel 1934, Solos and chorus with piano (or harpsichord). Three printed editions SHN 1934, Faith Press 1935, RSCM 1944. Three versions: full score, vocal score and libretto. "Written for the Choristers of The College of St Nicolas, Chislehurst on the SS Oronsay & SS Niagara 1934."

The Dandelion 1918, Unison voices with piano, published by Edward Arnold, London. *Singing Class Music Edward Arnold's Series No 23.*

The Diverting History of John Gilpin set to music for chorus of men's voices and orchestra 1908, TTBB with piano or orchestra, published by J Curwen & Sons, London. Curwen Edition 3517. Text by William Cowper. Several editions: full score, vocal score, Tonic Sol-fa edition and libretto.

The Hailstorm 1921, SS with piano, published by H F W Deane & Sons: The Year Book Press, London. *Unison and Part-Songs No 181.* No 4 of the Cycle 'Nature Songs'. Text by William Wordsworth.

The Jackdaw of Rheims: A Cantata for children's voices 1923, SS with piano, published by J Curwen & Sons, London. Curwen Edition 3649. The text is from the poem 'The Ingoldsby Legends' by the Rev Richard H Barham. Composed for the Morecombe Musical Festival 1924. A libretto illustrated by SHN's brothers Charles and Archie and printed on SHN's own printing press also exists.

The Lads of the Village 1926, SS with solos and piano, published by Stainer & Bell, London. The text is by SHN. 'Dedicated to W H Reid and the Children of the Carlisle Musical Festival.'

The Luck of Edenhall: Cantata for Treble Voices 1906, Two equal voices with string orchestra, Published by J Curwen & Sons, London. Curwen Edition 3275. 'Composed for the Carlisle & District Musical Festival (1907) and dedicated to Miss M. Goodwin.' Text from Walter White's 'Northumberland and the Border'.

The Mermaid: A Romantic Light Opera in Two Acts 1928, SATB and solos with orchestra or piano. Published by J Curwen & Sons, London. Curwen Edition 3677. Book by George Birmingham.

The Music-Makers 1919, Unison voices and piano, published by Stainer & Bell, London. *The Motherland Song Book for Unison and Mixed Voices Vol.1 No 15.* Later used as a hymn in *Songs of Praise* No 315(ii) [see Appendix G]. Another version of this work for string ensemble and unison voices also exists.

The Song for Me 1923, SS and piano, published by H F W Deane & Sons: The Year Book Press, London. *Unison and Part-Songs No 215.* No 1 of the Cycle 'Nature Songs'. Text by William Wordsworth.

Trowl, Trowl, the Bowl (undated), Tenor, Baritone, Bass, privately printed at the Academic Copying Office, Oxford. Possibly from Nicholson's University years.

Unto the Hills 1922, SATB unaccompanied, published by H F W Deane & Sons: The Year Book Press, London. *Unison and Part-Songs No 200.* Text by Joan Rundall.

Wee Happy Heardsmen 1918, SATB, published by the Faith Press, London. *The Faith Press Christmas Carols No III.* Text from an old 'Part-book' from Carlisle Cathedral 1637.

3) Instrumental music

Impromptu No 1 in A-flat (for organ) 1908, published by Stainer & Bell, London. Stainer & Bell's Organ Library No 20. Dedication: "To Theodore Walrond".

Impromptu No 2 in D (for organ) 1908, published by Stainer & Bell, London. Stainer & Bell's Organ Library No 21. Dedication: "To Arthur Harrison"."

4) Arrangements and compilations:

A Congregational Chant-Book 1907, SATB, published by Novello and Co, London. A compilation of 100 single and double chants by various composers.

Andante Larghetto from "Saul" by George Frederick Handel, 1926, arr for violin and piano by SHN, violin part edited by Ernest Yonge. published by H F W Deane & Sons: The Year Book Press, London.

Ave Radix Jesse (hymn tune) Melody from the Sens Processional 1728, harmonised by SHN for *Hymns Ancient & Modern Revised* 1950. Also previously published in the *Sydney Nicholson Commemoration Book*, Canterbury, RSCM, 1948.

British Songs for British Boys 1903, Unison voices with piano, published by MacMillan and Co, London. 'Dedicated to Sir Walter Parratt, Master of the King's Musick.' There are two Editions, a melody edition and the full score. Reprinted 1906, 1908, 1911, 1914, 1917 (with additions), 1919, 1921, 1924, 1927, 1930, 1934.

Twelve Carols reprinted from British Songs for British Boys 1924, Vocal score only, published by MacMillan and Co, London. Nos 97-108 from *British Songs for British Boys*.

Chanting Service No 1 1935, Unison or SATB with organ, published by the School of English Church Music in *SECM Choir Book No 4* 1935. The Magnificat uses a chant by Robert Cooke, the Nunc Dimittis a chant by W Tucker.

Chanting Service No 2 1936, Unison or SATB with organ, published by the School of English Church Music in *SECM Service Book No 1* 1936. The Magnificat uses a chant by John Goss, the Nunc Dimittis a chant by Thomas Kelway.

Chanting Service No 3 1939, Unison or SATB with organ, published by the School of English Church Music in *SECM Service Book No 4* 1939. The Magnificat uses a chant by J Jones, the Nunc Dimittis a chant by W Turner.

Four Settings of the Litany 1936, SATB unaccompanied, published by the Faith Press, London. Contains the Litanies of Cranmer, Tallis, Byrd and Anon, edited jointly by SHN and Dr E H Fellowes.

Free-Chant Canticles from the Unison Chant Book 1924, Unison or SATB, published by the Faith Press, London. [Te Deum, Benedictus, Magnificat, Nunc Dimittis].

Funeral March from 'Becket Op.48' by Sir Charles Villiers Stanford, arranged for organ solo by Sydney H Nicholson. 1925, published by Stainer & Bell, London.
Jerusalem by C H H Parry arranged for organ c 1945, an arrangement made for *Hymns A&M Revised* Hymn 578 but not used. Thalben-Ball's arrangement was used instead.

How dear are thy counsels by William Crotch (1775-1847), anthem for SATB edited by SHN 1938 for the SECM Regional Festivals. Copyright to SECM but printed by Novello and Co, London, in *Festival of English Church Music Regional Festivals 1938-1939*.

Let the Bright Seraphim: Air from "Samson" by George Frederick Handel, 1939, arr for voice and organ by SHN. published by Novello and Co, London.

Let Thy Hand Be Strengthened 'Anthem composed for the Coronation of James II' by John Blow (1649-1708), SATB with organ ad lib. Edited by SHN 1922, published by Novello and Co, London. *Novello's Octavo Anthems 1097*. Also in *SECM Service Book No 2* 1936.

Lift Up Your Heads by John Blow (1649-1708), anthem for SSATBB edited by SHN 1922 'For the Blow Commemoration Service held in Westminster Abbey, July 3, 1922.' Published by Novello and Co, London. *Novello's Octavo Anthems 1098*.

Litany for Five Voices by Thomas Tallis, 1926, SATBB, published by the Faith Press, London. Later incorporated into **Four Settings of the Litany** 1936 above.

Magnificat and Nunc Dimittis by Michael Wise (1648-1687), SATB and organ edited by SHN, published by the Oxford University Press, London, 1932 and in *SECM Choir Book No 2* 1932.

Magnificat and Nunc Dimittis in F by John Blow (1649-1708), SATB and organ, transposed to G and arranged by SHN 1930, published by Novello and Co, London. *Novello's Parish Choir Book 1071*.

Magnificat and Nunc Dimittis with Fauxbourdons by Thomas Morley SATB with organ, published by SECM in *Choir Book No 1* 1931.

Merbecke: From 'the Boke of Common Praier noted' (1550), Unison voices with organ accompaniment and optional descants arranged by SHN, published by the Faith Press, London, [Kyrie, Responses to the Commandments, Credo, Sursum Corda, Sanctus, Benedictus, Agnus Dei, Pater Noster, Gloria.]

O come, O come, Emmanuel c 1921, An arrangement of Veni Emmanuel for unison congregation (choir) with harmonization for choir and/or organ for Westminster Abbey Special Choir. Privately printed for Westminster Abbey.

St Nicholas Chant Book 1930, SATB, a compilation of chants used in *The Parish Psalter* published by the Faith Press, London. It contains three settings by SHN Ps 115 (single in E-minor, single in C), Ps 136 (single in E-flat) and Ps 148 (shortened double in B-flat). Re-printed 1974.

The Lord is King: Anthem for Men's Voices by William Boyce, ATB and organ, edited by SHN 1938 [The full choruses of the original anthem are omitted in this edition for ATB, the edition was made for the SECM Regional Festivals 1938/1939], published by Novello & Co, London. *Novello's Services, Anthems etc, for Men's Voices No 109.*

Unison Chants for the Psalms, a compilation of psalm chants with descants on some verses, arranged and compiled by Sydney Nicholson 1920. Published by the Faith Press, London. Two editions, a vocal edition and an organ accompaniment edition.

Upon a Quiet Conscience by Henry Purcell, 1924, duet with piano, published by Stainer & Bell, London. 'The words by King Charles the First.' Edited by Nicholson from *Harmonia Sacra* Playford, 1688.

Unpublished compositions

1) Liturgical and sacred choral music

Agnus Dei (undated), SSATB unaccompanied.

Before Jehovah's Awful Throne (undated anthem), SATB with treble solo and organ.

Behold the Lamb of God (undated anthem), SATB and organ.

Benedicite omnia opera in D 1946, SATB and organ [in 5/4].

Benedictus In G (undated), SATB and organ.

Blessed be God (undated anthem), SATB with bass solo and organ. "for *Musical Times* Competition: Motto 'Virtus sola nobilitas', text: Daniel II, 20-22 from *Novello's Anthem Book* No 804."

Canternus cuncti: The strain upraise of joy and praise 1941, boys and men with organ, Text by J M Neale (from the Latin.) "This anthem may be sung by a choir that is incomplete as regards the lower voices: or it may be sung by boys alone (singing the two parts if possible)."

Carlisle Cathedral Chants undated, SATB, A collection of 502 chants (two cycles) assembled by SHN for Carlisle Cathedral including some of his own chants. Ps 2 triple in C; Ps 40 triple in G; Ps 70 triple in F; Ps 41 triple in E-flat; Pss 42/43 single in B-flat, double in G-minor/D, single in D; Ps 57 single in C-minor, single in C-major; Ps 60 single in C-minor, single in F; Ps 108 single in C, single in F.

Chant Setting for Men's Voices No 1 (undated), Magnificat in E-flat on a chant by Jackson, Nunc Dimittis in E-flat on a chant by Felton.

Evensong orchestrated undated, SATB, organ brass and strings. The elements of Evensong are orchestrated 1 Processional Hymn [unknown tune], 2 Tallis Responses, 3 Hymn III [Croft's 136], 4 Hymn IV Recessional [Addisons], 5 The Psalms [glorias only] Psalm 122 [H West], Psalm 132 [unknown chant], Psalm 150 [full psalm with instruments, Chant P Humfrey].

God who hast made the valleys of England 1939, treble voice(s) and piano, composed just after the outbreak of WWII, author of text unknown.

Holy Spirit, Come, O Come (Veni sancte spiritus) 1900, SATB unaccompanied.

In thee O Lord: Anthem for Unaccompanied Singing (undated), SATB unaccompanied.

Introits (12) (undated), SATB unaccompanied. The copyright to five of these was purchased by the BBC in 1941.

Kyrie and Propria for Michaelmas (The Propers of the Mass for Dedication Festival and Michaelmas Day together with the Kyrie Eleison) 1941, SATB and organ "Written for the choir of St Michael's College, Tenbury. The main themes are taken from the Plainsong Melody 'Christe sanctorum deus angelorum'. In the gradual the melody of Sir F A Gore Ouseley's hymn tune 'Woolmer's' is used as a Canto Fermo."

Life through the Cross [Hymn Sequence] 1908, SATB, text by "F A of Brighton". There are five hymns 1 The Command, 2 The Answer, 3 The Encouragement, 4 The Resolve, 5 The Doxology.

Magnificat "The First Tune" / Nunc Dimittis "The Third Tune" [in G] (undated), SATB and organ.

Magnificat "The Second Tune" / Nunc Dimittis "The Fourth Tune" [in B-flat], SATB and organ.

Morning Anthem: My voice shalt thou hear betimes O Lord 1931, SATB with organ ad lib.

My son, forget not my law: Anthem for Boys' Voices 1941, SS and organ, "To the boys of St Michael's College, Tenbury:" Text from the Book of Proverbs.

My Song Is Love Unknown (undated anthem), SATB and organ.

O Lord support us all the day long (undated anthem), SATB unaccompanied.

O Quanta Qualia 1902, Soprano Solo and SSATB Chorus with string orchestra, [Mus Bac Exercise No 1 Chorus, No 2 Unaccompanied Quartet, No 3 Soprano Solo, No 4 Fugue.]

O Thou who camest from above: Anthem for Men's Voices 1941, AATTBB unaccompanied, Text by Charles Wesley. 'Written for Westminster Abbey Choir'. Xerox copy bound in Westminster Abbey covers but not formally printed.

Plainsong Magnificat (undated), SS and organ.

Ring out wild bells: Christmas & New Year's Song 1885/6, unison voices with piano. Text by Alfred Tennyson. 'Music composed for his mother by Sydney Nicholson in his 10th year.' The notation appears to be in Nicholson's own hand but it could be a parental copy.

Sanctus (in B-major, undated), SSATB with organ [The Sanctus leads into an incomplete Benedictus.]

Te Deum in E (undated), SATB and organ.

Teach me, my God and King 1929, unison voices with organ, text by George Herbert.

Urbs Beata Jerusalem set with Faux Bourdens 1924, SATB unaccompanied, privately printed facsimile copies of the composer's ms for Westminster Abbey Special Choir.

2) Secular vocal and choral music.

Folk Songs (undated), Unison voices, A series of 11 folk songs with a melody line and text, without harmonization, collected from local singers in Carlisle (so presumably 1904-1908).

A Love Symphony: 'Along the Garden Ways' (undated), SSATB unaccompanied, text by A H Fox O'Shaughnessy. [There is another version of this song for unison voice in 'Country Lyrics'.]

A Roundelay: Part Song for Male Voices (undated), ATTB unaccompanied, text by Thomas Lodge from 'England's Helicon' 1600.

A Song for Choirboys 1941, Unison voices with piano, Text by J M C Crum 'written in bed' in Edgbaston.

Country Lyrics [7 songs], Middle voice and piano (undated).

Four Songs in North Country Dialect 1937, Unison voices and piano, [No 1: A man wed be happy, No 2: There's better days to come, No 3: Laal Janet Bowe, No 4: O, Jobby, had thi tung].

Hymn of Pan for Soprano and Small Orchestra (undated), Scored for woodwind and strings.

In Love's Dispraise 1899, S and Ba with piano, text from Robert Greene's 'Menaphon' 1589.

Music to Hear: Sonnet No. 6 — Shakespeare c 1904, SSAATTBB unaccompanied, 'Dedicated to the Lay Clerks and Choristers of Eton College, Chapel'.

No 1: The Useful Plough (undated), Unison voices and piano, Text: Old English.

Passionate Peter a musical play 1931, Soloists with piano. [Also an instrumental 'Pot-Pourri' arrangement for two pianos by C H Philips.]

Song for Choristers To a Robin 1938, SS with piano, Full title 'To a Robin who attended regularly the statutory services in a cathedral.' Translated from a Latin poem by D Peter Du Moulin, Canon of Canterbury 1661-1684, by J M C Crum.

Songs of the Countryside 1928, unison voices with piano, texts by SHN. [No I: Early Spring. No II: Pine-Woods, No III: The Camp, No IV: The Village Maid, No V: The Road].

The Car (undated), a song for middle voice and piano. Unknown author of text.

The Children in the Wood or Nursery Melodrama Up to Date 1912, Treble voices and piano, 'Written for the Choristers of Manchester Cathedral — Christmas 1912.' Text by Theodore Walrond.

The Guggenheimer Emerald 1938, Soloists and piano, Act 1 Begun May 6th 1938 on SS Duchess of Belfast, Act 2 Begun July 9th 1938 on SS Empress of Britain, Finished Aug 12th 1938, Woodchurch.

The Jumblies (undated), SC and piano, text by Edward Lear.

The Lost Doll (undated) for voice and piano, text by Charles Kingsley.

The new boy loves not runs at first (undated) Voice and piano. A song (marked 'at Rugby' and initialled by SHN) The writing appears juvenile, probably a composition dating from his time at Rugby School. The 'runs' in the title refers to the game of cricket.

The Nightingale (undated) TrATB unaccompanied, text by Wordsworth.

The Thames: An Exercise for the Degree of B Mus 1898, SSATB with String Orchestra, Words from 'Cooper's Hill' by John Denham (1643).

The Town Crier's Wooing 1919, Soprano and bass duet with piano.

To a skylark 1937, High voice and piano, text by William Wordsworth.

Two Old English Songs arranged with accompaniment for String Orchestra 1917, Unison, No 1: Barbara Allen, No 2: O Willow, Willow.

Weep you no more, sad fountains 1899, S and piano.

What love is like? 1908, duet with piano, text by Thomas Middleton (1570-1627).

3) Instrumental music

Allegretto (undated) for organ.

A Miniature for String Quartet and Vocal Quartet (in D) 1918, SATB and string quartet, 'Lines written in early spring.' Dedicated to R H Wilson, text by William Wordsworth. 'Written at Allan Bank, Grasmere. (Wordsworth's home for three years, 1808-1811.)'

Coronation March 1902, for orchestra, Motto: Virtus sola nobilitas. Submitted anonymously for the 'Prize Coronation March' competition in 1902.

Estella Canziani 1887 for piano 'from Sydney Nicholson, aged 12 years 2 months.'

Hanover (undated) Chorale Prelude for organ on the hymn tune 'Hanover' with tune in the pedals.

Jubilee March 1887, for piano, harmonium, violin, fairy bells and cello, A childhood work incorporating the National Anthem.

String Quartet "Conatus" (undated).

Quintett for Pianoforte and Strings in E Major 1918, [Viola part missing].

Solemn March for Orchestra 1919, Written for the 'Order of the Bath Service.' Westminster Abbey. Rearranged for military band. Also an arrangement for solo organ.

Sonata for Cor Anglais and Pianoforte (in E-flat) 1941.

Sonata for the Pianoforte in D-Minor 1895, 'Composed for performance at the Oxford University Musical Union on December 4, 1895.'

Sonata in E-flat for Violin and Piano 1899/1900.

St Ann [an arrangement for orchestra of the hymn tune with seven verses set to various instrumentations.]

St Nicholas Voluntaries [for organ with pedals] 1937, 10 voluntaries, some based on hymn tunes. Also a printed copy typeset by John Henderson.

String Quartet in E-flat 1904 completed in Frankfurt Am Main [Four movements].

Suite for Orchestra "L'Allegro" 1921. Also an arrangement for two pianos.

Suite for Two Pianos (undated), five movements — Prelude, Minuet, Scherzo (with Trio), Air, March. [NB There is another suite for two pianos with only a first movement.]

Suite for Two Pianos (undated) Only the first movement is complete.

The Children of the Week: 7 Pianoforte Pieces [Monday's child is fair of face, Tuesday's child is full of grace, Wednesday's child is full of woe, Thursday's child has far to go, Friday's child is loving and giving, Saturday's child works hard for his living, A child that is born on the Sabbath day, is happy and gladsome and merry and gay.]

The Life of Saint Nicolas: Tone poem in the form of variations for two pianos 1933, 'To C S P' [The Rev C S Phillips], 'Written on the SS Oxford on the way from Naples to London, and finished on an influenza sickbed.'

Variations for Piano 1898 [33 Variations].

Variations on "O dear, what can the matter be?" for Two Pianos (undated).

Variations on an original theme [for piano] 1903.

Varied Accompaniments and Versets to Hymn Tunes a bound compilation of the accompaniments used for the ROX series of recordings made at St Sepulchre, Holborn, in 1939. A set of **Versets for 'Regent Square'** were added in 1947.

4) Arrangements and compilations:

Five Movements from the Water Music [for organ] by George Frederick Handel, undated, but the title information includes a reference to the "Coll of S Nic." which would place the arrangements after 1927.

God rest you merry gentlemen (undated), SATB and orchestra. An arrangement of the traditional carol for chorus and orchestra. "Vocal harmonies to suit arrangement in Stainer's and Bramley's Collection".

Marsch der Zwenge: Piano Duet by Ivan Knorr scored for orchestra by Sydney H Nicholson 1904.

Suite for organ by Henry Purcell 1923, "arranged from instrumental movements in the Dramatic Works by Sydney H Nicholson".

Unfinished compositions and fragments

III Allegro con brio: Scherzoso (undated) an instrumental movement in ABA form — only section A complete. For two unspecified instruments in C and one in D.

Anthem: While the earth remaineth (undated), SATB and organ.

Doth Not Wisdom Cry? (undated anthem), SATB and piano. The accompaniment is pianistic in compass.

Hail Thee, Nicolas, Patron Saint and Friend (undated anthem), SATB and organ. The manuscript is untitled, there is a long and florid organ introduction with optional repeats suggesting use in procession. Author of text unknown. It refers to 'sons of the college' so probably from the 1930's.

Hark to the song of the choristers undated music for a play or pageant. Movements 1 and 6 complete, movement 9 incomplete. No indication of title or author of text.

The Novelty Club: A Comic Opera in Three Acts (undated), Soloists and chorus with piano, Two copies of type-written libretto probably by SHN, Sketches for songs, some very rough pencil sketches, some ink fair copies.

Weep not my wanton voice and piano (undated).

Nicholson's published books and pamphlets

A Manual of Church Music edited by George Gardner and Sydney H Nicholson, London, SPCK 1923 reprinted 'with an Appendix bringing it up to date' 1936.

Beauty in Public Worship: A scheme for raising the standard, especially in parish churches, The Booklet Library No.82, London, Faith Press, 1927.

Boys' Choirs: Festival Booklets No 9, published in Glasgow, Paterson's Publications, 1922

Church Music: A Practical Handbook, London, The Faith Press 1920.

Peter: The adventures of a chorister 1137-1937, London, SPCK 1944. Illustrated by H Tisdall. 2nd ed [with a new foreword by Gerald H Knight.] 1963, reprinted Great Malvern, Cappella Archive, 2002.

Principles and Recommendations of the School of English Church Music: With notes and comments by Sir Sydney Nicholson [Articles reprinted from *English Church Music*.] Tenbury Wells, SECM, 1941, reprinted, RSCM, Canterbury, 1950.

Quires and Places where they Sing, London, G Bell and Sons Ltd, 1932, [With a facsimile reprint of the Communion Service from John Marbecke's "Booke of Common Praier noted," 1550.] reprinted SPCK in 1942 & 1958.

The Choirboy and his place in English Music, 1944, an extract from the *Proceedings of the Musical Association, Session LXX*.

The Elements of Extemporisation – an extract from *A Manual of Church Music* was reprinted as RSCM *Study Notes No. 14* in 1969.

The Improvement of Music in Parish Churches, Faith Press, 1920.

The Organ Voluntary Church Music Society 'Occasional Papers No 6', 1915.

Hymnbooks edited by Nicholson

A Plainsong Hymnbook (Hymns Ancient & Modern.) W. Clowes and Sons, 1932.

Hymns Ancient & Modern ... a second supplement to the old edition. W. Clowes & Sons, 1916.

Hymns Ancient & Modern ... with accompanying tunes. Old edition, 1889 edited by SHN William Clowes & Sons, 1916.

Hymns Ancient & Modern The Shortened Music edition, W. Clowes and Sons, 1939.

Hymns Ancient & Modern. Revised, William Clowes & Sons, 1951.

Appendix G: The original hymn tunes of Sydney Nicholson

In alphabetical order

Hymn book numbers:
- A&M — *Hymns Ancient & Modern* 1904
- A&MS — *Hymns Ancient & Modern Standard Edition* 1922
- A&MSE — *Shortened Music Edition* of *Hymns Ancient & Modern* 1939
- AMR — *Ancient & Modern Revised* 1950
- MMHB — *Mirfield Mission Hymn Book: Revised Edition* 1922
- SOP — *Songs of Praise* 1925
- Octavo — Several hymns were published in octavo editions.

AMR 143 **Aethelwold** (8 7 8 7 7 7 Trochaic):
Æthelwold was the first Bishop of Carlisle in 1133.
Text: "He is risen, he is risen!" [*English Hymnal* 132]
Composed for a reunion of Old Choristers of Carlisle Cathedral in 1931.
A version with descant and organ harmonies was published in the *Sydney Nicholson Commemoration Book*, Canterbury, RSCM, 1948.

AMR 453 **Airlie** (10 10 10 10 Anapaestic)
Nicholson's mother lived at 7, Airlie Gardens in Kensington from 1904 until her death in 1923.
Text: "Hosanna we sing, like the children dear"
Composed for the 1916 supplement to *Hymns Ancient & Modern*. Re-issued in the *Sydney Nicholson Commemoration Book*, Canterbury, RSCM, 1948.

'Airlie'
(mentioned in
Appendix F)

Octavo	**Appledore** (SM)	

Appledore is a small village close to Nicholson's Myrtle Cottage in Woodchurch.
Text: "I am the Bread of Life"
Three Hymns [Novello] 1945 No 3: Communion Hymn (text by Prebendary J E S Harrison, vicar of St Paul's, Weston-super-Mare.)

A&M 531   **Barnet** (8 7 8 7 D Iambic)

Chipping Barnet was Nicholson's first organist's post. In all his writing he never used the prefix 'Chipping', it was always just 'Barnet'.
Text: "O living God, whose voice of old"
Composed (for this text) for *Hymns Ancient & Modern* 1904.

A&MSE 661   **Boston** (irregular)

No obvious clue for the naming of this tune.
Text: "Lift up thyself, my soul"
Composed for the *Shortened Music Edition* of *Hymns Ancient & Modern* 1939.

AMR 215   **Bow Brickhill** (LM Iambic)

Bow Brickhill was the site of Nicholson's Scout/Chorister camp.
Text: "We sing the praise of him who died"
Composed (for this text) for his cantata *The Saviour of the World* 1924 and included in the *Shortened Music Edition* of *Hymns Ancient & Modern* 1939.

Octavo   **Carmen Civile** (8 8 7 8 8 7)

(The Westminster Hymn of Empire)
Text: "Quae sit patria Britannis/Dost thou ask what links entwine us" English translation by Canon H F Westlake of Westminster Abbey.
Privately printed for use in Westminster Abbey

AMR 610   **Chislehurst** (7 7 7 7 + Alleluias)

Chislehurst was the home of the *School of English Church Music*.
Text "Hail the day that sees him rise"
Composed for the *Shortened Music Edition* of *Hymns Ancient & Modern* 1939.

A&M 329   **Cosmos** (6 7 6 7 6 6 6 6)

The tune name may refer to the 'creation' content of the text.
Text: "Lord God! Our praise we give"
Composed (for this text) for *Hymns Ancient & Modern* 1904.

AMR 633   **Crucifer** (10 10 + Refrain)

No known reason for the naming of this tune, probably Nicholson's best-known, but he intended it as a processional hymn and so to follow the crucifer seems an apt title.
Text: "Lift high the Cross"
Composed (for this text) for the 1916 supplement to *Hymns Ancient & Modern*.

AMR 622	**Cumulus** (8 8 7 D) No obvious clue for the naming of this tune. Text "Praise, O Sion, praise thy Master" Composed for this text and AMR in 1946.
Octavo	**Dartmouth** (8 8 8 8 8 D) Text: "O God of Love" (C J Firth). Composed (for this text) in 1932 and published in 1933 by Oxford University Press.
AMR 392	**Feniton** (7 8 7 8 + Alleluias) Feniton Court was the home of Nicholson's friend and supporter Colonel Alfred Dyke Acland who had died in 1937. The tune name "Feniton Court" had already been used by E J Hopkins in *Hymns Ancient & Modern* 1904. Text: "Not a thought of earthly things" Composed for the *Shortened Music Edition* of *Hymns Ancient & Modern* 1939.
AMR 622	**Hayling** (8 7 8 7 4 7) No obvious clue for the naming of this tune. Text "Praise, O Sion, praise thy Master" Composed for the text "Praise, my soul, the king of heaven" by H F Lyte in 1908 and published in *The Church Monthly* Oct 1908.
AMR 421	**Hosanna in Excelsis** (irregular) Named after the text. Text: "Hosanna in the highest" Composed for the 1916 supplement to *Hymns Ancient & Modern*.
Octavo	**Kenardington** (6 5 6 5) Kenardington is a small village close to Nicholson's Myrtle Cottage in Woodchurch. Text: "Consecrate my Service" Three Hymns [Novello] 1945 No 1: Morning Hymn (text by Prebendary J E S Harrison, vicar of St Paul's, Weston-super-Mare.)
AMR 385	**Leamington** (10 10 10 10 Iambic) Nicholson and the SECM were based in Leamington when he extracted this from the cantata to become a hymn tune for *Ancient & Modern Revised* 1950. Text: "The we adore, O hidden Saviour, Thee" Composed for the cantata *The Saviour of the World* 1924.
AMR 587	**Litany of the Passion** (7 7 7 6) Named after the text. Text: "Litany of the Passion" Composed for this text and for *Ancient & Modern Revised* in 1946.

AMR 332		**Litlyngton** (irregular)

At the time he composed this, Nicholson's residence was Litlyngton Tower at Westminster Abbey.
Text: "God be in my head"
Composed for *The Winchester Hymn Supplement* 1928. Re-issued in the *Sydney Nicholson Commemoration Book*, Canterbury, RSCM, 1948.

SOP 315(ii) **Music Makers** (irregular)
The poem, by Arthur O'Shaughnessy (1844-1881), was the basis for Sir Edward Elgar's *The Music Makers* and the first verse begins 'We are the music-makers". Nicholson used three verses of the poem.
Text: "With wonderful deathless ditties"
Originally published in *Motherland Song Book Vol 1* 1919.

---------- **Myddle** (11 10 11 10)
Text by Rev Edgar Burford (d 1952) of Myddle, Shrewsbury
Text: "Ascended Lord, eternal intercessor"
1946, possibly unpublished but copyright to RSCM.

---------- **O perfect love** unpublished no date

---------- **O Joy of God** (11 10 11 10)
Text: "O Joy of God" by Bishop Cecil Boutflower (b 1863) unpublished.

MMHB 32 **St Denys** (8 5 8 5 8 8 8 5)
Text: "God of love and truth and beauty" by Timothy Rees (1874-1939), a Brother of the Community of the Resurrection at Mirfield in Yorkshire from 1907 and Warden from 1922. Nicholson composed the tune for this text and publication in the *Mirfield Mission Hymn Book New Edition* 1922.

---------- **St Edward** (8 8 7 D)
The tune was originally used by Nicholson in his *Sequence for St Edward's Day* composed for Westminster Abbey in 1921.
Text: "Campanarum Canticum" by Frederick Augustus Todd
Composed for this text in 1928 for the University of Sydney Carillon/Clock. The text was sung at the University on Armistice Day and Anzac Day.

St Edward

AMR 576	**St Nicolas** (LM Iambic)
	Hymn for St Nicolas' Day.
	Text: "Far-shining names from age to age" by W H Savile
	Composed for this text in 1927 at the suggestion of Rev G H Salter who wrote "we sang Savile's words and Nicholson's tune for the first time at the dedication of the Chapel [of the *School of English Church Music*] by Bishop Frere". [Note that there is no mention of it in the printed order of service for that day.]
Octavo	**Shadoxhurst** (6 4 6 4)
	Shadoxhurst is a small village close to Nicholson's Myrtle Cottage in Woodchurch.
	Text: "Once more the daylight falls"
	Three Hymns [Novello] 1945 No 2: Evening Hymn (text by Prebendary J E S Harrison, vicar of St Paul's, Weston-super-Mare.)

AMR 627	**Tenbury** (irregular)	

Nicholson and the SECM were based in Tenbury when this was written.
Text: "Let love arise and praise him"
Composed (for this text) in 1941 for the SECM *Choir Book of Music for Boys' Voices No.2*.

AMR 302	**Totteridge** (6 6 8 4)	

Totteridge was his family home.
Text: "Rise in the strength of God"
Composed (for this text) for the 1916 supplement to *Hymns Ancient & Modern*. Re-issued in the *Sydney Nicholson Commemoration Book*, Canterbury, RSCM, 1948.

A&MS 708	**Trafalgar** (8 8 8 8 8 D)	

Perhaps the militaristic style title reflects that this was composed during WWI.
Text: "God of our fathers, unto Thee"
Composed for *Hymns Ancient & Modern* 1922.

AMR 532	**Woodchurch** (10 10 10 4)	

Nicholson's retreat, Myrtle Cottage, was in Woodchurch, Kent.
Text: "We praise thee, Lord, for all the martyred throng"
Composed for the *Shortened Music Edition* of *Hymns Ancient & Modern* 1939.

Descants

Nicholson composed many hymn tune descants, especially in his role as music editor of *Hymns Ancient & Modern. Revised* 1951. Except for very few, it is not clear in this hymn book which descants were his own. As there is no manuscript or written evidence to support suspected attributions, the editors have decided not to list descants.

Appendix H

Leslie Heward

> Leslie Hays Heward was born in 1897. Something of a child prodigy, he started learning the organ at the age of five, and by the age of eight, was quoted as being able to accompany the whole of the Messiah. His father entered him for numerous Competition Festivals, at which he invariably won prizes for playing the piano and violin, and solo singing. He was eleven when Nicholson heard him sing, and offered him place in the Manchester Cathedral choir. In 1917 he moved to London, having won a composition scholarship to the Royal College of Music, where he studied composition under Stanford and Vaughan Williams, and conducting under Adrian Boult. After Heward's premature death in 1943, a memorial volume, edited by Eric Blom, was published by J M Dent in 1944. It included contributions from Nicholson, Eric Warr (a fellow chorister at Manchester) and Basil Johnson. It was sufficiently popular to require a second edition in 1946.

Nicholson's contribution to *Leslie Heward: A Memorial Volume (1897-1943)*

In looking back over a life-time there is nothing that seems to me more remarkable than the way in which happenings, which at the time seemed purely accidental and even trivial, have affected the whole future not only of my own life but of that of other people.

- It happened in 1910 that I was judging at the Morecambe Festival, shortly after I became organist at Manchester Cathedral.
- It happened that one of my co-judges was my old friend the Rev Henry Dams, who had been with me as Precentor at Carlisle.
- It happened that in the previous year he had been judging 'Ear-test' and 'Sight-reading' classes on the children's day, and a small boy had appeared who had 'completely stumped him.'
- It happened that the same small boy was due to come before him again, and he suggested that we might exchange duties, so that I could size him up.
- It happened that the Committee, not without some protest, agreed.

Had any of these apparently trivial things not happened I should probably have never known Leslie Heward; and though I am far from thinking that he would not have reached the top of the tree in any case, it is certain that the steps of the ladder would have led him by a different route and I should have missed one of the happiest associations of my life.

As it turned out, a rather small, delicate-looking boy presented himself in due course, and I gave him the usual preliminary tests — absolute pitch, naming notes in chords: in all of them he was perfect. Then I tried to invent new 'devilries' such as several notes struck together which had no sort of harmonic connection: he named them faultlessly, even when played in the top or bottom octave of the piano. I have never known this done with such absolute assurance — one might have been asking him merely to name the notes on the keyboard as he saw them. Then he read at sight, on the piano, some variations I had brought with me: he was in no way daunted by the most difficult.

I soon realized that I was dealing with a boy who was phenomenally gifted, and an idea entered my mind:—

> "Can you sing ?" I asked[1].
>
> "Not much, I'm afraid, sir."
>
> "Well, let's go into the church and have a try."

We did, and he sang me a bit of *Hear my prayer*, quite pleasantly but not showing promise of an exceptional voice. Then I asked him if he could play the organ:

> "A bit, sir, only I'm afraid I haven't brought any music."
>
> "Could you make up something, then, as you go along?"
>
> "I'll have a shot, sir."

So he got on to the organ stool and proceeded to devise a really remarkable extempore based on the themes he had just been singing: he managed the organ wonderfully though he could hardly reach the pedals.

His father was with him and we had a talk about the boy's future, for I now felt sure that here was a born musician.

I returned to Manchester, full of this wonderful boy, and immediately spoke to Bishop Welldon, the Dean, who was always ready to do anything to help and encourage the Cathedral music. The line I took with him was something like this:

> The Dean and Chapter are spending big sums on the Cathedral music each year. Now I want them to spend a little more and make it possible for a musical genius to come as a chorister. He may never be worth much as a singer, but the influence of his music will permeate the others and, further, the Cathedral will be giving him the chance of his life, for the music he will learn there will be the best possible foundation for his future.

Bishop Welldon was above all things a man of vision, and his reply was characteristic: "Bring the boy at once — anything for a genius!"

---

1   This account (1944) varies slightly in wording with Nicholson's other recollection (1939) in Chapter IV.

So Leslie came to Manchester. The Cathedral Choir School did not provide for boarders, the boys living with their parents ; so a home had to be found for the newcomer. At first it was arranged that he should live with another chorister, and various experiments were tried. But, to tell the truth, he was so naughty as well as so delicate that no one would keep him! So, as I had a rather large house and an excellent housekeeper, I decided to take him myself with two other boys to keep him company. Thus he came to live with me, I think in 1911, and remained till he went to London in 1916.

In spite of his abnormal gifts and poor health Leslie was in other ways a very normal boy: above the average in his school work, quite interested though not outstanding in games, a keen Boy Scout, and at times an imp of mischief: indeed he was seldom without some 'lark on.' Terrible were the pranks he would play upon my housekeeper: one night he appeared at the back door with his companions, 'The Terrible Three,' as they styled themselves, dressed up (probably in some of my clothes) complete with beards and moustaches and brandishing pistols, as a gang of house-breakers, frightening the lady almost to hysterics. Whenever there was mischief afoot Leslie was sure to be concerned in it; but he never 'made any bones' about owning up and he certainly suffered his full share of punishment in the form that was commoner for choristers in those days than it is now. He always 'took his gruel' in good part, with that cheery smile that never forsook him and certainly disarmed his critics.

When first he came to me he suffered terribly from eczema, and his hands and wrists were constantly bandaged; but in spite of this he would play the most complicated music without faltering. Then it was suggested that a course of baths at Harrogate would be beneficial, and he was sent there during one summer holiday. The treatment was effective, but when the eczema went its place was taken by asthma, and throughout his life he always suffered more or less from one or other of these distressing ailments. Several times, while a boy with me, he was very ill, running incredible temperatures, and once he had a very serious attack of pneumonia; but he always had an amazing power of recovery and before long was as fit and lively as ever.

At the time of the outbreak of the war in 1914 we were in camp at Rhyl: all the choristers were Scouts and he was the chief Patrol Leader. On our return to Manchester the Scouts were called upon to take their part in the national effort, and Bishop Welldon, who was a great stickler about the appearance of his choristers, was persuaded to a great concession — they were allowed to discard their 'Eton suits' and 'mortar-boards' for Scout uniform. School was closed down, and when they were not singing in the Cathedral they went 'on duty', assisting the police as messengers and so on. This suited Leslie splendidly; for these expeditions no doubt allowed all sorts of opportunities for such delights as illicit bicycle rides and surreptitious banquets of fish and chips; and the best of it was that 'The Boss' couldn't very well object! I remember his excitement when he returned late one evening, quite certain that he had discovered some German spies signalling with lights, and he had been able to put the police on their tracks! Be that as it may, the police expressed great appreciation of the services of the Scouts in those trying days, and it is certain that Leslie proved one of the most efficient of them.

With all his love of adventure there was, however, another side to his nature, and his association with the frequent Cathedral services was no mere formality. He was baptized after he came to Manchester (I was his godfather) and he took his Confirmation very seriously: he was much influenced by Canon Peter Green, who took great interest in him and loved to listen to his playing, and he became a regular Communicant, taking his turn as an Altar Server. As he grew older and more responsible his behaviour in the choir was a model, for he had, what is somewhat rare in a musician, an orderly mind; and when he became a leader he took great pride in such matters as the care of the music and insisted on smartness of appearance and all-round efficiency.

I am well aware that this picture of Leslie as a chorister may seem to some of his friends who only knew him in later life as over-drawn and impossible; but it is none the less a true picture. He was, in fact, a typical example of the best kind of product of a Cathedral choir and, though the circumstances of his career drew him largely out of contact with the Church, I know that he often regretted it, and on the occasions when he was able to meet his old friends at some reunion of ex-choristers no one was more pleased than he to get into his robes once more and take his place in the choir stalls. The lovely *Choral Song for a Reunion* which he wrote for one of these occasions (published by the SPCK) is too little known. It should be sung by ex-choristers whenever they meet together in their old haunts. I remember his telling me how on his first visit to Manchester after the 'blitz' he spent a quiet hour in the shattered Cathedral, looking at the place where he used to sit and conjuring up old memories. After all it was his first love!

He had only had an elementary school education, but he could learn easily though he liked to do it in his own way. His headmaster, the Rev R M Tuke, realized that he had an exceptional boy to deal with; and at times when the spirit moved him he was allowed to lay aside his exercise book and to turn his attention to music-paper. Nevertheless he did well in his ordinary lessons, soon getting to the top of the school, and he developed an interest in literature and poetry. On the occasion of school plays he soon eclipsed all others in his power of acting, and in his spare time he was never without some hobby: butterflies, guinea-pigs, editing magazines, printing, photography, sketching, and even gardening — all had their turns, though none of them lasted very long.

As to his music, I soon found that I could teach him little — it was just a matter of guidance. Everything seemed to come to him naturally, whether piano, organ or composition; but he was somewhat impatient of technique of any kind, and I felt it was wise, as far as possible, to keep him up to it; so I made him be careful of his fingering and acquire proper control of the organ pedals and go through the drudgery of strict counterpoint. But all these things were a bit distasteful to him and, if he had not been so gifted, he would have found it heavy going. However, I was really more concerned to guide him to the knowledge of great music of all styles and periods, for it was obvious that he must develop on his own lines: so we spent many happy hours playing on two pianos, he revelling in the solo part of some concerto — how he loved the Tchaikovsky in those days — while I struggled with an arrangement of the orchestral parts.

But the best musical education that I could give him was what came in the course of his work in the Cathedral choir. He often told me in after-years how much he felt he owed to this splendid grounding. He entered into his duties as a chorister with the same absorption and entire lack of self-consciousness that were so marked a feature of his conducting later on. I like to think of him, as I so often watched him, standing in his surplice and purple cassock with the background of the lovely old choir-stalls, singing some fine music, heart and soul in his job and determined to get the best out of it. I think it was this absorption in the music for its own sake that caused him to be so completely free all through his life of any trace of personal conceit: with him it was always the music that mattered and not his personal share in its rendering; far from seeking admiration, he almost disliked praise.

Though he never had an exceptionally beautiful voice his musical comprehension made him quite a good soloist, and of course in chorus he was invaluable.

At that time we had at Manchester a really remarkable choir: at least four boys who have since won distinction in the musical world were singing together — Eric Fogg, Crawford McNair, Eric Warr and Leslie Heward. There were others too of great ability, some of them with splendid voices, so it was no wonder that we were able to tackle a very large repertory, even rising to such things as the big Bach motets, Reger's *Palm-Sunday Morning* or the motets of Cornelius, and regularly performing on Sunday afternoons a series of short cantatas, including many of Bach's, or the shorter works of Parry and Stanford, Verdi's *Stabat Mater*, and of course selections from the longer oratorios. But the basis of the music was the English Service and Anthem, and of these the choir sang all the best examples that were available. The Tudor music series had not yet been issued, so that the repertory was, unfortunately, not as representative of that great period as it would have been a few years later. Still we tried to do the best of all styles, and as we sang two full choral services every day throughout the year there was plenty of opportunity.

The other great influence on his music at this time was the Halle Orchestra. As soon as he came to live with me I took him every Thursday to these famous concerts, at that time conducted by Richter. I remember his enthusiasm the first time he ever heard a full orchestra, and how he said "Shouldn't I like to conduct that band some day, sir!" It is pleasant to think that he was offered the conductorship of the Halle shortly before his death: I think it was always his ambition.

Even as a small boy he showed his extraordinary power of reading from a full score. He would take the score of a Beethoven symphony and give a very passable performance of it on the piano or organ; even huge scores like those of *Meistersinger* or Strauss's tone-poems presented no terrors to him: he seemed to understand them almost intuitively. Often, of course, he was provided with a score at the concerts, and I should think that in this way he laid the foundation of his amazing knowledge of the orchestra. As he began to experiment with orchestration on his own account I was able to help him in a way that I had found invaluable when studying with Ivan Knorr at Frankfort. He would write several variations for some orchestral instrument, the horn perhaps, or the oboe or bassoon, or trombone, and when they were completed I would get one of the Halle orchestra to come and play them for him and criticize them from the player's point of view. I do not think there is any better method of learning about the orchestra.

It was soon after he had come to Manchester that Sir Charles Stanford came to stay with me and met Leslie. He was astonished at his gifts and urged me to bring him up to London. I still have his letter:

Jan. 30, 1911

My dear Nicholson,

I've been talking to Walter P [Parratt] and Hubert P [Parry] about the amazing youth: and we should all like very much to 'vet' him here some day. It would be invaluable, I think, to get their united opinion (and Franklin Taylor's also) upon the tendency he should take during the next three years. They all agree with you and me about his staying with you at Manchester Cathedral until he is fifteen. But so much depends upon what line he should develop most, and eventually stand for a scholarship on, that I think it is very important to get the views of two or three brains like theirs. Will you try and arrange it ?

Yours very sincerely,

C V Stanford

In due course I took him for his first visit to London and to the Royal College, where he was put through his paces. Parry's comment to me was "This is the kind of phenomenon that appears once in a generation."

About the time of the outbreak of war his voice was changing, but he stayed on at the Cathedral, often playing for services and taking boys' practices, and enjoying his 'first job' as organist and choirmaster at St Andrew's, Ancoats, where his great friend Canon Scott was Rector. When Ernest Bullock, who was my sub-organist, joined the Forces, Leslie took his place. Old boys of that time will remember his magnificent playing and how he revelled in the splendid organ, especially when it had to take the place of an orchestra in the accompaniments to the cantatas. It says much for his force of character and winning personality that the lay clerks were as ready as the choristers to accept him as their master when he was in charge of the choir during my absence. His powers as a conductor were evidently already showing themselves.

By this time he was attracting the attention of the leading Manchester musicians outside the Cathedral circle. He frequently appeared at the Tuesday Midday Concerts, which were started during the war, and he played (when still a boy in an Eton suit) a Mozart concerto with the Beethoven Society's orchestra in the Town Hall. On several occasions he played in chamber music with Dr Brodsky, who had the highest appreciation of his powers.

So his experience was widening: first there was his constant attendance at the Halle concerts and sometimes at the rehearsals as well ; and then came that wonderful series of operas produced by Sir Thomas Beecham and the BNOC[2] with which he was later to become so closely connected.

But it became evident that the time was approaching when he should move on, and a scholarship at the RCM. seemed the obvious opening, as he was utterly unfit for any form of military service. As I have already said, Leslie never cared about the drudgery needed to acquire a very brilliant keyboard technique, and at this time he was inclining more and more to composition. He had written some charming partsongs, particularly one called *Bunches of Grapes*, which was performed by his fellow-choristers at a school concert, and later a most exceedingly difficult partsong (his first published composition except the tune that he wrote when still a choirboy for the Second Supplement of *Hymns Ancient and Modern* — No. 699, 'Wyke.'[3]) This piece was called *The Witches' Sabbath* and was fittingly performed at the Morecambe Festival and nearly defeated even those superb north-country choirs. It was a *tour de force*, but it made a great effect.

He duly entered for the examination and it was a foregone conclusion that he should be awarded an open scholarship in composition; so he went to the Royal College and took up his studies, mainly with Sir Charles Stanford and Adrian Boult. Some place had to be found where he could live and at the same time augment his maintenance allowance, so he was taken on to the teaching staff at Eton College under Basil Johnson and for some time also acted as organist at Holy Trinity, Windsor.

But this part of his life belongs to a period of which others are better qualified to write, and I conclude these reminiscences of his boyhood by quoting a letter from Bishop Welldon on his winning the scholarship:

---

2 British National Opera Company

3 'Wyke' was named after the village near Bradford, where Heward was born and it was included in *Hymns Ancient & Modern Standard* (2nd Supplement, 1916) as No 699(i) and in *Ancient & Modern. Revised* 1951 as No 359.

The Deanery, Manchester

My dear Nicholson,

> I congratulate you with all my heart upon Heward's excellent initiation into a public musical career.
>
> There is scarcely any richer pleasure in life than to watch over genius in its early days.
>
> Heward owes everything to you, but I think you will be fully repaid.
>
> Sincerely yours,
> J E C Welldon

I cannot quote this delightful letter without dissenting from one part of it. He certainly did *not* owe everything to me; he owed his success to three things — his marvellous gifts, his own industry and his delightful nature. Indeed, looking back over a long musical life, I cannot but feel that I owe far more to him than I could ever have repaid. It is a rare privilege to live in daily touch and mutual affection with a genius and to realize that no one is too young to learn from.

So, though our lives were widely separated in later years, I am proud to think of him as one of my most loved friends and thankful to have had the chance of doing something to help him to get a start in life.

Sydney H Nicholson

Leslie Heward (1897-1943) conductor of the BBC Midland Orchestra, and latterly Principal Conductor of the City of Birmingham Orchestra

My song is love unknown

Anthem for SATB and Organ

Text: Samuel Crossman (1624-1684)

Music: Sydney Hugo Nicholson (1875-1947)
Edited by John Henderson

Andante moderato
♩ = 70

My song is love unknown, my Saviour's love to me, love to the loveless shown, that they might

© The Royal School of Church Music, 19 The Close, Salisbury, SP1 2EB. All Rights Reserved
It is ILLEGAL to photocopy this copyright work.

love-ly be. O who am I, that for my sake my Lord should take frail flesh, and die?

He came from his blest throne, salvation to bestow; but men made strange, and none the longed-for Christ would know. But O, my Friend, my Friend indeed, who at my need his life did spend.

Poco meno mosso 𝅗𝅥 = 65
Trebles only
Some - times they strew his way, and his sweet
Without pedals
55
prai - ses sing; re - soun-ding all the day ho - san - nas to their
King.
60
Then 'Cru - ci - fy', 'Cru - ci - fy' is all their breath, and
Ped.

for his death they thirst and cry.

mp Why, *mf* what hath my Lord done? What makes this rage and spite? *mp* He made the lame to run, he gave the blind their sight. Sweet in-ju-ries! yet they at these them-selves dis-please, and 'gainst him rise.

[Tempo primo]

95
f Here might I stay and sing: no sto - ry
100
so di - vine; ne - ver was love, dear King, ne - ver was
105
grief like thine!
This is my Friend, in whose sweet
This is my Friend, in whose sweet
This is my Friend, in whose sweet
This is my Friend, in whose sweet

Nicholson's manuscript is undated. This piece seems to be part of a Passiontide sequence. It is immediately followed by a Bible reading (Isaiah 53. 1-6) and an organ interlude leading into another SATB anthem *Behold the Lamb of God* which uses the tune 'Adeste fideles'. The ms. concludes with a setting of the Prayer of St Richard of Chichester and a further Bible reading.